Protestants, Catholics and Jews in Germany, 1800–1914

Protestants, Catholics and Jews in Germany, 1800–1914

Edited by
Helmut Walser Smith

Oxford • New York

First published in 2001 by
Berg
Editorial offices:
150 Cowley Road, Oxford, OX4 1JJ, UK
838 Broadway, Third Floor, New York, NY 10003-4812, USA

Berg is an imprint of Oxford International Publishers Ltd.

Library of Congress Cataloging-in-Publication Data
A catalogue record for this book is available from the Library of Congress.

British Library Cataloguing-in-Publication Data
A catalogue record for this book is available from the British Library.

ISBN 1 85973 560 6 (Cloth)
1 85973 565 7 (Paper)

Typeset by JS Typesetting, Wellingborough, Northants.
Printed in the United Kingdom by Biddles Ltd, Guildford and King's Lynn.

For Michael and Kimberly Bess
Good Friends

Contents

Acknowledgements   ix

Notes on Contributors   xi

Part I Introduction

1   The Fate of Nathan   3
     Helmut Walser Smith and *Chris Clark*

Part II Outlines

2   The Religious Divide: Piety in Nineteenth-Century
     Germany   33
     Lucian Hölscher

3   Religion, Denomination and Nationalism in
     Nineteenth-Century Germany   49
     Wolfgang Altgeld

4   The "Christian" State and the "Jewish Citizen" in
     Nineteenth-Century Prussia   67
     Chris Clark

Part III Religious Difference, National Culture and Identity

5   The Cult of Gustavus Adolphus: Protestant Identity
     and German Nationalism   97
     Kevin Cramer

6   The Process of Confessional Inculturation: Catholic
     Reading in the "Long Nineteenth Century"   121
     Jeffrey T. Zalar

Contents

7   Anti-Jesuitism in Imperial Germany: The Jesuit as
    Androgyne   153
    Róisín Healy

Part IV Religious Difference, Local Politics, and Pluralism

8   The Rise of the Religious Right and the Recasting of
    the "Jewish Question": Baden in the 1840s   185
    Dagmar Herzog

9   Unity, Diversity, and Difference: Jews, Protestants, and
    Catholics in Breslau Schools During the *Kulturkampf*   217
    Till van Rahden

Part V From Conflict to Coexistence

10 The Catholics' Missionary Crusade and the Protestant
    Revival in Nineteenth-Century Germany   245
    Michael B. Gross

11 Building Religious Community: Worship Space and
    Experience in Strasburg after the Franco-Prussian War   267
    Anthony J. Steinhoff

12 The Development and Destruction of a Social Institution:
    How Jews, Catholics and Protestants Lived Together in
    Rural Baden, 1862–1940   297
    Ulrich Baumann

Part VI Afterword

13 Living Apart and Together in Germany   317
    Margaret Lavinia Anderson

Index   333

Acknowledgements

The idea for this volume started with a conversation with Maike Bohn. We were sitting in two plush chairs around a small round table on the right side of a hotel lobby in Salt Lake City, Seattle, or somewhere else. If I have forgotten where this took place, I will not soon forget the energy and excitement, and later encouragement and work and camaraderie that Maike Bohn brought to this project. Without her ideas and help, it would never have seen the light of day. I also want to thank Kathryn Earle of Berg Publishers for her encouragement and patience and good humor, especially as the manuscript did not always arrive at her desk on time.

Jan Palmowski of King's College, London, read the manuscript and offered insightful and constructive advice. In addition to writing the afterword, Margaret Lavinia Anderson of the University of California, Berkeley, suggested a series of revisions and, at a critical juncture, offered good advice. Chris Clark of Cambridge University invited me to present the ideas behind the volume to an engaged and critical audience at the German Historical Institute in London. I am grateful for that invitation, not the least because Chris and I realized that the ideas we presented to this audience were of a piece, and belonged together. I also received help preparing the manuscript in its various stages from Vicki Crothers and Lori Cohen, two wonderful administrative assistants in the Department of History at Vanderbilt. Jane Landers, my colleague who understands editing better than I, also offered encouragement and advice, and tried to keep me from doing too much myself.

My wife Meike – with irony and a smile – is happy that this one is finished.

Notes on Contributors

Wolfgang Altgeld is Professor of Modern and Contemporary History at the University of Würzburg. He is the author of *Das politische Italien-bild der Deutschen zwischen Aufklärung und europäischer Revolution* (Tübingen, 1984) and *Katholizismus, Protestantismus, Judentum: Über religiös begründete Gegensätze und nationalreligiöse Ideen in der Geschichte des deutschen Nationalismus* (Mainz, 1992). He is also the co-editor of and a contributor to a series of books on the European resistance in the era of National Socialism, as well as the author of scholarly contributions to the history of Italy.

Margaret Lavinia Anderson is Professor of History at the University of California at Berkeley. She is the author of articles on politics and religion in the German Empire and on European Catholicism, as well as of *Windthorst: A Political Biography* (Oxford, 1981; in Germany: *Windthorst: Zentrumspolitiker und Gegenspieler Bismarcks*, published by Droste in 1988) and *Practicing Democracy: Elections and Political Culture in Imperial Germany* (Princeton, NJ, 2001). She is currently working on German involvement in the fate of the Armenians in the Ottoman Empire.

Ulrich Baumann is the author of *Zerstörte Nachbarschaften. Christen und Juden in badischen Landgemeinden 1862–1940* (Hamburg, 2000) and is currently a post-doctoral fellow in the special research area entitled "Gruppen–Schichten–Klassen" at the University of Bielefeld.

Christopher Clark is a Lecturer in Modern European History at St. Catharine's College, Cambridge. He is the author of *The Politics of Conversion. Missionary Protestantism and the Jews in Prussia 1728–1941* (Oxford, 1995) and *Kaiser Wilhelm II. A Profile in Power* (London, 2000), and has published widely in the area of modern Prussian and German history. He is currently involved in a collaborative project on Catholic–secular conflict in nineteenth-century Europe and is working on a general history of Prussia for the Penguin Press.

Kevin Cramer is Assistant Professor of German and Central European History at Indiana University-Indianapolis. He is completing a manuscript entitled "The Lamentations of Germany: The Historiography of the Thirty Years' War, 1790–1890." His current research focuses on the "Protestant Diaspora" and German nationalism.

Michael B. Gross is Assistant Professor of Modern Germany in the Department of History at East Carolina University, Greenville, North Carolina. His essay here is part of a larger study of liberal identity and the anti-Catholic imagination in nineteenth-century Germany. He is currently examining *Majestätsbeleidigung*, state authority, discipline and popular culture in the Wilhelmine period.

Róisín Healy is Assistant Professor of History at the National University of Ireland, Galway. In 1999 she completed a dissertation at Georgetown University entitled "The Jesuit as Enemy: Anti-Jesuitism and the Protestant Bourgeoisie in Imperial Germany, 1890–1917." Her research interests are in modern German history, the history of religion in the nineteenth and twentieth centuries, and modern European social history.

Dagmar Herzog is Associate Professor of History at Michigan State University and is the author of *Intimacy and Exclusion: Religious Politics in Pre-Revolutionary Baden* (Princeton, NJ, 1996). She has written widely on religion and gender in the nineteenth century and is now working on a study of "sex and memory in postfascist Germany."

Lucian Hölscher is Professor of Modern History at the University of Bochum. He is the author of *Öffentlichkeit und Geheimnis. Zur Entstehung der Öffentlichkeit in der frühen Neuzeit* (Stuttgart, 1979), *Weltgericht oder Revolution. Protestantische und sozialistische Zukunftsvorstellungen im deutschen Kaiserreich* (Stuttgart, 1989), *Die Entdeckung der Zukunft* (Frankfurt, 1999), and, most recently, an *Atlas zur religiösen Geographie im protestantischen Deutschland zwischen der Mitte des 19. Jahrhunderts und dem Zweiten Weltkrieg* (Berlin, 2001). He also publishes widely in the theory of history.

Anthony J. Steinhoff is Assistant Professor of Modern European History at the University of Tennessee-Chattanooga. A specialist in both French and German history, he is the author of a dissertation, completed in 1996, entitled "Protestants in Strasbourg 1870–1914: Religion and Society in the Late Nineteenth-Century Europe."

Notes on Contributors

Till van Rahden is Assistant Professor of History at the University of Cologne. He is the author of *Juden und andere Breslauer. Die Beziehungen zwischen Juden, Protestanten und Katholiken in einer deutschen Großstadt von 1860 bis 1925* (Göttingen, 2000), which received the Fraenkel Prize in Contemporary History, and is co-editor of *Bürger, Juden, Deutsche. Zur Geschichte von Vielfalt und Differenz seit dem späten 18. Jahrhundert* (Tübingen, 2000). He is currently working on a social and cultural history of fatherhood in twentieth-century Germany.

Helmut Walser Smith is Associate Professor of History at Vanderbilt University. He is the author of *German Nationalism and Religious Conflict* (Princeton, NJ, 1995) and, forthcoming, *The Butcher's Tale: Murder and Anti-Semitism in a German Town* (New York, 2002). He is also a co-editor of *"Exclusionary Violence": Antisemitic Riots in Modern Germany* (Ann Arbor, MI, 2002) and *The Holocaust and Other Genocides* (Nashville, TN, 2002).

Jeffrey T. Zalar is a Ph.D. candidate in modern German cultural and religious history studying under the direction of Professor Roger Chickering at Georgetown University. His dissertation is entitled "Knowledge and Nationalism in Imperial Germany: A Cultural History of the Association of Saint Charles Borromeo, 1890–1914." He is the author of several articles and book chapters on Catholic intellectual culture and religious *mentalité*.

Part I
Introduction

–1–

The Fate of Nathan
Helmut Walser Smith and *Chris Clark*

"The one is darker and turned inward, the other outgoing and industrious. The one is meatier and redder in the face, often blood red; the other is somewhat more angular in the bone structure of the face, and the color in his face is not as pronounced."[1] This is how Nicolai observed Catholics and Protestants in Augsburg in 1781. In the same year, and in Nicolai's publishing house, Christian Wilhelm Dohm published *On the Civic Improvement of the Jews*. Like Nicolai with respect to Catholics, Dohm observed that the Jews lived in a world apart, and that this constituted a deplorable state of affairs. Unlike Nicolai, however, Dohm did not blame the Jews as such. Instead, he attributed their "miserable condition to . . . inhuman prejudice from the darkest ages," and argued that this condition "was not worthy to continue in our time."[2] This too was a widely shared assumption of the Enlightenment. Kant had argued that the progress of civilization would ameliorate divisive differences, especially of religion.[3] Most famously, Lessing attributed the voice of enlightened religious tolerance to Nathan the Wise. And Nathan, in his parable of the rings, hoped for a future in which the rancor of religious difference and division would be rendered a peaceful competition of piety and good works.

The future was to be otherwise. In the course of the succeeding century, the border that divided Protestants, Catholics and Jews would be challenged, redrawn, rendered porous, and built anew. This volume addresses this redrawing. It considers the relations of three religious groups – Protestants, Catholics, and Jews – and asks how, by dint of their interaction, they affected one another. It therefore addresses the nature of religious prejudice. But it also looks at cooperation across what Etienne François has called "the invisible boundary," and attempts to recast the history of religion in nineteenth-century Germany as a history of relations between religious groups.[4] In short, this volume asks about the fate of Nathan.

The story begins in 1800, when, to cite Thomas Nipperdey, "nation and national unity first became decisive forces of the time."[5] It ends, provisionally, in 1914, with the outbreak of the Great War. The chronological markers thus establish nationalism and the rise of the nation-state as the main stages for the working out of these relations. This is not just a matter of convenience. For nationalism and the nation-state powerfully influenced the terms of religious conflict, supplying weapons to aggressors as well as shields to defenders. But the nation was not the only stage. There was also the local: individual states, communities, neighborhoods. And there was the personal – the religious determination of what it means to be a citizen, a man or woman, an individual.

I

The study of religious groups in modern German history has long been an established historiographical field of inquiry. Yet three salient features stand out in the landscape.

First, religion has only recently been reintegrated into broader historical interpretations. Influenced by the normative implications of modernization theory, historians used to treat religion, and religious conflict, as a historical atavism, consigning it to a subsidiary role in the historical process. To these historians, the powerful but anonymous force of industrialization, not the seemingly irrational whispers of mentalities, constituted the real motor driving history forward. Class, not religion, was the crucial category.[6]

The publication in 1988 of Thomas' Nipperdey's *Religion im Umbruch, 1870-1914* signaled a change.[7] Although there had been important and innovative works on nineteenth-century religion before, they had not found their way into the historiographical mainstream. Moreover, historians in England and the United States penned many of these works, especially concerning Catholics and Jews, and their reception among German colleagues was often sluggish.[8] Nipperdey's volume marked the rediscovery of a forgotten terrain. He not only offered a cogent critique of existing historiography, he also summarized the state of knowledge, at least for Imperial Germany.

Yet the contours of scholarly terrains shift slowly. Even after Nipperdey's volume, historians of religion lamented the continued indifference of the mainstream historical profession in Germany to the social, cultural and political impact of religion. On the one hand, it was argued, the entrenched disciplinary divide between Church history (*Kirchengeschichte*) and secular history (*Profangeschichte*) obstructed the analysis of religion as a wider social and cultural phenomenon.[9] On the other hand, the neo-Weberian modernization paradigm that underwrote so much of the best social history generated an approach that all too often seemed deaf to the modern resonances of confessional allegiances and confessional conflicts.

Today, such complaints have an obsolete ring. Since the 1980s, we have seen a stream of innovative work on the societal history of religion. The impact of work by scholars such as Wolfgang Schieder, Jonathan Sperber, Thomas Nipperdey and Urs Altermatt, to name just a very few, was not simply to draw attention to a neglected field on the margins of mainstream research, but, more importantly, to show how widely and deeply religion was woven into the fabric of modern politics and society. Religion was no longer perceived simply as an instrument of social or institutional hegemony, but as a social force capable of shaping and bestowing meaning upon political, social and cultural action. Not only is there now more scholarship on religious communities than ever, but also, and of equal importance, the best scholarship on other topics, whether concerning nation, class, or gender, typically considers the religious dimension. To this end, fields as diverse as intellectual history and the social history of madness have been significantly reconstituted by, so to speak, "bringing religion back in."[10] "Religion," as Nipperdey put it in 1988, "is no isolated province of life, [but rather] part of an interpretative culture which constitutes the entire reality of lived experience . . .".[11]

For well over a decade, historians of modern Germany have taken up Nipperdey's insight, turning what was in the 1980s a modest stream of works on religion into a veritable torrent. Various factors have contributed to this renewed interest, including an expansion of interest in the forces of cohesion at work in the electoral "milieu," growing skepticism about the validity of linear concepts of secularization (along with many other such "master narratives"), and the "cultural turn" in German historiography. Consequently, the new work is more expansive, sophisticated, and cutting-edge than the old. The faintly musty and embarrassing whiff once attached to religious history has as a result been dispelled, the ghetto of the *Kirchenhistoriker* has been gentrified, and this field is now surely one of the most vibrant growth areas in German historical studies.

If the generic boundaries between the history of religion and that of society now seem very porous, the same cannot be said for the internal divisions that still separate the historical study of each of the three religious communities. Put simply, one set of scholars writes on Protestants, another on Catholics, a third on Jews. This practice is anchored in scholarly networks (which in Germany have profound implications for university positions) and in publishing venues. In Germany, separate journals publish works on the history of Catholicism, Protestantism, and, with the recent proliferation in Germany of institutes of Jewish studies, now Jewish history as well.

In Germany, the segmentation of religious history has deep roots, typically reaching back to the religious entanglements of the nineteenth century. For it was amidst the throes of late nineteenth-century religious conflict that many of the major journals that publish scholarship in religious history were first founded. This is true of the *Archiv für Reformationsgeschichte*, established in 1883 on the quatercentenary of Luther's birth, but also as a reaction to the founding of the Catholic *Historisches Jahrbuch* in 1880. Against the backdrop of the persecution of the Kulturkampf, the *Historisches Jahrbuch* called for an explicitly Catholic historiography, and invited as contributors historians "who place Christ in the center of history and for whom the Catholic church is the God-willed educational institution of humanity."[12] Academic venues of modern Jewish history were similarly established within the wider context of religious coexistence and conflict. In 1835, Abraham Geiger founded the *Wissenschaftliche Zeitschrift für Theologie*, which, at base, and despite its title, was a historical journal that probed the essence of historical Judaism, an enterprise all the more important in the post-emancipation period. Tellingly, his son, Ludwig Geiger, the editor of the *Goethe Jahrbuch*, would later establish a more explicitly historical journal: *Die Zeitschrift für die Geschichte der Juden in Deutschland*.[13]

The segregation of historical studies along religious lines evinced a concomitant disdain, indeed rancor, across these lines. The Protestant historian Heinrich von Treitschke's comment on the Jewish historian Heinrich Graetz remains the most egregious example. "Graetz," Treitschke wrote, "is an alien [*Fremdling*] on the soil of his fortuitous host country, an oriental who neither understands our people nor wants to . . .".[14] A generation later, less caustic and less implicated in racist logic," Friedrich Meinecke would pronounce that "Catholic history professors are and remain a monstrosity."[15] If the articulation of such sentiments no longer seems publicly acceptable, it is nevertheless true that the prejudices that underlie them persisted for a very long time.

This too has changed, and confessional divisions and animosities have slowly ceded to scholarly interest in how they came about to begin with, and how they shape individual and collective behaviors. Indeed this theme has tended to become more and more prominent as historians have realized how interdependent confessional identities were and are, how they thrive on mutual misunderstandings, how impossible it is to make sense of one confessional affiliation without reference to the others by which, or against which, it defines itself. Kurt Nowak exemplified this trend when he announced in the foreword to his *Geschichte des Christentums in Deutschland* that the historiography of confessional monocultures was now a thing of the past and that it was time for a genuinely "tri-confessional" history of German Christianity, in which attention would be given not only to "the conflicts, the exchanges and commonalities" between Protestants and Catholics, but also to the complex Christian encounter with Judaism.[16]

The new emphasis on multiconfessionality has already transformed our understanding of the high politics of the old German Reich, the Holy Roman Empire. Eighteenth-century observers objected to the Machiavellian character of the *Staatsräson* that informed the relations among modern territorial states, and this view used to be accepted by historians of the post-1648 era. But some of the most interesting recent work on the Reich has highlighted the continuing importance of confessional tensions in imperial high politics.[17] A case in point is Mack Walker's subtle account of the "Salzburg Transaction" – an inter-territorially negotiated exercise in confessional cleansing by which some 20,000 Protestant dissenters from the alpine districts of Catholic Salzburg were transferred *en masse* in the early 1730s to be resettled on the lowlands of Prussian Lithuania. Walker's book demonstrated the capacity of confessional issues to divide and mobilize public opinion – one of the most interesting chapters in this work reflected on the enduring impact of the Salzburg migration on the print culture of German Protestantism. But the book also offered a fascinating glimpse of the biconfessional machinery of the Reich in action. With its separate confessional caucuses, the *corpus evangelicorum* and the *corpus catholicorum*, the Reichstag provided a forum for the perpetration of the confessional divide, not only in political action, but in public awareness.[18]

Of course, even within the history of Christianity, the Catholic–Protestant divide is not the only confessional division that deserves our attention. Historians of Prussia have, for example, long been alert to the importance of the divide between Lutherans and Reformed Protestants, and to the formative impact of the stand-off between Calvinist court and Lutheran province on the development of the Prussian state and its political culture. Carl Hinrichs pioneered this line of inquiry in his wide-ranging essays on Pietism as a force for political, cultural and spiritual renewal, but it has since been taken up by the likes of Klaus Deppermann, Hartmut Lehmann, Mary Fulbrook and Martin Greschat.[19] Its apotheosis may be found in Richard L. Gawthrop's stimulating, if sometimes overstated, book on Pietism and the making of eighteenth-century Prussia, which argued that the emergence of Prussia as a potential

German hegemon was driven by a process of Pietist confessional trans-formation from within.[20] When we celebrate the interdisciplinary vigor of the new wave of confessional historiography or deplore the narrowness of the old Church history, it is well to remember the subtlety and intel-lectual breadth with which the historiography of Pietism wove together social, political, economic and spiritual themes.

It is the nineteenth century above all that has seen productive new research on the confessional divide. On the one hand, historians have begun to attend in a more differentiated way to the phenomenon of secularization. Rudolf Schlögel and Thomas Mergel, for example, have argued that urbanization and the emergence of a culturally confident *Bürgertum* created new patterns of solidarity that crossed and muted the confessional divide.[21] On the other hand, it has long been observed that secularization was much more a Protestant than a Catholic phenomenon, and many scholars have placed this problem at the center of their work. There is increasing skepticism about whether such differences can be adequately explained by urbanization, industrialization and proletarian-ization – those mainstays of the modernization paradigm. Whereas some scholars, like Willfried Spohn, point to the very different political environments created by church–state relations, others, like Antonius Liedhegener, focus on the distinctive doctrinal, liturgical and spiritual cultures of the respective confessions.[22]

The questions these studies ask are still in a sense dictated by the familiar secularization paradigm. The decline of religious observance, albeit at variable speeds, is the phenomenon that is deemed to need explaining. Very different questions are raised by the mysterious but important phenomenon of religious renewal. It is self-evident to the point of banality that the nineteenth century saw not only the gradual dilution of confessional affiliations, but also massive periodic expansions of confessional commitment. Although there has been much interesting work on Protestant revivalism, it is Catholic renewal that has received the lion's share of the attention – one thinks here of Wolfgang Schieder's pioneering study of the Trier pilgrimage, or Otto Weiss's rich and compendious study of the Redemptorists, or Christoph Weber's work on Rhenish Catholic circles, or a string of suggestive articles by Margaret Lavinia Anderson, or David Blackbourn's justly celebrated study of the Marian visions at Marpingen.[23] These are important works of history, and, at least for the Catholic community, they have put the reconfessionalization of social and political life squarely in the center of things. In fact, so central does reconfessionalization now seem that the Bielefeld historian Olaf Blaschke, in a boisterous historiographical review published in *Geschichte und*

Gesellschaft, has urged that the nineteenth century be seen as a "second confessional era."[24] The reference here is of course to the "first confessional era" of the Reformation itself and to the "confessionalization" paradigm expounded some twenty years ago by Heinz Schilling and Wolfgang Reinhard. Indeed Blaschke's essay culminates in the proposal that the interpretative apparatus of "confessionalization" can, with some adjustments, be just as well applied to the nineteenth as to the sixteenth and seventeenth centuries. Ironically, although the term is now a fixture within the historiography, it remains controversial in its field of origin, above all for its emphasis on the close connections between state-building and the fixing of confessional identities.[25]

This intensified interest in the forces of religious renewal has also transformed our understanding of the Kulturkampf. One of the strengths of the best recent work on the Kulturkampf – in particular Ronald J. Ross's work – is that it brings to light the extraordinary social depth of a conflict that used to be seen in terms of policies and parties.[26] As Oded Heilbronner has recently observed, the new wave of research on German Catholicism has rescued the Catholics from the ghetto of historiographical neglect only to reincarcerate them in a historical ghetto, supposedly of their own making, that cut most of them off from all that was modern and progressive in German life.[27] The Catholic milieu, it is widely alleged, was involuted and backward-looking. But there is a danger here of taking at face value the back-to-basics rhetoric of revival. To take an analogy: those mid-nineteenth-century bourgeois artists who left the cities to settle in tiny villages, claiming, as they put it, that they were "returning to nature," were doing nothing of the sort. They were "returning" to something that had never existed, that had been constructed in the imagination of the urban middle classes. In other words, the quest for tradition (*Rückbesinnung*) was in this case a quintessentially modern enterprise.[28] And the same can surely be said for the wholly new quality of mid-to-late nineteenth-century Catholicism and the thoroughly modern technologies – railways, mass circulation journals, photography and so on – that sustained its devotional culture. It is interesting in this connection to consider Margaret Lavinia Anderson's recent reflections on the role of revival in stimulating and facilitating political mobilization; or to ponder more generally on the role of Catholic revival in creating wider communities of sentiment and solidarity that crossed the boundaries of the nation-states.[29]

Still, most of this work has focused on the one or the other religious group, and has rarely crossed "the invisible boundary." In addition to force of habit, there has been a methodological reason for staying within the boundaries of religious denomination. Historians of modern Germany have been at pains to tie the study of religion to the study of politics. This is a further prominent feature of the historiographical landscape, and, to this end, the concept of the "socio-moral milieu," as adumbrated by the sociologist M. R. Lepsius, has exercised an important influence. Lepsius argued that, by the end of the nineteenth century, four distinct social milieux had crystallized – a Catholic, a Conservative, a bourgeois-Protestant, and a Socialist milieu. Each constituted a dense cultural system of shared values supported by interlocking elites, common institutions, and a vast array of organizational networks. More than the narrow interest defined by class, that milieux structured political allegiances. They also ensured that German political life remained highly organized, if poorly integrated.[30] As people were socialized in their respective milieux, they rarely looked beyond the invisible borders.

The concept of milieu has had a profound influence on the study of political Catholicism, which at first glance it seems to fit like a well-made glove. Indeed, the reigning image of political Catholicism was a fortress tower guarding against the outside world, or, to adopt a modern-ized image of the same, a Taylorist corporation controlled in all its parts by "milieu managers."[31] Yet this image suggests an intentionalist, top-down model of how ideas are formed that would be seen as method-ologically primitive in any other context. Moreover, it leads historians to share the assumptions of the liberal anti-clericals of the nineteenth century, to whom "the Catholic people often appear to be putty in the clergy's hands, too dumb to know what is good for them."[32] The problem is, more-over, compounded when applied to other milieux, for this would cause us to conclude that Protestant peasants think and do as the lords of the manor instruct; and that, were it not for the rabbis, poor Jews would throw off the shackles of orthodoxy.[33] This top-down perspective informed the observations of many contemporaries and has exercised an enduring influence on the twentieth-century historiography. By contrast, present-day historians working in the tradition established by E. P. Thompson, Fernand Braudel, and Carlo Ginzburg are more sensitive to the kinds of resistance, negotiation and compromise that attend the exercise of authority within cultural systems.

Concentrating the focus of research on the making of milieux has also obfuscated the margins of these milieux and has dulled our sensibilities for the possibilities of hybridity, or, to use an older vocabulary, multiple affiliations.[34] As a consequence, it is difficult to situate Catholic workers engaged in the politics of Socialism, or middle-class Catholic men whose ties to the Church proved tenuous. Yet, as the researches of Raymond Sun, Thomas Mergel, Oded Heilbronner, and Jonathan Sperber have shown, their numbers and their influence remained profound.[35] Moreover, it was not just a question of their numbers. For the milieu theory also offered little in the way of understanding multiple affiliations. How, for example, should one analyze the Catholic worker in Cologne who helped found the local Catholic workers' club but who nevertheless voted Socialist?[36] Milieux, even the Catholic milieu, were not timeless fortresses but bastions whose walls required constant buttressing.

The creation of milieux remains a legitimate research concern.[37] Yet because the predominant paradigm has focused on the mechanisms that create consensus within a milieu, relations across religious groups, and their corresponding milieux, have remained largely outside the historian's purview. If this is true of the study of Catholicism, it also rings right for the emerging work on Protestantism. Here a central debate has been between historians who argue for polarization within the milieu and historians who see an emerging unity despite socially and religiously based differences.[38] This new work is of immense importance, as Protestants constituted the largest religious group in Imperial Germany. Yet until recently, the social history of this group has seemed exceedingly anemic, especially compared to the well-developed social histories of Catholics and Jews in Germany.[39] Precisely because this new research focuses on the construction of coherent mentalities and milieux, it has tended to overlook the way in which interaction with other groups influenced Protestantism. This problem has been exacerbated by the lack of close studies of Protestants at the communal level, where, in many parts of Germany, Protestants lived in religiously mixed villages, towns, and cities.

The historiography of German Jews faces a different set of problems. Although German Jews shared common interests, these interests never coalesced into a national milieu, and a Jewish "Center Party" never existed, though the possibility was not beyond the pale of discussion. Partly, tensions between Orthodox and Liberal Jews precluded a "Jewish Center." So too did the fact that Jews only made up 1 per cent of the population. Moreover, no single organization tied the myriad Jewish organizations together.[40] And Jews who eagerly participated in Jewish organizations as eagerly participated in non-Jewish organizations (unless discrimination precluded it). All of this meant that Jewish identity, for from resting on the networks and institutions of a closed and coherent social-moral milieu, depended, instead, on what Till van Rahden has called "situative" constellations.[41] In essence, Jewish identity was powerfully relational.

Yet the historiography on German Jews has been slow to consider the full import of this fact, and the greatest part of the history of German

Jews has been written as if either Jews lived among themselves, or Jews lived as a religious group in the context of a largely monolithic "gentile" culture, or that Christian–Jewish relations mainly concerned the problem of anti-Semitism.[42] In fact, however, Jews lived in communities where they interacted in myriad ways now with Catholics (some liberal, some conservative), now with Protestants. Moreover, the attribute of the "other" had profound influence on the quality and kind of interaction. In the German southwest, to take one example, Catholic villagers expressed considerable antipathy towards assimilated Jews, especially if they hailed from the city. Yet these same Catholics respected Jews whom they considered observant. In his immensely popular almanacs, Alban Stolz enjoined Catholics to consider rural Jews exemplary for their devotion, for their work, and for their abstinence from drink. Not rural Jews, but city Jews were the object of Stolz's anti-Semitic diatribes. But these diatribes were also directed against other city people: Old Catholics, Freemasons, Protestant professors.[43] Similarly, rural Jews – cattle traders, village rabbis, schoolmasters, tailors, seamstresses, and homemakers – knew and understood a great deal about the rhythms and rituals of religious life across the divide.[44] In the religiously mixed communities of Germany, the fault lines were not so self-evident, and the ties that bound sometimes surprisingly strong.

Concentration on milieu obscures these complicating moments in German religious history. It also undermines a sense for the common structural underpinnings of religious life. Not until recently have historians fixed their analysis on the ways in which social phenomena structure religious communities despite the lines separating them. In his masterful work on Catholics and Protestants in Münster and Bochum in the period 1830–1933, Antonius Liedhegener has, for example, addressed how Catholic and Protestant communities fared when faced with the myriad social and economic challenges of the modern world. Paradoxically, Catholic communities successfully reconstituted themselves, while Protestant communities suffered a persistent downward slide outwardly marked by a deep decline in church attendance. By isolating variables, Liedhegener shows precisely why different responses to modernity led to radically different outcomes: secularization for Protestants, religious revival for Catholics.[45]

A focus on the structural underpinnings of religious life also suggests new possibilities for comparative work. Consider some rudimentary statistics on the structure of Jewish communities and the size of the local population in Prussia in 1905. At first, the obvious stands out: more than 50 per cent of Christians still live in small villages, while nearly 50 per cent of Jews live in large cities. But between these two markers there is the whole world of German hometowns and small cities that Jews and Christians shared in equal proportions. They shared, in this sense, something of a common geography.[46] Further, there may be some similarities in the geography of religious institutions. We know that, with important exceptions, there was a north/south split in Protestant religiosity, and that, with further caveats, the areas of greatest observance are to be found to the south and west.[47] What of Jews? Here we do not have the same kind of statistics on observance, but statistics on religious infrastructure hint at similarities. Consider three such indexes: Synagogues per Jewish inhabitant; Jewish *Kultusbeamte* per Jewish inhabitant; and the number of Jewish communities in which services were held daily. Especially when we focus on the last figure, we can discern a weaker religious infrastructure for East Prussia, Brandenburg, Pomerania, Silesia (though here the numbers are complicated by Breslau), Westphalia, and the Rhine Province than for Posen, Hesse-Nassau, Bavaria, Württemberg, Baden, Hesse, and Alsace-Lorraine.[48] Similarly, the numbers of inter-faith marriages were especially low in areas like Posen, Baden and Alsace-Lorraine, where Jews continued to live in small communities, and where religious life centered on a rural synagogue in which services were held day after day. Compare Berlin, the object of anxiety of the editors of the *Zeitschrift für Demographie und Statistik der Juden*. Here the number of Jews who left their religion behind was prodigious (especially among young men and across all social classes); the number of inter-faith marriages roughly a third of the overall figure; and the religious infrastructure, as was the case for Protestants in Berlin, a catastrophe.[49]

All too typically such issues are treated separately. Yet it might make more sense to reverse this assumption, and to consider religious life as fundamentally structured, synchronically and diachronically, by common facts of religious geography. Thus, for example, the fact that severe and lasting intra-religious divisions occurred in the 1840s, especially in the cities, among Jews (between liberals and the neo-orthodoxy of Samuel Raphael Hirsch) among Catholics (Ultramontanes, liberal Catholics and German-Catholics) and among Protestants (the awakening on one side, the Friends of Light on the other) is rarely considered as part of a collective history with common antecedents.[50] As Antonius Liedhegener has brilliantly shown in his study of Protestants and Catholics in Bochum, focusing on common antecedents does not imply determinism. It does, however, suggest a research agenda, and it does give us a sense for the common challenges that confronted Protestants, Catholics, and Jews alike.

II

This research agenda may well bring us into a terrain that, from the standpoint of approach, is new, and, from the standpoint of the perspective that emerges, potentially exciting.

The work of Clifford Geertz may serve as a starting-point, for, as is well known, he suggested a way to go beyond studying culture as an epiphenomenon of a previously understood hierarchy of causality. When trained on the major religious groups of nineteenth-century Germany, this approach also encouraged us to look beyond the assumed social structuring of religious milieux implicit in the approach of Lepsius and very much at the center of the volume on *Religion im Kaiserreich*, edited by Frank-Michael Kuhleman and Olaf Blaschke. In another sense, however, Geertz's approach did not necessarily conflict with the emphasis of the Bielefeld school on the cohesion of social-moral milieux. Where one approach saw causal structuring forces, the other saw meaning. Both fixed their focus on cultural coherence.

Yet this is precisely the point on which the work of Geertz, in particular his concept of culture, has come under criticism. The idea that culture is contained, bounded, attached to a particular group in a particular place may reflect more the heritage and assumptions of spatially circumscribed fieldwork than the reality of how culture actually exists as publicly available symbols. This critique has been particularly strong from postmodern theorists, especially those who work on borderlands – zones of cultural cooperation, collision, and contention, but also of annihilation. Here cultural collision is the motor of historical change, of mutual understanding, as well as of misunderstanding, of what makes history move. Work on borderlands has also reconfigured our understanding of the coherence of cultures, especially cultures that coexist, interact, and compete. As William H. Sewell Jr. has recently put it: "Once we admit social diversity, we can no longer see cultural systems as always self-reinforcing; instead they must also be seen as sites of conflict, dialogue, and change."[51] Transferred to our narrower field, this insight would suggest a history of religious groups that takes culture seriously, but does not see culture, or mentality, as enclosed, as self-referential, as largely determined from within. This would open the history of religious groups not only to comparative study across the confessional divide but also to the history of the actual interaction of religious groups. Moreover, and following the lead of historians and anthropologists who write on borderlands and contact zones, it would make, to quote the anthropologist Sherry Ortner, "the clash of power and meaning the stuff of change and transformation."[52]

In a sense, this work has already begun, in particular concerning the centuries-old encounter between Christians and Jews. One approach has been to probe the ways in which Christian confessional conflicts shaped attitudes towards the Jews – Wolfgang Altgeld's subtle and learned survey of the turn into the nineteenth century, for example, or Dagmar Herzog's fascinating study of the Baden Landtag in the 1840s, which showed how Protestant–Catholic animosities could help to generate a parliamentary consensus in favor of Jewish emancipation.[53] There is also an emerging literature on the role of confessional affiliations in muting or intensifying the susceptibility of communities to the appeal of anti-Semitism.[54] But the logic of such arguments assigns a purely passive role to the Jews, whose function is merely to register the impact of developments within the Christian fold. By contrast, the confessional dimension in the Christian–Jewish encounter has received very little attention. That this encounter was formative – for the Christians too! – is evident, if one thinks for example of the anti-Judaizing campaigns of the Reformation era or of the fact that the Pietist movement began with Philip Jakob Spener's rethinking of the place of the Jews in the prophesied future of Christianity, or of the emergence of Christian statism in response to calls for Jewish emancipation after 1815.[55] Considering the interaction of religious communities may lead us to recast the history of the whole; it may also change our view of the individual parts.

To focus on the interaction, or clash and collision of cultural groups, may also help us set our sights to the everyday. A second critique of Geertz concerns his own tendency, and still more that of his followers, to reify culture, treating it as if it possessed foundational status – the irreducible kith and kin of older notions of structure. This, in turn, has contributed to what seems like a set of perpetual oppositions between culture and power, culture and function. In the Geertz paradigm, the questions of culture – multilayered, infinitely complex, a web of signif-ication – always seemed more interesting and innocent than questions of sheer power – who's got the maxim gun? Nor is this problem so far from the barely concealed assumptions of historians working in an ethnological mode. Consider here David Blackbourn's prescient remark in the introduc-tion to *Marpingen*: "Easier by far to summon up empathy for an oppressed Saarland villager seeking solace in the Blessed Virgin than to understand the martinets of modernity."[56] Protestants often, the martinets possessed power, and that, paradoxically, has kept historians of recent vintage from looking at their culture in quite the same way.

There is another dimension. Increasingly, historians and ethnologists are focusing less on culture as representation than on the interested way in which people deploy cultural symbols to achieve ends. This brings the study of culture back to the social process (where it had always been for the Turnerians), and back to the microanalysis of power. It enjoins us to focus on practice, on how culture is actually put to work, to what end, and with what degree of success.[57] "Function and meaning," Peter Sahlins writes, "are not alternatives, but stand in relation to each other: the practical reason of an act is an interested deployment of meanings."[58] Although this may seem more obvious with respect to the cross-dressing peasants of the Pyrenees whom Sahlins describes in *Forest Rites*, it is also an insight of larger methodological import. And it bears on an emerging historiography of religious groups who compete and who clash, not least over cultural symbols, and whose collision, at the micro and macro level, had everything to do with the interested deployment of meaning.

Finally, imagining the history of religious groups in Germany as fundamentally a history of religious cultures in coexistence and conflict places not so much religion as the plurality of religious groups in the center of things. This is important, but not just as a matter of painting in a patch of white on our mental map of the nineteenth century. Rather, it changes the way we see the whole as well as its parts. In a very recent review of research on Catholicism, Karl-Egon Lönne pointed out that the attraction of this field has to do with the fact that Catholics represented "a certain resistance against the general stream of development," and that, precisely in research into this aspect of Catholicism, historians can in a comparative way illuminate "the seemingly 'normal' developments."[59] We would argue the reverse: that cultural differentiation constituted the center; that this is what made the nineteenth century a period of cultural collision; and that this was the norm. An analytical framework burdened by the normative ballast of modernization theory and by the dystopia of cultural homogeneity will necessarily overlook this "normality." In the process it will flatten out a history that, for all its unfortunate turns, was in some ways extraordinarily rich. It is time, we think, to restore the deep, difficult, sometimes disturbing contours to the terrain.

III

The chapters that follow constitute an entry into a different way of writing the history of the major religious groups in Germany. The authors are from both sides of the Atlantic, indeed from the United States, England, Ireland, and Germany. They are also indebted to different historiographical traditions, whether Anglo-American social history, or the Bielefeld school of the history of society, or the history of concepts (*Begriffsgeschichte*).

This methodological pluralism constitutes a *novum* in a field hitherto marked by the conspicuous absence of collective work across both methodological and confessional borders. What follows, then, is decidedly not a collection of "in-house" histories: Catholics do not necessarily write about Catholics, Protestants about Protestants or Jews about Jews. We try instead to break away from paradigms centered on cohesive and bounded religious identities. Yet two threads powerfully bind the chapters together. The first is the idea that religious groups in Germany can no longer be treated in isolation. The second is that bringing previously separated histories together adds immeasurably to the richness and complexity of the story.

The chapters in this volume powerfully suggest that the trajectory of each religious group cannot be understood without carefully considering its relationship to the other major confessional groups. This is true not just at one level but at many. Wolfgang Altgeld, for example, shows how Protestant theologians fundamentally shaped the idea of nationalism and, as a result, brought to a powerful discourse of community a religious language of inclusion and exclusion. The insight is important in many ways, not least because it dispels the notion that nationalism was at its core a secular phenomenon. Yes, nationalism partook of the modern; but that did not necessarily make it secular. The ongoing debate between Catholics and Protestants on the suitability of Gustavus Adolphus as a national hero would not, as Kevin Cramer demonstrates, make sense otherwise. Ideas also have a materiality, as Jeff Zalar shows with respect to the different but overlapping and competing worlds of confessional printing and publishing. Indeed, this element of competition often had surprising results, especially in politics. The nineteenth-century trajectory of Jewish emancipation, as both Chris Clark and Dagmar Herzog argue, cannot be understood without reference to the religious revivals among Protestants and Catholics. But reason, as Hegel knew, is cunning. Chris Clark sees the Protestant Awakening as a powerful force shifting Prussian policies towards Jews. Against a well-established historiography, he argues that the politics of Jewish emancipation cannot be understood as the slow, but sure breakthrough of Enlightened measures but must, instead, be seen in the context of the Protestant revival that shaped these measures. Dagmar Herzog also sees religious revival as powerfully shaping the possibilities of Jewish emancipation, but in a different way. In Baden, it was the liberal deputies reacting against the gathering storm of Catholic revival that shaped a consensus for Jewish emancipation. In either case, however, the notion that Jewish emancipation happened within a fundamentally secular frame needs to be reconsidered. In fact, it happened within a context of now Protestant, now Catholic revival.

Introduction

Historians have considered these revivals, or awakenings, before; but we have yet to consider the full extent of their interrelation. Lucian Hölscher and Michael Gross look at this from two very different angles. Lucian Hölscher, who has written extensively on Protestant piety, addresses the awakening within the general context of long-term shifts in religiosity. These shifts were marked, according to Hölscher, by the individualization of belief, by the increasing separation of personal faith from Church doctrine, by the importance of the home as the locus of religious socialization, and by the influence of science on the possibilities of religious certainty. Shifts in piety also engendered a reshaping of confessional boundaries, which Hölscher sees as a constituent element of modernization, and which was absorbed by new forms of religious community that, in turn, shaped social and political conflicts. Michael Gross focuses initially on the revivals themselves, revealing how tremendously successful they were in the 1850s, especially in the countryside and in small towns. They were not only successful; they also drew attention, not least from Protestants, many of whom actually went to the revivals. In reaction, Protestant pastors redoubled their efforts to distinguish Protestant from Catholic. In no small sense, then, late-nineteenth-century understandings of confessional differences derived from the competitive pressures of the religion next door.

By the late-nineteenth-century, this aspect of the formation of confessional communities emerges even more clearly. It emerges in Róisín Healy's discussion of the bourgeois Protestant construction of the Jesuit as an androgyne – at once masculine and feminine, active and passive, cunning and malleable, insistent on authority and slavish towards superiors. Healy suggests that, for liberal Protestants, seeing Jesuits as figures that transgressed fixed sexual identities imparted an explosive *élan* to the Jesuit question. As a discourse, "anti-Jesuitism" revealed less about the handful of Jesuits in Germany than it did about middle-class anxieties concerning the manliness of liberal Protestantism. The anxiety of demarcation is also the theme of Anthony Steinhoff's essay on "building religious community." In Strasbourg, consideration of the differences between Protestant and Catholic fundamentally influenced the space of Protestant religiosity and the concrete aspects of the Protestant imagined community. Steinhoff considers how, after 1870, the Protestant community in Strasbourg went about reconstructing the "Lutheran New Church," which had been destroyed in the war. Historians, he insists, have written a great deal about community without looking at the actual space and the actual rituals that create it. Among the Protestants of Strasbourg, these spaces and rituals were in a competitive field – in the shadow of, and with an eye to, the towering spires of Strasbourg's Catholic cathedral. On the other side of the Empire, the Jews of Breslau felt the limits of religious pluralism, despite formal emancipation. The liberal city council insisted that in the new *Gymnasium*, pupils from each of the three religious groups should receive religious instruction, and that Judaism, like Protestantism and Catholicism, ought to be represented as a compulsory subject. Yet this idea broke apart on the shoals of intra-religious conflict, especially between Old Catholics and Roman Catholics, and the stubborn rock of a Prussian bureaucracy beholden to the notion of a Christian state. Although some liberals clung tenaciously to an abstract pluralism that granted the three religious communities equal rights, others universalized positions that essentially derived from the ethical precepts of cultural Protestantism. In the end, and with considerable consequence for the future, neither Protestants nor Catholics developed a discourse of rights centered on the right to be different.

Nevertheless, living together entailed arrangement. Historians have often overlooked this rich world of give and take, knowledge and ignorance, living together and apart. The large questions of history, and the analytical tools we use to examine the past, all too often push us to see difference where commonality also existed, conflict where there was also neighborliness. In his chapter entitled "How Jews, Catholics and Protestants Lived Together in Rural Baden, 1862–1940," Uli Baumann addresses what he calls the "social institutions" of the village and small town, the sites – formal and informal – of everyday contact, ordinary relations, and all too ordinary kinds of conflict. He shows not only that these social institutions existed, but also that for a myriad reasons they unraveled in the inter-war period, and were destroyed in the Third Reich.

These chapters also suggest that the experience of Protestants, Catholics and Jews as groups "living apart and together" partook of wider dilemmas involved in modern societies negotiating between the hunger for wholeness and the pull of particularity. Margaret Lavinia Anderson addresses this dilemma of unity and difference in her afterword to this volume. She reminds us that while many aspects of the German experience placed it on a special path, the problem of how to navigate the dilemma of pluralist societies does not have a self-evident solution. Yet if there is a lesson to be learned, it surely concerns the dangers inherent in a dystopia of imagined unity, especially when purchased with what seems like the small change of the particular, religious or otherwise.

In the chapters that follow, we attempt to demarcate the territory of German religious history as the interaction of the major religious groups. Part II of the volume introduces the topic in broad outline. It begins with the text of Lucian Hölscher's inaugural lecture, one of the first forays into the field of genuine comparison, Protestant with Catholic. It is followed by Wolfgang Altgeld's trenchant analysis of the way in which Protestant ideas of the nation were soaked in anti-Catholic ideas, and how these ideas, in turn, powerfully shaped Protestant views of Jews. Chris Clark takes this analysis from the realm of print culture and ideology to the state and its policies, and shows how Prussia's conception of itself as a Christian state, and not its secular agenda, structured Jewish emancipation in the nineteenth century. Conversely, Prussia's emerging Jewish policy influenced, in turn, what it meant to be a Christian state. These are sweeping essays that stake out the wide boundaries of the territory.

In Part III, the terrain is considered in more detail. Kevin Cremer focuses on how Gustavus Adolphus, the Swedish king and military hero (or anti-hero) of the Thirty Years War, became a flashpoint of debates between Protestants and Catholics about the character of the German nation. It is followed by a methodologically innovative chapter by Jeffrey T. Zalar, who argues that Catholic reading was not as separate from Protestant as some historians have supposed, and shows how religious cultures were, in fact, deeply intertwined. Thereafter, Róisín Healy reveals the gendered construction of Protestant images of Jesuits in Imperial Germany, and how these images reflected anxieties about the manliness of liberal Protestantism.

In Part IV, on religious difference, local politics, and pluralism, two chapters that are in interpretative tension are placed next to each other. Originally published in 1995, Dagmar Herzog's "The Rise of the Religious Right and the Recasting of the 'Jewish Question'" was one of the first essays to demonstrate that debates over Jewish rights were set within intra-Christian discourses. It is followed by Till van Rahden's chapter on "Pluralism in School Politics," which shows how important issues of local religious politics revealed cracks in liberalism's universalist claims.

The final Part, "From Conflict to Coexistence," is about the impact of the major religious communities on each other. In an important revisionist essay, Michael Gross argues that the example of Catholic missionaries shaped the Protestant revival in important ways. In a similar manner, if with different conclusions, Anthony J. Steinhoff demonstrates that Protestant church-builders in Strasbourg were at pains to create Protestant worship spaces that looked different from Catholic spaces. Finally, Ulrich Baumann probes in considerable local detail the possibilities for cooperation and coexistence between Jews, Catholics and Protestants in Baden. Anti-Semitism certainly existed in this region, but this never exhausted the local possibilities of interaction between Jews and other confessions.

There is then an afterword by Margaret Lavinia Anderson, who offers a panoramic survey of the interactions of Protestants, Catholics, and Jews in nineteenth-century Germany, and places the German experience in a wider European context.

Notes

1. Friedrich Nicolai, *Beschreibung einer Reise durch Deutschland und die Schweiz im Jahre 1781*, Vol. 7 (Berlin and Stettin: F. Nicolai, 1786), p. 63.
2. Christian Konrad Wilhelm Dohm, *Ueber die bürgerliche Verbesserung der Juden* (Berlin and Stettin: F. Nicolai, 1781), p. 3.
3. Immanuel Kant, *Zum Ewigen Frieden*, ed. Theodor Valentiner (Stuttgart: Reclam, 1954), p. 49.
4. Etienne François, *Die unsichtbare Grenze: Protestanten und Katholiken in Augsburg, 1648–1806* (Sigmaringen: Jan Thorbecke Verlag, 1991).
5. Thomas Nipperdey, *Nachdenken über die deutsche Geschichte* (Munich: C. H. Beck, 1986), p. 207.
6. The *locus classicus* was Hans-Ulrich Wehler, *Das deutsche Kaiserreich 1871-1918*, 4th edn. (Göttingen: Vandenhoeck and Ruprecht, 1980), pp. 118–21, where religion was considered an "ideology of legitimation." For a more nuanced view, reflecting shifts in the discipline, but structurally indebted to older hierarchies of causality that privilege class over culture, see H.-U. Wehler, *Deutsche Gesellschaftsgeschichte*, vols. 2–3 (Munich: C. H. Beck, 1989–1995).
7. Thomas Nipperdey, *Religion im Umbruch. Deutschland 1870–1918* (Munich: C. H. Beck, 1988).
8. Some prominent examples include Robert Liberles, *Religious Conflict in Social Context: The Resurgence of Orthodox Judaism in Frankfurt am Main, 1838–1877* (Westport, CT:Greenwood Press, 1985); Steven M. Lowenstein, *The Mechanics of Change: Essays in the Social History of German Jewry* (Atlanta, NJ: Scholars Press, 1992); Jonathan Sperber, *Popular Catholicism in Nineteenth-Century Germany* (Princeton, NJ: Princeton University Press, 1985), which however was widely received; and Margaret L. Anderson and Kenneth L. Barkin, "The Myth of the Puttkamer Purge and the Reality of the Kulturkampf: Some Reflections on the Historiography of Imperial Germany," *Journal of Modern History*, 54,4 (1982): 647–86, a pathbreaking article whose problematic reception is worth a study in itself.
9. See the trenchant analysis in Jonathan Sperber, "Kirchengeschichte or the Social and Cultural History of Religion," *Neue Politische*

Literatur 43 (1998): 13–35; and the searching essays in Anselm Doering-Manteuffel and Kurt Nowak (eds), *Kirchliche Zeitgeschichte* (Stuttgart: W. Kohlhammer, 1996).

10. In intellectual history, see especially George Williamson, "The Longing for Myth in Germany: Culture, Religion, and Politics, 1790–1878" (Ph.D. dissertation, Yale, 1996) and Warren Breckman, *Marx, the Young Hegelians, and the Origins of Radical Social Theory* (Cambridge: Cambridge University Press, 1999). See also Ann Goldberg, *Sex, Religion, and the Making of Modern Madness: The Eberbach Asylum and German Society 1815–1849* (New York: Oxford University Press, 1999). Another straw in the wind is the fact that for the first time in recent memory a work focused on a religious group received the "Nachwuchs" prize of the Deutscher Historikerverband: see Ulrich Sieg, "Jüdische Intellektuelle im Ersten Weltkrieg. Kriegserfahrungen, weltanschauliche Debatten und kulturelle Neuentwürfe" (Habilitation, University of Marburg, 2000).

11. Nipperdey, *Religion im Umbruch*, p. 7.

12. *Historisches Jahrbuch* 1(1888). "Programm der von der historischen Section der Görres-Gesellschaft zu gründenden Zeitschrift für Geschichte."

13. Michael A. Meyer, "The Emergence of Modern Jewish Historiography: Motives and Motifs," *History and Theory* 27(1988): 160–75.

14. Cited in Ulrich Langer, *Heinrich von Treitschke: Politische Biographie eines deutschen Nationalisten* (Düsseldorf: Droste, 1998), p. 311. On the failure of dialogue between Jewish and Christian scholars of religious history, see Susannah Heschel, *Abraham Geiger and the Jewish Jesus* (Chicago: Chicago University Press, 1998). On anti-Jewish attitudes in later nineteenth-century Protestant publications, see now the exhaustive treatment by Wolfgang Heinrichs, *Das Judenbild im Protestantismus des deutschen Kaiserreichs* (Cologne: Rheinland-Verlag, 2000).

15. Cited in Ronald Ross, *Beleaguered Tower: The Dilemma of Political Catholicism in Wilhelmine Germany* (Notre Dame, IN: University of Notre Dame Press, 1976), p. 26.

16. Kurt Nowak, *Geschichte des Christentums in Deutschland: Religion, Politik und Gesellschaft vom Ende der Aufklärung bis zur Mitte des 20. Jahrhunderts* (Munich: C. H. Beck, 1995), pp. 10–11. Whether the book as a whole succeeds in realizing this laudable objective is a matter for debate; but the intention itself is noteworthy. For an innovative, and genuinely tri-confessional, approach to European history in the nineteenth century, though one in which religious

groups are treated separately, see Rainer Liedtke and Stephan Wendehorst (eds), *The Emancipation of Catholics, Jews and Protestants* (Manchester: Manchester University Press, 1999).

17. For an overview of this literature, see Joel F. Harrington and Helmut Walser Smith, "Confessionalization, Community, and State Building in Germany, 1555–1870," *Journal of Modern History* 69,1 (March, 1997): 77–101.

18. Mack Walker, *The Salzburg Transaction: Expulsion and Redemption in Eighteenth-Century Germany* (Ithaca, NY: Cornell University Press, 1992). Similar themes surfaced in Gabriele Haug-Moritz's *Württembergischer Ständekonflikt und deutscher Dualismus* (Stuttgart: W. Kohlhammer, 1992). Haug-Moritz's central concern was the structure of domestic political conflict in mid-eighteenth-century Württemberg, but her book also shed much light on the continuing importance of interterritorial networks of confessional solidarity. Both books, in other words, point to the importance of the confessional divide in projects of political aggrandizement, and both hint at the ways in which the exploitation of a confessionally polarized public opinion could hollow out the legitimacy of an imperial sovereignty increasingly seen as the instrument of only one confessional party.

19. Martin Greschat, *Orthodoxie und Pietismus* (Stuttgart: W. Kohlhammer, 1982); Klaus Deppermann, *Der hallesche Pietismus und der Preussische Staat unter Friedrich III.* (Göttingen: Vandenhoeck and Ruprecht, 1961); Hartmut Lehmann, *Pietismus und weltliche Ordnung in Württemberg vom 17. bis zum 20. Jahrhundert* (Stuttgart: W. Kohlhammer, 1969); Mary Fulbrook, *Piety in Politics: Religion and the Rise of Absolutism in England, Württemberg and Prussia* (Cambridge: Cambridge University Press, 1983); Martin Greschat (ed.), *Zur neueren Pietismusforschung* (Darmstadt: Wissenschaftliche Verlagsanstalt, 1977).

20. Richard Gawthrop, *Piety and the Making of Eighteenth-century Prussia* (Cambridge: Cambridge University Press, 1993).

21. Thomas Mergel, *Zwischen Klasse und Konfession: Katholisches Bürgertum im Rheinland* (Göttingen: Vandenhoeck and Ruprecht, 1994); Rudolf Schlögel, *Glaube und Religion in der Säkularisierung: Die katholische Stadt – Köln, Aachen, Münster – 1700–1840* (Munich: Oldenbourg, 1995).

22. Wilfried Spohn, "Religion and Working-Class Formation," *in Society, Culture and the State in Germany 1870–1930*, ed. Geoff Eley (Ann Arbor, MI: University of Michigan Press, 1996), 163–88; Antonius Liedhegener, *Christentum und Urbanisierung: Katholiken und*

Protestanten in Münster und Bochum 1880–1933 (Paderborn: Ferdinand Schöningh, 1997). For an international collection of essays summarizing much of the current state of research, see Hartmut Lehmann (ed.), *Säkularisierung, Dechristianisierung, Rechristianisierung im neuzeitlichen Europa* (Göttingen: Vandenhoeck and Ruprecht, 1997).

23. On Protestant revivalism, see especially Josef Mooser (ed.), *Frommes Volk und Patrioten: Erweckungsbewegung und soziale Frage im östlichen Westfalen, 1800–1900* (Bielefeld: Verlag für Regionalgeschichte, 1989). See also the exciting dissertation of David Ellis, "A Foot in Each Kingdom: Politics and Piety in the Protestant 'Awakening' in Brandenburg and Pomerania, 1816–1858," (Ph.D. Thesis, University of Chicago, 2001). On Catholic revival, see Wolfgang Schieder, "Kirche und Revolution. Sozialgeschichtliche Aspekte der Trierer Wallfahrt von 1844," *Archiv für Sozialgeschichte* 14 (1974), 419–54 (but see also the sharp criticisms of social reductionism in Rudolf Lill, "Kirche und Revolution. Zu den Anfängen der katholischen Bewegung im Jahrhundert vor 1848," *Archiv für Sozialgeschichte* 18(1978): 565–75); Otto Weiss, *Die Redemptoristen in Bayern (1790–1909)* (St Ottilien: EOS, 1983); Christoph Weber, *Aufklärung und Orthodoxie am Mittelrhein 1820–1850* (Munich: Ferdinand Schöningh, 1973); Margaret Lavinia Anderson, "The Limits of Secularization: On the Problem of the Catholic Revival in Nineteenth-Century Germany," *The Historical Journal* 38,3 (September 1995); M. L. Anderson, "The Kulturkampf and the Course of German History," *Central European History* 19,1 (1986): 82–115; David Blackbourn, *Marpingen: Apparitions of the Virgin Mary in a Nineteenth-Century German Village* (New York, Alfred A. Knopf, 1994).

24. Olaf Blaschke, "Das 19. Jahrhundert: Ein Zweites Konfessionelles Zeitalter?" *Geschichte und Gesellschaft* 26 (2000): 38–75. At one level, the thesis is hardly new. Consider Harold J. Laski, *Studies in the Problem of Sovereignty* (New Haven, CT: Yale University Press, 1917): "The Catholic revival and the growth of nationalism are perhaps the two most fundamental facts in the history of the nineteenth century" (cited in Margaret Lavinia Anderson, "The Divisions of the Pope: The Catholic Revival and Europe's Transition to Democracy," in Austen Ivereigh (ed.), *The Politics of Religion in an Age of Revival*, (London: *ILAS Nineteenth Century Latin America Series*, 2000). Blaschke's thesis, on the other hand, overshoots the mark (see Anderson in the afterword to this volume).

25. The most recent (1990) edition of the *Theologische Realenzyklopädie* was the first to include an entry on confessionalization. For recent studies that raise doubts about the impact of top-down "confessionalization", see C. Scott Dixon, *The Reformation and Rural Society, The Parishes of Brandenburg-Ansbach-Kulmbach, 1528–1603* (Cambridge: Cambridge University Press, 1996), which is skeptical of the Brandenburg state's capacity to enforce confessional conformity, and Bodo Nischan, *Prince, People and Confession. The Second Reformation in Brandenburg* (Philadelphia: University of Pennsylvania Press, 1994), which raises similar doubts in connection with Calvinist efforts at confessionalization in Brandenburg. For a general account of modern Protestantism in the German states that emphasizes the relative immunity of the Lutheran "parishscape" to interventions from above, see Nicholas Hope, *German and Scandinavian Protestantism 1700 to 1918* (Oxford: Oxford University Press, 1995). Heinz Schilling discusses many of the objections to the confessionalization paradigm in "Die Konfessionalisierung von Kirche, Staat und Gesellschaft – Profil, Leistung, Defizite und Perspektiven eines geschichtswissenschaftlichen Paradigmas," in W. Reinhard and H. Schilling (eds), *Die Katholische Konfessionalisierung. Wissenschaftliches Symposion der Gesellschaft zur Herausgabe des Corpus Catholicorum und des Vereins für Reformationsgeschichte* (Münster: Aschendorff, 1995), pp. 1–49.
26. Ronald J. Ross, *The Failure of Bismarck's Kulturkampf: Catholicism and State Power in Imperial Germany, 1871–1887* (Washington, DC: Catholic University of America Press, 1998). See also, for a fine local study, Norbert Schloßmacher, *Düsseldorf im Bismarckreich* (Düsseldorf: Schwann, 1985).
27. Oded Heilbronner, "From Ghetto to Ghetto; The Place of German Catholic Society in Recent Historiography," *Journal of Modern History* 72,2(June 2000): 453–95.
28. For reflections along these lines on the paradoxical centrality of "nostalgia" to modern consciousness, see Nina Lübbren, *Rural Artists' Colonies in Nineteenth-Century Europe* (Manchester: Manchester University Press, 2001).
29. See Margaret Lavinia Anderson, "Voter, Landrat, Junker, Priest: The Old Authorities and the New Franchise in Imperial Germany," *American Historical Review* 98,5 (December, 1993), 14448–74; and, in more detail, Margaret Lavinia Anderson, *Practicing Democracy: Elections and Political Culture in Imperial Germany* (Princeton, NJ: Princeton University Press, 2000).

30. M. Rainer Lepsius, "Parteiensystem und Sozialstruktur: Zum Problem der Demokratisierung der deutschen Gesellschaft," in *Deutsche Parteien vor 1918*, ed. Gerhard A. Ritter (Cologne: Kiepenheuer and Witsch, 1990), pp. 56–80.

31. Olaf Blaschke, "Die Kolonisierung der Laienwelt: Priester als Milieumanager und die Kanäle klerikaler Kuratel," in *Religion im Kaiserreich*, ed. Olaf Blaschke and Frank-Michael Kuhlemann (Gütersloh: Chr. Kaiser, 1996), pp. 93–135.

32. Anderson, "The Limits of Secularization," p. 651.

33. The analogous position in the field of labor history, represented in the historiography of the SPD in the 1960s, is that the worldview of workers was at one with the political imperatives of trade unionists and SPD functionaries.

34. Gary B. Cohen, "Jews in German Society: Prague, 1860–1914," *Central European History* 10 (1977): 28–54.

35. Mergel, *Zwischen Klasse und Konfession*; Raymond Chien Sun, *Before the Enemy is Within Our Walls: Catholic Workers in Cologne, 1885–1912* (Boston: Humanities Press, 1999); Jonathan Sperber, *The Kaiser's Voters: Electors and Elections in Imperial Germany* (New York: Cambridge University Press, 1997); Oded Heibronner, *Catholicism, Political Culture, and the Countryside: A Social History of the Nazi Party in South Germany* (Ann Arbor, MI: University of Michigan Press, 1998).

36. Sun, *Before the Enemy is Within Our Walls*, p. 283.

37. The most forceful defense is Blaschke and Kuhlemann (eds), *Religion im Kaiserreich*, pp. 7–56. See also, in the same volume, Siegfried Weichlein, "Konfession und Region: Katholische Milieubildung am Beispiel Fuldas," pp. 193–232. Note the "we'll-stay-with-the-ship-come-what-may" tone in Peter Lösche and Franz Walter, 'Katholiken, Konservative und Liberale: Milieus und Lebenswelten bürgerlicher Parteien in Deutschland während des 20. Jahrhunderts," *Geschichte und Gesellschaft* 26 (2000): 471–92, which begins: "Despite the dirges, 'milieu' remains an important category of research."

38. Compare Gangolf Hübinger, *Kulturprotestantismus und Politik: Zum Verhältnis von Liberalismus und Protestantismus im wilhelminischen Deutschland* (Tübingen: Mohr Siebeck, 1994) with Dietmar von Reeken, *Kirchen im Umbruch zur Moderne: Milieubildungsprozesse im nordwestdeutschen Protestantismus 1849–1914* (Gütersloh: Chr. Kaiser, 1999). See also the important review of Hübinger by Frank-Michael Kuhlemann, "Das protestantische Milieu auf dem Prüfstand," *Zeitschrift für neuere Theologiegeschichte* 3 (1996): 303–12. For the

gravity of division in the first half of the nineteenth century, see the extremely insightful essay of Friedrich Wilhelm Graf, "Die Spaltung des Protestantismus. Zum Verhältnis von evangelischer Kirche, Staat und 'Gesellschaft' im frühen 19. Jahrhundert," in *Religion und Gesellschaft*, ed. Wolfgang Schieder (Stuttgart: Klett-Cotta, 1993), pp. 157–90.

39. See von Reeken, *Kirchen im Umbruch zur Moderne*.

40. For a discussion of this problem by a Jewish civil rights activist, see Landgerichtsrat Wollstein, "Unser Verhalten gegen den Antisemitismus in politischer, sittlicher und gesellschaftlicher Beziehung," *Im Deutschen Reich* 6 (April 1900): 177–91. On these issues more generally, see Christopher Clark, "The Jews and the German State in the Wilhelmine Era," in *Two Nations. British and German Jews in Comparative Perspective*, ed. Michael Brenner, Rainer Liedtke and David Rechter (Tübingen: Mohr Siebeck, 1999); Peter Pulzer, *Jews and the German State. The Political History of a Minority, 1848–1933* (Oxford: Oxford University Press, 1992).

41. Till van Rahden, "Weder Milieu noch Konfession. Die situative Ethnizität der deutschen Juden im Kaiserreich in vergleichender Perspektive," in Blaschke and Kuhlemann (eds), *Religion im Kaiserreich*, pp. 409–34, esp. pp. 423–4.

42. A useful, if dated, review of the literature may be found in Shulamit Volkov, *Die Juden in Deutschland 1780–1918* (Munich: Oldenbourg, 1994). See also Michael Meyer (ed.), *German-Jewish History in Modern Times*, vols. 2 and 3 (New York: Columbia University Press, 1997). An early and important exception to the tendency to paint Christianity with a large brush was Uriel Tal, *Christians and Jews in Germany: Religion, Politics, and Ideology in the Second Reich, 1870–1914*, trans. Noah Jonathan Jacobs (Ithaca, NY: Cornell University Press, 1975). As the social history of Jews in Germany and of anti-Semitism becomes more developed, the image of the Christian "other" has necessarily become more complex. Two examples include Till van Rahden, *Juden und andere Breslauer: Die Beziehungen zwischen Juden, Protestanten und Katholiken in einer deutschen Großstadt von 1860 bis 1925* (Göttingen: Vandenhoeck and Ruprecht, 2000) and the essays on anti-Semitic violence in Werner Bergmann, Christhard Hoffmann and Helmut Walser Smith, eds. *Exclusionary Violence: Antisemitic Riots in Modern German History* (Ann Arbor, MI: Michigan University Press, 2002).

43. On Stolz, see Helmut Walser Smith, "Religion and Conflict: Protestants, Catholics, and Anti-Semitism in the State of Baden in the Era

of Wilhelm II," *Central European History* 27,3 (1994): 312–13. For a different view, see Dagmar Herzog, "Anti-Judaism in Intra-Christian Conflict: Catholics and Liberals in Baden in the 1840s," *Central European History* 27,3 (1994): 273–5.

44. Steven M. Lowenstein, "Jüdisches religiöses Leben in deutschen Dörfern. Regionale Unterschiede im 19. und frühen 20. Jahrhundert," in *Jüdisches Leben auf dem Lande*, ed. Monika Richarz and Reinhard Rürup (Tübingen: Mohr Siebeck, 1997), pp. 219–30.

45. Antonius Liedhegener, *Christentum und Urbanisierung: Katholiken und Protestanten in Münster und Bochum 1880–1933* (Paderborn: Ferdinand Schöningh, 1997). See also Stefan J. Dietrich, *Christentum und Revolution: Die christlichen Kirchen in Württemberg 1848–1952* (Paderborn: Ferdinand Schöningh,1996).

46. *Zeitschrift für Demographie und Statistik der Juden* 2,12 (December, 1906): 187–9.

47. Lucian Hölscher, *Weltgericht oder Revolution: Protestantische und sozialistische Zukunftsvorstellungen im deutschen Kaiserreich* (Stuttgart: Klett-Cotta, 1989), p. 143.

48. *Zeitschrift für Demographie und Statistik der Juden* 1,9 (September, 1905): 1–5.

49. *Zeitschrift für Demographie und Statistik der Juden* 3,5 (May, 1907): 79–80. See now also the detailed work of Kerstin Meiring, *Die Christlich-jüdische Mischehe in Deutschland 1840–1933* (Hamburg: Dölling and Galitz, 1988), pp. 91–101.

50. For a start, see Werner Blessing, "Reform, Restauration, Rezession: Kirchenreligion und Volksreligiösität zwischen Aufklärung und Industrialisierung," in *Volksreligiösität in der modernen Sozialgeschichte*, ed. Wolfgang Schieder (Göttingen: Vandenhoeck and Ruprecht, 1986), pp. 97–122.

51. William H. Sewell Jr., "Geertz, Cultural Systems, and History: From Synchrony to Transformation," in Sherry B. Ortner (ed.), *The Fate of "Culture": Geertz and Beyond* (Berkeley, CA: University of California Press, 1991), p. 51.

52. Ortner, *The Fate of "Culture."* p. 8.

53. Wolfgang Altgeld, *Katholizismus, Protestantismus, Judentum: Über religiös begründete Gegensätze und nationalreligiöse Ideen in der Geschichte des deutschen Nationalismus* (Mainz: Matthias-Grünewald-Verlag, 1992); Dagmar Herzog, *Intimacy and Exclusion: Religious Politics in Pre-Revolutionary Baden* (Princeton, NJ: Princeton University Press, 1996).

54. Smith, "Religion and Conflict."

55. On these issues, see Christopher Clark, *The Politics of Conversion. Missionary Protestantism and the Jews in Prussia, 1728–1941* (Oxford: Oxford University Press, 1995).
56. Blackbourn, *Marpingen*, xxxiv.
57. See Richard Biernacki, "Method and Metaphor after the New Cultural History," in *Beyond the Cultural Turn*, ed. Victoria E. Bonnell and Lynn Hunt (Berkeley, CA: University of California Press, 1999), pp. 62–94. See also Till van Rahden, "Words and Actions: Rethinking the Social History of German Antisemitism, Breslau, 1870–1914," *German History* 18,4 (2000): 416.
58. Peter Sahlins, *Forest Rites: The War of the Demoiselles in Nineteenth-Century France* (Cambridge, MA: Harvard University Press, 1994), p. 129.
59. Karl-Egon Lönne, "Katholizismus-Forschung," *Geschichte und Gesellschaft* 26 (2000): 128, fn.1.

Part II
Outlines

–2–

The Religious Divide: Piety in Nineteenth-Century Germany

Lucian Hölscher

On 30 July 1911 the Protestant Vicar of Cologne, Carl Jatho, turned to the famous Berlin Church historian, Adolph von Harnack, to ask him in an open letter for his support: "Full of hope and trust the free theological youth looks to you. It sees you as a leader who can show a safe path through the labyrinth of theological speculation . . . you know as much as I do that true science has no other boundaries than those drawn by the reason and conscience of the researcher. Let us therefore work together, my dear Professor, in the great and glorious endeavor to preserve this noble principle and to apply it also to Protestant theology and its priest-hood."[1]

Four weeks earlier, Carl Jatho had been dismissed from office for his "heretical" views by an official Church ruling of the doctrinal body (*Spruchkollegium*) of the Prussian Church. Although Harnack, a deputy member of the Spruchkollegium, did not support this judgment, he left no doubt that Jatho's "whole theological position was outside the realm of ideas supported by the [Prussian] Church."[2] Yet Jatho had fought for Harnack's consent. Did they not both reject the belief in a personal God? Did they not see Christ as an exemplary man in search of God and not as a divine being? Had Harnack's criticism of the history of dogmatic theology not shown the extent to which concepts of God and Christ had changed over time? And did not academic freedom allow him to defend himself against all dogmatic truth claims of church orthodoxy? But Harnack brusquely rejected Jatho. Harnack had never defined Christ as merely a man seeking God, but instead always taught that Christ was the Messiah and Lord of the Church. Nor had it ever occurred to Harnack to equate God with natural law in a pantheistic or monistic way as Jatho had done. There was also no question of a threat to scientific freedom as Jatho had claimed, for, according to Harnack, what was at stake here was whether the Church "could and should tolerate preachers who make no distinction between God and the world."[3]

The controversy between Jatho and Harnack shows all the symptoms of the religious divide within Protestant piety on the eve of the First World War: the contradiction between religion and science; i.e. the deep disagreement about the significance of historical and scientific findings for Christian tradition; the contrast between personal and impersonal faith; and the contrast between Jatho's claim to profess his individual, free belief and Harnack's holding on to the identity of essential, historically unchanging, Christian doctrines. Jatho's dismissal from office provoked a huge outcry among the German public. An absolutely irreproachable minister, Jatho was well connected, with a faithful following in Cologne and in neighboring cities deep into the Ruhr area. Well-respected theologians like Otto Baumgarten in Kiel had pleaded for him to stay; and Jatho's liberal colleague in Dortmund, Gottfried Traub, even risked losing his own office by insulting the Berlin *Spruchkollegium* over the issue.

Similar long-standing internal conflicts, more moderate but nevertheless important, could also be seen in the Catholic Church. The tensions between ecclesiastical tradition and modern culture had likewise come to a head in Catholicism. Following the frontal assault against modern culture and science represented by the "Syllabus of Errors" of 1864, and the declaration of papal infallibility during the first Vatican Council in 1870, an anti-modern oath required all Catholic priests after 1910 to reject a detailed corpus of modern theological principles and insights. When in 1905 the radical separation of church and state in France signaled a permanent marginalization of the church in state and society, many Germans felt that the end of both Churches was near.

Historians of religion have mainly interpreted religious tensions within nineteenth-century society as a matter of church politics and not as manifestations of a much deeper and more rooted religious division within nineteenth-century piety. Here I want to address this split, its origins, and its consequences for the general history of the nineteenth century. First of all: how do we define piety? The following inquiry defines piety as a way of thinking and behaving that justifies itself as "pious" because it relates to a common religious ground. Piety is thus not a normative definition of the "right," God-pleasing life but instead a category of subjective self-understanding, a form of discursive and pragmatic self-definition. Piety is understood here as a kind of mental interior within which individuals interpret the outside world and which guides their actions.

The following sketch of a history of piety in the nineteenth century consists of seven theses.

1. *Within the history of piety, the eighteenth century marks an epochal caesura that fundamentally separates modern and pre-modern devotional culture.* The decisive elements of this caesura are the separation of confession (*Konfession*) and belief (*Bekenntnis*), of official Church doctrine and personal faith.

The transition in devotional culture can be seen from the changing religious and social meanings of communion in the eighteenth century. In the constitution of early modern religious communities, communion was mainly a judgement of conscience (*Gewissensgericht*). Regular attendance at communion constituted a basic duty of every adult Christian. At least among members of the middle class and the peasantry, attendance was also rigorously enforced. The conscience of the people was sharpened above all by the threat of divine and Church punishment if someone participated in communion without having made his or her peace with God and man through absolution. In political terms, the purpose of communion was to safeguard or to restore social peace within the Christian community; in religious terms, it opened up the possibility of participating in a spiritual community of God's true children that was based on the miraculous union with the body and spirit of Christ.

In the course of the eighteenth century communion slowly but irreversibly lost this meaning and function: on the one hand science took away the material basis of the traditional understanding of the miracle of Christ; on the other hand state and society withdrew the worldly arm that had reinforced penance and communion. As a consequence, communion lost its power of socio-political and physiological-spiritual integration. However, when the socio-political and magical function receded into the background, the original religious significance of communion became more evident. Modern society understood this as the voluntary participation in communion and its spiritual and metaphorical interpretation. Changes similar to this replacement of material and empirical with religious and spiritual symbolism can be observed in many Christian *topoi* in the eighteenth century. In the culture of modern piety, "heaven" and "hell" are no longer places in the universe; the biblical narratives of the beginning and end of the World have their place in mythology but no longer in history; even "God" and the "Devil" have turned from cosmological into mythological beings and ethical principles.

Modern piety has become more private and more spiritual. The close connection of public confession and private belief has vanished to the degree that confessional conflicts – surrounding doctrines such as transubstantiation, the trinity of God, and the dual nature of Christ – are understood as theological and ecclesiastical conflicts but not as the expression of individual piety. The often-told story of Frederick the Great shouting at his theologians that they ought to stop their superfluous theological hair-splitting is not only an expression of his personal contempt for religion. It also demonstrates the eighteenth century's lack of understanding of the doctrinal conflicts of the Reformation period. Despite its critique of the superficial rationalism of the Enlightenment, modern piety has nevertheless maintained this distance from early modern confessional theology.

There are also semantic indicators of this change in devotional culture. Since around 1770 the theology of the Protestant Enlightenment distinguishes between a "public" and a "private," an "outer" and an "inner" religion. In doing so it followed the equally new semantic distinction between "confession" (*Konfession*) as the predominantly negative expression of the religious doctrines and traditions that cemented the Church as an institution and distinguished it from other denominations, and "belief" (*Bekenntnis*) as the fairly positive expression of subjective truthfulness and the focal point of individual and collective identity. Thus the 1792 "profession of faith" (*Glaubensbekenntnis*) by the Enlightenment theologian Johann Salomo Semler says about "inner religion": "The individual inner religion is not subject to a human way of thinking but to God and conscience alone . . .".[4]

This inner religion was also described by the term "religiosity" (*Religiosität*), which was borrowed from the French in the 1780s. It went hand in hand with the concept of piety (*Frömmigkeit*), which had been narrowed down from its original secular meaning (hardworking goodness and honesty) to a specific religious virtue. Together, both concepts described a newly-found general religiousness of man, an almost anthropological orientation towards the divine: "Religiosity describes the vigorous moral character who follows his conscience in all his dealings out of love to God," the *Brockhaus Encyclopedia* of 1820 states, "religiosity and religion relate to each other like morality and reason . . . as the fruit relates to the blossom, religiosity is a moral feeling that relates to the Eternal and Divine."[5]

2. *Characteristic of the devotional culture since the Enlightenment is the individualization of belief.* This individualization is unevenly distributed among religious and social groups; it is more pronounced among Protestants than Catholics, and more developed among the educated than among popular classes.

The new concepts of "inner religion" and "religiosity," of "belief" and "piety", underline the individualization of Protestant piety since the middle of the eighteenth century. The confessional doctrines of the Church did not become obsolete for most believers; the majority still subscribed to them even in the nineteenth century. This official declaration of faith was however not enough for a growing minority of mostly educated bourgeois. They demanded a personal reception and interpretation of official Church doctrine, a critical attitude towards religious tradition, and, if in doubt and at odds with the official doctrine, the possibility of remaining faithful to personal belief against all dogmas of the Church.

Subjective truthfulness had replaced objective religious truth as the greatest good of bourgeois piety. This individualizing tendency was not entirely absent from Catholic piety, but certainly less pronounced. Proof of this confessional imbalance can be found in the predominance of Protestant autobiographies: the ratio of Protestant to Catholic auto-biographies was roughly ten to one, and this not only in Germany but surprisingly also in France, where a strong Catholic bourgeoisie should have generated a wealth of autobiographical literature. More important than numerical difference as such are the differences in the religious styles of bourgeois life. When they offered a religious interpretation of their own lives, nineteenth-century Catholic autobiographers tended to follow the Catholic lives of Saints. Protestant authors on the other hand avoid modeling their self-portrayal on a stereotype of the pious life. Typical for them is the search for their own individuality, which they interpreted as a fulfillment of divine providence.

From the eighteenth century onwards bourgeois-Protestant piety centers around the individual as a spiritual unit, the "entelechy" or "monad." The bourgeois defines himself as pious through the connection between the outward circumstances of his life and his inner spiritual development. Fate and providence guide his journey through life. His divine destiny is expressed in his "profession" (*Beruf*) – understood in the dual sense of career and divine calling to an individual task in the world. The bourgeois proves to be pious and God-fearing not by acting according to God's commandments but by thankfully acknowledging the guiding hand of God in his life and by being aware of God's miraculous ways. This religious self-stylization found its literary expression in the German *Bildungsroman*, a literary form that hardly finds an equivalent in other European countries.

A typical element of nineteenth-century Protestant piety is the sys-tematic cultivation of individual religious belief. The educated of all confessions had always doubted the truthfulness of religious dogmas and tradition, particularly as adolescents. In modern Protestantism, however, these doubts became an integral part of religious socialization. Religious doubts were widely tolerated, especially among young men, and they were even encouraged by extensive discussions in confirmation classes and between father and son at home. They were seen as the seed of the young man's future personality. Even strictly orthodox fathers honored their sons' different religious views as an inviolable part of their personal dignity.

This attitude was expressed in the widespread habit among the Protestant bourgeoisie of drawing up an individual declaration of faith (*Glaubensbekenntnis*). Parish priests often asked candidates for confirmation to write down their interpretation of the Apostles' Creed, which would describe their personal view of religious tradition. The future socialist Lily Braun, for example, invested this "personal declaration of faith" with all her resentment for the ideas of her confirmation teacher, whom she hated.

> – I believe in God, the father, almighty creator of heaven and earth.
> – I don't believe in this God. I don't believe that he created the world in six days and man in his own image. I believe in science more than in the unknown narrators of the fables of the Old Testament.
>
> – I believe in Jesus Christ, God's own son . . .
> – I do not believe in this Jesus Christ, for I consider it pagan to believe that God becomes man . . . I do believe in a higher authority that we call God, the origin of life that filled the first atom with the power of creation. My spirit is part of this divine spirit. I believe in Jesus as a noble man who was the first to preach the commandment of human love and who lived accordingly . . . I believe in the spirit of God that reveals itself in beauty and greatness that lives on in others once the body dies, either above or on the earth. I regard the Church and its dogmas as human institutions that cannot command a free spirit. However, I hope time will show me whether the Christian tradition that I am being taught will prove to be the true one. If it is a crime that I am now turning away from the Church, it seems to me an even larger crime to support the Church against the knowledge of my heart.[6]

The search for individual faith went far beyond the realm of the Church. In 1912, the *Yearbook of the Schopenhauer Society* published the declaration of faith of a certain Maria Groener. Its strict analogy to the Apostles' Creed demonstrates this vision of philosophical pessimism: "I believe in the will, the father of the world, by virtue of its affirmation. I believe in the negation of the will to live that results from voluntary self-annulment of the will . . ." and so on.

The culture of nineteenth-century Catholic piety revealed this compulsion for individual confession to a much lesser extent. This had to do with, on the one hand, the influence of ultramontanism, particularly strong in Germany, and on the other with the specific form of Catholic piety. Material religious symbols such as relics and holy pictures remained meaningful parts of daily life, regardless of their rationality.

The desire for religious depth and discussion in times of religious fervor, above all in puberty, manifested itself in lively private and public prayers rather than in the development of personal religious views. There was little room for religious doubts in Catholic religious teaching and in communion classes; at least doubts were not encouraged as a form of individual learning of religious tradition. When doubts hardened into principles the rupture with the Church was often more radical and abrupt. Unless converting to Protestantism, Catholic dissidents since the end of the nineteenth century tended to turn into radical atheists when they renounced their confession. Consequently, a post-Enlightenment culture of free Catholicism is only now developing again.

3. *Cultures of piety are handed down in modern society less through confessional, corporate* (ständisch), *and socio-economically defined communities; instead, piety is increasingly a consequence of religious socialization at home.*

Any analysis of modern piety is confronted with the empirical problem that piety cannot be delimited by confessionally defined region, social stratum, or class. Cultures of piety in modern society cut across religious communities as well as across socio-economic and political groups. Each of them contains liberal and orthodox, indifferent and strongly religious elements. If we want to draw up a profile of a person's piety, it is more important to look at religious socialization in the family and the effect this has on the life of an individual than to examine the local milieu of Church, profession, estate, and class. Religious statistics have shown that in all today's Christian confessions there is a connection between the frequency of parental churchgoing and that of children, as well as between their beliefs. These links are much stronger than any similarities between members of the same profession or social stratum.

Basic ways of family piety often live on for generations. They can be traced in children who uphold the same personal or conceptual image of God as their parents; in the everyday retention of piety, whether in their social professions or in active solidarity with those around them; in the preservation or rejection of a certain aesthetics of living, and in many other ways. Often forms of piety even survive deep political and confessional ruptures and divisions. Thus, for example, although Marx and Engels had broken demonstratively with all forms of religion in the early 1840s, and despite their close friendship, their different religious upbringings nevertheless had considerable influence on their respective visions of a socialist future. Born into the pious milieu of Elberfeld, Engels always tended to draw up a realistic picture of the social state of the future that had replaced, in religious terms, his pious image of the Kingdom of God. Marx, on the other hand, had been immunized against such utopian descriptions by an enlightened Jewish upbringing. Analogous connections between the profiles of pious family traditions can easily be drawn from the biographies of many National Socialists and their anti-fascist children.

4. *Next to the family, the level of education forms the individual profile of piety. Scientific and historical knowledge helped substantially to revolutionize traditional piety in the eighteenth and nineteenth centuries; it both bridged confessional divides and brought about the religious split of modern society.*

For a long time, school and university education opened the door to religious self-reflection. It created a difference – much more pronounced in earlier centuries – between an educated high religion, open to philosophical and scientific impulses, and an uneducated popular religion, replete with superstition and utilitarian elements. Even when the educated withdrew in the eighteenth century in large part from Church life and confessional tradition in favor of new *Bildungsreligionen*, it was self-evident that "the people" were in need of traditional religion. To quote Goethe: "Who has science and art/ also has religion/ who doesn't have those two/ has to have religion."[7] In the nineteenth century, education constituted the basis of a bourgeois community of piety that remained influential beyond just the criticism of Church dogma. Thus, for example, New Humanism became the common religious belief of intellectuals because it was exclusively taught in the Humanist *gymnasia* during the first half of the century.

With respect to gender, the difference in education contributed to the formation of a specifically female devotional culture, at least in the upper layers of the bourgeoisie. The following complaint of a wealthy lady, printed in the *Lausitzisches Magazin* in 1789, illustrates the threat that education, especially in its utility for a critique of religion, posed to marriage. She wrote that her husband's acquaintances regarded it as "bad form if any of his friends should find a religious book on my table."[8] She turned to a friend of her husband for advice and the clergyman responded that her husband was by no means the victim of bad company or conviction. Nevertheless, the pastor said, in school her husband had already encountered religion as a dead subject of rote memorization, and later experiences at the university and in so-called high society offered no opportunity to experience something better. Conversely, Friederike Baldinger, the wife of a Göttingen Court Councillor, described in a short autobiographical sketch in 1783 how difficult it was for her as a young girl to break the male privilege of education through clandestine reading and intense discussions with her brother: "You must be pious and chaste," was her mother's description of the ideal feminine way of life.[9] Until the twentieth century this attitude distinguished the religious socialization of women from that of their male contemporaries.

Education could overcome confessional boundaries and facilitate a common faith in new beliefs; but education also estranged people of similar backgrounds. Thus the founder of the Schopenhauer Society and the son of a humble country parson, Paul Deussen, shared his admiration for Schopenhauer with his boarding-school friend at *Schulpforta*, Friedrich Nietzsche, also the son of a pastor. But with his own mother, a pious woman whose spiritual and social narrow-mindedness Deussen had with difficulty left behind upon entering Gymnasium, the possibility of religious understanding no longer existed.[10] Education thus not only contributed to religious harmony in society as the Enlightenment and its liberal and socialist heirs had hoped. It also brought about religious division.

5. *Germany's religious divide was a constituent element of nineteenth-century social modernization more generally . It was not solely or primarily a result of the immanent principles of Protestantism; rather it was a consequence of the ecclesiastical split and the demographic mixing of confessions in the early modern period.*

Around 1900, cultural critics like Max Weber, Werner Sombart and Ernst Troeltsch shared the undisputed conviction that the social modernization of Europe could be traced back to the economic and cultural superiority of "Protestantism" over "Catholicism," and that this was in itself a result of immanent religious principles of "Protestantism." In his famous work, *The Protestant Ethic and the Spirit of Capitalism*, Max Weber attributed this superiority to the Calvinist doctrine of predestination and in its wake the inner-worldly asceticism of the reformed Calvinist bourgeoisie. Conversely, Ernst Troeltsch traced this superiority to Lutheran notions of religious freedom and individual responsibility. Yet these explanatory models largely ignored the exogenous factor of different confessions and cultures of piety living together in an often limited amount of space, i.e. the religious geography of those countries and regions in which the process of modernization began. Cultural Protestantism regarded the religious divide within modern societies as a regrettable negative side-effect of uneven regional and social modernization. In reality, however, the religious divide played a constitutive role.

The confessional map of early modern Europe assigns Germany a special position among the European nations. Located between the Protestant countries of the north and west and the Catholic countries in the east, west and southwest, Germany constituted a land in-between and a zone of transition. Unlike Germany's neighbors, which in terms of confession were significantly more homogeneous, the religious stalemate in Germany created areas of confessional tolerance and mixture as early as the late seventeenth century. The Peace of Westphalia had tried to create uniform confessional territories in 1648. Yet the resettlement of persecuted religious minorities in territories of a different confession soon led to increasing confessional mixture in many German lands.

To this exogenous immigration, the onset of mixed confessional states in the eighteenth and early nineteenth centuries added an internal confessional migration. This occurred early on in Prussia, with the annexation of largely Catholic Silesia in 1740, and in Bavaria with the acquisition of the mostly Protestant Palatinate in 1777. This internal shift occurred even more dramatically at the beginning of the nineteenth century, when the Kingdoms of Württemberg and Hanover as well as the Grand Duchies of Baden and Hesse were transformed into confessionally mixed states. In the new regions of the confessional minorities, the extension of the state, manifested in new garrisons and cadres of administrative officials, encouraged confessional mixing, especially among the military and the bureaucracy in towns and cities. Also since the beginning of the nineteenth century, marriages between partners of different confessions had become easier, and this too accelerated the dissolution of confessionally homogeneous regions. By 1910, 45 per cent of Prussia's "smaller administrative units" had already registered confessional minorities of more than 10 per cent. And nearly 10 per cent of all marriages were inter-faith marriages.

The mixture of regional confessions had grave consequences for the transformation of traditional devotional cultures. In the early modern period, these cultures had been largely homogeneous within their specific regions, but had differed in terms of religion and ethnic characteristics from other lands. The inhabitants of Lower Saxony and Westphalia, for example, were known for their religious reserve and devotion to pre-Christian, "superstitious" rituals; the people in the Rhineland for their religious openness and receptiveness; the Franconians for their directness; and the Swabians and Alemanians for their tendency to separatism and self-absorption.

These stereotypes may provoke skepticism, but one cannot get around the demonstrably different forms of religious life that coexisted within confessionally homogeneous zones. A nineteenth-century traveler from Württemberg to Saxony, from Bavaria to Hanover, or from Westphalia to West Prussia would encounter a completely different form of piety, even among his Lutheran companions. Church attendance was at one place traditionally frequent, at another sparse; here Church feasts and rituals were rich and popular, there they were meager and strictly orthodox; at another place, the relationship with other confessions was tolerant and cooperative, at still another, intolerant and acrimonious.

Given the variety and disparity of early modern piety, religious minorities often faced serious pressures in their attempt to maintain their religious integrity in an alien environment. These pressures encouraged them to strive for economic and cultural success. That in Germany these groups were mostly Protestant was less a consequence of Protestant ethics and Lutheran demands for individual freedom than the willingness of German princes and city councils to take in Protestant refugees from culturally advanced regions. Here one need only recall the settlement of Dutch and Belgian Protestants in the Catholic lower and central Rhineland since the middle of the sixteenth century, the absorption of French-reformed Huguenots by the largely Catholic Palatinate and the predominantly Lutheran states of Hesse, Brunswick and Brandenburg at the end of the seventeenth century, the Calvinist dissidents of Salzburg, or the Waldenser in Württemberg. Most of these groups, along with Jewish minorities in Berlin, Hamburg and Frankfurt, became foci of social modernization in their new homeland. Collectively, they shared the need to assert themselves as a religious minority through cultural and economic success, which they often achieved as a result of their often superior economic and intellectual abilities.

6. *The confessional mixture of society was absorbed by the Churches through new forms of religious community, which can, from the standpoint of the history of piety, be classified according to social composition and spatial structure.*

Among the local and regional minorities of the late eighteenth century, above all in the large trading and residential cities, the confessional mixture of the population provoked two diametrically opposite reactions. On the one hand, large parts of the often-mobile industrial and educated bourgeoisie tried to mediate between the confessions in the name of an educated worldview. Since 1760, the educated high society of Berlin had been attending church together in the French Cathedral, regardless of confession. In the salons members of different confessions met on an equal basis; even educated Jews were welcome at the end of the eighteenth century. In educated circles and learned journals, confessional polemics were forbidden. In the wake of a new religion of the reason and sentiment, dogmatic controversies lost their divisiveness.

This favored in particular the Masonic Lodges, which pronounced a new interdenominational religion based on humanism and spiritual equality. From a sociological point of view, their incredible resonance among the educated and industrial bourgeoisie around 1800 resulted in part from factors of religious geography. As an isolated but mobile minority within regionally established cultures of piety, these classes attempted over long distances to maintain religious ties that protected them from the arm of the local Church and provided a spiritual home during travel or when moving from place to place.

On the other hand, religious minorities who were much less mobile and firmly rooted in a traditional devotional culture reacted very differently to increasing confessional mixture. To establish a religious identity, they insisted on local Church rights and stressed their confessional and ritual difference from their religious environment. This was true for most communities of refugees in the early modern period, be it in Cologne, Berlin, Hamburg or Kassel. Even under the changed conditions of civic equality in the nineteenth century, traditionalist groups sought their religious identity in confessional delimitation and the self-assertion of the Church. In the decades after 1815 the Silesian and Rhenish resistance of the Calvinist and Lutheran communities against the Prussian Union drew on this as much as did the Catholic communities, with their ultra-montane criticism of the Prussian policy of mixed marriages. Throughout the nineteenth century, the fear of confessional infiltration remained the main obstacle to political reconciliation between the Churches.

The varied reaction to regional confessional mixture can be traced back to the sociological structure of religious communities. Religious groups whose devotional culture was rooted in the Enlightenment (in the Protestant Church, for example, the Protestantenverein in the 1860s or the Evangelische Bund and the Evangelisch-soziale Kongreß at the end of the nineteenth century) had a socially homogeneous membership, attracted few members from the petty bourgeoisie or the proletariat and were mostly organized in supra-regional unions and associations. Traditionalist religious communities on the other hand (such as the predominantly orthodox societies for the propagation of the bible and religious pamphlets, as well as many associations linked to internal and external missionary activity) revealed a vertical social structure, i.e. they were composed of a number of social groups: landed gentry, bourgeois dignitaries and pensioners, small businessmen, craftsmen and many female workers.

In-between we find the pious revivalist movement of the late eighteenth and early nineteenth centuries: here, a vertical social community was combined with a disapproval of local associations and a surprisingly wide network of supra-regional contacts. This special, intermediate, movement notwithstanding, it is nevertheless noticeable that pious communities contained social and organizational models for the differentiation of Protestant piety. As such, they became an important sounding board for the internal division of Protestant pious culture in the nineteenth century.

7. More than in its European neighbor-states, the religious divide in Germany charged nineteenth-century political and social conflicts with a complicating ideological element. The history of piety thus helps to explain Germany's unique political path in the twentieth century.

In the nineteenth century the religious divide of German piety constituted a specific development of Germany within an international framework. Protestant England, Catholic France, Italy and Spain all witnessed the Church's growing resentment of religious enlightenment after the Napoleonic Wars. Increasingly, the clergy distanced itself socially from the enlightened bourgeois groups, whose social gatherings and ideas it had supported until around 1800. The result was an ecclesiastical form of piety that dissociated itself firmly from the worldly culture of the bourgeoisie. In terms of religion, this alienated an enlightened bourgeoisie from a traditional bourgeoisie, and led in all countries to a political division of society into a liberal-critical and a conservative-confessional group.

In Germany alone the confessional mixture of the population in a delimited space created individual, social and regional breaches that rendered a *weltanschaulich* integration of society more and more difficult in the course of the nineteenth century. On a regional level, sects and Free Churches settled in the border-zones between Catholic and Protestant regions, for example in the Swabian area around Stuttgart, the Saxon Vogtland and the Erzgebirge, in eastern Westphalia and the Wupper valley. Together with the pious communities they often became centers of fundamentalist opposition against the established Church and its political allies in governments and bureaucracies. In the early-industrialized west of the Kingdom of Saxony it was above all Social Democracy that benefited after 1850 from the confessional mixture.

On an individual level this mixture led to an increase in mixed marriages. Children of these marriages were particularly restless and active when it came to religion – one thinks of Franz Overbeck or Bertolt

Outlines

Brecht – which further contributed to the differentiation of the religious spectrum in Germany. The Churches tried hard to hold the children from mixed marriages; but in the long run with only limited success.

The confessional mixture had its greatest effect, however, on the religious spectrum in conjunction with political and social tensions in Germany. Already before 1848 entire professions, including doctors, engineers and other scientific groups but also teachers of all levels and philologists in particular, had begun to distance themselves from their confessional Churches. For these groups, the Revolution of 1848 meant an important caesura, in particular when the old alliance of throne and altar suppressed the Revolution and thus for the first time turned against the liberal bourgeoisie. Henceforth, religious conflict turned into open rejection of the major Churches.

Among the Catholic bourgeoisie in Germany, as opposed to their French counterparts, their opposition to the religious proselytism emanating from Prussia and the Reich eclipsed this rejection. But even the Catholic bourgeoisie was slowly driven to a sort of internal exile out of disappointment with the conservative attitude of the clergy. People resigned themselves to the bare essentials of religious duty or stayed away from the Church altogether, leaving, like their Protestant counterparts, religious life to the urban and rural petty bourgeoisie.

More important for a social history of piety and its underlying mentality, however, is the astonishing number of religious mutations caused by the mixture of confessions. We can say without exaggeration that no European country has produced a comparable multitude of revisionist groups and movements: a whole vast religious spectrum unfolds in Germany from the fundamentalist renaissance of piety in the Awakening to the materialistic and monistic unions and associations of the educated bourgeoisie and the workers: the freethinkers, the Giordano Bruno Association, the society for ethical culture and so on. It ranges from the many variants of the movement for life-reform – modernism in architecture and the national dress, vegetarian, nudist, and garden city movements – to the educated bourgeois circles and societies that had sprung up out of quasi-religious admiration for the works of Goethe and Schiller, Schopenhauer and Nietzsche. Finally, this spectrum stretches from the Socialist workers' movement, which Marxism turned into a quasi-religious Weltanschauung with an enormous international aura, to many variants of German-Christian, German-religious and *völkisch* religiosity. If difficult to classify, these movements nevertheless collectively became a national movement of enormous strength.

The consequences of this social fragmentation into competing ideological communities for the political culture of Germany are well known. Most of these communities, even those that proclaimed their tolerance, put forward their claims to truth with missionary zeal. Through their religions of the future, they promised to overcome the fissures in the ideological landscape of German society. They could also rely on a widespread need for ideological harmony. In fact, however, they further reinforced the battlefronts. With their all-encompassing claims for religious comprehensivity, they infused religious elements into political and social conflicts, thus rendering them difficult to solve through rational political compromise. As a result these conflicts assumed the vehement nature of a latent civil war, defined in terms of Weltanschauung, which after the defeat of the First World War proved decisive for Germany's political journey towards the Third Reich.

Translated by Maike Bohn

Notes

1. Carl Jatho, *Briefe,* ed. Carl O. Jatho (Jena: Eugen Diederichs, 1914), pp. 313 ff.
2. Ibid., p. 311.
3. Ibid., p. 315.
4. *Johann Salomo Semlers letztes Glaubensbekenntnis über natürliche und christliche Religion*, ed. Christian Gottfried Schütz (Königsberg: Nicolovius, 1792), p. 137.
5. *Allgemeine deutsche Real-Enzyklopädie für die gebildeten Stände*, 5th. edn., Vol. 8 (Leipzig: Brockhaus, 1820), p. 200.
6. Lily Braun, *Memoiren einer Sozialistin*, reprint (Munich: Piper, 1908), p. 83.
7. *Goethes Werke*, ed. Erich Trunz, Vol.1 (Hamburg: Christian Wegner, 1969), p. 367.
8. "Antwortschreiben an eine Dame, betreffend den Unglauben ihres Gatten," in *Lausitzisches Magazin oder Sammlung verschiedener Abhandlungen und Nachrichten . . .*, 22(1789): 278.
9. *Lebensbeschreibung von Friderike Baldinger von ihr selbst verfaßt*, ed. Sophie von La Roche (Offenbach: Ulrich Weiss and Carl Ludwig Brede, 1791), p. 18.
10. Paul Deussen, *Mein Leben*, ed. Erika Rosenthal-Deussen (Leipzig: Brockhaus, 1922).

-3-

Religion, Denomination and Nationalism in Nineteenth-century Germany
Wolfgang Altgeld

In older treatments of Germany in the nineteenth century, a self-evident, ubiquitous process of modernization dominated the historical narrative. The *telos* of this narrative served to structure history in such a way that the multiplicity and openness of the past was sacrificed to an all-too-simple pattern of progress and reaction. As secularization was deemed an essential aspect of social and cultural modernization, religious belief and affiliation was considered at best a historical phenomenon of secondary importance, but more often as a drag on the forces of progress and modernity.[1]

This way of writing modern German history can no longer be seen as representing the current state of research, which has powerfully shown that religion, Christianity and the various denominations were extremely important forces in the nineteenth century, and, indeed, became more important as the nineteenth century wore on. Historians do not dispute that secularization as a phenomenon existed. But with respect to the nineteenth century, and to other centuries as well, one must be careful not to misinterpret individual instances of atheism as well as new, irreligious and post-Christian worldviews as testimonies to a deep-seated and all-embracing process of secularization. Similarly, empirically demonstrable declines in church attendance cannot self-evidently be seen as the equivalent of dechristianization. Decline in church attendance affected the urban bourgeoisie and proletariat, mainly in Protestant Germany. Contemporary Protestant liberals as well as liberal theologians by no means always perceived this in negative terms, but felt that the rational modern citizen in the modern ethical state could receive the message of God without the help of an external institution such as the Church. To them, a good Christian meant a good citizen! In large parts of Catholic Germany, the opposite experience held.[2] By the late eighteenth and early nineteenth century, Catholic popular piety and the Catholic

Church had been in ruins, but in the course of the nineteenth century Catholicism witnessed a stupendous renewal of neo-traditional forms of mass-religiosity that went hand-in-hand with an equally stupendous renewal of the ultramontane Church.[3] Both developments (as well as other Christian religious movements, which we cannot consider here) were so massive that upon closer inspection they reveal the nineteenth century, which had seemed to be so essentially marked by secularization, to be instead a century of reconfessionalization.[4] The lines of conflict did not run simply between the major confessions, Protestant and Catholic. Rather, they ran between the mainly Catholic defenders of orthodoxy and the mainly Protestant advocates of enlightened or liberal Christianity. But as these antagonisms became more and more pronounced, they came to be reinforced by fundamental social, cultural and political differences, and these differences powerfully shaped the two milieux, the one bourgeois, the other not. Moreover, in the process, both cultural Protestantism (*Kulturprotestantismus*) and ultramontane Catholicism developed new forms of integration, demarcation, and identity.[5] These processes count as integral parts of the history of Christianity in Germany; they are modern phenomena, and aspects of the modernization process.

Most nationalists, and until recently most historians, have for a long time uncritically subscribed to the following interpretation of the relationships between nation, national movement and nation-state. The nation exists, ready-made from the beginning of history, or at least from very, very ancient times. Varying circumstances have continually or over long periods of time prevented the nation's political unification. For the national movement it is always a given that the nation, typically in some heroic struggle, will achieve its statehood. Yet Massimo D'Azeglio, an Italian nationalist and like Cavour a liberal realist, came much closer to the truth of things when he declared in the first session of the chamber proclaiming the Kingdom of Italy in 1861: "We have made Italy, now must make Italians!" How true this was. And how universally true! Nationalists could not start from the assumption of a pre-existing nation, or at least not from the pre-existence at the nation's inception of a culturally defined national sphere. Rather, it was more accurate to see in the modern nation a product of the multiple and multi-layered efforts of the nationalists. This involved the work of finding pre-existing older, smaller cultures within the projected nation-state; the work of selecting from or excluding these cultures from what the nationalists defined as the "national"; and the work of integrating their constructed nation-state with the conditions dictated by economic, social and structural modernization. This process of becoming a nation did not end with the foundation of the national state, but instead merely entered a new stage.[6]

The problem was not one of a homogeneous national movement *vis-à-vis* a-national and anti-national forces, but rather of competing national forces, indeed one should say competing national movements. The goal was however the same. The foundation of a nation-state (although with significantly different conceptions about the extent and scope of the state) and the aim were based on the shared premise that the nation already existed. Competition centered on which older cultural facts and points of orientation the nation should take up, and which it should exclude. This was not a small matter, because few people either were able to or wanted to step out of their older attachments simply because the nation demanded it or because the nation needed to build bridges between older, pre-national and modern national identities. At the same time, social redistribution of opportunities was at the heart of this process, because groups who would successfully transform pre-national historical and cultural traditions into a national mold would self-evidently be privileged in the prospective nation state. Yet religion and religious communities shaped these pre-national cultures, including the particularistic cultures endemic to the long nineteenth century of transition to modern industrial society. Among populations with completely or relatively homogeneous religious compositions, the formerly ubiquitous influence of religion and the Church only played (and play) a role in the process of nation building in cases where new lay elites clash with those parts of the population still tied to the Church. However, in places where for historical or ethnic reasons the idea of the nation was (and is) related to religiously or denominationally heterogeneous populations, not only the possibility of national cultural unification becomes (and has become) questionable, but also the idea of the nation itself, and thus the foundation and preservation of a nation-state.

Catholicism, Protestantism and German Nationalism

In the German Reich that ended in 1806 the population (including Prussian Silesia) was roughly divided into 60 per cent Catholics and 40 per cent Protestants. The German *Bund* of 1815 brought these percentages more into line with each other. A small Catholic preponderance remained, but more than three million Catholics lived under Protestant sovereigns as a result of decisions made in 1803, and the previous dominance of the Catholics in the *Reichsrat* became reversed in the new *Bundesrat*. Finally, in the Second Empire founded in 1871 the Catholic proportion, including the French- and Polish-speaking populations, shrank to only one-third of the citizenry. In the three-quarters of a century from the end of the first

Empire to the beginning of the second, the Jews made up just under 1 per cent of the total population; by the time National Socialism took power in 1933 this number, as is well known, fell to around 0.5 per cent.[7] It is important to note that Catholics outside Bavaria and German Austria – which in the system of Metternich had been closed off from German cultural developments as if behind (as Goethe put it in 1818) a Chinese wall – had felt like a minority since 1815. They were often a disadvantaged minority in an enlarged Prussia, and still more so in several of the smaller states, and even to some degree in Baden, which had a Catholic majority but was ruled by Protestant grand dukes.[8]

In Germany, the idea of the nation and nationalism are in the first analysis the fruit of certain intellectual, and not least certain theological, developments in Protestant Germany. This becomes evident when we consider the famous early champions of the national idea. Against Herder, Schleiermacher, Arndt, and Jahn (all Protestant) and many others, there is only the name of one Catholic: Josef Görres (and situating his political worldview and religious development in any case calls for more clarification). In this sense, converts to Catholicism, like Friedrich Schlegel and Adam Müller, confirm the rule. Many among these Protestant protagonists were theologians or pastors, or had at least studied theology. The consequences were significant. On the one hand, the language and emotions of German nationalism, or at least its main current, were filled with pietistic images (for example "brothers and sisters" as a metaphor for co-nationals) and concepts (for example the importance of language for the creation of community and identity). On the other hand, the idea of the nation as the highest unity in the order of Creation became a central part of modern, enlightened and later liberal Protestant theology.[9] Many contemporary commentaries give the impression that the nation was not understood as the replacement of religion or Christendom, but rather as an *ersatz* for the Church.

This religious paternity did not come from just anywhere. It was already part of the thought of the early nationalists of Protestant Germany; it was still more a part of their descendants who fought the *Kuturkampf* and who waged battle for the *Evangelischer Bund*. "Germany is the land of Protestantism," Ernst Moritz Arndt declared in his writings following the so-called Wars of Liberation, because "Protestantism seems to be purely Germanic . . . it effortlessly attracts all things Germanic to it."[10] Had the German Reformation not freed spirit and politics from the fetters of the essentially Latin (indeed Jewish-Latin) Catholic Church, which was authoritarian and foreign in the same measure? And had Luther not won back the German language and with it the essence of the German nation through his translation of the Bible? It was only all too consistent to then celebrate the Austrian defeat at Königgrätz as a "victory for Luther" (as Ferdinand Gregorovius for example did) and five years later to praise the foundation of the "Protestant Empire of the German Nation" (*Evangelische Reich deutscher Nation*) with jubilation.[11]

Nationalism became a permanent part of the ideological structure, first of pre-March political currents and then of the political parties gradually organized after 1848. On the one hand, nationalism had as many faces as the different aims of liberalism, democracy, conservatism and even socialism; on the other hand, it supplied those parties with similar motives, although different in the specific importance attributed to them in each case. Nationalism comprised the idea of a national state as being desirable in itself, but also in combination with other fundamental motives. In the case of progressive factions and later also in modern Conservatism, these fundamental motives included a deeply rooted anti-Catholicism which, through nationalism, penetrated democratic movements and liberalism in Germany.

Throughout the long nineteenth century most proponents of the cultural and political idea of the nation regarded confessional diversity – its long-term effects on high and popular culture, on society, ethics and even language – as a problem of the first order in creating a German nation-state. Partly, this was a problem because of the estrangement between Protestantism and Catholicism. In his observations on the pilgrimages and processions, holy services and churches replete with baroque splend-our that he witnessed in Catholic Upper Germany, the famous enlightened traveler, Friedrich Nicolai, commented: "A Protestant believes himself in a different world seeing all this," and he wanted to thank God from now on "for freedom from hierarchy and for the benefits brought to the German Protestant lands by the Reformation and the true, free spirit of Protestantism."[12] Similar testimonies of alienation, coupled with arro-gance, could be found in the one-sided North German Protestant travel literature from the eighteenth and nineteenth centuries, as well as in letters exchanged between "northern academic luminaries" who had taken posts in Bavaria – or even in Thomas Mann's *Buddenbrooks*.[13] This aspect of confessional alienation became less important with the increase in social mobility; but it remained, however, and even intensified with mass manifestations of modern Catholic piety in the wake of reconfessional-ization and Catholic-ecclesiastical renewal in the second third of the nineteenth century. Heinrich von Sybel's essay on the Trier pilgrimage of 1844 or the brochure in a series of the *Evangelischer Bund* describing a procession in an Alsatian town in 1898 are good examples.[14]

Aside from the negative aspect of alienation and estrangement between Catholic and Protestant Germans, there was another issue that from the beginning and throughout affected the problem of nationalism in Germany. At the core of nationalist thought in its dominantly Protestant incarnation was the conviction that a unified, indivisible nation, as both a cultural and as a political nation, unconditionally required a common, singular religion. This religion, as Hegel put it, "expresses the innermost being of all people, so that all external and diffuse matters aside, they can find a common focus and, despite inequality and transformations in other spheres and conditions, are still able to trust and rely on each other."[15] German nationalists also expressed the further conviction that the essence of a nation was revealed by God and thus had to be rooted in a specific religion. About a century later, the historian Max Lenz found that the nation had hardly come closer to achieving this foundation; on the contrary: "National unity is not achieved as long as our worship of God does not have the same basis," Lenz wrote, "the powerful will that created our empire would weaken, the vital force, the belief in our fatherland would die, if our innermost [. . .] national conscience did not contain the same holy and divine thoughts."[16]

In this context nationalists often recalled the example of the Jews; they had kept their national character by sticking to their religion "in all nations and climates," as Herder noted. Arndt wrote: "You children of Abraham, although spread throughout this world, you still are an honorable people because you steadfastly love and defend your own. May we Germans follow your example!"[17] For this very reason, however, Arndt strongly opposed the civic emancipation of the Jews on German national territory. But how should Germans fulfil the desire for national unity in the face of confessional division? Not at all, better not to, was one of the answers given by the young, subsequently famous theologian Karl Bretschneider in 1806: "The dissimilarity between the North and South of Germany is immense; and the difference in customs and intellectual culture is striking." Even if a few writers were able to spread a pan-German "patriotism" this would, he argued, "never unite the German-speaking people. Because what nature has divided man cannot bring together!" Reformation and Counter-Reformation were possibly not the cause but much more the consequence of this division. For Bretschneider only the creation of a North German nation-state under Prussian leadership seemed imaginable. Where else in Germany could the "noble German fatherland . . ., the splendid Germanic tribe in its unity and power . . ., in its unity and culture and enlightenment, in its unity of a political bond and German sentiment" be found but in the "purely German Prussia and among the 'peoples' between Westphalia, Mecklenburg, Franconia and Saxony? . . . This is where culture thrives [and] religious culture in particular."[18] As late as 1869, Bismarck offered similar reflections on the incompatibility of North and South as a nation or even a nation-state.[19]

If the thesis that secularization is connected with the rise, or success, of nationalism is historically correct, the problem of a nation divided along denominational lines can be solved in a fairly simple way: by denying the religious element altogether, by making the nation the ideological measure of the thoughts and actions of all Germans, and by elevating nationalism to a political religion. Naturally, we find statements confirming this view, seldom in the first half of the nineteenth century, more often thereafter. To a surprising extent, however, German nationalists were occupied with conceiving an individual religion, a national religion, linked to the national state but primarily concerned with overcoming the problem of confessional difference, which after 1815, and especially after 1830, had become more severe.

What could this Germanic religion be? There were a number of answers. Both Fichte and the philosopher Jacob Fries, who had shot to prominence during the *Wartburgfest*, believed that a national religion entailed a post-Church or even post-Christian civil religion. For Fichte, this meant a national elite of "Christians."[20] For Fries it meant a national religion of the masses, pious but outside the confines of Christianity and thus beyond all national problems of confessional division. "One God, one German sword, one German God for honor and justice," was the motto. This idea went beyond the national religious conceptions of the Wartburg fraternities in 1817, and it was further developed by Paul A. Pfizer, David Friedrich Strauss, Bruno Bauer, and others.[21] Another response was not to go beyond the confessional splits of Christianity but back to the pre-Christian religion of the Teutons, thus going behind the religious estrangement of the German people. As Jacob Grimm commented: "Our ancestors were Germans before they converted to Christianity; we have to start from the still older state of affairs, when we were united with a common bond."[22] Discussed and half-heartedly dismissed by Herder around 1800, Grimm's comment was made into verse by Johann Heinrich Voß and became publicized during the Wars of Liberation, especially in the writing of the now-forgotten publicist Ernst Trautvetter.[23] A critic warned in 1817 of these radical religious *Deutschtümler*, who believed that the "altars of Germany will only become truly German altars again when they are consecrated to Thor and Wodan instead of the religion of the Cross, and when the Nordic Edda has replaced the Gospel."[24] This view was not further developed in the following decades;

but it did not disappear wholly from nationalist discussions. It returned more powerfully in the wake of the *völkisch* movement in the 1890s, when it led to the creation of many Aryan, Germanic, or German religious communities.

But the most frequent answer throughout the nineteenth century was simply this: the national religion of the Germans best suited to their national spirit is Christianity, but only in its Protestant, in particular in its Lutheran manifestation. This answer was given decisively but in a mild-mannered tone as long as the Catholic Church seemed to be heading for complete dissolution; it became harsher following the success of the Catholic revival and the victory, especially since it was unrivaled in popular religiosity, of Ultramontanism. "If we allow the Catholic priests to carry on like this," Brettschneider opined, "German unity is beyond reach."[25] What remained, according to another Protestant publicist, "was to ask the Catholic Germans 'to become better Germans than Christians,' to break the yoke of the pope completely to gain German independence."[26]

The modern idea of the nation – first as an ethnic, hereditary community; second as it was manifested in specific cultural characteristics and achievements; which, thirdly, were to be the basis for demanding political unification of all co-nationals – originated from Protestant Germany. But within one or two generations it also took hold in Catholic Germany, as it did in other places as well, gradually moving from elite to mass nationalism. Research has shown delays as well as weaker and more exclusive variations of this development (as documented for example by an analysis of the NSDAP electorate where Catholics, the only easily identifiable social group, were under-represented).[27] These differences have to be further explained and quantified by comparative social history (for instance in relation to the relative differences in secularization between Catholic and Protestant Germany). My own research points to the central motive for this difference as well as for a distinct Catholic national consciousness, both as a reflex and as a part of this difference. Catholic thinkers, clergy as well as laity, did not oppose the modern idea of the nation. As an idea, the nation was neither opposed by Görres nor by both Reichenspergers, neither by Ketteler nor by Buß, neither by the Catholic deputies from the Rhineland, Westphalia, Bavaria and Austria in the Frankfurt National Assembly nor by the deputies of the Center Party, neither at the time of the *Kuturkampf* nor even after its official end. What they did oppose was the equation of the national idea with religion! As one priest put it during the early disputes with the radical German nationalists and the national-Protestant demonstration of students at the Wartburg in 1817: "The founder of Christian religion obviously did not intended a national but a universal religion which embraces all people, empires, states and individuals."[28] The so-called *großdeutsch*, Austrian preferences of most nationalistic Catholics before 1866 (and in many cases long after this first German partition) are not simply caused by fear of becoming a native minority in the case of a *kleindeutsch*, Prussian solution of the national-political problem. Rather, the idea of the bygone Reich as historical memory and the *großdeutsch* projection of a new German Empire under Catholic Habsburg rule, which evoked that very memory, expressed the need to make both possible: to put the national idea into political practice and to maintain the universal bond of the Christian Church, and to safeguard the dual identity of German and Catholic. Consequently, the Catholics were skeptical of, indeed averse to, the nationalist, Protestant and Lutheran Borussianism and the *kleindeutsch* tendencies of the liberal bourgeoisie, which were increasingly motivated by economic policy. These aversions were further fueled by social discrimination and an officious Church policy toward Prussian Catholics, who now communicated their ire in a newly emergent Catholic public sphere, itself the product of pre-March journalistic debates. What also followed was a counter-image of national history that opposed the Protestant, "national liberal" and "national democratic" visions in all main points. In view of the general importance of constructions of national history for the process of nation-building, this counter-image of national history might have been as important to Catholic politics as their general opposition to Prussia.[29] One argument followed another; the most prominent dispute in a debate dating back to Herder was the debate in 1860 between Sybel, Julius Ficker and others about medieval Italian foreign policy.[30] Debate centered on Charles the Great and the compulsory conversion to Christianity of the Saxons, on the dispute over Boniface that caused such a stir during Ketteler's celebrations in 1854, on arguments about Luther and the Reformation and whether it had been the latter or the counter-Reformation that had split the nation, on the meaning of the medieval papacy in general and for Germany in particular, on Gustavus Adolphus and how the German Protestants might feel if a Catholic association were to name itself after Tilly following their example, and on Frederick the Great and Prussia's separate peace in 1795.

In 1871, representatives of Catholic Germany tried to bring a small part of this specific idea of the nation into the new nation-state. In the Reichstag, they raised the issue of a diplomatic intervention of the Reich on behalf of the pope, who had been deprived of his other Roman estates by Italy, the other recent nation-state. National-Liberals like Sybel reacted as if the Reich was to be involved in an Italian campaign similar to the one that led to the foundation of the medieval Empire.[31] This became one more trigger for the fast track to the so-called *Kuturkampf*, which had many causes but one goal above all: to establish a unified, leveled and almost total nation whose members were to know no other authority or higher morality than the national, and therefore the national-religious. The massive attack on the everyday life of many Catholics through a growing suppression of Church activities welded them together as a minority; the rest of Germany saw them more than ever as dyed-in-the-wool, incorrigible enemies of the Reich who should be excluded from all the important posts in state and society, in cultural life, and at the very least in higher education.[32] In 1880, Ludwig Windthorst, the leader of the Center Party and a parliamentary opponent of Bismarck and other National-Liberal chiefs, rightly told the Prussian diet during a debate of the blown-up, so-called Jewish question: "Political and religious toleration is the only ground on which state and civic society, under currently existing circumstances, can thrive."[33] But religion and denomination, at least their collective and profane manifestations, were deemed as too important, the rifts in the recent national political debates too open and deep, to be simply depoliticized and smoothed out by mutual toleration.

Nationalistic Anti-Judaism

The possible relationships between anti-Catholicism and anti-Judaism in certain forms of mainstream nationalism can be touched on only briefly in this context. These relationships had their origins in the late eighteenth century, and thus before the beginning of political nationalism, when thinkers of the Enlightenment, and in particular enlightened Protestant theologians, denounced Judaism as the origin of Christian, and specifically Catholic, orthodoxy. Schleiermacher and others transferred this motif to important segments of German nationalism. The Enlightenment, on the other hand, denied that Judaism was essentially a religion; this view, held by Kant for example, saw Judaism as a political constitution clothed in a religion that was especially suited to maintain the unity of the Jews during the eighteen centuries following the loss of their state.[34] When enlightened thinkers talked of the Jews as a "state within the state," this was easily translated into the nationalist maxim a "people within the people" (*"Volk im Volk"*). In principle this excluded a bourgeois emancipation of the Jews within the imagined German nation. Yet the Jews also represented a living example of the significance of religious unity for the constitution of a unique and indivisible nation. Fundamentalist nationalists thus discredited

Catholic faith not only as being a Christian confession foreign to the people but as being a foreign religion inspired by the Jews, which was international and therefore as hostile as Judaism towards the political ambitions of nations before or after unification. Towards the end of the nineteenth century the radical successors to this view consequently talked of the threat to the Empire from the black (Catholic), gold (Jewish) and red (Socialist) International and supported Georg von Schönerer's German-Austrian *Los-von-Rom* movement with the slogan: "Without Jews, without Rome, do we build the German dome" ("*Ohne Juda, ohne Rom bauen wir Großdeutschlands Dom*")![35]

National anti-Judaism was also often used as a vehicle to disguise the reality of confessional, and thus cultural, rifts in a nation imagined as united in a trans-confessional German Christianity. Nationalists then promoted this imagined community against the "other," the excluded Jew. According to the Jewish journalist Saul Ascher, writing at the time of the *Wartburgfest*, the "Germanomaniacs" (*Germanomanen*) saw the greatest obstacle to national unity "in the religious rift in Germany, in the antagonism between Catholics and Protestants." Their ideas revolved around "the matter of uniting all Germany in one faith" and "establishing Protestantism as the only source of Germany's salvation." As Ascher put it: "they would rather like to pursue the [nationalistic-Protestant] system than the ultra-German [i.e. universal] Christianity if they did not have to fear reprisals. However, the anti-Judaism that has become fashionable in Protestant Germany shows that they try this wherever they don't have this worry." Following Ascher, this surrogate discrimination was no surprise, since the Jews constituted a negative point of reference for an ideology of national-religious integration. "People say that the Jews are neither Germans nor Christians and therefore can never become German. As Jews they oppose Germanness and thus cannot treat Christians like their own kind."[36] Ascher knew about the dangers of this hopeless ideologization. Early on it had provoked ideas of total expulsion and annihilation that oscillated between incendiary metaphors, like those of the young Fichte, and the "Germanomaniacs" proposals of extermination in the wake of the Hep-Hep unrest of 1819. Among those proposing such ideas was the Prussian officer and later emigrant, Hartwig von Hundt-Radowski, whose malicious writings were particularly effective.[37] In this sense, racist anti-Semitism stood directly in line with nationalist anti-Judaism. The latter's radicalism bordered, and often turned into, a biologically motivated hostility towards Jews, and we can assume that this nationalistic anti-Judaism opened the way for general racism in Germany, and not the other way round, i.e. racist ideas leading to modern anti-Semitism.

Against the background of the *Kuturkampf* many German advocates of Catholic rights resorted to similar arguments that were nationalistic but not aimed at eliminating the Jews. They portrayed the assimilated bourgeois Jews and liberalism – which had supported their emancipation and was now justifying and carrying out the persecution of the Catholic Church and its followers – as truly hostile to the Reich. Windthorst fought against this too – successfully inasmuch as nationalistic anti-Judaism remained a marginal problem for political Catholicism in Germany; the latter's racist radicalization was prevented because the Catholic Church and Catholicism did not accept religion as a function of nation, of anything national, or even of race. Anti-Semitism however went hand in hand with racist distortions of the image of Christianity and finally with the breakthrough of anti-Christian neo-pagan movements.[38]

Translated by Maike Bohn

Notes

1. On modernization theory, see Hans-Ulrich Wehler, *Modernisierungs-theorie und Geschichte* (Göttingen: Vandenhoeck and Ruprecht, 1975). On the centrality of the idea of progress to post-war historiography, see Karsten Ruppert, *Die Idee des Fortschritts in der neueren Geschichte* (Eichstätt: Katholische Universität Eichstätt, 2000). For an older text centrally structured by modernization theory, see H.-U. Wehler, *Das deutsche Kaiserreich 1871–1918* (Göttingen: Vandenhoeck and Ruprecht, 1973). See, for a contrary view, Thomas Nipperdey, *Deutsche Geschichte 1866–1918*, 2 vols (Munich: C. H. Beck, 1990, 1992).

2. See Walter Nigg, *Geschichte des religiösen Liberalismus. Entstehung, Blütezeit, Ausklang* (Zürich: Niehaus, 1937); Martin Greschat, *Das Zeitalter der industriellen Revolution. Das Christentum vor der Moderne* (Stuttgart: W. Kohlhammer, 1980); *Zur Soziologie des Katholizismus*, ed. Karl Gabriel and Franz Xaver Kaufmann (Mainz: Matthias-Grünewald Verlag, 1980); *Entwicklungslinien des deutschen Katholizismus*, ed. Anton Rauscher (Munich: Schöningh, 1973).

3. See the exemplary study of Jonathan Sperber, *Popular Catholicism in Nineteenth-Century Germany* (Princeton, NJ: Princeton University Press, 1984); David Blackbourn, *Marpingen. Apparitions of the Virgin Mary in Nineteenth-Century Germany* (New York: Alfred A. Knopf, 1994); Heinz Hürten, *Kurze Geschichte des deutschen Katholizismus 1800–1960* (Mainz: Matthias-Grünewald, 1986); Otto Weiss, "Der Ultramontanismus. Grundlagen, Vorgeschichte, Struktur," *Zeitschrift für Bayerische Landesgeschichte* 41 (1978): 821–77.

4. See *Zwischen Polemik und Irenik. Untersuchungen zum Verhältnis der Konfessionen im späten 18. und frühen 19. Jahrhundert*, ed. Georg Schwaiger (Göttingen: Vandenhoeck and Ruprecht, 1977); *Probleme des Konfessionalismus in Deutschland seit 1800*, ed. Anton Rauscher (Paderborn: Ferdinand Schöningh, 1984); *Säkularisierung, Dechristianisierung, Rechristianisierung im neuzeitlichen Europa*, ed. Hartmut Lehmann (Göttingen: Vandenhoeck and Ruprecht, 1997).

5. On the history of the concept of "cultural Protestantism" see Friedrich W. Graf, "Kulturprotestantismus. Zur Begriffsgeschichte einer theologiegeschichtlichen Chiffre," *Archiv für Begriffsgeschichte* 27 (1984): 214–68. See also Heinz Gollwitzer, *Vorüberlegungen zu einer Geschichte des politischen Protestantismus* (Opladen: Westdeutscher Verlag, 1981).

6. See Benedict Anderson, *Imagined Communities. Reflections on the Origin and Spread of Nationalism*. 2nd edn (London: Verso, 1991); Ernest Gellner, *Nations and Nationalism* (Oxford: Oxford University Press, 1983); Hagen Schulze, *Gibt es überhaupt eine deutsche Geschichte?* (Berlin: Siedler, 1989). See also the stimulating account by Michael Hechter, *International Colonialism. The Celtic Fringe in British National Development* (London: Routledge and Kegan Paul, 1975).

7. For denominational statistics for nineteenth-century Germany see Peter Claus Hartmann, "Bevölkerungszahlen und Konfessionsverhältnisse des Heiligen Römischen Reiches Deutscher Nation und der Reichskreise am Ende des 18. Jahrhunderts," *Zeitschrift für Historische Forschung* 22 (1995): 345–69; *Bevölkerungsgeschichte*, ed. Wolfgang Köllmann and Peter Marschalk (Cologne: Kiepenheuer and Witsch, 1972).

8. See Wolfgang Altgeld, "German Catholics," in *The Emancipation of Catholics, Jews and Protestants. Minorities and the Nation State in Nineteenth-Century Europe*, ed. Rainer Liedtke and Stephan Wendehorst (Manchester: University of Manchester Press, 1999), pp. 100–21.

9. See Koppel S. Pinson, *Pietism as a Factor in the Rise of German Nationalism* (New York: Columbia University Press, 1934); Gerhard Kaiser, *Pietismus und Patriotismus im literarischen Deutschland. Ein Beitrag zum Problem der Säkularisation*, 2nd edn (Frankfurt: Athenäum, 1973); Wolfgang Tilgner, *Volksnomostheologie und Schöpfungsglaube. Ein Beitrag zur Geschichte des Kirchenkampfes* (Göttingen: Vandenhoeck and Ruprecht, 1966); Arlie J. Hoover, *The Gospel of Nationalism. German Patriotic Preaching from Napoleon to Versailles* (Stuttgart: Franz Steiner, 1986).

10. Ernst Moritz Arndt, "Über alte Zeit und neue Zeit," in E. M. Arndt, *Blick aus der Zeit* (Germanien, 1814), 111–46, 142; Arndt, "Zum neuen Jahr," *Der Wächter* 3 (1816): 13–206, 161. See Wolfgang Altgeld, *Katholizismus, Protestantismus, Judentum. Über religiös begründete Gegensätze und nationalreligiöse Ideen in der Geschichte des deutschen Nationalismus* (Mainz: Matthias-Grünewald Verlag, 1992).

11. Wolfgang Altgeld, "Gregorovius und die Entstehung des italienischen Nationalstaats," *Jahrbuch des Italienisch-Deutschen Historischen Instituts in Trient* 18 (1992): 223–38. See also *Volk, Nation, Vaterland. Der deutsche Protestantismus und der Nationalismus*, ed. Horst Zillessen (Gütersloh: G. Mohr, 1970); *Religion im Kaiserreich. Milieus, Mentalitäten, Krisen*, ed. Olaf Blaschke and Frank-Michael Kuhlemann (Gütersloh: Chr. Kaiser, 1996). The essay by Claudia Lepp, "Protestanten feiern ihre Nation. Die kulturprotestantischen Ursprünge des Sedantages," *Historisches Jahrbuch der Görres-Gesellschaft* 118 (1998): 201–22, sheds an interesting light on this.

12. Friedrich Nicolai, *Beschreibung einer Reise durch Deutschland und die Schweiz im Jahre 1871*, 12 Vols (Berlin, 1783–1796), Vol. 5 (1785), p. 17, Vol. 4 (1784), p. 710.

13. See Wolfgang Altgeld, "'Akademische Nordlichter.' Ein Streit um Aufklärung, Religion und Nation nach der Neueröffnung der Bayerischen Akademie der Wissenschaften im Jahr 1807," *Archiv für Kulturgeschichte* 67 (1985): 339–88.

14. Heinrich von Sybel and Johann G. Gildemeister, *Der Heilige Rock und die zwanzig anderen heiligen Ungenähten Röcke. Eine historische Untersuchung* (Düsseldorf: J. Buddens, 1844). Otto Schulze, *Die "lebenden Bilder" der Alberschweiler Fronleichnamsprozession vor Gericht* (Leipzig: Carl Braun, 1898). For the context of the *Evangelischer Bund*, see in particular Helmut Walser Smith, *German Nationalism and Religious Conflict. Culture, Ideology, Politics 1870–1914* (Princeton, NJ: Princeton University Press, 1995).

15. G. W. F. Hegel, *Die Verfassung Deutschlands* (first edition 1802, reprinted 1893), in Hegel, *Politische Schriften*, ed. Hans Blumenberg *et al.* (Frankfurt: Suhrkamp, 1966) pp. 23–139, 37.

16. Max Lenz, "Nationalität und Religion," *Preußische Jahrbücher* 127 (1907): 385–408, 404.

17. Johann G. Herder, *Von Religion, Lehrmeinungen und Gebräuchen* (Leipzig: J. F. Hartknoch, 1798), in J. G. Herder, *Sämtliche Werke*, ed. B. Suphan, Vol. 20 (Berlin: Weidmann, 1880), pp. 133–265, 223;

Ernst Moritz Arndt, *Der Rhein, Deutschlands Strom, aber nicht Deutschlands Grenze* (first in 1813), in E. M. Arndt, *Schriften für und an seine lieben Deutschen*, Part 2 (Leipzig: Insel, 1845), pp. 1–66, 58.

18. Karl G. Bretschneider, *Teutschland und Preußen, oder: Das Interesse Teutschlands am preußischen Staat* (Berlin: Unger, 1806), pp. 7, 16.

19. Otto von Bismarck to Robert Graf von der Goltz, 9.7.1866, in Otto von Bismarck, *Werke in Auswahl*, ed. G. A. Rein, Vol. 3 (Darmstadt: Wissenschaftliche Buchgesellschaft, 1965), p. 755. Similar contemporary comments by Hermann Baumgarten, Sybel and Wilhelm Wehrenpfennig in *Deutscher Liberalismus im Zeitalter Bismarcks. Eine politische Briefsammlung*, Vol. 1, ed. Julius Heyderhoff (Bonn: K. Schroeder, 1925), no. 259, 260, 327.

20. Johann G. Fichte, "Republik der Deutschen, zu Anfang des zweiundzwanzigsten Jahrhunderts (um 1808)," in J. G. Fichte, *Sämtliche Werke*, ed. J. G. Fichte, Vol. 7 (Berlin: Veit, 1846), pp. 531–45, 537.

21. Jakob F. Fries, "Anruf an die Wartburgversammlung," in *Das Wartburgfest am 18. Oktober 1817*, ed. H. Kühn (Weimar: A. Duncker, 1913), p. 49. See also J. F. Fries, *Bekehrt Euch!* (Heidelberg: Mohr and Winter, 1814). Fries was not just by chance one of the most radical champions of a nationalistic anti-Judaism: see J. F. Fries, *Über die Gefährdung des Wohlstandes und Charakters der Deutschen durch die Juden*, 2nd edn (Heidelberg: Mohr, 1816); Ulrich von Hehl, "Zwei Kulturen – eine Nation? Die frühburschenschaftliche Einheitsbewegung und das Wartburgfest," *Historisches Jahrbuch der Görres-Gesellschaft* 111 (1991): 28–52.

22. Jakob Grimm, "Rede auf dem Frankfurter Germanistentag," in *Verhandlungen der Germanisten zu Frankfurt am Main am 24., 25. und 26. September 1846* (Frankfurt: Sauerländer in Komm., 1847), p. 17.

23. See Johann G. Herder, "Über National-Religionen" (first published in Hender, 1802), in *Sämtliche Werke*, ed. B. Suphan, Vol. 24, pp. 38–60; Ernst Chr. Trautvetter, *Der Bardenhain* (Berlin: Schöne, 1812); ibid., *Der Schlüssel zur Edda* (Berlin: J. W. Schmidts Erben, 1815). For the wide-ranging writings of Trautvetter and Johann Heinrich Voss see Altgeld, *Katholizismus, Protestantismus, Judentum*, pp. 178–81, 110–12.

24. Karl A. Menzel, *Über die Undeutschheit des neuesten Deutschtums* (Breslau: Graß, Barth, 1818), p. 54.

25. Karl G. Bretschneider, *Für die Deutsch-Katholiken* (Jena: Frommann, 1845), p. 45.

26. Wilhelm M. L. de Wette, "Katholizismus und Protestantismus im Verhältnis zur christlichen Offenbarung," in de Wette, *Zur christlichen Belehrung und Ermahnung*, Vol. 1 (Berlin: G. Reimer, 1819), pp. 1–90, 89. For the same reason the efforts to establish a national Church around Heinrich Ignaz von Wessenberg, and later spin-offs like the German-Catholicism and Old Catholicism were widely praised. See Friedrich W. Graf, *Die Politisierung des religiösen Bewußtseins. Die bürgerlichen Religionsparteien im deutschen Vormärz: Das Beispiel des Deutschkatholizismus* (Stuttgart-Bad Cannstatt: Frommann-Holzboog, 1986); Olaf R. Blaschke, "Der Altkatholizismus 1870–1945: Nationalismus, Antisemitismus und Nationalsozialismus," *Historische Zeitschrift* 261 (1995): 51–99.

27. See Jürgen W. Falter, *Hitlers Wähler* (Munich: C. H. Beck, 1991), pp. 169–193.

28. Augustin B. Hille, *Soll die Scheidewand unter Katholiken und Protestanten noch länger fortbestehen?* 2nd edn (Augsburg: Doll, 1819), p. 85. See also *Katholizismus, nationaler Gedanke und Europa seit 1800*, ed. Albrecht Langner (Paderborn: Ferdinand Schöningh, 1985).

29. See Matthias Klug, *Rückwendung zum Mittelalter? Geschichtsbilder und historische Argumentation im politischen Katholizismus des Vormärz* (Paderborn: Ferdinand Schöningh, 1995); Thomas Brechenmacher, *Großdeutsche Geschichtsschreibung im neunzehnten Jahrhundert. Die erste Generation 1830–48* (Berlin: Duncker and Humblot, 1996). The central contemporary theme is outlined in Bernhard Schneider, *Katholiken auf die Barrikaden? Europäische Revolutionen und deutsche katholische Presse 1815–1848* (Paderborn: Ferdinand Schöningh, 1998). For the controversy that was especially relevant for German historiography, see Wolfgang Hardtwig, "Von Preußens Aufgabe in Deutschland zu Deutschlands Aufgabe in der Welt. Liberalismus und borussianisches Geschichtsbild zwischen Revolution und Imperialismus" in Hardtwig, *Geschichtskultur und Wissenschaft* (Munich: Deutscher Taschenbuch Verlag, 1990), pp. 103–160.

30. *Universalstaat oder Nationalstaat. Die Streitschriften von Heinrich von Sybel und Julius Ficker zur Kaiserpolitik des Mittelalters*, ed. Friedrich Schneider (Innsbruck: Universitätsverlag Wagner, 1941).

31. See Rudolf Lill, "Die deutschen Katholiken und Bismarcks Reichsgründung," in *Reichsgründung 1870/71*, ed. Theodor Schieder and Ernst Deuerlein (Stuttgart: Seewald, 1970), pp. 345–65. The *Kulturkampf* legislation and its legitimization through press and propaganda

are now available in *Der Kulturkampf*, ed. Rudolf Lill (Paderborn: Ferdinand Schöningh, 1997).

32. See Martin Baumeister, *Parität und katholische Inferiorität. Untersuchungen zur Stellung des Katholizismus im Deutschen Kaiserreich* (Paderborn: Ferdinand Schöningh, 1987); *Katholizismus, Bildung und Wissenschaft im 19. und 20. Jahrhundert*, ed. Anton Rauscher (Paderborn: Ferdinand Schöningh, 1987). The massive repression by the state during the *Kulturkampf* is described in Ronald J. Ross, *The Failure of Bismarck's Kulturkampf. Catholicism and State Power in Imperial Germany, 1871–1887* (Washington, DC: The Catholic University of America Press, 1998). The debate about this failure ought to take into account the fact that the social, cultural and, to some extent, political *Kulturkampf* continued unabated because of this very consent of the Reich and of the individual states.

33. *Stenographische Berichte über die Verhandlungen des Preussischen Hauses der Abgeordneten, 20.11.1880*, 248. The context is described in Margaret L. Anderson, *Windthorst* (Oxford: Oxford University Press, 1981), Chapter 9.

34. See Imanuel Kant, *Die Religion innerhalb der Grenzen der bloßen Vernunft* (first in 1793), in I. Kant, *Werke. Akademie-Textausgabe*, Vol. 6 (Berlin: Weichert, 1907), pp. 1–202, 123. On the enlightened stereotype see Jacob Katz, "A State within a State. The History of an Antisemitic Slogan," in J. Katz, *Zur Assimilation und Emanzipation der Juden* (Darmstadt: Wissenschaftliche Buchgesellschaft, 1982), pp. 124–53. For its almost *völkisch* transformation see Altgeld, *Katholizismus, Protestantismus, Judentum*, pp. 91–107.

35. See Lothar Albertin, "Nationalismus und Protestantismus in der österreichischen Los-von-Rom Bewegung um 1900" (Ph. D. dissertation, University of Cologne, 1953), and for the larger context, see Smith, *German Nationalism and Religious Conflict*, pp. 206–232.

36. Saul Ascher, *Die Germanomanie. Skizze zu einem Zeitgemälde* (Berlin: Aschenwall, 1815), pp. 11, 14; idem, *Der deutsche Geistesaristokratismus. Ein Beitrag zur Charakteristik des zeitigen politischen Geistes in Deutschland* (Leipzig, 1819), p. 65.

37. See Hartwig von Hundt-Radowsky, *Judenspiegel. Ein Schand- und Sittengemälde alter und neuer Zeit*, 1st edn 1819 (Reutlingen: J. N. Ennslin'sche Buchhandlung, 1821).

38. Uriel Tal, *Christians and Jews in Germany. Religion, Politics and Ideology in the Second Reich 1870–1914* (Ithaca, NY: Cornell University Press, 1975). Olaf Blaschke offers a different view in *Katholizismus und Antisemitismus im Deutschen Kaiserreich* (Göttingen: Vandenhoeck and Ruprecht, 1997).

–4–

The "Christian" State and the "Jewish Citizen" in Nineteenth-Century Prussia

Chris Clark

This chapter focuses on the impact of Christian religious concerns on the debate over Jewish emancipation in Prussia. In doing so it swims against the current of the historiography in this field, which has generally seen Jewish policy in the German states as driven by secular preoccupations. I argue that the debate over Jewish entitlements – initially conducted under secular auspices – was reframed in the confessionally charged environment of post-Napoleonic Prussia as a question touching on the identity and purpose of the state. The "Christian state" so often invoked in the 1840s was conceived in part as an argument against the legal emancipation of Jews; but it also expressed authentically religious aspirations. Jewish policy and "Christian policy" were intertwined, both for the Prussian state authorities and for an influential sector of the political elite. It was of course the liberals, not the partisans of the Christian state, who ultimately won the argument over legal emancipation. However, as I argue below, the continuing impact of the concept should not be underestimated. It was enshrined in fragmentary form in the new Prussian constitution of January 1850 and it enjoyed a long afterlife – albeit in a debased and philosophically impoverished form – as a conservative slogan.

* * *

Religion does not loom large in the historical literature on the development of Jewish policy in the early-nineteenth-century German states, and it is easy to see why. The Enlightenment, one might argue, had recast the terms of the confessional opposition between Christianity and Judaism in a secular mold, and thereby cleared the way for the later emergence of a post-Christian anti-Semitism founded on ethnic categories. The Protestant philosophers and publicists of the revolutionary and Napoleonic eras conflated the religious category "Judaism" with the secular concept of a "Jewish nation." They defined the Jewish religion as an oppressive system of purely legal obligations, and denied that it possessed any genuinely religious or transcendent moral content.[1] Drawing on a long-standing trend in German Protestant perceptions of the Jewish minority, both the supporters and the opponents of emancipation saw the Jews as a "caste," whose distinctive characteristics were sociological and economic rather than confessional, though they differed as to whether these distinctive features were the consequence of external coercion or of endogenous, group-specific factors. Accordingly, as Wolfgang Altgeld has pointed out in a wide-ranging study of the periodical literature of the late eighteenth and early nineteenth centuries, virtually none of the early opponents of Jewish emancipation cited Christian imperatives, or the Christian character of the state, as an obstacle to the acceptance of Jewish civic equality. Most of those who participated in the debate triggered by Dohm's famous reformist essay, *Concerning the Civic Betterment of the Jews* (1781), shared the author's enlightened, skeptical standpoint on positive religion and a correspondingly secular conception of the state's tasks and responsibilities; none was prepared to argue that religion provided adequate grounds for civic discrimination against the Jews, and none identified the adoption by Jews of the Christian faith as either the sole or a necessary means of resolving the problem of Jewish status.

What the enlightened reformers sought was not the religious but the secular "conversion" of the Jews, from the supposedly narrow particularism of their customs, laws and communal life to the rational civic, "universal" morality of the "total citizen."[2] Once the pressures of legal discrimination were removed, Dohm had argued, it would become possible to "woo the Jews away from the sophistic sayings of their rabbis" and to divest them of their "clannish religious opinions," inspiring them instead with "patriotism and love for the state." And since it was primarily the "limitation of the Jews to commerce which has had a detrimental influence on their moral and political character," Dohm proposed that the state might take action to "dissuade the Jews from commercial occupations" and direct them towards professions – by which he meant above all the skilled crafts – that would foster a "diametrically opposed spirit and character."[3]

The development of government "Jewish policy" in most of the German states reflected the persistence of this secular, ameliorative approach to the question of Jewish entitlements. The renowned edicts of the Napoleonic era – most famous among them the Prussian Edict of 11 March 1812, to which we return below – removed specific Jewish disabilities, but withheld crucial entitlements, such as the right to occupy public office, on the grounds that, as one Prussian official put it: "repression had made the Jews treacherous" and the "sudden concession of liberty" would not suffice to "reconstitute all at once the natural human nobility within them."[4] The trend throughout the German states after 1815 was to insist on social restructuring as the precondition for legal emancipation; there was thus a proliferation of decrees that aimed to lever the Jews out of their traditional economic niches into allegedly less harmful and more "productive" areas of the economy. The aim, as one resolution by the administration of Hesse-Cassel put it, was to "sever" the Jews "from activities dishonourable to the citizen . . . [such as] brokering, peddling, personal loans and the sale of second-hand goods."[5] The oppressive Bavarian law of 1813, which remained in force until 1861, made permission to reside in the kingdom dependent on possession of a "matricular number" which could only be bequeathed to the eldest son; younger sons were only permitted to settle if they earned their livelihood from a craft trade, agriculture or manufacturing.[6] All of this would suggest that the governments of the post-Napoleonic era continued to frame the problem of Jewish entitlements in the fundamentally secular categories that had established themselves during the Enlightenment. This would bear out the view that, notwithstanding the restorative energies released by the defeat of Napoleon, the bureaucratic projects inaugurated during the late Enlightenment continued largely unabated in the post-Napoleonic era.[7]

However, a survey of the evolution of "Jewish policy" in Prussia, home of the largest Jewish population within the boundaries of the German Confederation, reveals a more complex picture than this paradigm can accommodate. For perhaps the most striking aspect of Prussian policy discussions and administrative action with regard to Jewish entitlements after 1815 was a new emphasis on religion, and specifically upon conversion, as the key to the resolution of the "Jewish question." In the course of debate over these matters within the Ministerial Council in 1816, the Ministry of Finance submitted a long memorandum that opened with some general reflections on the role of religion as the only true foundation for a confident and independent state: "A cohesive, independent people," it argued, should consist of members who share the same "basic ideas that are most dear to them"; religion was the only bond powerful enough to transform a people into a "unanimous whole" capable of unified and determined action in "times of external threat." The report went on to set out its recommendations in a list of key points: "1. It would be ideal if there were no Jews in the country at all. 2. Those that we have we must tolerate, but we must always be at pains to make them as harmless as possible. [. . .] 4. The conversion of Jews to the Christian faith must be made easier and should entail the granting of all civil rights. [. . .] 6. As long as the Jew remains a Jew, he must not be permitted to take up a position in the state . . .".[8] Conversion was taken no less seriously in local government circles. In a report of 1819, the district government of Arnsberg affirmed that religion was the main hindrance to Jewish emancipation. It proposed that the state should introduce measures to encourage Jewish conversions. A report of 1820 from the district magistrates of Münster recommended mandatory Christian adult education for Jews and special benefits for converts to Christianity who took up a "Christian profession." The provincial government of Minden expressed its preference for "indirect" forms of conversionary pressure that would neither compromise the state's commitment to freedom of conscience, nor burden its finances.[9]

These views were endorsed by King Frederick William III himself. When the Jewish mathematician David Unger, a citizen of Prussia, applied for a teaching position at the Berlin *Bauakademie*, he was advised by the monarch personally that his application would be reconsidered after his "conversion to the Evangelical Church."[10] In the widely-discussed case of the Jewish lieutenant Meno Burg, who was due in 1830 to be promoted to the rank of captain, the king issued a cabinet order in which he expressed his assumption that, in view of his education and position, Burg would have the sense to come to a recognition of the truth and redeeming power of the Christian faith and thus "clear away any obstacle to his promotion."[11]

In addition to this kind of *ad hoc* intervention, Frederick William III actively encouraged conversion by introducing a royal bounty for Jewish converts who had the name of the sovereign entered in the church records as their nominal "godfather."[12] Frederick William also took an intense personal interest in the *prevention* of conversions in the other direction, i.e. from Christianity to Judaism. In a Cabinet Order of November 1814, he announced that conversions from Christianity to Judaism were not to be permitted. Persons who persisted in this intention were to forfeit their rights as Prussian citizens and therefore to be treated as "alien Jews" and expelled from the kingdom.[13] In 1834, having been advised of a number of cases in which "Christian females of low estate" made pregnant by Jewish men had sought to convert to Judaism, Frederick William ordered that rabbis and Jewish elders be warned that they would be punished if they accepted into their "religious society" (*Religionsgesellschaft*) converts from the "Christian community" (*Gemeinschaft der Christen*) before these had been "released" by the Christian Church authorities. At around the same time he issued an order stating that Christian clergymen were forbidden to issue formal permissions of any kind to Christians seeking to convert to Judaism. Persons who expressed a desire to convert were furthermore to be "taught and warned" of the legal consequences of such a step.[14]

By contrast with the enlightened emancipationists, who argued that the removal of legal boundaries would in time result in the merging of the Jewish and Christian communities, Frederick William sought to uphold and fortify the social frontier between the two religions. He forbade, for example, Christian clergymen to attend Jewish "religious celebrations" such as bar mitzvahs, even if they did so in a purely private capacity as friends or neighbors of a Jewish family. Failure to abide by this ruling, he argued in a Cabinet Order of 1821, would result in a "cooling of respect for the value of Christianity" and a form of *rapprochement* (*Annäherung*) between the two faiths that would be alien to the "system" of Christian religion.[15] In order to prevent the emergence of a secular third option between Judaism and Christianity, he also prohibited Jews from leaving their own communities without converting to the Christian faith. The king also made repeated attempts (in 1816, 1836, and 1839) to forbid the carrying of "Christian" first names by Jewish subjects.[16]

This reorientation in policy was supported by trends in contemporary intellectual and religious life. In an influential rejoinder to those who pressed for emancipation on secular grounds, Friedrich Rühs, a professor at the University of Berlin, argued that conversion to Christianity was the crucial precondition for any authentic process of emancipation. The Jews, he argued in 1816, should be granted human rights (i.e. freedom from onerous and demeaning restrictions), but the concession of full civil rights (i.e. the right to participate as equals in the public life of the polity) should be contingent upon their acceptance of Christianity. Every effort should be made to give them access to the ennobling rewards of the Christian faith. In a second work published in the same year, Rühs drew attention to the traditional Christian belief in a prophesied general conversion of the Jews and suggested that everything possible should be done to bring this great event nearer.[17] Similar positions were taken up by other less prominent figures who joined the debate over emancipation with pamphlets calling for measures to preserve the Christian character of the polity and to "educate" the Jews towards conversion.[18]

Rühs's call for a campaign to convert the Jews coincided with that phase of heightened religious activism in the capital that was later to be known as the "Berlin Awakening." In the years following the end of the Wars of Liberation against Napoleon, a distinctly patrician revivalism emerged in Berlin. It was not unusual during the early post-war years for generals and senior officials of noble lineage who spent their mornings in ministries and staff offices to spend their evening at prayer with a circle of devout friends. Charismatic individuals such as the born-again noble-man Baron Kottwitz, or the evangelical preachers Hermes, Jänicke and Anders provided the focus of religious life in what became a cohesive "awakened" community. Neo-pietist noblemen met at the churches of the Moravian brethren, frequented each other's houses and country estates, formed close friendships and married each other's relatives. They read the same edifying texts, experienced traumatic "conversions," often in each other's company, and went on long journeys to meet the gurus of the Protestant awakening in southern Germany. Many of those who passed through the awakening subsequently became involved in voluntary religious societies. They directed missions, religious book clubs and Bible societies, founded poor-schools and visited the inmates of prisons.[19]

One variety of Christian activism that attracted a particularly broad cross-section of the awakened community was the mission to the Jews. A society founded in Berlin in 1822 to evangelize the Jews reflected faithfully the social composition and conservative political complexion of post-war revivalism in the capital. And the participation of powerful individuals from ministerial and administrative circles – senior civil servants and high-ranking officers – reflected the importance that the political and social elite now attached to conversion as an answer to the problems allegedly posed by the existence of the Jewish minority. The Berlin Society for the Promotion of Christianity among the Jews founded in January 1822 at the house of General Job von Witzleben soon gave rise to a string of daughter-foundations dispersed across the Prussian provinces, in Detmold, Rackschütz, Posen, Minden, Oletzko, Stettin, Ratibor, Danzig, Frankfurt an der Oder, Potsdam, Bröskerfelde, Thorn, Gleiwitz, Fraustadt, Kalningken, Proeculs and Preußisch Eylau. In the Province of Posen in particular, the Posen mission was able, with the assistance of subsidies from the London Society for the Promotion of Christianity among the Jews, to finance a network of "free schools" that catered for Jewish children in communities too poor to establish schools of their own. By presenting themselves in non-denominational language as free schools for the Jewish communities and thus veiling their mission-ary purpose, these institutions succeeded in attracting substantial numbers of Jewish children from some of the poorest districts in the Province of Posen. They profited from new laws requiring all Jewish children of school age to attend properly certified schools, regardless of whether specifically Jewish schooling was locally available. In addition to these activities, the societies employed professional missionaries, some with a knowledge of Yiddish, who were employed to travel from town to town evangelizing the Jewish communities.[20]

In all these enterprises, the missionary societies and their influential backers enjoyed the full support of the state authorities. Frederick William had informed the Society's director personally in February 1822 that the new foundation expressed his "innermost wishes", and that he intended to assist it in achieving its goals. The king authorized an annual donation from his own funds and exempted the mission societies from the payment of postal fees, an important provision, since so much of their activity consisted in the distribution by post of Bibles, missionary pamphlets and pious tracts.[21] In 1827, he issued a Cabinet Order authorizing the Berlin Society to appoint a clergyman especially for the purpose of holding services and Bible-study hours for Jews and converts in the city.[22] Throughout his reign, Prussia remained a "missionary state," both in the passive sense that it withheld emancipation from Jews who chose not to convert and in the active sense that it encouraged and celebrated the act of conversion.

The evangelizing work, literary output and impact of the missions have been analyzed in detail elsewhere. The point to be made here is that this collusion between the monarch and the forces of Protestant voluntarism within Prussian society signaled a new point of departure. The contrast with the vehemently secular tone of the debate on Jewish entitlements in the 1780s and 1790s could have not have been greater. Why did this transformation occur?

The most obvious answer to this question would appear to be the upsurge of revivalist religion known as the Awakening. This variegated, multilayered phenomenon drew on disenchantment with the secular prescriptions of the Enlightenment and the French revolution, and was nourished by the dislocation and suffering caused by the Napoleonic wars. There were also strands of continuity with the earlier pietist revivals of eighteenth-century Protestant northern Europe. The activists who founded the missionary movement in Prussia came, as we saw, from the heart of the Berlin Awakening, and the movement's rural support network reflected the resonance of revivalist Christianity among pious artisans, those "quiet ones in the land" whose devotional culture remained recognizably pietist.[23] Their activism reflected the characteristic emphasis of the "awakened" on practical piety, and their faith in an ultimate prophesied general conversion of the Jews drew on a strand of chiliastic expectation that had motivated the earlier utopian projects of the Prussian pietist movement in Halle and Königsberg.

The link between the passionate commitment of the Awakened and the confessional activism of the monarch after 1815 is more complex and less direct. Frederick William was certainly a believing Christian who attended church regularly. In 1808, during his exile in East Prussia (after the catastrophic defeats of Jena and Auerstedt), he experienced a religious awakening of sorts, brought on by the preaching of Pastor Borowski in Königsberg. The duress of exile and the struggle and exaltation of the Wars of Liberation appear to have awakened in him faith in a providential God, whose hand could be seen in the restoration of Prussian fortunes.[24] But Frederick William III was and remained in many respects a child of the Enlightenment, who had grown up with a basically functional understanding of the role of religion in a Christian polity. As a young man, he had declared in his confession of faith that he held the church to be the "best pillar of the state" and the "best means of promoting the peace and welfare of civil society."[25]

Frederick William's support for missionary activism and his insistence upon conversion as a criterion for entry into the political life of the state should be seen in the context of the king's broader involvement in efforts to create a homogeneous Protestant confessional culture in Prussia after 1815. Frederick William's personal commitment to the establishment of a state-sponsored "Church of the Prussian Union" that would merge the Calvinist and Lutheran strands of North German Protestantism was doubtless reinforced by a range of contemporary political exigencies: the need to integrate the newly-acquired territories in east and west (including the presbyterial Calvinists of the Rhenish districts), the desire to reinforce the primacy of Protestantism in the face of an enlarged Catholic minority and the wish to secure the reputation of the Brandenburg monarchy as the foremost German Protestant house. What matters for the present purpose is that the consequence was a period of unprecedented confessional interventionism on the part of the monarch and his administration. In the place of the diverse and localized structures of the Lutheran and Reformed churches of the Prussian lands in the eighteenth century, Frederick William sought to install a unified and centralized Church regime with edifying and accessible rituals that would arrest the centrifugal pull of sectarian formations and draw the Protestant populace together into "One flock," united in "One love and in One hope . . . under One communal shepherd."[26]

At the heart of Frederick William's Church reform project was an uncompromising drive for uniformity that was recognizably post-Napoleonic: the simplification and homogenization of vestments at the altar as on the field of battle, liturgical conformity down to the most minute detail, even modular *Normkirchen* designed to be built from prefabricated parts and available in different sizes to suit villages and towns. Although entry into the Union Church was theoretically voluntary, Frederick William regarded those who resisted co-option or sought to leave the Union as troublemakers and subversives. The last decade of his reign saw extensive police action against congregations of "Old Lutherans" who insisted that they remained a distinct and autonomous Protestant "confession."[27]

In some respects, this project represented a continuation of the agenda set out by the Prussian reformers, who had also favored the rationalization of Church administration, but in the fullness of its ambition it constituted a departure from the secular principles that had motivated the key reformers. The unity of religious practice was to provide the spiritual and emotional basis for the state-oriented sense of commitment that the reformers had aimed to stimulate within the population. In this sense, the union was a church–state organism of a new type. It did not entail, as Marx wishfully diagnosed in an influential essay of 1844, the banishment of religion from the state into society. Nor did it bring about the enslavement of the Church by the state, as the critics of the Union have sometimes claimed. Rather it inaugurated an era of symbiosis and interdependency, in which state and clerical competences were blended. As Hans-Dietrich Loock has shown, there was a utopian element in the drive to establish the Union: the aim was ultimately to create a new order that would overcome the church–state divide, at once disciplining the Church and sacralizing the state.[28] This program was not conducive to the concession of full political entitlements to unconverted Jewish subjects.

An earlier development that helps to explain the new emphasis on religion as the key issue in deliberations on Jewish entitlements was the "Edict of Emancipation" issued under the auspices of the Hardenberg administration on 11 March 1812. The edict announced that all Jews resident in Prussia and in possession of general privileges, naturalization certificates, letters of protection, or special concessions should henceforth be regarded as inhabitants (*Einländer*) and citizens of the state (*Staatsbürger*) of Prussia. The emancipation thereby made available to Prussian Jews was limited in a number of important respects. Firstly, it was only issued with respect to the four core provinces that remained under Prussian control after the French invasion and occupation, namely Brandenburg, Silesia, Pomerania and East Prussia. It was not extended to the territories ceded or returned to Prussia after 1814/15 (namely the Rhineland, Posen, the Prussian Province of Saxony and so on). Secondly, while the Edict removed important civil disabilities, such as the restrictions on freedom of movement, occupation, marriage and property acquisition, it withheld – thanks to the monarch's personal intervention – crucial political rights. In particular the question of whether positions in government service ought to be made available to Jewish applicants was left open, to be determined "at a later time."[29]

Opinions differ as to the significance of the "March edict." In a classic résumé of the legal emancipation of the Jews in Germany, Reinhard Rürup described it as "a remarkable document, which to this day must be valued as one of the greatest documents of the history of emancipation in Europe."[30] According to this view, the stagnation and even partial reversal of the emancipation after 1815 constituted an abandonment of the initiative launched in 1812. An alternative view stresses the Edict's limitations and argues that it amounted to little more in reality than an "extended and generally decreed privilege" issued to certain Jews for the purpose of removing certain anomalous restrictions.[31] According to this view, it is mistaken to see the edict of March 1812 as embodying the potential for a new progressive legislative climate, since officials were concerned only with applying the letter of the new legislation and "had no reason to attend to its 'spirit' over and above its literal content."[32] But however one assesses the place of the Edict in the history of Jewish policy in Prussia and the German states, it is clear that it was perceived by contemporaries as a moment of epochal significance. The Jewish journal *Sulamith* welcomed it as the inauguration of a "new and happy era," and the new legislation was imitated in other German states.[33] Nor is it by any means clear that Prussian officials were indifferent to the "spirit of 1812." On the contrary, a government survey of 1842 revealed that many officials in the district and provincial administrations saw the Edict as the high-water mark of forward-thinking state legislation on Jewish affairs and regarded it as the inauguration of and basis for a continuing process of Jewish social and moral assimilation.[34]

The point – to return to the main argument – is that the Edict, regardless of its limitations, had placed the question of Jewish entitlements on a new footing. For the Jews were no longer "foreigners" dwelling on Prussian soil on His Majesty's sufferance, but "citizens of the state" along with their fellow citizens of Christian faith (though the precise meaning of the term *Staatsbürger* remained unclear). In other words, the boundaries in the debate over entitlements had to be redrawn. The question now was: should the Jews, having already been allowed to participate on an equal footing as *private individuals* in the sphere of economy and society, be admitted to participation in the organs of the state? Answering this question involved making claims about the purposes for which the state and its organs existed. A taciturn and unintellectual figure, Frederick

William was not given to synthetic formulations on matters of political principle. However, the trend in his policy after 1815 suggests that he gradually moved away from the functional conception of the role of religion that he had imbibed from the enlightened tutors of his youth towards a viewpoint that at least encompassed the possibility that the state might exist to pursue ends defined by religion. "However strong the claim to tolerance may become," he observed in 1821, "a borderline [*Grenze*] must be drawn wherever this implies a step backwards on the road to the redemption of mankind."[35] But if the state existed, among other things, for the purpose of providing a platform for the expansion of (Protestant) Christianity as a community of faith, did this mean that the state itself was – in diametrical opposition to the tenets of the enlightened political theory that had underwritten the emancipation debate of the 1780s – a Christian institution?

Although the assumption that the state was in some sense Christian clearly underlay government policies during the decades following the liberation of Prussia from French occupation, it was not until the 1840s, during intensified public discussion of Jewish emancipation, that coherent theories were formulated outlining the precise nature of the relationship between state structures and Christian principles. In August 1842, when the emancipation question was debated in the Baden Chamber of Deputies, opponents founded their case on the claim that Baden was a "Christian state," and therefore could not tolerate the admission of Jews into its public life. In Prussia, the stage was set from 1840 by the new monarch, Frederick William IV, the "awakened Christian on the throne," as Hans-Joachim Schoeps called him, who saw the Prussian state as the arena for a variety of state-sponsored Christian projects and warmly supported Jewish-missionary activity.[36] In 1841, with the establishment of the Anglo-Prussian bishopric in Jerusalem, the mission to the Jews at home and abroad became official Prussian policy. General Ludwig August von Thile, Count Anton Stolberg-Wernigerode, Count von der Gröben and Baron Senfft von Pilsach, all directors of the Berlin Society, had all been close to Frederick William as Crown Prince and were among the new king's most trusted friends and personal advisers; indeed their proximity to him fueled liberal suspicions that the throne had fallen under the influence of "pietists and reactionaries."[37] Soon after his accession, Frederick William made it known, in a document accidentally leaked to the public, that he intended to reorganize the Jews of his kingdom in neo-medieval corporations to be known as *Judenschaften*, a measure that, had it been enacted, would have reversed the thirty-year process of legal and societal assimilation set in train by the edict of March 1812.

Throughout Prussia, the Christian state concept became a common-place in debates that touched on the emancipation of the Jewish minority. During a dispute in the Rhenish provincial assembly over the exclusion of Jews from the right to be elected to communal councils (*Gemeinderäte*), the exponents of exclusion argued that "in a Christian state only those who profess an allegiance to Christianity can become members of admin-istrative bodies."[38] The debate provoked in the Brandenburg provincial assembly in March 1845 by a petition calling for full legal emancipation saw a polarization of the participants into "liberals" on the one hand, and "exponents of the Christian state" on the other.[39] Even some liberal com-mentators co-opted the slogan "Christian state" for their own ends, arguing, for example, that full emancipation would "extend the Christian state" by "drawing the Jews closer to us" or that a state that was truly Christian must in the spirit of good-neighborly love concede entitlements to an oppressed minority.[40] Nothing could better illustrate the degree to which the term had established itself as central fixture in public debate.

Jewish journals were quick to take note of these developments. An article written in September 1842 for Julius Fürst's journal *Der Orient*, the most zestfully critical of the Jewish periodicals of this era, observed that although the idea of the Christian state had hitherto been little discussed, if at all, in Prussia, it appeared to be the underlying principle of the monarch's new legislative proposal. A further article printed in the following year observed that "the phantom of the Christian state" was "the very latest pretext for refusing us our rights."[41] "More than ever," the liberal journal *Die Zeitinteressen* noted, "Christianity is being questioned on the one hand, and defended on the other [by those who seek] to prove that the essence of our contemporary political life is intrinsically Christian, that our states are Christian."[42] However, although it was alluded to with increasing frequency, the notion of the Christian state remained poorly defined and was only applied in a piecemeal way to public debate on the question of emancipation. Jewish and liberal journalists responded by pointing up the practical and theoretical incoherence of the idea. The Christian state was an empire of pious wishes, or a theocratic utopia based upon a fundamental misunderstanding of the modern state and its relationship with society.[43]

In 1847 a book appeared in Berlin that claimed to have raised the idea of the Christian state to the level of ideological coherence. The fact that its author, Friedrich Julius Stahl, was for many years a director of the Berlin Society for the Promotion of Christianity among the Jews was hardly fortuitous. Stahl, a convert from Judaism who had been called to the University of Berlin by Frederick William IV in 1840, announced in the introduction to his book, *The Christian State*, that the question of Jewish entitlements was one of the most fundamental that had faced the United Prussian Diet of 1847. The liberal faction at the Diet had called for emancipation on the basis of equal rights for all, Stahl argued, but to have granted this request would have amounted to denying that the state itself had any Christian content. The issue therefore touched upon the constitution, laws, administration and church-state relations in Prussia. "It is the cardinal question of our time," Stahl declared, "not merely in Prussia, but in all Germany."[44]

Because the state concerned itself with so many facets of human activity – war, welfare, education, the family – it was, Stahl maintained, the highest expression of a people's "legal, ethical and religious worth." However, since laws were based upon ethical life, and ethical life in turn upon religion, it was above all the shared religious conviction of a nation that found expression in the state. In a characteristically Hegelian form-ulation, Stahl concluded that "the state is a revelation of the ethical spirit of the nation."[45] The "Christian state" would therefore seek to regulate public affairs in a way which expressed the "spirit of a Christian people." It would be marked by the acknowledgement of Christian truth in its official documents and by the application of Christian principles to the spheres of legislation and administration. However, Christianity was not merely the "norm and foundation" of the Christian State, but also its "purpose." In other words, the state existed not merely to express, but also to propagate and realize in practice, the values of Christianity.[46] During his years as a teacher of law at the University of Erlangen, Stahl had attended the conventicles and prayer-meetings of neo-pietists in the Erlangen district, and his political thought reflected the Christian activist assumptions of the awakened. Like many of the awakened, he could not accept the (traditional Lutheran) view that the earthly realm and the king-dom of God were two distinct and separate spheres. If the idea of God were not to be an absurdity, then the world must strive to attain its ideal condition. Christianity was thus, in Stahl's view, more than a set of ethical principles. It was a force for the transformation of the worldly order work-ing through the legal and political framework of the state.[47] There was a certain circularity here: on the one hand, the Christian character of the state was justified by reference to the Christian cultures and values of the people whose "ethical substance" it expressed and represented; on the other hand, it was the state that bore the responsibility for maintaining and extending the influence of Christianity in the public life of the nation.

One consequence of the Christian character of the state was the restriction of political rights to members of the "official Christian church."

It was unthinkable that Jews (and other non-believers, such as deists) should occupy state offices in such a polity. Even in areas not directly concerned with religion, they would spread the notion that the highest things are those which best serve the needs of men and thereby propagate a profane understanding of the state's function and essence. As for those areas of administration that did concern morality and religion – marital law, education, church–state relations – the admission of non-Christians would lead to the "complete dechristianisation of the state."[48] Among the God-given duties of the Christian State, Stahl continued, was the obligation to encourage the conversion to Christianity of the Jews in its midst. He acknowledged that the work of the missions to the Jews had not so far been very successful, but it should not be forgotten that God had provided, in the co-existence of Jews and Christians, the means by which they would all eventually be converted.[49] One of the achievements of the Emancipation edict of 1812 had been that it "tolerated" the Jews as citizens, thereby exemplifying the generosity of the Protestant spirit, but did not elevate them to the status of "active citizens," thereby safeguarding the integrity of the Christian state. Since the Christian state of Prussia was effectively a missionary institute intended by God to bring on a mass conversion of Jewry, it was fitting that the Jews should continue to live and flourish within it, albeit in a negatively privileged condition.[50]

Viewed from a present-day standpoint, with knowledge of the imminent Revolution of 1848 and of the triumph of the liberal, secular definition of citizenship in the emancipation legislation of the 1860s, Stahl's Christian state concept has the odor of a doomed idea. Opponents were quick to pounce on its internal contradictions; among other things, they asked: was the "Christianity" of the Christian state of the Protestant or of the Catholic variety? This was a sore point, given that memories of the bitter Prussian church–state struggle of the 1830s over Protestant–Catholic mixed marriages were still fresh in the minds of Catholic contemporaries. But it also drew attention to the specifically Protestant character of the concept as it was expounded by Prussian conservatives. Stahl's concept of the role of secular authority in assimilating earthly affairs to an eternal order and thereby hastening the completion of a divine plan carried the stamp of the Protestant awakening Stahl had encountered as a young man. His (closely related) notion that state and Church were "separate" but not "apart," and his organicist metaphors, in which religion figured as the "single life-force" that permeated the public affairs of the nation[51] implied an identity of interest between Church, nation and state that held little plausibility for German Catholics. Catholic national consciousness tended, by contrast, as Wolfgang Altgeld has shown, to problematize the relationship between Church and state and to insist upon "the universal religious affinities of the individual."[52] Moreover, the term "Christian state" carried a specifically Protestant historical resonance, since it was widely associated with the confessional polities established in the aftermath of the Reformation.[53] Stahl dodged this issue by arguing that Protestantism and Catholicism constituted parts of the one Christian "religion" and were thus interchangeable from the standpoint of his theory,[54] but he did make a telling – if indirect – allusion to the competitive relationship between the two confessions when he warned that allowing Jews to marry Christians would benefit the German Catholics at the expense of the Protestants, since it was the latter, with their more tolerant way of life who would be more prepared to accept the compromises involved in a mixed union. "Thus after a half-century, the Catholic church, in addition to its other external advantages, would gain the further advantage that it could say of the Protestants that their church is a blend of Christianity and Judaism."[55]

Critics also doubted whether the Christian state was compatible with the venerable concept of the *Rechtsstaat*, the state ruled by codified law.[56] In *The Christian State*, Stahl insisted that it was: "The *Rechtsstaat* does indeed prevent intervention for Christian motives and purposes in the legal order, but it does not prevent the form of the legal order from being based on Christian ideas."[57] And yet the history of Frederick William III's confessional interventions in the 1820s and 1830s had suggested precisely the opposite, for the reality was that the legal fabric of the Prussian state was fundamentally secular, with the consequence that the constitutional basis for state interventions in the religious sphere was often found to be lacking. In the matter of conversions to Judaism, for example, an administration bent on outright prohibition was forced to act against the letter of the *Allgemeines Landrecht* and the Edict of 1812, which in combination seemed to stipulate that any Prussian subject over the age of fourteen and in possession of a sane mind was at liberty to change his or her confessional affiliation. The contradiction between the existing legal provisions and the will of the executive led to protracted confusion, as the cases of women seeking to convert in order to marry Jewish men were passed up the ranks of the district, provincial, and central admin- istrations, only to be decided by an extra-constitutional royal fiat. Similar problems dogged the government's efforts to safeguard the Union against dissenting groups like the Old Lutherans and the pietist separatists in the 1830s.[58] Stahl may well have been right in arguing that a *Rechtsstaat* compatible with the Christian state principle was *theoretically* possible, but it was also clear that the *Rechtsstaat* as it had actually evolved in

Prussia since the late eighteenth century posed serious obstacles to any government bent on enforcing religious conformity through state action.

To the extent that it depended upon the collusion of voluntarist forces from the awakened elements within the Protestant community, moreover, the confessional activism of the Prussian administration under Frederick William III had run into a further problem: the priorities of the "awakened" and those of the state were not always compatible. In the wake of the early-nineteenth-century revival came a proliferation of sectarian and separatist groups whose need for a more authentic and intense religious experience could not be satisfied within the confines of the official Church. It is thus no coincidence that separatists of various stripe were disportionately represented within the ranks of the missionary movement. This naturally brought the missionary societies into conflict with the state Church that Frederick William had labored so ardently to establish. In May 1826, for example, tension between the missionary movement and the Church administration came to a head when the Protestant consistory of the province of Prussia accused Missionary Händes, an employee of the Berlin Society for the Promotion of Christianity among the Jews, of having started a "sect" in the town of Neidenburg. Reporting to the ministry for Church, health and educational affairs in Berlin, the consistory alleged that Händes had gathered about him "in particular the inexperienced female youth of Neidenburg, so that after his departure a regular society for religious purposes had formed in the house of the dyer Oettinger." The consistory argued that the meetings in Oettinger's house constituted a "sect" in the "general sense of any separatist gathering." The "excessive prayer" (*Andächtelei*) that characterized these meetings allegedly left the young women of Neidenburg in a state of "mental confusion and even physical collapse." It was reported that the daughter of the district doctor had returned from Oettinger's house "filled with fantasy, unfit for chores and numb to all appeals."[59] In later years, concern over the sectarian sympathies of awakened missionaries was overshadowed by – justified – apprehensions about the close links between the missionary scene and the movement of Old Lutheran dissent based in Silesia that became Frederick William III's bugbear during the last decade of his reign.

In other words: Christian statism had never been a viable operational basis for political action in Prussia, and it appeared fundamentally incompatible with the wave of liberal legislation that undid the bond between Christianity and citizenship rights in *Reich* law after 1871. Indeed, it could be argued that the incoherence of the Christian state idea and the contradictions exposed by its sporadic translation into government practice eased the way for those liberals who sought to set citizenship upon a secular foundation: what the Prussian monarchy had found it so difficult to weld together, liberals found it beguilingly easy to tear asunder. We might thus take the view, with one recent commentator, that Stahl and his idea should be counted among "the losers of history."[60]

This conclusion would be premature, for two reasons. Firstly, as historians of mid-century German conservatism have often acknowledged, Stahl was crucially involved during and after the revolution in the emergence of a constitutional conservatism in Prussia that was flexible enough in its principles to subsist in the new parliamentary environment of the post-revolutionary era. But, more importantly for our purposes, he also played a central role in the campaign to have the Christian character, if not of the state as such, then at least of its key public institutions, protected under the new dispensation. The result of these efforts was article 14 of the revised constitution of 31 January 1850, which stated: "The Christian religion is taken to be the basis of those institutions of the state that are connected with the practice of religion, regardless of the freedom of religion guaranteed in article 12." "Some people," Stahl noted smugly in the foreword to a second edition of *The Christian State* in 1857, "may have voted for this article on the assumption that it sole purpose was to preserve Christian holidays and the Christian calendar", but the reality was that it could also be deployed much more widely as "an effective protection" of the state's "Christian institutions."[61] This was a matter of some significance, for the Reich constitution promulgated in 1871 did not automatically abrogate the constitutions of the member states. The *Reich* may have done away – in theory at least – with all positive confessional discrimination, but the Prussian state in which three-fifths of its subjects resided remained a "Christian state" in the sense set out in article 14. Here, in the state that employed Germany's largest public service and presided over the recruitment of the small Reich bureaucracy, it was possible to legitimate discriminatory action against Jewish applicants to public office by reference to the Christian character of all institutions connected – however tenuously – with religious observance. Precisely this principle was invoked in the repeated controversies of the late 1880s over the recruitment of Jewish jurors, in which debate turned, among other things, on the supposedly "religious" character of the judicial oath.[62]

The Prussian constitution thus continued, thanks to Stahl's efforts, to supply grist for the mills of those conservatives who continued after his death – and often with explicit reference to his thought – to invoke the concept of the "Christian state." In an important study of anti-Jewish and anti-Semitic mentalities after 1871, Uriel Tal showed how central the slogan of the "Christian state" was to the evolution of conservative ideologies in the Wilhelmine era.[63] The growing respectability of this idea in the decades following the "second foundation" of the Reich must help to explain the growing willingness of ministerial officials within and outside Prussia to defend discriminatory appointment policies on the grounds that it was legitimate for a Christian population to demand Christian officials, doctors and notaries and so on. During a sensational debate triggered by an interpellation in the Prussian Landtag regarding discrimination against Jewish candidates for notarial office, the Prussian minister of justice Karl Heinrich von Schönstedt affirmed that he had to take account of local opinion when making judicial appointments. "I cannot, when appointing notaries," Schönstedt declared, "simply treat Jewish advocates on the same basis as Christian ones, since the broadest strata of the population are not willing to have their affairs managed by Jewish notaries."[64] To be sure: the argument implied here drew in a very selective way on the Christian statist position set out in the 1840s. There was no reference to the role of the state in maintaining or extending the influence of Christianity on public life, only to its alleged obligation to reflect or accommodate in its policies, the supposedly Christian preferences of the great majority of the population. In 1903, when the emblematically named Jewish civil rights organisation *Centralverein, für deutsche Staatsbürger jüdischen Glaubens*, complained to the Saxon district authorities of discrimination against Jewish medical trainees at the City Hospital of Chemnitz, it was informed that "since the City Council is free, for example, to limit the circle of candidates for intern posts at the City Hospital to married doctors, doctors of a certain age, or [doctors] who have acquired a certain examination result, so it would be inadmissible for the authorities to intervene with prohibitions if [the Council] wishes to see only *Christian* doctors employed at the City Hospital. This is a matter for its free decision." The district authorities were supported in this view by the Saxon ministry. When the same issue was aired in the Saxon parliament, Freiherr von Groß, acting Minister of State, used exactly the same line of argument: "We can't hold it against the [hospital] if, [. . .] when it seeks to acquire a physician, it must ask itself whether [his] religion accords with that of the majority of the patients, or whether perhaps conflicts could arise . . .".[65] The same issue stirred controversy in the legislatures of other German states, and the same arguments were adduced to justify the exclusion of Jews from teaching positions in primary and secondary education with such frequency that the journal of the Centralverein felt justified in warning in 1903 of a "revival of the Christian state."[66] It should be noted that the arguments outlined here exploited an aspect of Stahl's Christian statism that proved enduringly attractive to conservatives, namely the appeal to confession as the foundation for an idealized, pseudo-democratic identity between government and governed. In this sense, the increasingly frequent invocation of the "Christian state" from the 1880s onwards should be seen in the context of the broader shift towards demagogical formulae that characterized German political culture in the *fin-de-siècle*.[67]

The aim of these reflections has not been to diminish the significance of the emergence of an "ethnic" anti-Semitism in nineteenth-century Germany. In any case, the dividing line between "Christian" and "ethnic" arguments was never clearly drawn. As early as the 1730s, the Pietist missionaries of the *Institutum Judaicum* in Halle had begun to redefine "conversion" from Judaism to Christianity in occupational and socio-logical terms that prefigured the debates of the later Enlightenment.[68] Herder's influential proposition that the culture, national identity and religiosity of a *Volk* were of the same substance and the rise of "national-religious" ideas within the intellectual milieu of North German Protestant-ism helped to create an environment in which religious and ethno-cultural arguments flowed into each other.[69]

On the other hand, the concerns we have addressed in this chapter should not be seen as mere camouflage for a fundamentally racist political vision. The Christian statism of the Restoration era took root in part because it provided an outlet for the activist, utopian, evangelizing strand in contemporary Protestantism. The commitment of Prussian administrations under Frederick William III and his successor to the Christianization of the polity went beyond the minimum required to justify the exclusion of the Jewish minority from civil equality – the Edict concerning the Estates of 1823, for example, excluded not only Jews, but also Christian non-conformists from the exercise of *ständisch* rights.[70] Moreover, Christian statism generated an account, however limited, of the monarchical state's ultimate moral purpose. It thereby provided a legitimating rationale that appealed to the idea of an identity of interest and culture between state and society, but was not dependent upon the ethnic categories of the early nationalist movement, whose broader arguments were so threatening to the particularist polities of the German princes after 1815. In any case, the ardor of some *Vormärz* conservatives for a more close-meshed relation-ship between Church and state was not a uniquely Prussian phenomenon. In a treatise of 1838 on "the State in its relations with the Church," a young William Ewart Gladstone observed, in terms strongly anticipatory of Stahl's later pamphlet, that a properly constituted government ought to "profess and maintain" the national religion, on the grounds both that it was the "organ" of the "national personality," which was Christian in its essence, and that it was "preeminently qualified to extend religion in the nation."[71] Gladstone's Christian idealist effusion remained, as an insightful analyst of the evangelical politics of this era has shown, a brief and ultimately uncharacteristic episode,[72] but it reflected a broader conservative Protestant interest in ways of consolidating and protecting the Christian character of public life without resort to "Roman theocracy."[73]

Christian statism as a mode of political action proved too self-contradictory to sustain itself over the longer term. But the idea survived the débâcle of the practice, both in the form of a legal provision that provided a fig-leaf of constitutional probity for the increasingly discriminatory handling of public appointments, and as a slogan in later-nineteenth-century conservative political discourse. Yet it would be mistaken to see the "Christian state" invoked in support of discriminatory practice by late-nineteenth-century legislators and ideologues as a straightforward continuation of the concept elaborated by Stahl. For Stahl's Christian statism was above all a set of ideas about what the state was for; its purpose, by his account (as in Gladstone's treatise on the same subject), was not merely to mirror the preoccupations of the nation, but also to further the evangelization of society and, ultimately, to assimilate worldly affairs to a heavenly order. But the "Christian state" so widely invoked by the late-nineteenth-century ideologues lacked this reflexive Hegelian logic. It concerned itself above all with the putative aspirations of a Germanic-Christian *Volk* and the obligations these imposed upon the state authority. It thus signaled an abdication of the autonomous, transcendent function that Stahl had assigned to the state. Shorn of its statist elements and reduced to a populist formula, the "Christian state" became a appealing slogan for those increasingly numerous critics of the post-emancipation order who wished to see the state demoted to the status of a mere instrument of the *Volksgemeinschaft*.[74]

Notes

1. See e.g. I. Kant, *Religion within the Limits of Reason Alone*, trans. T. M. Greene (La Salle, IL, 1960), pp. 74, 116, 122; G.W.F. Hegel, "The Positivity of the Christian Religion," in *On Christianity*, trans. T. M. Knox (Gloucester, MA: Peter Smith, 1970), pt. 1, p. 68 and pt. 3, p. 178; id., *Vorlesungen über die Philosophie der Geschichte*, ed. F. Brunstäd (Stuttgart: Reclam,1961), pp. 35–8, 285–6. More generally on these issues, see H. Liebeschütz, *Das Judentum im deutschen*

Geschichtsbild von Hegel bis Max Weber (Tübingen: Mohr Siebeck, 1967); B. Lang, *Act and Idea in the Nazi Genocide* (Chicago and London: University of Chicago Press, 1990), pp. 186–9; P. L. Rose, *Revolutionary Antisemitism in Germany from Kant to Wagner* (Princeton, NJ: Princeton University Press, 1990), pp. 87–90 and *passim*; W. Altgeld, *Katholizismus, Protestantismus, Judentum. Über religiös begründete Gegensätze und nationalreligiöse Ideen in der Geschichte des deutschen Nationalismus* (Mainz: Matthiäs-Grünewald Verlag, 1992), pp. 47–8.

2. Altgeld, *Nationalreligiöse Ideen*, p. 54.

3. C. W. Dohm, *Über die bürgerliche Verbesserung der Juden* (Berlin and Stettin: F. Nicolai, 1781); on the impact of Dohm's essay, see esp. H. Möller, "Aufklärung, Judenemanzipation und Staat. Ursprung und Wirkung von Dohms Schrift über die bürgerliche Verbesserung der Juden," in W. Grab (ed.), *Deutsche Aufklärung und Judenemanzipation. Internationales Symposium anläßlich der 250. Geburtstage Lessings und Mendelssohns* (Jahrbuch des Instituts für deutsche Geschichte, Suppl. 3; Tel Aviv, 1980). The translations given here are based on the excerpts in P. Mendes-Flohr and J. Reinharz (eds), *The Jew in the Modern World: A Documentary History* (New York: Oxford University Press, 1980), pp. 27–34.

4. Memorandum of 13 May 1809 by Staatsrat Köhler in I. Freund, *Die Emanzipation der Juden in Preußen unter besonderer Berücksichtigung des Gesetzes vom 11. März 1812. Ein Beitrag zur Rechtsgeschichte der Juden in Preußen*, 2 vols (Berlin: M. Poppelauer, 1912), vol. 2, pp. 251–2.

5. G. Hentsch, *Gewerbeordnung und Emanzipation der Juden im Kurfürstentum Hessen* (Wiesbaden: Kommission für die Geschichte der Juden in Hessen, 1979), p. 43.

6. M. Richarz, *Jüdisches Leben in Deutschland: Selbstzeugnisse zur Sozialgeschichte 1780–1871* (Stuttgart: Deutsche Verlagsanstalt, 1976), p. 24.

7. A strong general case for such continuities between the enlightened and "restoration" eras is made in Walter Demel, *Vom aufgeklärten Reformstaat zum bürokratischen Staatsabsolutismus* (Munich: Oldenbourg, 1993).

8. Recommendation from the Ministry of Finance, 28 November 1816, in I. Freund, *Die Emanzipation der Juden in Preußen*, vol. 2, pp. 475–96, here pp. 479, 482–3.

9. H. Fischer, *Juden, Staat und Heer in Preussen im frühen 19. Jahrhundert* (Tübingen: Mohr Siebeck, 1968), p. 95.

10. Frederick William III, cabinet order of 14 June 1824, reproduced in Bildarchiv Preußischer Kulturbesitz, *Juden in Preußen: Ein Kapitel deutscher Geschichte* (Dortmund: Harenberg, 1981), p. 195.
11. Cited in N. Samter, *Judentaufen im 19. Jahrhundert* (Berlin: M. Poppelauer, 1906), p. 37.
12. GStA Berlin – Dahlem, Geheimes Zivilkabinett, 2.2.1., 4541–4, Der Übertritt der Juden zum Christentum und die bei dieser Gelegenheit Seiner Majestät angetragenen Pathenstellen.
13. On this policy, see C. M. Clark, "The Limits of the Confessional State: Conversions to Judaism in Prussia 1814–1843," *Past & Present* 147 (1995): 159–79.
14. Minister of the Interior and of Police (Rochow) to all Royal Governments, Berlin 28 December 1834, Geheimes Staatsarchiv Berlin-Dahlem, XX 2/2282. See also Frederick William III to Rochow, Berlin 21 December 1834, Evangelisches Zentralarchiv Berlin, G III 13 9/35.
15. Documents relating to this policy may be found in Consistorium der Provinz Brandenburg, Acta Generalia betreffend die Theilnahme christlicher Prediger an jüdischen Religions-Feierlichkeiten, Evangelisches Zentralarchiv Berlin, G III 22 9/37.
16. On this policy, which caused considerable administrative confusion and was not faithfully carried out in practice, see T. Stamm-Kuhlmann, *König in Preußens großer Zeit. Friedrich Wilhelm III., der Melancholiker auf dem Thron* (Berlin: Siedler, 1992), pp. 548–51; also D. Bering, *Der Name als Stigma. Antisemitismus im deutschen Alltag 1812–1933* (Stuttgart: Klett-Cotta, 1988), pp. 63–105.
17. F. Rühs, *Über die Ansprüche der Juden an das deutsche Bürgerrecht* (Berlin: Realschulebuchhandlung, 1916); id., *Das Recht des Christenthums und des deutschen Reiches vertheidigt gegen die Ansprüche der Juden und ihrer Verfechter* (Berlin: Realschulebuchhandlung, 1916); Altgeld, *Katholizismus, Protestantismus, Judentum*, p. 50; C. M. Clark, *The Politics of Conversion. Missionary Protestantism and the Jews in Prussia 1728–1941* (Oxford: Oxford University Press, 1995), p. 98.
18. A. H. Brammer, *Judenpolitik und Judengesetzgebung in Preußen 1812 bis 1847* (Berlin: Schelzky and Jeep, 1987), pp. 147, 449; on this debate more generally, see S. Stern-Täubler, "Der literarische Kampf um die Emanzipation in den Jahren 1816–1820 und seine ideologischen und soziologischen Voraussetzungen," *Hebrew Union College Annual* 23/2 (1950–1): 171–96.

19. See C. M. Clark, "The Politics of Revival: Pietists, Aristocrats, and the State Church in Early Nineteenth-Century Prussia," in L. E. Jones and J. Retallack (eds), *Between Reform, Reaction and Resistance. Studies in the History of German Conservatism from 1789 to 1945* (Providence, RI and Oxford: Berghahn, 1993), pp. 31–60.

20. Clark, *Politics of Conversion*, pp. 124–43, 201–11.

21. R. Bieling, *Die Juden vornehmlich. Ein geschichtlicher Überblick über die Arbeiten der Gesellschaft zur Beförderung des Christenthums unter den Juden* (Berlin: Selbstverlag, 1913), p. 12; J. De le Roi, *Die evangelische Christenheit und die Juden unter dem Gesichtspunkte der Mission geschichtlich betrachtet,* 3 vols (Karlsruhe and Leipzig: H. Reuter, 1884–1892), vol. 2, p. 142.

22. Frederick William III, Cabinet Order to Altenstein, 23 November 1827, Evangelisches Zentralarchiv, Berlin, 7/2912.

23. On these continuities, see H. Weigelt, *Lavater und die Stillen im Lande, Distanz und Nähe: die Beziehungen Lavaters zu Frömmigkeitsbewegungen im 18. Jahrhundert* (Göttingen: Vandenhoeck and Ruprecht, 1988), *passim*; F. W. Krummacher, *Gottfried Daniel Krummacher und die Niederrheinische Erweckungsbewegung* (Berlin and Leipzig: W. de Gruyter, 1935), esp. pp. 62–3.

24. Stamm-Kuhlmann, *König in Preußens großer Zeit*, pp. 478–9.

25. Cited in G. Ruhbach, "Die Religionspolitik Friedrich Wilhelms III von Preußen," in B. Moeller and G. Ruhbach, *Bleibendes im Wandel der Kirchengeschichte. Kirchenhistorische Studien* (Tübingen: Mohr Siebeck, 1973), p. 310; C. M. Clark, "The Napoleonic Moment in Prussian Church Policy," in D. Laven and L. Riall (eds), *Napoleon's Legacy. Problems of Government in Restoration Europe* (Oxford, New York: Berg Publishers, 2000), pp. 217–35.

26. C. M. Clark, "Confessional Policy and the Limits of State Action: Frederick William III and the Prussian Church Union 1817–40," *Historical Journal* 39 (1996): 985–1004, citation p. 985.

27. Clark, "Confessional Policy," pp. 988–1004; W. H. Neuser, "Agende, Agendenstreit und Provinzialagenden" and W. Nixdorf, "Die Lutherische Separation. Union und Bekenntnis," both in J. F. G. Goeters and R. Mau (eds), *Die Geschichte der evangelischen Kirche der Union,* Vol. 1, *Die Anfänge der Union unter landesherrlichem Kirchenregiment (1817–1850)* (Leipzig: Evangelische Verlagsanstalt, 1992), pp. 134–59 and 220–40; W. Klän, "Die altlutherische Kirchenbildung in Preußen," in W. D. Hauschild (ed.), *Das deutsche Luthertum und die Unionsproblematik im 19. Jahrhundert* (Gütersloh: G. Mohr, 1991), pp. 153–70.

28. H.-D. Loock, "Die preußische Union, der Streit um die Kirchenverfassung 1808–1817 und die Reaktion der brandenburgischen Landpfarrer," in A. M. Birke and K. Kluxen (eds), *Kirche, Staat und Gesellschaft im 19. Jahrhundert. Ein deutsch–englischer Vergleich* (Munich: Saur, 1984), pp. 45–65.

29. The text of the Edict may be found in A. Doll, H.-J. Schmidt, M. Wilmanns (eds), *Der Weg zur Gleichberechtigung der Juden. Dokumente zur Geschichte der jüdischen Bevölkerung in Rheinland-Pfalz und im Saarland von 1800 bis 1945* (Koblenz: Selbstverlag der Landesarchivverwaltung Rheinland-Pfalz, 1979), vol. 2, pp. 45–8; for an illuminating recent discussion of the background to the Edict, see T. Stamm-Kuhlmann, "'Man vertraue doch der Administration!' Staatsverständnis und Regierungshandeln des preußischen Staatskanzlers Karl August von Hardenberg," *Historische Zeitschrift* 264 (1997): 613–54.

30. R. Rürup, "The tortuous and thorny path to legal equality: 'Jew laws' and emancipatory legislation in Germany from the late eighteenth century," *Leo Baeck Institute Yearbook* 31 (1986): 3–33, here p. 15.

31. R. Koselleck, *Preußen zwischen Reform und Revolution. Allgemeines Landrecht, Verwaltung und soziale Bewegung von 1791 bis 1848, 3rd edn* (Stuttgart: Klett-Cotta, 1981), p. 60.

32. M. Jehle (ed.), *Die Juden und die jüdischen Gemeinden Preußens in amtlichen Enquêten des Vormärz,* 4 vols (Munich: K. G. Saur, 1998), vol. 1, p. lxviii (introduction by Jehle).

33. Citation in Brammer, *Judenpolitik*, p. 67; for similar Jewish responses see also p. 425; on emulation in other states, see C. M. Clark, "German Jews," in R. Liedtke and S. Wendehorst (eds), *The Emancipation of Catholics, Jews and Protestants. Minorities and the State in Nineteenth-Century Europe* (Manchester: Manchester University Press, 1999), pp. 122–47, here p. 127.

34. This emerges from Manfred Jehle's excellent edition of the voluminous correspondence generated by the ministerial enquiries of 1842–5 into Jewish affairs in the kingdom of Prussia, *Die Juden und die jüdischen Gemeinden*, esp. Part One (vols 1–2), *Enquête des Ministeriums des Innern und der Polizei über die Rechtsverhältnisse der Juden in den preußischen Provinzen 1842–1843,* see esp. vol. 1, pp. 16, 38, 78–9, 141, 148, 261, 268, 274, 292.

35. Circular issued by the ministry for church, health and education to all superintendents, with excerpts from Frederick William's cabinet order, 18 October 1821, Evangelisches Zentralarchiv, Berlin, 9/37.

36. H.-J. Schoeps, "Der Erweckungschrist auf dem Thron. Friedrich Wilhelm IV," in Friedrich Wilhelm Prinz von Preußen (ed.), *Preußens Könige* (Munich: Bertelsmann Sachbuchverlag, 1971), pp. 159–72.
37. H. Wagener, *Die Politik Friedrich Wilhelms IV* (Berlin: Pohl, 1883), pp. 12, 17.
38. 15th plenary session of the 7th Rhenish Provincial Parliament, 10 June 1843 concerning §48 of the draft Communal Law for the province, in Landesarchivverwaltung Rheinland-Pfalz (ed.), *Dokumentation zur Geschichte der jüdischen Bevölkerung in Rheinland-Pfalz und im Saarland von 1800 bis 1945*, Vol. 2; A. Doll, H.-J. Schmidt and M. Wilmanns (eds), *Der Weg zur Gleichberechtigung der Juden* (Koblenz: Selbstverlag der Landesarchivverwaltung Rheinland-Pfalz, 1979), vol. 2, doc. 29, pp. 123–6. citation from p. 125.
39. Brammer, *Judenpolitik*, p. 313.
40. Brammer, *Judenpolitik*, pp. 298, 313.
41. For Jewish comments on the Christian state, see esp. "Ulm, 12 September," *Der Orient* 3 (1942): 342–3; "Vorwärts oder Rückwärts in der Judenemancipation: Ein offenes Sendschreiben," *Der Orient* 4 (1843): 106; "Tübingen, im Februar," *Der Orient* 5 (1844): 68.
42. This article from *Die Zeitinteressen* is reprinted in *Der Orient* 3 (1842): 342–3.
43. For a general, though partisan, outline of liberal objections, see F. J. Stahl, *Der christliche Staat und sein Verhältniß zum Deismus und Judenthum. Eine durch die Verhandlungen des vereinigten Landtages hervorgerufene Abhandlung* (Berlin: Ochmigke, 1847), pp. 57–70.
44. Stahl, *Der christliche Staat*, p. 5. For an outline of the issues raised in the debate at the Diet, see W. Kampmann, *Deutsche und Juden. Studien zur Geschichte des deutschen Judentums* (Heidelberg: L. Schneider, 1963), pp. 189–205.
45. Stahl, *Der christliche Staat*, p. 7.
46. Ibid., p. 27.
47. W. Füßl, *Professor in der Politik. Friedrich Julius Stahl (1802–1861)* (Göttingen: Vandenhoeck and Ruprecht, 1988), pp. 26–7.
48. Stahl, *Der christliche Staat*, pp. 31–3.
49. Stahl, *Der christliche Staat*, pp. 53–4.
50. Ibid., p. 55.
51. Ibid., p. 63.
52. Altgeld, *Katholizismus, Protestantismus, Judentum*, p. 209; for related observations on later nineteenth-century German Catholicism, see Helmut Walser Smith, *German Nationalism and Religious Conflict:*

Culture, Ideology, Politics, 1870–1914 (Princeton, NJ: Princeton University Press, 1995), pp. 70–1.

53. S. J. Dietrich, *Christentum und Revolution. Die christlichen Kirchen in Württemberg 1848–1852* (Paderborn: Ferdinand Schöningh, 1996), pp. 181–2.
54. Stahl, *Der christliche Staat*, p. 61
55. Ibid., p. 46.
56. Brammer, *Judenpolitik*, pp. 340–2.
57. Ibid., p. 61.
58. Clark, "Limits of the Confessional State," pp. 162–77; id., "Confessional Policy," pp. 993–1004.
59. Prussian consistory to the ministry for church, health and educational affairs, Königsberg, 18 May 1826, GStA Merseburg, Rep. 76 III Sekt. 1, Abt. XIV, Bl. 55–57.
60. See E. Feuchtwanger, "The Jewishness of Conservative Politicians: Disraeli and Stahl," in M. Brenner, R. Liedtke and D. Rechter (eds), *Two Nations: British and German Jews in Comparative Perspective* (Tübingen: Mohr Siebeck, 1999), pp. 223–39; here p. 227.
61. F. J. Stahl, *Der christliche Staat* (2nd edn, Berlin, 1858), pp. xii–xiii.
62. J. Toury, "Die Bangen Jahre (1887–1891). Juden in Deutschland zwischen Integrationshoffnung und Isolationsfurcht" in P. Freimark, A. Jankowski and I.S. Lorenz (eds), *Juden in Deutschland. Emanzipation, Integration, Hoffnung und Vernichtung* (Hamburg: H. Christian, 1991), pp. 164–85; here 177–8.
63. U. Tal, *Christians and Jews in Germany. Religion, Politics and Ideology in the Second Reich 1870–1914* (Ithaca, NY and London: Cornell University Press, 1975), pp. 121–59.
64. On the context of these remarks made by the Minister of Justice before the Prussian Landtag in 1901, see E. Hamburger, *Juden im öffentlichen Leben Deutschlands* (Tübingen: Mohr Siebeck, 1968), p. 47; Schönstedt cited in anon., "Justizminister a.D. Schönstedt," *Im Deutschen Reich* 11 (1905): 623–6.
65. Both cited in J. Lewy, "Die staatsbürgerliche Gleichberechtigung und die jüdischen Ärzte," *Im Deutschen Reich* 9 (1903): 150–6, here pp. 155–6.
66. E. Fuchs, "Rückblick auf die zehnjährige Tätigkeit des Central-Vereins deutscher Staatsbürger jüdischen Glaubens," *Im Deutschen Reich* 9 (1903): 197–214; here p. 198.
67. See especially D. Blackbourn, "The Politics of Demagogy in Imperial Germany," in idem, *Populists and Patricians. Essays in Modern German History* (London: Allen and Unwin, 1987), pp. 246–64.

68. Clark, *Politics of Conversion*, pp. 55–7, 66–71.
69. See esp. Rose, *Revolutionary Antisemitism*, pp. 97–109; Altgeld, *Katholizismus, Protestantismus, Judentum, passim*.
70. For the debate over the relevant section (§5,2) of the Prussian estates law, see the official record of the Herrenkurie of the United Diet of 1847, in E. Bleich (ed.), *Der Erste Vereinigte Landtag in Berlin 1847, 4 vols* (Berlin: K. Reimarus, 1847), here vol. 4, pp. 2351, 2354.
71. W. E. Gladstone, *The State in Its Relations with the Church* (London: J. Murray, 1838), p. 40; see also pp. 3, 4, 6, 20, 26, 27, 37, 233.
72. A. J. B. Hilton, *The Age of Atonement. The Influence of Evangelicalism in Social and Economic Thought, 1785–1865* (Oxford: Oxford University Press, 1988), pp. 340–1, 350.
73. On similar aspirations amongst American Protestants at this time (a "Christian people should be governed by Christian rulers;" government should be "administered on Christian principles and with Christian ends in view"), see R. J. Cawardine, *Evangelicals and Politics in Antebellum America* (New Haven, CT and London: Yale University Press, 1993), pp. 20–2.
74. On this trend in late-nineteenth-century German politics and its implications for the Jewish minority, see P. Pulzer, *Jews and the German State. The Political History of a Minority, 1848–1933* (Oxford: Oxford University Press, 1992), esp. pp. 44–68 and C. M. Clark, "The Jews and the German State in the Wilhelmine Empire," in Brenner, Liedtke and Rechter (eds), *Two Nations*, pp. 163–84.

Part III
Religious Difference, National Culture and Identity

–5–

The Cult of Gustavus Adolphus: Protestant Identity and German Nationalism

Kevin Cramer

"Thousands and thousands of voices called and prayed to God: have you then, Lord our God, completely forsaken us? Oh, make an end to our misfortune and misery, dry our tears, still our sighs! Send us an angel of deliverance in our distress and affliction!" This was the prayer of Protestant Germany *in extremis*, *circa* 1629, as imagined in 1844 by Friedrich Moser of Zwickau. The angel of deliverance was the Swedish king Gustavus Adolphus. The passage is from a pamphlet that described the dedication of the Gustavus Adolphus memorial at Lützen in 1837. Moser claimed that his imaginative flight was inspired by his contemplation of the "holy land" of the battlefield in its symbolic proximity to Leipzig, site of the *Völkersschlacht* of 1813. [1]

The mythogenesis of Gustavus Adolphus as a German national hero in the early nineteenth century illustrates a significant blurring of the boundaries between religion and nationalism in German intellectual and cultural life. The devotion of Germany's Protestants to the memory of the Swedish king is a well known, but unexamined, phenomenon of popular culture in the first half of the nineteenth century. [2] Before 1871, Gustavus Adolphus was one of the most powerful symbols of unity in the political folklore of Germany. His story, as shaped by Protestant historians, became the centerpiece of a national narrative founded on an idealization of those Protestant-German virtues that had defied Rome and France for three hundred years. His legend cast him as the savior of a Germany suffering under the yoke of a foreign and Catholic empire – the true heir of Luther. [3] Gustavus Adolphus's nationalist symbolism embodied visions of a unified Protestant *Reich* on the *kleindeutsch* model and an idea of the nation that excluded Catholics as un-German. This chapter will examine a moment in the battle between Protestant and

Catholic ideas of the nation as it was fought in the historiography of the Thirty Years War.

The study of nationalism has thoroughly examined the phenomenon as a consequence of secularization, modernization, and institutional state-building. It has devoted less attention to the enduring influence of confessional allegiances on nationalist thinking.[4] The cult of Gustavus Adolphus arose out of the confluence of traditional cultural allegiances and modern desires for national unity. The Swedish king became the figurehead of an inchoate Protestant nationalism that reflected a range of opinion, from the democratic aspirations of the *Burschenschaften* through constitutional liberalism to the militant demands of Pan-Germanism. But at its core was the idea that Protestantism constituted the essence of the German national character.[5] As this chapter examines the cultural and intellectual foundations of Ludwig von Gerlach's conviction that "[The Germans] must give [their] consciousness of God a political form," Horst Zillessen's observation that this spirit was "apolitical in its expression, but not unpolitical" has particular resonance as a description of the dynamics of the conflict between Protestant and Catholic ideas of the German nation.[6] On both sides of the confessional divide nationalist thinking put religion at the service of political ends. The conflict between Protestant and Catholic was not ameliorated by the demands of modernization. Instead, the three-hundred-year-old battle was renewed in a modern context as a fight over the structure and mission of the nation.[7] Protestant histories of Gustavus Adolphus, in creating a narrative link between past and present, played a crucial role in establishing what Helmut Smith has called "the cultural criteria for national authenticity."[8] The nineteenth-century Protestant historiography dealing with Gustavus Adolphus (and the Thirty Years War in general) based these criteria on three assumptions: Protestantism and the spirit of the Reformation embodied the core values that defined the German national community; this community was bound together by a notion of "chosen-ness" and thus covenanted with God; and this convenant implied a national mission that conceived the nation in moral, as well as political, terms.

This national mission was at the heart of the so-called "Gustavus Adolphus Problem" that animated historical debate for much of the nineteenth century. Protestant and Catholic historians argued bitterly over the answers to two questions: Why did Gustavus Adolphus intervene in a German war? What were his ultimate goals? This argument began in the optimistic years between the victory over Napoleon and the republican festival at Hambach in 1832. In the idealistic spirit of 1813, the memory of the Swedish king was refashioned during this period as a parable of liberation and unification for Germany's Protestants. As political folklore, this new tradition took shape most clearly in the commemorative ceremonies at Breitenfeld and Lützen in 1831 and 1832. While the policies of the Restoration-era rulers temporarily quieted calls for political reform, the confessional divide continued to strain the bonds of the German Confederation. Prussia's increasing economic and political power manifested itself in the historians' debate over Gustavus Adolphus. The advocacy of the Protestant *Reich* he symbolized became more shrill and chauvinistic. As Protestant historiography acquired marked "national-German" overtones, especially in the unsettled 1840s, Catholic historians (and a small group of anti-Prussian Protestants) responded with counter-histories. These alternative national narratives invoked the memories of Napoleon to paint a picture of Gustavus Adolphus as a foreign conqueror. In resisting the establishment of a history that excluded Catholic participation, these historians took pains to point out the manifest absurdity of a national idea that turned a Swedish king into a German hero.

During the first decades of the Restoration period the elevation of Gustavus Adolphus attempted to link interpretations of his motivations with the aspirations of 1813. The war against Napoleon had led to calls for a German renewal and rebirth in language that appealed to the tradition of the liberation of the Reformation. The national narrative built on the symbolism of Gustavus Adolphus attempted not only to legitimate a new idea of Germany, but also a new moral and political order in Europe. This Protestant nationalist history told the compelling story of a Protestant monarch uniting northern Germany in a crusade against foreign tyranny and Catholic despotism. This history legitimated a popular belief in the German national mission that began in the Reformation and was continued in the war against Napoleon.[9]

German political thought during the late Enlightenment defined the German mission as providing the keystone of a stable European state system. In the late eighteenth century proposals for modernizing the settlement of 1648 assumed that a reorganized German empire would be at the center of a new moral and political order in Europe.[10] Niklas Vogt (1756–1836), a professor at Mainz and an important figure of the late Enlightenment in Germany, placed Gustavus Adolphus at the center of his speculations on creating a new order in Europe. Though he was a Catholic, Vogt was of Febronian inclination as well as a student of the Göttingen School. This background accounts for his admiration of the Teutonic kings, which was more in sympathy with Protestant celebrations of the Germanic virtues of liberty and independence than the legitimist arguments of most Catholic intellectuals. Vogt was also an early supporter of Napoleon. In Vogt's political thought Napoleon was the successor to Gustavus Adolphus in pursuing the project of the territorial consolidation of Germany within a broader reconfiguration of the European state system. In Vogt's analysis both men fought an obsolete tyranny to establish a monarchical, federative, and united Germany.[11] In his major theoretical work *Über die Europäische Republik* (1787) Vogt envisioned a Germany organized as a constitutional union of sovereign states as the nexus of a new European balance of power. Vogt also claimed that this was the grand design behind Gustavus Adolphus's intervention in Germany.[12] In 1790 Vogt wrote a verse drama as a "supplement" to the earlier work in which he created a fictional dialogue between Gustavus Adolphus and his chancellor Oxenstierna that included walk-on roles for the approving spirits of Charlemagne and Otto the Great. Vogt imagined Gustav Adolf proposing a grand vision of a redesigned *Reich*, ruled by him as the new "Roman King" of Germany, that excluded Austria.[13] Vogt's eventual disenchantment with Napoleon did not alter his conviction that he had created the possibility of a fundamental political and territorial reorganization of Germany. Vogt was convinced that Gustav Adolf had pursued this goal two hundred years earlier in a plan to consolidate the northern German states, a scheme that included combining Holstein and Pomerania into a new electoral territory.[14] Vogt's interpretation of the motives of the Swedish king represented an intermediate definition of the German role in Europe. This idea of the German state was located between the constitutional conceptions of Pütter, Gatterer and Spittler and the nationalist conceptions of the nineteenth century. It combined admiration of Hohenzollern bureaucratic absolutism, the constitutional theories coming out of Göttingen and a faith in the rational and progressive dynamic of Protestantism.[15]

Vogt's vision of a new Germany within a new Europe was part of the optimism that drove the German national movement in the early nineteenth century. However, the exhilarating feeling of unity following the expulsion of the French soon dissipated. The line between reaction and reform in German politics roughly divided those who saw the defeat of France as a Prussian achievement and those who saw it as a German victory. But in the first decades of the nineteenth century, a period that saw the first flowering of German nationalism, the historical mythologizing of Gustavus Adolphus made him a symbol of the possibilities of binding the idea of the Protestant nation to a conception of a unified state. This process began with the bicentennial commemorations of his victory at Breitenfeld in 1831 and his death at Lützen in 1832. These ceremonies were an important expression of the popular demands for *"Einheit und*

Freiheit" after the defeat of Napoleon. Arising out of the general European flux of revolution and repression in this period and given the increasing risk of explicit demands for reform, the celebration of the heroic myth of Gustavus Adolphus covered a multitude of sins. It is important to note that these commemorations derived much of their symbolic power from the sites' fortunate proximity to the hallowed ground of the Leipzig *Völkersschlacht* of 1813. As acts of remembrance they integrated the nationalist themes of liberation and unity within the narrative of the Protestant German nation. They were also acts of political pedagogy: the mythic event was recreated at a sacred site of pilgrimage for a chosen community.[16] They were patriotic communions with the dead that linked the years 1632 and 1813 in a narrative of a struggle for liberty, independence, and unity.

Protestant nationalism gave eloquence to the sentimental patriotic outpourings that followed the defeat of Napoleon. Friedrich Ludwig von Rango, a Silesian grenadier officer who won the Iron Cross in 1813, memorialized the "holy fight for freedom" in his poem *Mein deutsches Vaterland*. Rango, writing in 1815, celebrated the victory over France by summoning the avenging spirit of Hermann, who had once "shattered the chains of Rome."[17] Ten years later Rango wrote a hagiography of Gustavus Adolphus dedicated to Friedrich Wilhelm III and the soldiers that fought at Leipzig in 1813. The dedicatory verse bound together Vasa and Hohenzollern in the opening lines ". . . God and king leading the victorious soldiers to bring Europe's freedom out of the ruins":

> Da war ich plötzlich jenem Denkmal nahe,
> Das so bescheiden aus dem Schoss der Zeit
> Dem Wandrer liebend still zu stehn gebietet;
> Ich stand vor Lützens heil'gem Schwedenstein.[18]

> There I was suddenly close to the monument
> That so modestly from the lap of time
> Presents itself lovingly to the wanderer;
> I stood before Lützens sacred Sweden stone.

Fifteen years later Otto Jacobi, a dramatist well regarded by contemporaries, if not posterity, made the mystical connection between 1632 and 1813 even more explicit:

> So sehen wir in unsern Tagen auch,
> Wie hier um Recht und Freiheit ward gestritten.
> Dieselben Felder tränkten sich mit Blut,
> Dieselben Felder brachten uns den Ruhm,
> Und ehrne Ketten fielen von uns ab.[19]

So we see ourselves in our own day,
As here they fought for justice and freedom.
The same fields soaked with blood,
The same fields brought us glory,
And iron chains fell from us.

Bounded by Lützen, Breitenfeld, and Leipzig (Witttenberg was thirty miles to the north), this tiny triangle of German soil in western Saxony (ceded to Prussia in 1815), by virtue of its close connection to the history of Protestantism, had become the center of gravity for German nationalism in the early nineteenth century.

The commemoration of the two-hundredth anniversary of Gustavus Adolphus's victory over Tilly at Breitenfeld marked the beginning of the nationalist cult devoted to the memory of the Swedish king. The anonymous account of the ceremony left by a participant stressed the spiritual connection between Breitenfeld and the *Völkerschlacht*. In both battles, the author contended, the cause of German liberty had been at stake. On a warm afternoon on 7 September 1831 the people of Breitenfeld and environs, local notables, and clergy gathered around the shrouded monument on the battle site. Children held small wreaths and small flags bearing the arms of Saxony and Sweden. The memorial of polished Mannsdorfer stone was unveiled to hymns and prayers that gave thanks for the deliverance of the German Protestant Church and the freedom of belief. On each face of the stone was carved:

> Glaubensfreiheit für die Welt
> Rettete bei Breitenfeld
> Gustav Adolf, Christ und Held
> Am 7ten September 1631.

> Religious Freedom for the World
> Saved at Breitenfeld
> Gustavus Adolphus, Christian and Hero
> On 7 September 1631.

Stepping to the rostrum, *Kirchenrat* Gottlob Grossman of Leipzig dedicated the memorial in the name of the Swedish and Saxon people and the "renewed and redeemed" German nation. Grossman went on to remind his audience that without the victory at Breitenfeld they would still be ruled by the cruel tyranny that oppressed the people of southern and central Europe. In conclusion he observed that the monument to Gustavus Adolphus's victory marked not only a great turning-point in

German history but also served as a boundary stone in the German lands between delusion and belief and freedom and slavery.[20]

Even under the cloak of the rhetoric of the pulpit, the spirit of the Wars of Liberation lingered in these careful *bürgerliche* nationalist sentiments. But more radical voices also found inspiration in the symbolism of Breitenfeld. Ernst Ortlepp, a political poet who shared the radical enthusiasms of Herwegh and Büchner, envisioned the clash between the armies of light and darkness:

> Zerissen lag die Welt vom Meinungskampfe,
> Die finstere Religion der Nacht
> Sie zog mit Wolkendunst und Nebeldampfe
> Heran – geschützt von eines Kaisers Macht,
> Durchzucket schon von leisen Todeskrampfe
> Sah sie des neuen Tages Siegespracht,
> Sah sie aus Norden eine Sonne steigen,
> Wie nie noch keine stieg aus Ostens Reichen . . .[21]

> The world lay torn by religious war,
> The dark religion of night
> Moved in musket smoke and cannon's roar
> Shielded by a Kaiser's might,
> But already racked by faint death throes
> It saw the new day's magnificent light,
> It saw a sun rise out of the North,
> As never before climbed from the East.

The symbolism of Breitenfeld represented more than emerging bourgeois aspirations for a unified Protestant Germany. The battle also symbolized the possibility of Germany's liberation from the forces of reaction.

Nineteenth-century chroniclers turned the story of the Swedish king's advance into central Germany after Breitenfeld into a coronation procession. According to these accounts, the "Nordic Lion" was greeted by cheering crowds and ringing bells as his army passed through Naumburg, Erfurt, Frankfurt am Main, and Nuremberg.[22] In one recreation of the triumphal march, the Elector of Saxony supposedly toasted Gustavus Adolphus with the words, "The crown of king belongs to the worthiest – hail Germany's king, Gustavus Adolphus!" His audience, which included Georg Wilhelm of Brandenburg, thereupon rose to demand that Gustavus Adolphus accept the *römische Königskrone*, or at the very least, according to this author, the crown of a united Swedish–German kingdom.[23] There was an old German saying that whoever occupied Frankfurt for a year would become emperor. This made the symbolism of Gustavus Adolphus's brief residence in the city, the traditional site for the coronations of the Holy Roman Emporors, particularly compelling. Promoters and critics of the king's burgeoning cult claimed that he was well aware of this legend and that "he felt so at home in Frankfurt that he sent for his queen."[24] Friedrich Förster (1791–1868), a student of Hegel and a prominent historian of the Prussian state, wrote a "historical drama" about Gustavus Adolphus in honor of the 1832 anniversary. Förster imagined excited Germans discussing the possibilities that Breitenfeld had opened up:

> Kommt er erst auf die Spur,
> Daß wir den Kaiser-Krönungs-Apparat,
> Die Reichskleinode, Karls des Großen Krone,
> Auf unsrer Burg verwahren, wandelt ihn
> Der Appetit wohl an, den goldnen Apfel
> Des heil'gen römischen Reiches anzubeißen.

> When he finds out
> That we have the imperial regalia,
> The crown jewels, and the crown of Charlemagne
> Protected at our castle, the appetite might
> Come to him, to bite the golden apple
> Of the Holy Roman Empire.

Förster shifted the scene to Nuremberg and the room in the fortress in which the imperial regalia were kept. The king and his queen soberly contemplate the crown of Charlemagne:

> Dies ist die Krone, die des großen Karls
> Ruhmwürdig Haupt geschmückt, für wahr, das ist
> Ein schwer gewicht'ger Riesen, schwer an Gold,
> Und schwerer noch an Sorgen.

> This is the Crown that adorned Karl's
> Glorious Head; true, it is
> A heavy-weighted giant, heavy in gold,
> And heavier still in worries.

Whereupon Gustavus Adolphus and Eleanora put on the imperial robes and he takes up the scepter as Eleanora exclaims, "Your arm is strong enough to rule!"[25]

Nationalist thinking transformed the Protestant legend of Gustavus Adolphus into the unifying story at the center of a German national narrative. Protestant nationalism found its clearest expression in the commemoration in 1832 of his death at Lützen and the subsequent foundation of the Gustav-Adolf-Verein in 1833. For two hundred years local tradition claimed that the *Schwedenstein*, a large granite boulder in a field north-east of the village of Lützen near the road to Leipzig, marked the spot where Gustavus Adolphus had died. The boulder was about four feet tall and was inscribed "G A 1632." Some of the tales maintained that it had set up by the king's valet. Other accounts claimed that it was a sixteenth-century milestone.[26] In 1803 eight poplar trees were planted around the stone and in 1813 a Prussian general laid stones in the shape of a cross around the boulder. A painted wooden sign faced the road, informing passers-by that "Gustavus Adolphus, King of Sweden, fell here in battle for religious freedom on 6 November 1632."[27] This was the general appearance of the site in 1832. According to the historian J. C. Pfister the first calls for a more elaborate memorial came in 1798 in the *Philosophische Monatsschrift* and Leopold von Göckingk's liberal *Journal von und für Teutschland*.[28] In 1830 a Lützen official, one F. C. F. Philippi, also proposed that a new memorial be built. The mayor of Lützen endorsed the plan, and in August a collection was announced to collect funds for a general improvement of the site and the building of a more imposing monument.[29] However, the fund-raising drive only gained real impetus two years later.

The commemorative ceremonies at Lützen were documented in a collection of poems, recollections, and historical notes published in 1833 by C. H. F. Hartmann, a Leipzig book dealer and one of the participants. In his preface Hartmann lamented that Germany had yet to achieve the unity that best served her national interests. He added that, in any case, the act of remembrance demonstrated that the sparks of national feeling and confessional unity had not been completely extinguished.[30] The ceremony began on 5 November in the church in the nearby village of Meuchen, where the king's body had been brought after the battle. The church had long been a popular destination of Protestant pilgrimages from all over Europe. [31] Philippi was in attendance, as was *Kirchenrat* Grossmann, who gave a short sermon. Philippi hoped that such services showed the possibilities of raising national consciousness in Germany.[32]

The next morning the celebrants, who included Grossmann, *Konsistorialrat* Haasenritter from Merseberg and the French ambassador to the Saxon court, made their way to the battlefield. They were accompanied by schoolchildren wearing blue and yellow and escorted by mounted

Prussian and Saxon gendarmes. At the *Schwedenstein* Haasenritter gave a speech in which he asked those assembled to remember Gustavus Adolphus's sacrifice to re-establish the lawful constitution of Germany and to deliver her princes and people from slavery. Young women laid wreaths and garlands at the base of the stone as they intoned these words:

> Nur im schwachen Gebild zeigt diese erinnerende Feier
> Tiefe Gefühle der Brust und Dank dem höchsten der Wesen,
> Der dies Schlachtenfeld auch unserm Heile bereitet,
> Hier, Dich Gustav! Helden des Glaubens, zu sich erhöhte.

> This celebration of memory, that serves only as a pale reflection
> Of deep thoughts in the breast, and praise to the highest essence
> Of you who saved this battlefield to our eternal good,
> To you, Gustavus, Hero of Faith, is here offered up.

A blue silk cushion bearing the three crowns of Sweden was laid on the stone, the blessing was spoken, and after singing a hymn in the Lützen Square, everybody went home.[33]

At the concluding banquet that evening conversation turned to the idea of building a monument to the Swedish king, and it was decided to announce a new public subscription to raise the funds. Philippi started things off with a contribution of 400 talers. A committee proposed a design for the monument: a colossal granite cube. The cost was estimated at 3000 talers.[34] On 7 December the *Leipziger Tageblatt* announced an English-style "penny subscription," the brainchild of C. A. Schild, a Leipzig merchant motivated as much by commercial as patriotic motives. Schild declared that the idea of national unity was manifest in the historical solidarity of Protestant Germany. He felt strongly that the building of a memorial to Gustavus Adolphus offered a unique opportunity to unite Germany in remembrance: "Obviously, our poor Fatherland is divided into many small states, but it still lives in a unity of conviction despite the different flags that fly on the border posts that keep our brothers from freely pursuing their business . . . Let us erect a memorial that will also be a monument to the German national character."[35] The campaign quickly gained momentum. The Kingdom of Saxony donated 1,000 talers. The enterprising Hartmann sent copies of his commemorative anthology to the Grand Duke of Weimar. The package was returned with no reply. But the secretary of the Saxon legation forwarded a copy to the Prussian king in his capacity as the guardian of the Protestant Church in Germany. Friedrich Wilhelm III donated 100 talers.[36] More importantly, Friedrich Wilhelm directed the architect Karl Friedrich Schinkel to work up some ideas for a design. Schinkel initially proposed an open stone temple to be erected over the *Schwedenstein*. A variation of this design, a ten-meter-high cast-iron baldachin, was finally executed.[37] On 6 November 1837 the new monument was dedicated in the presence of an estimated 25,000 festive spectators. Appropriately enough, the caretaker of the grounds was an invalided veteran of the *Völkerschlacht*.[38]

The fund-raising campaign also inspired the creation of a foundation dedicated to the spiritual and financial support of oppressed and impoverished Protestants in Catholic lands, the so-called "diaspora." This institution, the Gustav-Adolf-Verein, held its first meeting on 6 November 1833. Schild and Grossmann, among others, had called for the establishment of such an organization in an article in the *Tageblatt* that appeared in December 1832.[39] The idea of the "Protestant diaspora," and its manifestation in the historiographical and popular remembrance of Gustavus Adolphus was fundamental to early-nineteenth-century Protestant nationalism.[40] The commemorations located German identity and unity in a vanished kingdom resembling George Mosse's description of the mystical Fatherland of German Pietism: a "magic and hidden space."[41] Grossmann's use of the metaphor of the "boundary marker" is, in this context, very revealing. The commemorations became rituals of demarcation (and exclusion), the setting of boundary stones, which marked and defined the sacred soil of the community.[42] The concept of the diaspora was a complex and contradictory expression of cultural and confessional solidarity, political fragmentation and the potential for unity. The cult of Gustavus Adolphus that emerged from this sense of powerlessness was an act of national self-definition. The monuments dedicated to the memory of the Swedish king, by making the mystical connection between 1632 and 1813, made concrete an incorporeal idea of the nation. They manifested the *bürgerlich* ideas of monarchy, liberty, independence and unity.

The patriotic spirit generated by the Wars of Liberation dissipated under the reactionary regime of Congress Europe. The ceremony at Lützen and the dedication of the Gustavus Adolphus memorial in 1837 can be seen to have marked the end of the idealistic phase of German nationalist thinking in the nineteenth century. In the following decades the perspective of Protestant historiography shifted from hagiography. The emphasis was less on Gustavus Adolphus as a symbol of confessional solidarity than on the lessons his policies offered for a modern project of state-building. A maturing nationalist historiography writing speculated on how Gustavus Adolphus might have carried out the unification of a Protestant Reich. A more pragmatic political history of the Swedish king began to emerge, which interpreted his plans as a blueprint for a confederation of Protestant states governed from Mainz or Frankfurt. These narratives deplored the weakness of the *Kleinstaaterei* in resisting the ever-present French danger.[43]

The Protestant historiography of the 1840s had not lost its confessional edge. But there were signs of an increasing animus toward Prussian absolutism and pretensions to German leadership. The iconoclast Karl Menzel (1784–1855) pointed out that, in occupying Frankfurt and Nuremberg, Gustavus Adolphus had revealed his plan to "declare himself the supreme ruler of the German Reich" in prioritizing the occupation of those cities "which bound the political imagination of the nation."[44] It was Menzel's view that Gustavus Adolphus intended to secularize and consolidate the German states, but only to preserve and modify the *Reichsverfassung*: "Prussia would never have risen to its position in Germany as a significant European power had Gustavus Adolphus consolidated the Swedish protectorate over Protestant Germany and produced a male heir."[45]

Friedrich Wilhelm Barthold (1799–1858) took Menzel's anti-Prussian thesis even further. Barthold was openly contemptuous of those "credulous souls, inflamed by the traditions of their school years" who accepted a naïve manipulation of the history of Gustavus Adolphus. Barthold was influenced by the constitutional ideas of his teacher Friedrich von Raumer. He rejected the schoolmasters' patriotic idealization of Gustavus Adolphus as the savior of German liberties. Barthold argued that he was a foreign conqueror who would have eventually delivered Germany into the hands of Richelieu or, at best, those princes who sought to expand their own power by undermining or destroying the German constitution: "The events reported here are old, but the lessons that they teach, are they superfluous for our day?"[46]

Most critics were naturally outraged at Menzel and Barthold's accu-sations that historians were manipulating the symbolism of Gustavus Adolphus to justify Prussian hegemony. These two revisionists had struck a nerve in pointing out the peculiarity of anointing a Swedish king as a German hero. Before 1848 any uneasiness about this fact had been partially relieved by those who noted that Sweden ruled territories that were *Reichskörper* and that the House of Vasa was linked to several German dynasties. One critic was of the opinion that, if the "what if game" was to be played, he was inclined to Barthold Georg Niebuhr's view that "[H]ad Gustavus Adolphus won the imperial crown he would have been considered a German by the entire country."[47] Protestant historians clung tenaciously to the folklore of Gustavus Adolphus's triumphal march into central Germany. If this was taken as evidence of his ambitions to make himself Kaiser of a Protestant Reich, well, what of it? " . . . a free and independent Germany, would that have been such a misfortune? It is hard to grasp in these times."[48] The belief in the Protestant foundation of German national identity continued to make Gustavus Adolphus a powerful nationalist symbol at mid-century.

This nationalist symbolism was also used to articulate a German mission in Europe. Wilhelm Bötticher invoked the "evangelical and godly unity" of the German *Volk*, for which Gustavus Adolphus had sacrificed his life, in the eternal battle against the "Roman and Slavic peoples." In comparing the king's attempt to create a "monarchical, Protestant Germany" as a bulwark against the despotism of the Habsburgs to the ambitions of the Hohenzollerns, Bötticher wondered if a German union with Sweden would have been more shameful than the rule of Hanover by England or Holstein by Denmark. Bötticher was convinced that "history will show the fulfillment of the prophetic designs and visions of the great Swedish king."[49] The nationalist cult of Gustavus Adolphus promoted the idea of Germany as northern Europe's cultural, racial, and political glacis against the threat of Habsburg despotism, Slavic barbarism, and French conquest. Ludwig Flathe, a professor of history at the University of Leipzig, claimed that Protestantism was "the essential religion of the German tribe" and that the German princes' alliance with Gustavus Adolphus was the reunion of a great racial family. Flathe believed that a nation's "German-ness" was directly proportional to its distance from the Catholic world. This conviction led to the claim that Roman Catholics were essentially "un-German." His conclusion was that Gustavus Adolphus had demonstrated that the French threat could only be countered through the creation of a unified Protestant Reich founded on the "*deutsch-nationale Gesinnung*."[50]

Protestant historians such as Menzel and Barthold, whose anti-Prussian animus targeted the selfish particularism of the *kleinstaaterei* as the cause of Germany's political weakness, advanced many of the arguments implicit in *großdeutsch* Catholic historiography. At the turn of the century Catholic historians such as Michael Ignatz Schmidt (1736–1794) and Lorenz von Westenrieder (1748–1829) had used legitimist arguments in an attempt to create an inclusive "national-Catholic" history that went beyond the defense of traditional liberties found in the obsolescent *Reichshistorie* of Justus Möser.[51] Westenrieder, the doyen of Bavarian historians, used a combination of legitimist claims and anti-French rhetoric in his rejection of the idea of Gustavus Adolphus as a liberator. Westenrieder compared the Swedish king to Napoleon in a portrayal of a conqueror who had similarly aimed at the complete transformation of the political structure of Germany. Westenrieder complained that "a whole flood of panegyrics, poems, songs, tales and eulogies in which everything that the king thought, said, did, or could and should have thought, said, or done . . ." could not alter the fact that the liberator had pursued territorial aggrandizement and one-man rule in Germany.[52]

Westenrieder felt that the liberation of the German princes was not identical to the liberation of the German people, just as Menzel and Barthold felt that Prussian interests were not identical to aspirations for an independent and unified Reich. The most influential expression of this view came in a best-selling biography of Gustavus Adolphus written by the Swabian historian and archivist August Friedrich Gfrörer (1803–1861). *Gustav Adolph, König von Schweden und seine Zeit* went through four editions and sold more than 15,000 copies between 1835 and 1864. Until Gustav Droysen's biography appeared in 1869, Gfrörer's book was the most widely read work on the Swedish king. Gfrörer, the son of Protestant clergyman who had converted to Catholicism in 1853, was, like his friend Heinrich Leo, a liberal opponent of Prussian ambitions who also objected to Ranke's influence on history writing. Gfrörer believed that history-writing had a "present usefulness" in addressing contemporary social and political issues.[53]

The first edition of 1835 sold well. The much revised version that appeared in 1837 did even better. Gfrörer's changes placed even more emphasis on a defense of the policies of Ferdinand II and Wallenstein, contrasting the latter's efforts to unify the Reich on a non-confessional basis with the Swedish king's lust for territory and power. Gfrörer claimed that Gustavus Adolphus had schemed to find a pretext for invading Germany as far back as 1629, motivated by a "lust for military glory and the spirit of conquest, veiled by the glitter of religious ideas, which drove the Swedes across the Baltic." In Gfrörer's view, Gustavus Adolphus's decision to invade central Germany after Breitenfeld, instead of marching directly on Vienna, betrayed his true intentions: "As soon as Protestants and Catholics united against him and public opinion turned, the mask of the *Glaubensheld* fell away and out stretched the hated hand of the conqueror . . . No one summoned him to Germany, he broke into our Reich like a thief . . . our nation was not so stupid, as some theologians would have it, to put a royal adventurer at its head." Gfrörer was convinced that had Gustavus Adolphus lived he would have established a cruel military dictatorship in Germany. His conclusion warned against the prevailing misinterpretation of Gustavus Adolphus by Protestant historians and asserted that " . . . if the German nation is again to be united, it will be only as a constitutional monarchy on the English model."[54]

This liberal core of Gfrörer's attack on the cult of Gustavus Adolphus was rejected by the ultramontane historians that succeeded him. Onno Klopp (1822–1903), a notorious Catholic critic of the Prussian state (he was a convert) who edited the fourth revised edition of the Swabian's work, criticized him for his neglect of important political issues.[55] Klopp was writing in a period when the Protestant threat, in the shape of Prussian ascendancy, was much more menacing and clearly defined than it had been for Gfrörer. The ultramontane reaction to the cult of Gustavus Adolphus, represented most prominently in the work of Klopp and the biographer and defender of Ferdinand II, Friedrich von Hurter (1787–1865), contended that the Swedish king had intervened in German affairs in order to destroy the rejuvenated empire of Ferdinand II. On the ruins of the old empire Gustavus Adolphus would have, according to Klopp and Hurter, erected a completely new constitutional structure ruled by a Protestant emperor supported by the Protestant estates.[56] Like their Protestant counterparts, Klopp and Hurter had looked into the past and seen the future.

The Catholic journal *Historisch-politische Blätter für das katholische Deutschland* [*HpB*] had been in the vanguard in responding to the exclusionary claims of Protestant historiography during the 1830s and 1840s, a period that Klopp labeled the "Third Phase of Protestantism," which he characterized as a time of restored seventeenth-century orthodoxy.[57] The *HpB*'s editors were also alarmed at the appeal of what they saw as a foreign adventurer's intervention in a German civil war: "Here is an example warning us that we should never again let a foreigner, whether he comes from the north like Gustavus Adolphus, or the west like Louis XIV, intervene in our internal affairs, because the price we pay in honor, in wealth, and in blood is too dear, much too dear."[58] An article that attacked the Gustav-Adolf-Verein lamented that only a country so lacking in self-esteem as Germany would erect monuments celebrating the memory of a foreign conqueror.[59] It was in the pages of the *HpB* during the 1840s that Albert Heising, a Catholic polemicist and amateur historian, gained as much notoriety as Gfrörer because of his assault on the Protestant conception of Gustavus Adolphus as liberator. This reappraisal was paired with an equally controversial rehabilitation of the reputation of Tilly, the *Mordbrenner* of Magdeburg, which was largely responsible for igniting a long-running *Historikerstreit* over who was responsible for the infamous sacking of that Protestant city in 1631. Heising compared Gustavus Adolphus to Napoleon, and condemned the idea that the Swedish king was anything more than an "interloper and conqueror." According to Heising, historians were not "theologians," and they were obliged to judge

Gustavus Adolphus on the basis of his actions. There could be only one conclusion: Gustavus Adolphus was a conqueror who, like Napoleon, had robbed the Germans of their wealth, exiled their princes, and expropriated their lands. Heising carried this comparison further when he claimed that the Swedish king had intended to establish an independent Protestant confederation that would have resembled nothing so much as the Confederation of the Rhine. Heising deplored the fact that for two hundred years Protestant historians had "treasonously" celebrated a robber, a sad circumstance that, in his view, only provided "further evidence that the Germans valued their confession more than their nation."[60] In comparing Gustavus Adolphus to Napoleon, Heising aimed a telling blow at the keystone of Protestant historiography, the mystical connection between 1632 and 1813. This comparison was also part of Johannes Janssen's claim that Catholic historiography, in offering a rebuttal to the Gustavus Adolphus myth, represented the triumph of a "German-national" historical perspective over the partisan and confessional "rational-scientific" perspective: "any German that celebrates Gustavus Adolphus must also celebrate Napoleon, and the celebration of Napoleon is as base a sin against German national feeling and the honor of the nation as any that pays homage to the Swedish conqueror."[61]

The commemoration of Gustavus Adolphus's deeds in 1832 had been characterized as establishing a line of demarcation between two ages. In the ceremonies at Breitenfeld this imagery had been used to contrast the spiritual and civil liberation of the Reformation with the benighted political, cultural, and intellectual traditions of Catholicism. By mid-century this view had begun to be altered. The confessional content of German nationalism had by no means diminished; but the Protestant historiography of Gustavus Adolphus increasingly held up the policies and plans of the Swedish king as models of a *Realpolitik* solution to the problem of German unification. In 1866, the *annus horribilis* for German Catholics, a Protestant historian noted the prophetic example of Gustavus Adolphus: "What could have been better for the German Reich than the replacement of the Roman Catholic imperium, with all of its southern European dead weight, with a German kingdom that embraced the new age and the noblest aspirations of humanity? If the dissolution of the German Reich was to be avoided, the only possible solution was the ascension of a German federative monarchy in place of the Roman Catholic imperium's caesaristic majesty . . .[in this regard] if Gustavus Adolphus had a failing, it was that he was more German than the German princes."[62] Gustav Droysen's (1838–1908) influential 1869 biography of the Swedish king firmly established this *Realpolitik* interpretation by asserting that Gustavus Adolphus's intervention in Germany had been driven by strategic considerations that aimed at the creation of a unified state that would guarantee the balance of power in Europe.[63] Or as the rabid nationalist Wolfgang Menzel (1798–1873) put it, "The unifying force of the German nation, or the strivings toward this goal, have always come from the north, all divisive tendencies from the south."[64] The utility of the symbolism of Gustavus Adolphus during the nineteenth century was closely connected to assumptions about the Protestant origins of the German national consciousness and the nature of the German mission in Europe. Along with England and Scandinavia, Germany was seen as an integral part of a northern European Protestant bulwark against the encircling Catholic threats of French expansionism, southern despotism, and Slavic barbarism. In the period of German unification Gustavus Adolphus was still important as a symbol of confessional solidarity; but his achievements increasingly came to represent the possibilities of German power. His elevation to heroic status was a palliative for apprehensions about German weakness. In a response to Catholic attempts at revising the myth, one commentator noted that to dismiss his symbolism for Germany's Protestants as inherently divisive was to miss the point: what mattered was that, in honoring him, Germans were finally acknowledging the revitalization of a power and a "unitary national consciousness" that heralded the advent of a *deutsche Partei* that would find its fulfillment in the rise of Prussia.[65]

Notes

1. Friedrich Salomo Moser, *Gustav Adolph und die dankbare Nachwelt* (Zwickau: Klinckhardt, 1844), pp. 12–13, 50, 77–80.
2. Modern scholarship dealing with Gustavus Adolphus has been traditionally and primarily confined to the field of political history. The historiography of the Thirties was inclined to see Gustavus Adolphus's Swedish–German alliance as an example of an imperialistic *Weltpolitik* based on common racial-cultural origins. See Johannes Paul, *Gustav Adolf. Erster Band: Schwedens Aufsteig zur Großmachtstellung* (Leipzig: Quelle and Meyer, 1927), *Gustav Adolf. Dritter Band: Von Breitenfeld bis Lützen* (Leipzig: Quelle and Meyer, 1932) and "Gustaf Adolf in der deutschen Geschichtsschreibung," *Historische Vierteljahrsschrift* 25, no. 3 (September 1930): 415–29. For this interpretation see also Richard Schmidt, "Gustav Adolf. Die Bedeutung seiner Erscheinung für die europäische Politik und für den deutschen Volksgeist," *Zeitschrift für Politik* 22, no. 11 (February, 1933): 701–19

and Gerhard Ritter, "Gustav Adolf, Deutschland und das nordische Luthertum," in *Die Weltwirkung der Reformation* (Munich: R. Oldenbourg, 1959), pp. 134–45. For surveys of the Gustavus Adolphus historiography, see Ernst Ekman, "Three Decades of Research on Gustav Adolphus," *The Journal of Modern History* 38, no. 3 (September, 1966): 243–55; Werner Buchholz, "Der Eintritt Schwedens in den Dreißigjährigen Krieg in der Schwedischen und Deutschen Historiographie des 19. und 20. Jahrhunderts," *Historische Zeitschrift* 245, no. 2 (1987): 291–314; and Sverker Oredsson, *Geschichtsschreibung und Kult. Gustav Adolf, Schweden und der Dreißigjährige Krieg*, trans. Klaus Böhme (Berlin: Duncker und Humblot, 1994). Oredsson only cursorily focuses on the Gustavus Adolphus phenomenon before 1914. On nineteenth-century German historiography of the Thirty Years War in general, see Kevin Cramer, "The Lamentations of Germany: The Historiography of the Thirty Years' War, 1790–1890" (Ph.D. diss., Harvard University, 1998).

3. Hartmut Lehmann, "Martin Luther als Deutscher Nationalheld im 19. Jahrhundert," *Luther. Zeitschrift der Luther-Gesellschaft* 55, no. 2 (1984): 57–9.

4. Joel F. Harrington and Helmut Walser Smith, "Confessionalization, Community, and State Building in Germany, 1555–1870," *The Journal of Modern History* 69, no. 1 (March 1997): 77.

5. See the essays in *Volk–Nation–Vaterland. Der deutsche Patriotismus und der Nationalismus*, ed. Horst Zillessen (Gütersloh: G. Mohn, 1970).

6. Horst Zillessen, *Protestantismus und politische Form. Eine Untersuchung zum protestantischen Verfassungsverständnis* (Gütersloh: G. Mohn, 1971), pp. 42–5. The Gerlach quote is from Robert Bigler, "The Rise of Political Protestantism in Nineteenth-Century Germany," *Church History* 34, no. 4 (December, 1965): 440.

7. Wolfgang Altgeld, *Katholizismus, Protestantismus, Judentum* (Mainz: Matthias-Grünewald-Verlag, 1992), pp. 4, 22, 64–5, 125–36, 160.

8. Helmut Walser Smith, *German Nationalism and Religious Conflict: Culture, Ideology and Politics, 1870–1914* (Princeton, NJ: Princeton University Press, 1995), pp. 20–24, 33.

9. On the impact of the Wars of Liberation on German nationalism see Christopher Clark, "The Wars of Liberation in Prussian Memory: Reflections on the Memorialization of War in Early Nineteenth-Century Germany," *The Journal of Modern History* 68, no. 3 (September, 1996): 550–76 and the essays in *Öffentliche Festkultur: Politische Feste in Deutschland von der Aufklärung bis zum Ersten*

Weltkrieg, ed. Dieter Düding, Peter Friedeman and Paul Münch (Hamburg: Rowohlt, 1988).

10. Heinz Gollwitzer, *Europabild und Europagedanke* (Munich: C. H. Beck, 1964), pp. 53–66, 81–2.

11. Ursula Berg, *Niklas Vogt (1756–1836). Weltsicht und Politische Ordnungsvorstellungen zwischen Aufklärung und Romantik*, Beiträge zur Geschichte der Universität Mainz, 16 (Stuttgart: F. Steiner, 1992), pp. 138–42, 236–47, 262–4.

12. Niklas Vogt, *Ueber die Europäische Republik*, 2 vols (Frankfurt am Main: Varrentrapp und Wenner, 1787), vol. 1, pp. 7, 95, 127.

13. Niklas Vogt, *Gustav Adolph, König in Schweden: als Nachtrag zur europäischen Republik* (Frankfurt am Main: Varrentrapp und Wenner, 1790), Part II, pp. 1–11, 24–8.

14. Niklas Vogt, *Historische Darstellung des europäischen Völkerbundes. Erster Theil* (Frankfurt am Main: Andreäische Buchhandlung, 1808), pp. 3, 49, 235–37, and *Gustav Adolph*, p. 10.

15. Pro-Prussian historians followed Vogt in viewing the idea of a Swedish-led North German confederation as a seventeenth-century blueprint for achieving a unified Germany. See O. Friedrich Rühs, *Geschichte Schwedens*, Vol. 4 (Halle: J. J. Gebauer, 1810), 226, 244; Ludwig Flathe, *Geschichte des Kampfes zwischen dem alten und dem neuen Verfassungsprincip der Staaten der neuesten Zeit. Erster Theil. 1789–1791* (Leipzig: J. A. Barth, 1813), pp. 22–3; and Friedrich von Raumer, *Geschichte Deutschlands von der Abdankung Karls V. bis zum westphälischen Frieden. Zweite Hälfte von 1630–1648*, Historisches Taschenbuch 3 (Leipzig: F.A. Brockhaus, 1831–1832), pp. 3, 60, 95–6.

16. See Patrick H. Hutton, *History as an Art of Memory* (Hanover, VT: University Press of New England, 1993), pp. 79–80.

17. Friedrich Ludwig von Rango, *Denkmal der verhängnißvollen Jahre 1813 und 1814: jedem deutschen Biedermann gewidmet; zum Besten der im heiligen Freiheitskampf verstümmelten Königl. Preuß. Krieger* (Berlin: C. Voss, 1815), p.v.

18. Friedrich Ludwig von Rango, *Gustav Adolph der Große König von Schweden. Ein historisches Gemälde* (Leipzig: C. H. F. Hartmann, 1824), pp. i–vii. A second edition of this book was issued for the *Säcularfeier* of 1832. As an indication of the reverence with which the author regarded the memory of the Swedish king, note his observation of the "unusual size" of Gustav Adolf's heart revealed at the embalming (a favorite detail of the folklore) and his sober description of the king's *Zauberschwert*, said to be covered with

talismanic signs and figures. In common with other tales of such relics, the magic weapon was reported to have resided in multiple locations: Stockholm, Aix-en-Provence, and the Büchersaal in Leipzig. See p. 386 and *"Anhang,"* pp. 127–8.

19. Otto von Ravensberg [Otto Jacobi], *Gustav Adolph und Wallenstein. Tragödie in fünf Akten* (Berlin: G. Reimer, 1840), p. 8.
20. *Errinnerung an die Schlacht bei Breitenfeld am 7ten September und deren Feier am 7. September 1831* (Leipzig: C. Voss, 1831), pp. 5, 15–44. The language of the dedications at Breitenfeld and Lützen tends to contradict Christopher Clark's assertion that the "patriotic memory" of the Wars of Liberation found no representation in public monuments in the immediate post-war decades. See Clark, "The Wars of Liberation in Prussian Memory," p. 576.
21. Ernst Ortlepp, *Gustav Adolph. Eine lyrische Phantasie zu dem zweihundertjährigen Jubiläum der Breitenfelder–Leipziger Schlacht am 7ten September 1631* (Leipzig: W. Zirges, 1831), pp. 8–9.
22. *Die Schlacht bei Lützen, am 6. November 1632* (Naumburg: K. A. Klassenbach, 1832), pp. 3–4.
23. Gerhard Friederich, *Gustav Adolf's Heldentod für Teutschlands Freiheit: Ein historisches Gedicht in vier Gesängen* (Frankfurt am Main: Streng, 1834), pp. 72–8.
24. Dietrich Freiherr von Bülow, *Gustav Adolph in Deutschland. Kritische Geschichte seiner Feldzüge* (Berlin: Himburg, 1808), Vol. 2: pp. 111–114. See also Andreas Buchner, *Geschichte von Bayern während des dreißigjährigen Krieges* (Munich: Lindauer, 1851), p. 169.
25. Friedrich Förster, *Gustav Adolph. Ein historisches Drama* (Berlin: G. Reimer, 1832), pp. 140, 161–3.
26. Hartmut Mai and Kurt Schneider, *Die Stadtkirche St. Viti und die Gustav-Adolf-Gedenkstätte Zu Lützen*. Das Christliche Denkmal, no. 115 (Berlin: Union Verlag, 1981), pp. 23–4. The exact location of the king's death was disputed. C.A. Jahn, who identified the marker as an old milestone, questioned Joseph de Francheville's location some 700 paces from the stone. Jahn claimed that the king had died exactly 83 paces from where the stone stood. See C. J. Jahn, *Ueber den Tod Gustav Adolph's, König in Schweden* (Weissenfels: L. F. Leyckam, 1806), p. 3 and Joseph du Fresne de Francheville, *La Mort de Gustave-Adolphe* (Breslau: Imprimerie priv. de Grass, 1799).
27. Hermann Wolfgang Beyer, *Die Geschichte des Gustav-Adolf-Vereins in ihren kirchen-und geistesgeschichtlichen Zusammenhängen* (Göttingen: Vandenhoeck and Ruprecht, 1932), p. 5 and Moser, *Gustav Adolph*, pp. 70–71.

28. J. C. Pfister, *Geschichte der Teutschen* (Hamburg: F. Perthes, 1829–1833), p. 537.

29. Beyer, *Gustav-Adolf-Verein*, p. 5.

30. C. H. F. Hartmann, *Der Schwedenstein. Die Zweite Säcularfeier der Schlacht bei Lützen am 6. November 1632 in allen ihren An- und Nachklängen. Ein Denkmal für Gustav Adolph, den Retter Deutschlands von geistlichen und weltlichem Sclavenjoche* (Leipzig: C. H. F. Hartmann, 1833), pp. 56–7.

31. In January 1832 F. C. F. Philippi had discovered, beneath a mural of the Swedish coat of arms, a decomposed oak urn beneath the floor of the church. He conjectured, based on local stories, that the urn had contained the viscera removed by the embalmers who had prepared the king's body for the trip back to Sweden. See F. C. F. Philippi, "Der Tod Gustav Adolph's, Königs von Schweden, in der Schlacht bei Lützen am 6. November 1632. Zur Erinnerung bei der zweiten Säcularfeier [1832]" in Hartmann, *Der Schwedenstein*, pp. 62–4. After extensive renovations in 1912 the urn was sealed in lead and placed in its original location. On 6 November 1912 the church was reconsecrated. In 1913 it was renamed the "König-Gustav-Adolf-Gedächtniskirche" by imperial decree. See Mai and Schneider, *Gustav-Adolph Gedenkstätte*, pp. 29–31.

32. Philippi, in Hartmann, *Der Schwedenstein*, pp. 65–7.

33. Friederich, *Gustav Adolf's Heldentod*, p. 197, and Hartmann, *Der Schwedenstein*, pp. 58–61, 102–3. On the ceremony, see also Moser, *Gustav Adolph*, pp. 71–5.

34. Hartmann, *Der Schwedenstein*, pp. 121–2. See also Beyer, *Gustav-Adolph*-Verein, p. 13 and Hermann von Criegern, *Geschichte des Gustav-Adolf-Vereins* (Hamburg: Gustav Schloessmann's Verlagsbuchhandlung, 1903), p. 10.

35. C. A. W. Schild, "Aufforderung zu einer Sechser-Subscription, zur Errichtung eines Denkmals," *Leipziger Tageblatt*, 7 December 1832 (no. 162), in Hartmann, *Der Schwedenstein*, pp. 123–5 and von Criegern, *Geschichte des Gustav-Adolf-Vereins*, pp. 11–12.

36. Hartmann, *Der Schwedenstein*, pp. 136–8.

37. Mai and Schneider, *Gustav-Adolf-Gedenkstätte*, p. 25. On 6 November 1907 a memorial chapel was built behind the site. For a guide to the various sites and monuments connected to Gustav Adolf's sojourn in Germany, see Otto Lerche, *Gustav Adolf. Deutsche Bilder und Stätten*, Das Bild zum Wort, vol. 1 (Hamburg: Ag.d. Rauhen Hauses, 1932).

38. F. Treumund [Eduard Sparfeld], *Gustav Adolf König von Schweden, der heldenmüthige Kämpfer für Deutschlands Religionsfreiheit. Ein Volksbuch für alle Stände* (Leipzig: R. Friese, 1845), pp. 460–2. See also Beyer, *Gustav-Adolf-Verein*, p. 6 and Moser, *Gustav Adolph*, pp. 77–82.

39. For full accounts of the founding of the Verein and its goals, organization, and history, see Beyer and von Criegern. For a prospectus of its religious, social, and political positions, see Otto Lerche, *Hundert Jahre Arbeit an der Diaspora* (Leipzig: Centralvorstand des Evangelischen Vereins der Gustav-Adolf-Stiftung, 1932). See also Heiner Grote, "Konfessionalistische und unionistische Orientierung am Beispiel des Gustav-Adolf-Vereins und des Evangelischen Bundes," in *Das Deutsche Luthertum und die Unionsproblematik im 19. Jahrhundert*, ed. Wolf-Dieter Hauschild (Gütersloh: G. Mohn, 1991), pp. 110–30.

40. Ernst Gellner's definition of "diaspora nationalism" cannot be applied in this case. Germany's Protestants might have seen themselves historically as a "pariah" group on a Catholic continent, but in "choosing nationalism" they were not seeking to legitimate a self-conceived minority status or specialized socioeconomic function. See his *Nations and Nationalism* (Ithaca, NY: Cornell University Press, 1983), pp. 101–9.

41. George L. Mosse, *The Nationalism of the Masses: Political Symbolism and Mass Movements in Germany from the Napoleonic Wars through the Third Reich* (New York: H. Fertig, 1975), pp. 50–1.

42. See Maurice Halbwachs, *On Collective Memory*, translated and edited by Lewis A. Coser (Chicago: University of Chicago Press, 1992), pp. 63–5 and Jacques Le Goff, *History and Memory*, trans. Steven Randall and Elizabeth Claman (New York: Columbia University Press, 1992), p. 59.

43. See J. C. Pfister, *Geschichte der Teutschen* (Hamburg: F. Perthes, 1833), Vol. 4: p. 537; Johann Michael Söltl, *Der Religionskrieg in Deutschland. Zweiter Theil. Des Krieges Fortgang und Ende* (Hamburg: J. A. Meissner, 1840), pp. 126, 144–5; and Carl August Mebold, *Der dreißigjährige Krieg, und die Helden desselben: Gustav Adolf, König von Schweden, und Wallenstein, Herzog von Friedland* (Stuttgart: Literatur-Comptoir, 1840), Vol. 2: p. 275.

44. Karl Adolf Menzel, *Geschichte des dreißigjährigen Krieges in Deutschland* (Breslau: Grass, Barth and Co., 1839), Vol. 2: pp. 319–20.

45. Ibid., pp. 343–4, 350–1. The possibility of a "Protestant constitutional alliance under the aegis of a Swedish protectorate" was also advanced much later by M. Doeberl, "Das Kaiserprojekt und die letzten Absichten König Gustav Adolfs von Schweden nach bayerischer Auffassung," *Forschungen zur Geschichte Bayerns. Vierteljahresschrift*, 15, no. 3 (1907): 202–8.

46. Friedrich Wilhelm Barthold, *Geschichte des großen deutschen Krieges: vom Tode Gustav Adolfs ab mit besonderer Rücksicht auf Frankreich* (Stuttgart: S. G. Liesching, 1842–1843), Vol. 1: pp. vii–x, 29; Vol. 2: p. vi. On Barthold and Raumer, see Werner Friedrich, *Friedrich von Raumer als Historiker und Politiker* (Dissertation, Universität Leipzig, 1930), pp. 41–3.

47. Gottlieb Mohnike, "Gustav Adolph, gezeichnet von Erich Gustav Geijer," *Zeitschrift für die historische Theologie*, no. 3 (Leipzig, 1844): 59–61. This was a review of a Swedish biography.

48. Treumund [Sparfeld], *Gustav Adolf*, pp. 390–3.

49. Wilhelm Bötticher, *Gustav Adolph, König von Schweden. Ein Buch für Fürst und Volk* (Kaiserswerth am Rhein: Fliedner, 1845), pp. vii, 2, 68–9, 171–5.

50. Ludwig Flathe, *Geschichte Gustav Adolf's und des dreißigjährigen Krieges*, 2nd edn, (Leipzig: Teubner, 1847), Vol. 1: pp. 1–5.

51. On the influence of Schmidt's multi-volume *Neuere Geschichte der Deutschen* (Frankenthal: Verlag der Gegelischen Buchdruckerey und Buchhandlung, 1783–1786). On this interpretation see Franz von Wegele, *Geschichte der deutschen Historiographie seit dem Auftreten des Humanismus* (Munich and Leipzig: R. Oldenbourg, 1885), pp. 912–13; and Eduard Fueter, *Geschichte der neueren Historiographie* (Munich and Berlin: R. Oldenbourg, 1911), pp. 371–7.

52. Lorenz von Westenrieder, *Beyträge zur vaterländischen Historie, Geographie, Statistik, etc.* (Munich: J. B. Strobl, 1806), Vol. 8: pp. 243–55; and idem, *Geschichte des dreißigjährigen Krieges* (Munich: J. Lindauer, 1805), Vol. 2: pp. 136–7, 233.

53. Hans Fenske, "Gelehrtenpolitik im liberalen Südwesten 1830–1880," in *Gelehrtenpolitik und politische Kultur in Deutschland 1830–1930*, ed. Gustav Schmidt and Jörn Rüsen (Bochum: N. Brockmeyer, 1986), pp. 39–41.

54. August Friedrich Gfrörer, *Gustav Adolph, König von Schweden und seine Zeit*, 3rd edn, (Stuttgart: A. Krabbe, 1852), pp. 149–50, 580–1, 749–50, 891, 897.

55. Klopp tried to remedy this failure in his introduction, emendations, and notes. See Christian d'Elvert, *Beiträge zur Geschichte der*

Rebellion, Reformation, des dreißigjährigen Krieges und der Neugestaltung Mährens im siebzehnten Jahrhunderte (Brno: A. Nitsch, 1867), p. vi.

56. [Onno Klopp], *Studien über Katholizismus, Protestantismus und Gewissensfreiheit in Deutschland* (Schaffhausen: F. Hurter, 1857), pp. 298–300; idem, *Der König Friedrich II. von Preussen und die deutsche Nation* (Schaffhausen: F. Hurter, 1860), pp. 4–5; idem, *Tilly im dreißigjährigen Kriege* (Stuttgart: J. G. Cotta, 1861), Vol. 2: pp. 59–64; and Friedrich von Hurter, *Geschichte Kaiser Ferdinands II* (Schaffhausen: F. Hurter, 1861), Vol. 3: pp. 427–32, 592. See Karl Helbig's attack on the "Hurter–Klopp clique" of *Geschichtsverfälscher* in "Stimmungen in Deutschland vor Gustav Adolf's Landung," *Die Grenzboten* 24, no. 2 (Leipzig, 1865): pp. 173–9.

57. [Klopp], *Studien über Katholizismus*, p. 417.

58. "Gustav Adolf und Kurfürst Georg Wilhelm," *Historisch-politische Blätter für das katholische Deutschland* [*HpB*] 1 (Munich, 1838): 81, 88–9.

59. "Wie Gustav Adolf die religiöse Freiheit der Katholiken verstand," *HpB* 11 (1844): 580–4.

60. Albert Heising, *Magdeburg nicht durch Tilly zerstört. Gustav Adolph in Deutschland. Zwei historische Abhandlungen* (Berlin: Baumann und Kuhn, 1846), pp. 137–41, 177–87. These two pieces originally appeared as articles in the *HpB*. In the foreword to the second revised edition Heising expressed regret for the controversy his book had provoked and claimed that it was only intended as a warning about the damage that confessional division inflicted on the German national sensibility. See *Magdeburg nicht durch Tilly zerstört. Die Politik Gustav Adolph's in Deutschland*, 2nd rev. edn, (Berlin: F. Schneider and Co., 1854).

61. Johannes Janssen, *Gustav Adolf in Deutschland*, Katholischer Broschüren-Verein, 1, no. 8 (Frankfurt am Main: G. J. Hamacher, 1865), pp. 3–4, 12, 32.

62. G. Trauttwein, *Der dreißigjährige Krieg und der westfälische Friede* (Berlin: G. Reimer, 1866), pp. 14–15.

63. Gustav Droysen, *Gustav Adolf* (Leipzig: Teubner, 1869–1870), Vol. 1: p. vii; Vol. 2: pp. 423–4.

64. Wolfgang Menzel, *Was hat Preussen für Deutschland geleistet?* (Stuttgart: A. Krabbe, 1870), p. 3.

65. Franz Mauritius, *Gustav Adolf, König von Schweden. Ein Lebensbild*, Unterhaltende Belehrungen zur Förderung allgemeiner Bildung, no. 26 (Leipzig: F. A. Brockhaus, 1856), pp. 1–6, 66–72.

–6–

The Process of Confessional Inculturation: Catholic Reading in the "Long Nineteenth Century"

Jeffrey T. Zalar

On 12 March 1907 a young man in his early twenties named Franz Versen wrote a letter to the vicar general of the Archdiocese of Cologne. "In view of the fact," he began, "that in today's society one hears so much about the so-called free literature, and given that I have until now refrained from looking at such works out of religious considerations, my ignorance regarding them is [often] a minor embarrassment. Since I am not afraid of any disadvantageous religious consequences from reading this free literature due to my worldview, I respectfully ask the . . . Vicar General to grant me the permission to read the works of Hauptmann, Zola, Ibsen and Immermann . . . and to be allowed to see their plays." An attached note from his parish priest testifying to his good morals and sincere Catholicism convinced the vicar, who thereupon granted Herr Versen a five-year dispensation to read from the Index of Forbidden Books.[1] Franz Versen was not alone in his search for what the English modernist George Tyrell called "a little more breathing-space than their forefathers."[2] After 1890 German Catholics of the lower middle and middle class in every region of the country flooded their diocesan offices with such requests, making the negotiation of faith, knowledge, and social status one of the most conspicuous pastoral dilemmas of the Imperial era.[3] Cultural accommodation had become a powerful desire among Catholics, who sought respectability as authentic Germans without forsaking the practices of their religious tradition. Why and how this desire took shape, how Catholics encountered the dominant cultural discourse and fit it within their spiritual panorama, is the topic of this chapter, which begins with an illiterate population reeling from Napoleonic spoliation and *Aufklärungsschock*.

The secularization of ecclesiastical territories under the *Reichsdeputationshauptschluss* of 1803 hamstrung the German Church just when the Enlightenment had secured a footing in its active intellectual centers.[4] Diminished university presence, the loss of schools and cultural influence, and the coerced transfer of riches to state bureaucracies ensured that Catholics would enter the "century of the book" with plundered resources. The torpid pace of Catholic literacy relative to Protestants and Jews, therefore, had to do not only with a rural religious culture centered on pictures and verbal narration, but with institutional inequalities quite beyond their own making.[5] As a result, a Catholic was as likely to be read to as to be found reading during the first quarter of the nineteenth century. Well into the 1820s priests as intellectual notables and local *Studierten* still drew crowds to hear lectures on health, practical living, economic improvement, and the proper way to honor the saints, "which among the common folk so lustily degenerates into superstition."[6] If they read at all, Catholics consumed the simple exegeses, lives of Christ, and saints' devotionals that made up the model home library, or cut their literary teeth on the more appetizing and abundant fare of magic, legends, hack medicine, and irreverent social commentary.[7] Making fun of the "orders," figuring out how to win the lottery, and learning how to divine dreams satisfied needs more immediate than those connected with dying and the last things.

These simple reading habits were ill suited to intellectual expansion. And while reading tastes among uneducated Protestants were just as rough-hewn – Catholics accused Protestants of spreading occult literature throughout the 1820s[8] – the Protestant *literati* made Catholic "backwardness" a central complaint in their broadening philippic against the Church. By 1800 Enlightenment thinkers had already discredited Catholicism as a pre-modern relic. But, as Wolfgang Altgeld has shown, the centuries-old religious polemic in Germany took on new hues in the creation of German national identity, in which apprehensions of knowledge became paramount.[9] "The majority of our *Tagesblätter*," one Catholic wrote in 1822, "set themselves increasingly to the task of identifying and dragging out everything from remote antiquity, even if fabricated and untrue, so that Catholics can be blamed for obscurantism and barbarism and so the highly praised Enlightenment can more quickly disseminate its lies and deceptions."[10] According to the "official" narrative, the folkways of Catholics from the lower orders had no place in a nation of bourgeois *Wissenschaftler*, entrepreneurs, and literary sophisticates. The "primitive spirituality" of the Catholic Church, moreover, was irreconcilable with the more fashionable principles of social and cultural progress embedded somehow in the very fabric of Protantism. Faith and tradition were insufficient prerequisites for civilization compared with education and culture, which were the new bases for social authority and the chevrons of social rank.[11]

This socio-cultural nexus of confession, knowledge, and respectability, in other words, which did so much to justify the superior power position Protestants assumed, had its deepest roots in perceptions of the Enlightenment. This nexus posed critical dilemmas for Catholics especially. Thrown on the defensive by stereotypes designed to emphasize the chasm between Protestant progress and Catholic reaction, Catholics struggled to fight back. Against a developing German historicism that purportedly objected to transcendent principles of change, Catholics recalled Christ's promise to sustain the Church until the End Times.[12] In response to the "chaos of unconnected, half-true, half-false ideas" represented by *Wissenschaft*, Catholics defended the unity of truth in religion.[13] The enshrinement of Protestant authors like Schiller, Goethe, and Klopstock in the canon of national literature returned educated Catholics to Chaucer, Dante, and Cervantes. Faced with the absolute idealism of Fichte and Hegel, they brought forward the speculative metaphysics of Neo-Thomism. This religious and cultural response did little to mollify Protestant fears, and less to upgrade the standing of Catholics among individuals who were already suspicious about why they "lagged behind" intellectually.[14] Hurling thunderbolts at each other across a widening cultural gap, Protestants and Catholics settled into positions that hardened as the discourse of German nationalism coalesced. Pervasive sarcasm and discrimination provoked fierce anti-liberalism and edgy alarm. Through a Manichean lens Protestants projected the light of *Bildung* and progress on to the black canvas of Catholic discipline and ignorance; Catholics, not to be outdone, cast the illumination and true freedom of the Gospel against the dread darkness of Protestant–Jewish *Heidentum*.[15]

Apart from the spread of literacy itself, then, there was no more crucial factor shaping the reading habits of Catholics than confessional animosity. And given the beating they took in the popular press, it is not surprising that they hunkered down in defensive mode. Protestants wrote of plotting Jesuits, inquisitorial bishops, and fat monks tumbling intoxicated nuns behind the cloister walls. Celibacy was "the most furious hostility" (*grimmigste Anfeindung*) against human nature. Pilgrimages, saints, relics, confession, and the Mass were frivolous manipulations. Catholics were untrustworthy subjects and enemies of religious tolerance and civil peace. The pope was a "wolf" to be avoided by anyone who did not want to be "devoured." He was the anti-Christ, a tyrant, and the leader of a political faction. Most troublesome of all to German nationalists, "the pope was a foreigner."[16]

Beset by what they determined to be a "legion" of "anti-Christian writers" who had seized "the whole of German literature," Catholics attempted to withdraw into a self-contained reading culture of their own.[17] Plotting and enforcing this withdrawal proved extremely difficult, however. According to Emmanuel Todd, literacy is not a "self-generated innovation" but results from a "process of diffusion."[18] Diffusion certainly occurred in mixed confessional communities, where Catholics read whatever was available, which often as not originated in a Protestant publishing house. A journal called "The Friend of the Poor" (*Der Armenfreund*), which was popular among neophyte Catholic readers in Baden and Württemberg in the 1820s, was actually a Protestant apologetic.[19] Reading material went from "hand to hand" in hospices, factories, train stations, and in the growing number of lending libraries and bookstores.[20] Catholic priests, who urged their parishioners to hand over questionable books before reading them, were overwhelmed by the responsibilities of literary policing. "In this local mixed community," one exasperated pastor wrote in 1869, "priests are almost daily in the situation of having to make judgments on books by non-Catholics."[21] For many priests, the confessional became a literary salon. In 1845 Father Heyden of Cologne wrote that he often encountered a youth in the confessional asking "whether or not he was permitted to read this or that book."[22] Father Zietz in Bochum complained in 1850 that he was tired of being pestered by people wanting to know which books were forbidden. It was "necessary," he concluded, to acquaint himself better with "the literature of the enemy" so that he could offer more helpful advice.[23]

Devotional reflection, it should be stressed, was the hallmark of Catholic reading throughout the nineteenth and early twentieth century. Nevertheless, the suspicion that Catholic communities of virtue were shot through with the "bad literature" of malignant Protestants and Jews made the establishment of a discrete reading culture of pious books a supreme *desideratum* by 1850.[24] In his 1853 Lenten pastoral letter, Wilhelm Arnoldi, the wildly popular bishop of Trier, warned his flock about the dangers of an expanding negative press and reminded them of the peril their souls fell into when they read from it. They were not to choose books written by non-Catholic authors. Nor were they to join the blossoming "bad societies" that "gloss over and justify" reading them. Reading circles and home libraries were to be purged of everything but instructional and edifying literature, which was the only antidote to the *Preßpest*. And "what a treasure a good book is for a poor child . . . what a guardian angel against seduction!"[25] Here the understanding of "ultramontanization" as an anti-modern fight with modern means seems particularly apt.[26] The priests of Cologne argued in 1849, "One must become familiar with the weapons of one's enemies [and] understand the times." Then one can identify and apply the best "remedies" (*Gegenmittel*).[27]

The best remedies included reinforcing the Catholic press and publishing houses, establishing confessionalized reading circles, building libraries and reading rooms, and exhorting the faithful constantly against religiously indifferent or anti-Catholic books, journals, and newspapers. The widening popularity of pious and instructional literature among the laity that resulted indicates that, as a pastoral strategy, the clergy's approach had struck a chord. Although they continued to buy almanacs, racy stories, and cheap books from the developing market in colportage *Trivialliteratur*, Catholics read religious works avidly: communion reflections, seasonal prayer books, Marian readers, hagiographies, pamphlets on the Immaculate Conception, prayer cards on papal piety and the Sacred Heart of Jesus, histories of the apostles, religious commentaries on the Revolution of 1848/9, church hymnals, and associational tracts.[28] This literature stressed the relevance and "beauty" of Catholic doctrine, the virtues of firm belief, and the importance of prayer in times of crisis. It also emphasized religious conflict in communities and the individual soul. A pilgrimage sheet from 1866 invoked Saint George for protection against all enemies "visible and invisible."[29] A prayer of 1858 asked Mary to "free us from our wicked enemies (*bösen Feinde*) and stand powerfully by us at death."[30] A poem inspired by the fifty-first psalm in 1862 went: "You have always loved the truth/ And have allowed me to profit from it;/ What darkness remains apart from wisdom,/ You make known to me./ With hyssop, Lord! refresh me!/ Cleanse me of my sins,/ And I will appear before your eyes whiter than the snow."[31] Complementing devotional texts at the humblest levels of the population were widely circulating calendars. Calendars provided an educational option not associated with the Enlightenment.[32] With didactic narratives, practical advice, daily prayers, and stories that illustrated Catholic moral teachings, folk calendars were displayed "in the room the whole year long in a place of honor."[33] Higher up the social ladder, among the lower middle class, the folk stories of Alban Stolz, Ida Hahn-Hahn, and Clemens Brentano attracted an enthusiastic readership. Stressing themes of family life and the moral rules of correct living, these books spoke to a widespread demand for reading material free of anti-Catholic bias and upbeat about the Church's future.[34] Catholics read political newspapers and fact sheets from a confessional perspective as well, especially after 1850, and they maintained allegiance to Sunday publications for entertainment and religious news.[35]

Although the Catholic reading culture was never as compartmentalized as historians have traditionally assumed, these tastes and the staid mental furniture they reflected lend support to Thomas Nipperdey's description of a mindset characterized by "a certain hardness [and] sometimes a nervous aggression against everything non-Catholic."[36] Mass literacy and mass production of books and pamphlets by 1870, much of it anti-Catholic in tone and content, sharpened this mindset, which was deployed in detrimental ways during the era of *Reichsgründung*. Catholics could have had little doubt about their unwelcome status in the new Reich. "Even you, my people," went the popular 1874 cavalry song, "centuries in the dust, have knelt before Roman tyranny. Your choicest members fell victim to the Church. Free yourselves finally from your yokes, stand up and storm the fortress of Rome with holy spears in a speedy victory charge!"[37] The perception of being flooded by negative literature had seethed below the surface since the 1820s. But in the bedeviling atmosphere of the *Kulturkampf*, feelings of disjointedness and vanishing intellectual control bubbled over. "Today it is not merely the learned bound works that lead the intellectual aristocracy on the path of error," one layman fumed in 1873. "Today the publishers send thousands more journals, brochures, and cheap serials everywhere that are [freely] selected, read, and discussed by all classes and occupations in guardrooms, attics, and children's bedrooms."[38] Parish communities had to be sternly reminded that it "is the duty of every Catholic pastor . . . to warn his children against reading and keeping journals and newspapers that are either openly or subtly opposed to Catholic belief and good morals, and it is the duty of every Catholic child to listen to and obey the warning of his priest."[39] This handwringing and defensiveness brought the expansion of literary tastes among Catholics to a standstill. Local newspapers that represented strict Catholic viewpoints began to achieve significant subscriptions. Book associations devoted to the spread of "good literature" removed the few titles from their lists that could be classified as *wissenschaftlich*, essentially delaying the beginnings of Catholic folk education by two decades. And in an era of stringent intellectual tests proctored by grim *Kulturkampf* Liberals, Catholics began recusing themselves from the public libraries.[40] The popular wisdom that stereotypes contain elements of truth may be difficult to prove. But it is not unfair to say that in the 1870s Catholic reading habits played into the axioms of Liberal-Protestant bias.

The denigration of culturally deficient, poorly read, and improperly bred Catholics became a common feature of official discourse in the German Empire, reflecting the institutionalization of religious inequality. Unification was understood to confirm Protestant values, philosophical idealism, and bourgeois neohumanism, and to lend divine confirmation to the positions of social and cultural prominence that Protestants already enjoyed. Accordingly, *Kulturkampf* rhetoric associated Catholics with customs and attitudes that were "inimical to Germany's economic and social modernization."[41] Dogmatism, ordained ministry, low educational attainment, and traditional corporate hierarchies posed critical obstacles to realizing the destiny of the nation. Catholics, therefore, who seemed to stand for all four, could be – indeed had to be – stigmatized and excluded from institutional power. They were consequently under-represented in banking, commerce, and industry, as well as the officer corps, the university professorate, and the higher bureaucracy. Political and social mobilization among Catholics, which contested this subordinate status, only fueled Protestant hostility in the decades before the First World War.[42] As Gangolf Hübinger has put it, "The boundaries between the confessions remained all but closed."[43]

In such a forbidding environment, Catholics developed a self-perception closely tied to their marginalization, estrangement, and lack of educational parity. Indeed, the view that the restrictive "milieu mentality" was a settled disposition in the Imperial era has sustained a significant body of research that has achieved the status of a master narrative. According to this narrative, Catholics, led by an arch-conservative, unified clergy, maintained their negative posture towards contemporary ideas and cultural values and held on to traditional piety, authority, and intellectual circumspection.[44] Yet even as they adopted concepts and practices that could strengthen a threatened identity, Catholics in the German Empire increasingly sought to make peace with the myths, motifs, and manners of modern German culture. The intra-confessional discussion of Catholic "educational deficiency," for example, which began in the 1880s, had a powerful effect on contemporaries. Martin Baumeister, who has written on this discussion so well, points out the flood of articles published in Catholic journals on the relationship of Catholicism to secular culture, their generally conservative tone, and yet their stress on necessary, if careful, assimilation.[45] And while historians' attention to *fin-de-siècle* reformist movements in the Catholic Church is usually limited to the literary circle around Karl Muth's *Hochland*, Julius Bachem's political ecumenism, interconfessional trade unions, and the wretched victims of the Modernist Crisis, there is evidence to suggest that the discourse of cultural accommodation among Catholics was far broader. The middle class seized upon education as the best way to crack the codes of polite sociability, and parents of both the old and the new lower middle class used the education system to enhance their children's prospects.[46] Catholic reading habits responded chiefly up to this point to the pleadings of an embattled spirituality. After 1890, however, Catholics, while never abandoning devotional texts, increasingly recognized the importance of book knowledge and craved the prestige that such knowledge bestowed.[47]

As for "ultramontane" priests in the *Kaiserreich*, they were hardly intellectual dinosaurs. As leaders of the emerging folk education movement, they themselves ensured that the shaping of a Catholic's inner life would not be limited by confessional identification. Clerics were unwilling to deny opportunities promised by social advancement through *Beruf*; they attempted to meet their parishioners' intellectual needs, and they hoped to avoid the dangers of ridicule and embarrassment surrounding censorship. "It is well known," one priest wrote in 1905, "that the Church is generous in granting dispensations to those who find themselves in need of reading forbidden books."[48] Religious faith may have been a central organizing principle of their lives, but Catholics also attended to other longings.

Many of these longings derived from the pain of being denied the laurels of middle-class standing. Admitting, albeit reluctantly, that some of this pain may have been self-inflicted, more and more Catholics took measures to facilitate social advancement. On the elite level, the prominent philosopher Georg von Hertling and modernist theologians such as Hermann Schell and Franz Xaver Kraus discussed these problems in detail and published reformist tracts. The Center Party established programs designed to expand the Catholic presence in the upper bureaucracy and in education.[49] Catholic periodicals and newspapers ran biting articles on the lackluster academic achievement of Catholics and their poor relationship to official German culture. In August 1896, the German bishops addressed the under-representation of Catholics studying in universities, a problem severe enough to shock even Roman authorities.[50] On the popular level, too, institutions and parishes mobilized to bring modern knowledge to a broader segment of the Catholic population. The massive Popular Association for Catholic Germany adopted an educational program intended, at least in part, to head off liberal and Social Democratic attacks on Catholics as enemies of culture and progress. Since its founding in 1845, the Association of Saint Charles Borromeo or *Borromäusverein* had been devoted above all to the preservation of Catholic identity through the diffusion of pious literature. By 1890, however, it constituted the vanguard of the Catholic folk education movement, whose primary goals were to distribute devotional books to the faithful, to be sure, but also to promote general knowledge in parish libraries, to "stimulate" and "arouse" an "interest in better professional training," and to grease the gears of social intercourse within the stubborn Protestant hegemony by improving the cultural profile of the average believer.[51] According to this association, authentic Catholicism in Imperial Germany meant dutiful consideration of religious texts as well as the enlargement of reading tastes commensurate with educational status and cultural competence.

These thousands of libraries and reading rooms spoke to the intense "lust for reading" and "hunger for education" that had seized the German population in general. "Education is the cry of the times," observed one speaker at the annual Catholic assembly in 1884. "There has probably never been a century in which striving for education has been so general, so widely diffused, so organized. At every level of human society families take pains to give their children intellectual instruction, not only the boys, but girls as well, oftentimes much higher than their position and occupation."[52] In similar terms a Paderborn priest wrote in 1895: "If one wants to judge the efforts of an age by what the high or the low fuss about, then the great effort of our time is directed towards education. Everyone clamors for education, as they do for daily bread."[53] The fact that membership in the *Borromäusverein* increased 425 per cent to a total of some 262,000 in the twenty years before 1914 gives some indication of the escalating interests Catholics demonstrated for self-education, to be sure, but also for the cultivation of status.[54] Thomas Mergel has studied the attempts of the Catholic middle class in the Rhineland to rise more rapidly in Protestant social circles by establishing their cultural legitimacy.[55] But the "average Catholic" was interested in climbing, too, especially via the "new *Mittelstand*" of white-collar workers and petty professionals who became, in the words of David Blackbourn, "the great conduit of social mobility."[56] Book-centered behavior at all levels of the Catholic population, in other words, was symbolically charged action oriented toward overthrowing stereotypes and relaxing institutional barriers. In a 1911 pamphlet for Catholic librarians Father Johannes Braun, the General Secretary of the *Borromäusverein*, wrote: "Given our difficult position, given the many efforts of the other side to make the Catholic folk out to be enemies of cultivation and dumb, it is extremely important for us to say to all these people: we have so and so many libraries, so and so many books, so and so often were they read."[57] Public displays of their cultural competence, Catholics reasoned, would encourage Protestant approbation and open cracks for social ascent. "Today a lack of education is the gravest danger for individuals as for society," one *Volksbildung* leader wrote in 1898. Accordingly, Catholics needed to address their *Bildungsdefizit* and demonstrate that faith and knowledge went "hand-in-hand," that they themselves were now as always "the most true guardians of cultivation."[58]

This discussion of the folk education movement is relevant to parish and *Verein* libraries, where Catholics met to mull over and discuss intellectual material. But it is also pertinent to libraries in Catholic homes, for within the Catholic "milieu" the public and private spheres overlapped.

The *Borromäusverein*, as well as other associations committed to cultural advance such as the Popular Association for Catholic Germany, also provided books for domestic reading.[59] In 1911 it was estimated that the *Borromäusverein* had spent fourteen million marks on books for Catholic home libraries since 1845, and had distributed some 220,000 books in 1911 alone.[60] The principles governing the consumption of books in public were also applicable to reading at home. "We must not only read books," one Catholic editor wrote, "but buy books as well . . . . We allow ourselves to become lovers and gourmets (*Feinschmeckern*) of literature. This is not a superfluous luxury. Things that are really valuable should become not only intellectual but material property as well."[61] Every member of the *Borromäusverein* was to have a "beautiful and decent" home library, every father was to collect books for the intellectual and moral needs of his family, and every worker was to have books on hand to "transfigure" the harsh realities of his domestic existence.[62] Just as Catholics were to demonstrate their ease with modernity by patronizing libraries, so also were they to create an atmosphere of middle-class decorum in the home with a collection of books to be read in the German tradition of self-cultivation or *Bildung*.[63] Possessing *Bildung*, being "cultivated" according to the standards of taste and sensibility of the dominant culture, was an important strategy for Catholics emerging from their nineteenth-century "Ghetto." By playing by the rules of contemporary intellectual development and aesthetic cultivation, they could give the lie to Protestant claims of their inferiority, and redefine the boundaries of national participation.[64]

But what did Catholics actually read at home? Of all the research dilemmas facing scholars interested in Catholic mentality and cultural *Alltag*, lifting the veil of private libraries is certainly one of the most challenging. Yet historians are not helpless. Given the close relationship between parish and home libraries, patronage statistics and book requests for the former shed some light on the likely contents of the latter. Data on literacy and publishing information indicate the development of reading tastes in Catholic areas. *Imprimatur* files at diocesan archives contain letters from authors hoping to reach domestic readers. And the letters contained in the Index of Forbidden Books files, as the case of young Franz Versen makes clear, provide striking examples of Catholic readers engaging literary culture independently.

These sources argue that Catholic reading tastes broadened significantly in the Imperial era, though not always in the noblest directions. The average Catholic reader, for example, like the average German, took advantage of an ever-expanding press by indulging large quantities of kitsch literature, which was often peddled door-to-door:[65] picture books, humorous sheets, *Heimat* literature, serialized stories of love and adventure, tracts on astrology and the occult, bawdy songsheets complete with "suggestive pictures" (*pikante Bilder*), and ubiquitous daily newspapers, which threatened the Catholic effort in dailies begun during the *Kulturkampf*.[66] Dime novels were popular as well, especially the so-called "behind the stairs novels" or *Hintertreppenromane*, whose themes of social democracy, violence, suicide, and easy morals provided grist for so many ethical mills after 1900.[67] Some of the books found in the hands of male Catholics caught *in flagrante* by their pastors included *Death on the Island of Love, The Pirates of the Spree, Poison and Dynamite, The Prince's Beloved, The Beautiful Nihilist* and, more attractive still, *The Beautiful Woman of the Harem*.[68]

Catholics, it seems, were susceptible to the philistine and the lowbrow. But it would be a mistake to conclude that this was all that they read, or that the clergy were obsessed with "dirty and trashy literature."[69] The evidence shows, in fact, that Catholics specifically asked for and obtained books that would display their cultural *bona fides* to the middle class. The pastor of St Joseph's Parish in Eupen wrote in 1893: "During the improvement of the library in recent years, primary consideration was given to the acquisition of popular-scientific works, which corresponds to the needs of the present. As a look at the inventory . . . shows, our library has been raised hereby to an all-round people's library, which even educated circles allow."[70] The secretary of a conference for *Borromäusverein* members in 1906 reported that "conspicuous this time were demands for more educational works. [In addition,] a number of *Verein* leaders wished that the newest literature were given more consideration, especially non-Catholic material . . .".[71] And a *Borromäusverein* report in 1909 concluded: "As to the question, which books in the associational and library lists were most often chosen, answers were given that show how important the enlightenment of the [Catholic library movement has become]."[72] Catholic readers in Imperial Germany, we may safely conclude, utilized both public and private space for resolving the demands of confession, knowledge, and respectability.

Showcasing one's regard for books as a way of marking social distinctions implied the development of tastes approved by the dominant elites. Books reflecting these tastes found their way into parish and home libraries. Such books included histories that established Germany's national superiority. Through publications like *The Fatherland's Home Library*, Catholics learned how to read history "correctly": how to recognize national heroes like Goethe, Fichte, and Kant; how to understand the Revolution of 1848/9 as a false beginning to Germany's national destiny because of the influence of "radicals" and the overwhelming strength of "particularism"; and how to revere the magical powers of Bismarck in bringing order out of chaos.[73] And while they would have objected to accounts placing the Reformation at the center of German history, Catholics eagerly supported much of the official narrative. The library at St. Walburga's parish in Bornheim, for example, offered a two-volume history of Prussia's greatest princes called *In the Brilliance of the King's Crown*, an illustrated work called *The Wars of Liberation 1813– 1815*, Theodor Fontane's *Prisoner of War*, and the obligatory biography of Bismarck.[74] Histories of the Franco-Prussian War, like the one that "thrilled" the young Catholic Adolf Hitler at his home in Linz, were increasingly attractive.[75] By checking out and purchasing these and other emblems of German nationalism, such as the poetry of Germany's classic authors, Catholics exhibited their immersion in the rhythms and myths of the German past. In this way, they hoped to establish themselves as custodians of the dominant culture, affirming their superior qualifications for citizenship.[76] "A hand edition of the classics for home use," one Catholic observed in 1912, is necessary "if the totality of their intellectual treasury is to be imparted to the German people."[77]

Another type of book to be found in a Catholic library would have to do with natural science. Catholics fervently embraced science and technology and passed over the threshold between faith and reason naturally. "We common children of man believe of course," a popular apologist wrote in 1899, "that the contemporary blossoming of natural science is the associated fruit of Christian culture."[78] Belief in the unity of truth, invoked earlier in the nineteenth century to forfend religion from the claims of science, was now to be understood as the grounds on which science was affirmed. The fathers at the First Vatican Council in 1869 lent authority to this view, when they refuted fideistic epistemologies that were insufficiently deferent to the positive contributions that reason makes to knowledge.[79] Accordingly, proposals for the improvement of parish libraries after 1890 included demands for more science books, and the *Borromäusverein* took steps to meet them.[80] In 1890 the *Verein*'s list of recommended books contained no scientific titles out of a collection of some 9,700. Ten years later, books had been added for the study of astronomy, anthropology, geology, botany, and zoology. By 1911, the association offered volumes on the scientific method, on conducting experiments at home, and on Darwinian theory.[81] Catholics also read special primers and instructional books on how to comprehend *wissenschaftliche* works without succumbing to a materialist ideology that makes people, according to one observer, "slaves of nature."[82] In and through their consumption of science, Catholics showed that they recognized both empirical and trans-empirical realities. They demonstrated their readiness to take part in a world dramatically shaped by the application of new scientific knowledge. Because this readiness was a requirement for inclusion in the culture, the accumulation of scientific knowledge amounted to cultural capital that could be drawn upon for negotiating social acceptance.

The presence of these books in parishes and in the Catholic home makes it quite plain that in the Imperial era there was no neat discrimination between Catholic and Protestant reading cultures,[83] no ready subscription to the rules and disciplines preserving Catholics from modern writing set on high, no set or accurate definition of what constituted acceptable cultural acquisition. But what about pious reading material? If there is to be a *Mentalitätsgeschichte* of German Catholics even in the early twentieth century, historians will have to take material such as prayer cards and pamphlets, parish congregationals, apologetic tracts, religious songbooks, catechisms, and first communion literature seriously.[84] The Catholic folk education movement, after all, which was structured as an understanding of faith in the light of what modern philosophy, science, and culture brought forward, was about adding books to parish and home libraries, not replacing what was already there. Does not such material, which filled bookshelves and sock drawers in homes all across Catholic Germany, establish the cultural particularism (read: ultramontane exclusivity) of the Catholic confessional "milieu?"

The evidence suggests otherwise. In their detailed 1993 study of the Catholic "milieu," the Working Circle for Contemporary Church History in Münster argued that catechisms helped Catholics form a traditionalist and consistent "view of reality."[85] Yet by the 1890s catechists were introducing works that followed the "scientific" and "pedagogical foundations of modernity," in part to meet the Protestant charge that priests were to blame for Catholic "inferiority."[86] By 1900, widely popular missionary literature was no longer cast in the time-honored hagiographic style, but presented "scientific" accounts of regions and peoples, often with disparaging ethnographic information included.[87] A 1908 songbook explained the meaning of the hymn "Oh Unconquered Hero of God, Saint Michael" (the Archangel), which was sung in the dioceses of Paderborn, Cologne, Osnabrück, and Hildesheim, by referring to the battle with the dragon in Schiller's *Siegfriedssage*.[88] Other hymns extolled both Pope and Kaiser, reflecting the broad nationalization of the Catholic masses.[89] An 1887 pamphlet on the holy scapular of Saint Simon Stock described the validity of the cult on the basis of Catholic tradition, but also on the basis of almost Rankean research into contemporary written testimonials in the relevant archives. These letters, wrote the author, were full "and detailed in all the particulars," which would remove doubt even from "the most incredulous intellect."[90] An 1846 confirmation prayer began with the words "You Spirit of Truth . . ."; a prayer for the same occasion in 1887 began: "Come, O Spirit of *Wissenschaft* . . ."[91]

These examples, drawn from the very heart of "ultramontane" religious culture, illustrate the depth to which modern ideas and values had penetrated German Catholicism by 1914. Put another way, they reflect an abiding commitment to traditional theologies even as these theologies were re-worked to encompass new ideas. This research cautions against over-emphasizing the success of the clergy in creating a reactionary subculture against modern influences.[92] Their reading habits suggest that Catholics in Imperial Germany divested themselves of some of their counter-cultural presumptions and became more comprehensively implicated in the discourses, vocabularies, and literature of "modern knowledge." Confessional distinctiveness and antimodernism were not fundamental constants of Catholic *mentalité* and ways of life. The boundaries separating official German intellectual and aesthetic culture from the Catholic "milieu," in other words, have been drawn too sharply. We need more studies that explore the innumerable shifts in perspective, intellectual changes, and attitudinal adjustments involved in marrying faith with the modern thought-world. One possible approach, demonstrated recently by Robert Bireley in his study of the Catholic Counter Reformation, stresses the supple process of negotiation that continuously fine-tunes Catholicism in changing circumstances. This "refashioning of Catholicism," Bireley wants to say, is threaded deeply and inextricably in the outlook of a religion that expresses itself as culture-forming.[93] Far from abandoning their faith tradition in Imperial Germany, Catholics sought to harmonize it with the attitudes, ideals, and axioms of the dominant culture. This "process of confessional inculturation," as it might be called, allowed Catholics to express traditional religious and modern secular identities simultaneously.[94] Catholics did not want to languish in the perilous no man's land between spiritual allegiance and cultural respectability; they desired cultural elision, a negotiated equipoise. The deportment and usage of parish reading rooms and home libraries after 1890 bear this interpretation out. In 1936, a member of the *Borromäusverein* observed what these libraries had in fact become: sources of religious renewal as well as "yardsticks for [measuring] the intellectual level and status of the family." A "house book must not only be authentically Catholic," he concluded, "but authentically German as well."[95]

Notes

1. Historisches Archiv des Erzbistums Köln (hereafter, AEK), Generalia I, 20.6, 5, Versen to Generalvikariat, 12 March 1907.
2. Quoted in Thomas Michael Loome, *Liberal Catholicism–Reform Catholicism–Modernism. A Contribution to a New Orientation in Modernist Research* (Mainz: Matthias-Grünewald-Verlag, 1979), p. 30.
3. At the August 1906 Fulda Bishops' Conference, every bishop in Germany endorsed a letter to the Holy See noting the "namentlich aus Laienkreisen stammenden Wünsche auf Erweiterung der Erlaubnis zum Lesen verbotener Bücher" and asking that parish priests be permitted to exercise the "Vollmacht dispensandi ad legendum libros prohibitos": Erwin Gatz (ed.), *Akten der Fuldaer Bischofskonferenz*, Vol. 3: *1900–1919* (Mainz: Matthias-Grünewald-Verlag, 1985), p. 93. See also "Der Index und die Seelsorge," *Pastoralblatt* 39 (1905): 8–9. Concerns over what Catholics read were always gravest in mixed confessional communities. See, for example, the letter of Father Baursch to Generalvikariat, AEK Generalia I, 20.6, 5, 18 June 1896.
4. For the effects of secularization on the Catholic Church in Germany, see James J. Sheehan, *German History, 1770–1866* (New York: Oxford University Press, 1989), pp. 243–6 and Karl Erlinghagen, *Katholisches Bildungsdefizit in Deutschland* (Freiburg: Herder Verlag, 1965), pp. 18–19. Secularization left a searing mark on Catholic memory throughout the nineteenth century. Hermann Herz, the central figure in the Catholic folk education movement during the Imperial era, had a lively bitterness towards the "Kirchenfeindliche Beamtenschaft" in Baden that had shut Catholics out of the universities and had forced them, "nach und nach," into a minority intellectual position: see Herz, *Alban Stolz* (Mönchen-Gladbach: Volksvereins-Verlag, 1916), pp. 8–14.
5. Most historians attribute accelerated literacy among Protestants to inherent theologies, such as Pietism and Sola Scriptura, not to the institutional advantages they enjoyed. See, for example, Susanna Schmidt, *"Handlanger der Vergänglichkeit." Zur Literatur des katholischen Milieus 1800–1950* (Paderborn: Ferdinand Schöningh, 1993), pp. 9–10 and Hans Maier, "Lese-Zeichen. 150 Jahre Borromäusverein," in Norbert Trippen and Horst Patenge (eds), *Bausteine für eine lesende Kirche. Borromäusverein und katholische Büchereiarbeit* (Mainz: Matthias-Grünewald-Verlag, 1996), pp. 14–35, here 22–6. Confession remained an important factor in German literacy throughout the

century. In 1871 Catholics were twice as likely as Protestants and Jews to be unable to read. See Harvey J. Graff, *The Legacies of Literacy. Continuities and Contradictions in Western Culture and Society* (Bloomington and Indianapolis, IN: Indiana University Press, 1987), p. 286.

6. Unsigned Article, "Vom gemeinverständlichen, populären Vortrag," *Beilagen zu der religiösen Zeitschrift: Der Katholik. Erster Supplementband* (1822), pp. 415–27. Plans for Bauern- and Dorfbibliotheken in the late eighteenth century saw a role for priests as librarians and teachers but primarily as "Vorleser": see Rudolf Schenda, *Volk ohne Buch. Studien zur Sozialgeschichte der populären Lesestoff, 1770–1910* (Frankfurt: Vittorio Klostermann, 1970), p. 215.

7. "Verzeichniß verbotener und der Confiskation unterliegender Schriften im Königreiche Baiern. Ausgezogen aus baierischen Intelligenzblättern," *Der Katholik* 4, 11 (1824): 251–6. One title of interest on p. 253: *Report of a Jew from Jerusalem named Ahasverus, who claims that he was at the crucifixion of Christ and until now has been kept alive by the almighty power of God.* See also Wolfram Siemann, "Ideenschmuggel. Probleme der Meinungskontrolle und das Los Deutscher Zensoren im 19. Jahrhundert," *Historische Zeitschrift* 245, 1 (1987): 92–4.

8. See, for example, Unsigned Article, "Unglauben und Aberglauben unsrer Zeit," *Der Katholik* 4, 11 (1824): 86–91.

9. Wolfgang Altgeld, *Katholizismus, Protestantismus, Judentum. Über religiös begründete Gegensätze und nationalreligiöse Ideen in der Geschichte des deutschen Nationalismus* (Mainz: Matthias-Grünewald-Verlag, 1992), pp. 160–1. See also Kurt Nowak, *Geschichte des Christentums in Deutschland. Religion, Politik und Gesellschaft vom Ende der Aufklärung bis zur Mitte des 20. Jahrhunderts* (Munich: Verlag C. H. Beck, 1995), pp. 65–6.

10. Unsigned Review of *Der Kampf der Finsterniß mit dem Lichte des neunzehnten Jahrhunderts* by Moriz von der Weser (Düsseldorf, 1822) in *Der Katholik* 2, 6 (1822): 201.

11. David Blackbourn, *The Long Nineteenth Century. A History of Germany, 1780–1914* (New York and Oxford: Oxford University Press, 1998), p. 41.

12. This was a frequent argument to protect Catholic truth claims against historical relativization. A Catholic might be disturbed by attacks on the historical validity of his Church, one writer observed in 1838. "Er wird aber auch nicht erschrecken, wenn das Schifflein Petri von den Wellen hart bedrängt wird, weil er weiß, daß der Herr, wenn er

auch zu schlafen scheint, dennoch wacht, und seine Kirche stets schützen wird": see Unsigned Article, "Vom Niederrhein," *Der Katholik* 18, 67 (1838): CXXV. See also Unsigned Article, "Betrachtung über die Erhaltung der christlichen Religion unter immerwährenden, ihr drohenden Gefahren bis auf unsere Tage," *Theologisch-praktische Monatschrift* 12 (1833): 12–3. For an excellent introduction to early Protestant historicism, see Kurt Nowak, "Geschichte–der höchste Gegenstand der Religion. Schleiermachers Beitrag zur Historik in den Reden 'Über die Religion' (1799)," *Theologische Literaturzeitung* 124, 6 (1999): 583–96.

13. Unsigned Review of *Ansichten und Vorschläge in Bezug auf das öffentliche Unterrichtswesen* (Innsbruck, 1836) in *Der Katholik* 17, 63 (1837): 92–3. The subsumption of secular knowledge within revealed truth was the backbone of Catholic epistemology. See M. X., review of *Jugendbibliothek*, Vol. 4: *Sittenschule zur Erziehung für Gott und Vaterland. Gesammelt von einem katholischen Geistlichen* (Munich, 1822) in *Der Katholik* 2, 4 (1822): 221 and Unsigned Article, "Die Popularisierung der Wissenschaft," *Historisch-politische Blätter* 45 (1860): 448–9.

14. *Ansichten und Vorschläge*, p. 95.

15. This interpretation admittedly needs to be balanced by recognizing that especially in the Vormärz, Catholic and Protestant conservatives adopted a similar posture towards the secularist foe, and that many individuals strove, unsuccessfully to be sure, towards the reunion of the Churches. See Christoph Weber, *Aufklärung und Orthodoxie am Mittelrhein 1820–1850* (Munich: Verlag Ferdinand Schöningh, 1973), p. 179 and Manfred Fleischer, "Lutheran and Catholic Reunionists in the Age of Bismarck," *Church History* 38, 1 (1969): 44. Light–dark imagery, however, was pervasive in early nineteenth-century popular readers and pious literature. For example, according to one Catholic author, "Nicht nur alle Zeitungsblätter, sondern selbst die meisten in einem bessern Tone abgefaßten protestantischen Schriften sind voll des eigenen Lobes und Rühmens, als Leuchte unter ihnen ein Licht, so hell wie die Mittagssonne; da hingegen bei uns Katholiken nichts als Blindheit und ewige Finsterniß zu Hause seyen": Franz Geiger, "Der lichtvolle Protestantismus," *Der Katholik* 3, 8 (1823): 35. In their stimulating essay on religious *mentalité*, Olaf Blaschke and Frank-Michael Kuhlemann discuss the power of the "dualistic disposition" in modern German Christian history: see Blaschke and Kuhlemann, "Religion in Geschichte und Gesellschaft. Sozialhistorische Perspektiven für die vergleichende Erforschung religiöser

Mentalitäten und Milieus," in Blaschke and Kuhlemann (eds), *Religion im Kaiserreich: Milieus–Mentalitäten–Krisen* (Gütersloh: Chr. Kaiser/Gütersloher Verlagshaus, 1996), p. 18.

16. Sources for this section include Unsigned Article, "Der positive Lichtkern des Protestantismus und der negativ protestierende Katholicismus," *Der Katholik* 2, 6 (1822): 354–7; Unsigned Article, "Wie Pabst, und katholische Fürsten noch heut zu Tage in öffentlichen Schriften behandelt werden," *Theologisch-praktische Monatschrift* 12 (1833): 41–51; Unsigned Review of *Katholisches Wochenblatt aus Ost- und Westpreußen für alle Stände* by Ed. Herzog (ed.) in *Historisch-politische Blätter* 10 (1842): 639–40; Unsigned Article, "Probestücke deutscher Preßfreiheit: Das Hetzbüchlein," *Der Katholik* 22, 84 (1842): 1–11; and Heinrich Keiter, *Konfessionelle Brunnenvergiftung. Die wahre Schmach des Jahrhunderts* (Regensburg and Leipzig: Verlag von Heinrich Keiter, 1896). For an excellent study of the "liberal anti-Catholic imagination," see Michael B. Gross, "The Strange Case of the Nun in the Dungeon, or German Liberalism as a Convent Atrocity Story," *German Studies Review* 23, 1 (2000): 69–84.

17. "Betrachtung über die Erhaltung der christlichen Religion," p. 7.

18. Emmanuel Todd, *The Causes of Progress: Culture, Authority and Change*, trans. Richard Boulind (Oxford: Basil Blackwell, 1987), p. 37.

19. R. R., "Nothwendige Warnung der Katholiken im Königreich Württemberg, Großherzogthum Baden und andern Ländern vor dem Lesen eines Unterhaltungsblattes, betitelt: Der Armen-Freund, und zu Stuttgart herauskommt," *Der Katholik* 1, 1 (1821): 256–81 and L. Wolf, "Der Armenfreund, ein Unterhaltungsblatt für alle Stände 1821," *Der Katholik* 1, 2 (1821): 89–94. One issue included this ode to Zwingli: "Die Tage jener Fey'r geweiht,/ Wo Zwingli einst in früh'rer Zeit/ Sein großes Werk begonnen,/ Wie waren sie dem Mann so theu'r,/ Er zeigte Klar, was später wir/ Durch dieses Werk gewonnen!/ Du lebst in deinen Schriften,/ Sie werden, wenn du droben bist,/ Wo dein geliebter Zwingli ist,/ Noch vielen Segen stiften": see pp. 89–90. On the problem of Catholics being exposed to Protestant reading material, see Pastar to Generalvikariat, AEK Generalia I, 20.6, 1, 26 August 1825 and Bierdranger to Generalvikariat, AEK Generalia I, 20.6, 1, 1 December 1826. Priests complained regularly about the circulation of Protestant Bibles among Catholics. See, for example, Waner to Generalvikariat, AEK Generalia I, 20.6, 2, 7 November 1854.

20. Letters by parish priests to their bishops and vicars general are powerful sources of information on the development of Catholic reading habits. See Marcos to Generalvikariat, AEK Generalia I, 20.6, 2, 29 February 1848 and Dolomen to Generalvikariat, AEK Generalia I, 20.6, 2, 13 August 1852. See also N. "Vorschlag zu einer zweckmäßigen Leihbibliothek von Erbauungsschriften für das Landvolk," *Der Katholik* 16, 62 (1836): 167–73 and Unsigned Article, "Rheinpreußen," *Der Katholik* 20, 78 (1840): CII. Priests noted that books with no imprimatur appeared with increasing frequency in Catholic bookstores. See the letter of Father Steinhausen, the pastor of St Martin's parish in Cologne, to the vicar general, AEK Generalia I, 18.1, 2, 19 October 1842.

21. Haap to Generalvikariat, AEK Generalia I, 20.6, 4, 17 November 1869. See also Heuser to Generalvikariat, AEK Generalia I, 20.6, 2, 13 January 1845.

22. Heyden to Generalvikariat, AEK Generalia I, 20.6, 2, 12 May 1846. Catholics read "unter Bestimmung meines Beichtvaters" into the twentieth century. See the letter of Lorenz Heitzer, a librarian in Altenessen, to authorities in Cologne, AEK Generalia I, 20.6, 5, 15 December 1901.

23. Zietz to Generalvikariat, AEK Generalia I, 20.6, 2, 6 November 1850.

24. Protestants were linked to the *schlechte Presse* throughout the first half of the century; Jews came under scrutiny especially after 1848/9, when they were associated with revolutionary journals and newspapers: "Viele unserer Zeitungen sind auch in den Händen von Juden, deren *spiritus principalis* ein grimmiger Haß gegen das Christenthum und alles christliche ist": Unsigned Article, "Die Zeitungspresse und das Volk," *Historisch-politische Blätter* 24 (1849): 1–2 and Unsigned Article, "Der Protestantismus und die schlechte Presse," *Der Katholik* 25 (1845): 1–2. Accordingly, devotionals after 1850 increasingly included prayers for the conversion of all non-Catholics: "Befreie die Unwissenden von der Verführung falscher Lehrer, die Gelehrten von der Täuschung ihrer Leidenschaften . . . Erhöre unser Gebet für das noch nicht gläubige Judenvolk. Laß dasselbe das wahre Licht, welches Christus ist, erkennen, damit es von seinem Unglauben befreit . . .": *Andacht der Filial-Bruderschaft des heiligen und unbefleckten Herzen Mariä zur Bekehrung der Sünder in der Pfarrkirche zu Bergheimerdorf*, AEK Generalia I, 18.1, 6, 1869. See also *Gedenkblatt der Filial-Bruderschaft des heiligen und unbefleckten Herzens Mariä zur Bekehrung der Sünder*, AEK Generalia I, 18.1, 6, 1856.

25. Quoted in Jakob Kraft, *Wilhelm Arnoldi, Bischof von Trier. Ein Lebensbild* (Trier: Verlag der Fr. Lintz'schen Buchhandlung, 1865), pp. 192–3.
26. This view is widely shared among scholars. See, for example, Thomas Nipperdey, *Deutsche Geschichte 1800–1866. Bürgerwelt und starker Staat* (Munich: Verlag C. H. Beck, 1983), pp. 412–13, Michael Klöcker, *Katholisch–von der Wiege bis zur Bahre. Eine Lebensmacht im Zerfall?* (Munich: Kösel-Verlag GmbH & Co., 1991), pp. 23–7, and Urs Altermatt, "Katholizismus: Antimodernismus mit modernen Mittlen?" in Urs Altermatt *et al.* (eds), *Moderne als Problem des Katholizismus* (Regensburg:Verlag Friedrich Pustet, 1995), pp. 33–50.
27. *Die katholische Kirche und die Forderungen der Jetztzeit. Ein Wort des Ernstes und der Mahnung an Alle, welche es mit der Kirche und Menschheit gut meinen, mit Rücksicht auf die Eingabe der 370 Geistlichen an den Erzbischof von Köln* (Cologne, 1849), p. 12 in AEK Generalia I, 18.1, 4, 1849.
28. AEK Generalia I, 18.1, 4–8, 1847–1870.
29. This card came from the pilgrimage church in Neuenhoven. AEK Generalia I, 18.1, 8, 1866.
30. *Ehren-Kranz der schönsten Blüthen und Früchte aus dem Garten der heiligen Kirche der ohne Makel der Erbsünde empfangenen allerseligsten Jungfrau-Mutter Maria* (Cologne, 1858), p. 58 in AEK Generalia I, 18.1, 8, 1858.
31. *Allerseelen-Octav in der Pfarrkirche zu Jackerath* (Erkelenz, 1862), p. 8 in AEK Generalia I, 18.1, 9, 1862.
32. Peter Uwe Hohendahl, *Building a National Literature. The Case of Germany, 1830–1870*, trans. Renate Baron Franciscono (Ithaca, NY and London: Cornell University Press, 1989), p. 303.
33. Unsigned Article, "In Sachen der katholischen Kalender," *Der Katholik* 3/4 (1851/52): 466–7.
34. Unsigned Article, "Katholische Volksliteratur," *Historish-politische Blätter* 32 (1853): 899–904. For a wonderful Catholic diatribe against the modern novel, see Unsigned Article, "Bücher and Broschüren-schau," *Historisch-politische Blätter* 58 (1866): 877–84. The best new studies of Catholic literature in the nineteenth century are Schmidt, *"Handlanger der Vergänglichkeit"* and Jutta Osinski, *Katholizismus und deutsche Literatur im 19. Jahrhundert* (Paderborn: F. Schöningh, 1993).
35. Simon Hyde, "Roman Catholicism and the Prussian State in the Early 1850s," *Central European History* 24, 2 (1991): 107–8; Ernst Heinen, *Katholizismus und Gesellschaft. Das katholische Vereinswesen*

zwischen Revolution und Reaktion (1848/49–1853/54) (Idstein: Wissenschaftlicher Verlag Dr. Ullrich Schulz-Kirchner, 1993), p. 50; and Ronald J. Ross, *The Failure of Bismarck's Kulturkampf. Catholicism and State Power in Imperial Germany, 1871–1887* (Washington, DC: The Catholic University of America Press, 1998), pp. 158–61.

36. Nipperdey *Deutsche Geschichte*, p. 413. For a description of how Catholics could be "completely" isolated intellectually and culturally by the 1870s, see Erlinghagen, *Katholisches Bildungsdefizit*, p. 17. Contemporary priests, with fingers closer to the literary pulse of the people, would have disagreed: "Leider ist die Indifferenz gegen die schlechte Presse im Allgemeinen schon so groß, daß das Halten und Lesen schlechter Bücher kaum als eine Sünde gilt": Unsigned Article, "Der katholische Seelsorger und die Presse," *Pastoralblatt* 2, 8 (1868): 101.

37. Keiter, *Konfessionelle Brunnenvergiftung*, p. 36.

38. *Der Görresverein zur Massenverbreitung guter Volksschriften für das Erzbistum Köln* (Cologne, 1873), p. 2. See also Matthias Schollen, *Echo der Gegenwart. Aelteste Aachener Zeitung 1848–1909. Blätter der Erinnerung zu seinem 60jährigen Bestehen* (Aachen: Verlag des Echo der Gegenwart, 1909), p. 15 and the letter from eight parish priests in Cologne to Generalvikariat, AEK Generalia I, 20.6, 4, 9 February 1871.

39. Unsigned Article, "Der katholische Seelsorger und die Presse," *Pastoralblatt* 2, 7 (1868): 86.

40. For an assortment of early 1870s newspapers in the Archdiocese of Cologne, see AEK Generalia I, 26.4, 1. On the "Ghettomentalität" of book associations during the *Kulturkampf*, see Andrea Asselmann, *Volksbüchereiarbeit im Spiegel der Zeitschrift "Borromäusblätter/ Die Bücherwelt" (1903–1933). Untersuchung und Bewertung ausgewählter Beiträge zu bibliothekarischen Fachfragen* (Bonn: Fachhochschule für das öffentliche Bibliothekswesen Bonn, 1992), p. 5 and Norbert Trippen, "150 Jahre katholische Büchereiarbeit. Von der Gründung des Borromäusvereins 1845 bis zu seiner Neustrukturierung 1995," in N. Trippen and H. Patenge (eds), *Bausteine für eine lesende Kirche*, pp. 41–2. The prominent editor Franz Hülskamp reported in 1871 that increasing numbers of Catholics formed reading circles to escape the "poison of the lending libraries": Franz Hülskamp, "Katholische Lesezirkel," *Literarischer Handweiser, zunächst für das katholische Deutschland* 10, 110 (1871): 522.

41. Ross, *Bismarck's Kulturkampf*, p. 5. See also Altermatt, "Katholizismus: Antimodernismus mit modernen Mitteln?", p. 38. For a

comprehensive investigation of the cultural implications of confessional acrimony in Imperial Germany, see Helmut Walser Smith's excellent *German Nationalism and Religious Conflict. Culture, Ideology, Politics, 1870–1914* (Princeton, NJ: Princeton University Press, 1995). Gangolf Hübinger also emphasizes culture in his concise essay "Confessionalism" in Roger Chickering (ed.), *Imperial Germany: A Historiographical Companion* (Westport, CT and London: Greenwood Press, 1996), pp. 156–84.

42. A succinct study of worsening confessional relations in Imperial Germany is Martin Baumeister, *Parität und katholische Inferiorität. Untersuchungen zur Stellung des Katholizismus im Deutschen Kaiserreich* (Paderborn: Ferdinand Schöningh, 1987). Konrad Jarausch discusses escalating fears of ultramontane Catholics among Protestant university students in *Students, Society, and Politics in Imperial Germany. The Rise of Academic Illiberalism* (Princeton, NJ: Princeton University Press, 1982), pp. 377–9. For rising anti-Catholic prejudice in Wilhelmine Politics, see Margaret Lavinia Anderson, "Interdenominationalism, Clericalism, Pluralism: The *Zentrumsstreit* and the Dilemma of Catholicism in Wilhelmine Germany," *Central European History* 21, 4 (1988): 371–2.

43. Hübinger, "Confessionalism," p. 159.

44. See, for example, Jonathan Sperber, *Popular Catholicism in Nineteenth-Century Germany* (Princeton, NJ: Princeton University Press, 1984); Irmtraud Götz von Olenhusen, "Die Ultramontanisierung des Klerus. Das Beispiel der Erzdiözese Freiburg," in Wilfried Loth (ed.), *Deutscher Katholizismus im Umbruch zur Moderne* (Stuttgart: Kohlhammer, 1991), pp. 46–75; and Christoph Weber, "Ultramontanismus als katholischer Fundamentalismus," in Loth (ed.), *Deutscher Katholizismus*, pp. 20–45.

45. Baumeister, *Parität und katholische Inferiorität*, pp. 89–91.

46. Thomas Mergel, *Zwischen Klasse und Konfession. Katholisches Bürgertum im Rheinland 1794–1914* (Göttingen: Vandenhoeck & Ruprecht, 1994), p. 161 and Blackbourn, *Long Nineteenth Century*, p. 363.

47. The need to read was firmly established by 1884: "Die großen Umgestaltungen, welche mit allen socialen Zuständen in den letzten fünfzig Jahren vorgegangen sind, haben auch in allen Klassen der Gesellschaft ein Bedürfniß genährt, das früher in einem solchen Grade unbekannt war. Dies ist das Bedürfniß, zu lesen, welches mit der fortschreitenden Leichtigkeit der Befriedigung tagtäglich allgemeiner hervortritt": see Der Central-Verwaltung-Ausschuß des

Vereins vom heil. Karl Borromäus, "Ueber den Verein vom heil. Karl Borromäus," *Der Katholik* 64, 2 (1884): 219–24. It is also interesting to note David Mitch's observation that literacy among the lower orders in Victorian England was "both a private and a public decision . . . For those segments of the English population for whom literacy clearly improved their earnings ability, this gain was almost certainly likely to outweigh the costs of acquiring literacy": David F. Mitch, *The Rise of Popular Literacy in Victorian England. The Influence of Private Choice and Public Policy* (Philadelphia: University of Pennsylvania Press, 1992), p. 201. There is little of the anti-intellectualism that supposedly characterized the Catholic "milieu" in *this* statement: "In unseren Tagen wird so viel von 'Gebildeten' gesprochen . . . 'Gebildete' gibt es überall, und jeder, auch der einfache Mann aus dem Volke denkt sich etwas Bestimmtes, wenn er von einem 'Gebildeten' reden hört": P. Dr. Hugo Höver, O. Cist., "Bildung und Wissen als Ziel des 'Gebildeten,'" *Der Katholik* 93, 1 (1913): 233.

48. Unsigned Article, "Der Index und die Seelsorge," *Pastoralblatt* 39 (1905): 12. Margaret Anderson points out that, in general, "the German church was less puritanical. And the constant, if unacknowledged, intellectual presence of the Protestant 'competition' made Germany from the outset unfavorable soil for any kind of anti-intellectual fideism": Margaret Lavinia Anderson, "The Limits of Secularization: On the Problem of the Catholic Revival in Nineteenth-Century Germany," *The Historical Journal* 38, 3 (1995): 657.

49. Baumeister, *Parität und katholische Inferiorität*, pp. 14–31. Baumeister relates the contemporary general rule: "Je höher die Regierungsebene, desto weniger Katholiken findet man" (see p. 22).

50. On 30 July 1896 Archbishop André Aiuti, the Apostolic Nuncio to Germany in Bavaria, sent a letter to Archbishop Krementz of Cologne expressing official concern about the disproportion in the universities by confession: "La question est de l'importance la plus grande. . . . [The German bishops should identify] la route à suivre pour arriver un jour à la résoudre ou du moins pour arriver à améliorer l'état actual de façon à conjurer les dangers ultérieurs que la continuation de cet état de choses inspire." The bishops assembled at Dortmund three weeks later and gave the matter their full attention: Erwin Gatz (ed.), *Akten der Fuldaer Bischofskonferenz*, Vol. 2: *1888–1899* (Mainz: Matthias-Grünewald-Verlag, 1979), pp. 393–4 and 400.

51. Hermann Herz, "Caritas, Volkslektüre und Borromäusverein," *Caritas. Zeitschrift für die Werke der Nächstenliebe im katholischen Deutschland* 10 (1905): 179–80. For the first fifty years of the *Borromäusverein*,

see August Reichensperger, *Die Gründung und Thätigkeit des Vereins vom heiligen Karl Borromäus* (Cologne: Bachem, 1895) and Meier, "Lese-Zeichen." pp. 14–35.

52. See the speech of Father Haffner, Domkapitular in Mainz, in the *Verhandlungen der XXXI. General-Versammlung der Katholiken Deutschlands in Amberg* (Amberg: Druck und Kommissions-Verlag von J. Habbel, 1884), pp. 179–80.

53. Fr. Otten, "Schriftenkunde und Bildung: Analphabetenstatistik," *Der katholische Seelsorger* 7 (1895): 510. For an informative study of the development of German "Leselust," see Rolf Engelsing, *Analphabetentum und Lektüre. Zur Sozialgeschichte des Lesens in Deutschland zwischen feudaler und industrieller Gesellschaft* (Stuttgart: J. B. Metzlersche Verlagsbuchhandlung, 1973).

54. Wilhelm Spael, *Das Buch im Geisteskampf. 100 Jahre Borromäusverein* (Bonn: Verlag des Borromäus-Vereins, 1950), p. 372.

55. Mergel, *Zwischen Klasse und Konfession*, p. 235.

56. Blackbourn, *Long Nineteenth Century*, pp. 361–2.

57. Johannes Braun, *Ausbau des Borromäus-Vereins* (Bonn, 1911), p. 6.

58. Unsigned Article, "Zur Verständigung," *Zeitschrift für das freie Bildungswesen und Literatur-Blatt* 1 (1898): 5–7 in AEK Generalia I, 18.1, 12, 1898.

59. A good summary of the network of Catholic associations devoted to popular education is G. Hölscher, "Die katholischen Organisationen für den Büchervertrieb," *Soziale Kultur* 32 (1912): 72–88. The original goal of the *Borromäusverein*, in fact, was not to build parish libraries but the creation of libraries in Catholic homes, which were to be domestic "apothecaries" for combating the "poison" of "trashy and dirty literature." Quoted in Oskar Köhler, "Bücher als Wegmarken des deutschen Katholizismus," in Die Vereinigung des katholischen Buchhandels, e.V. ed., *Der katholische Buchhandel Deutschlands. Seine Geschichte bis zum Jahre 1967* (Frankfurt a. M.: Vereinigung d. kath. Buchhandels e. V., 1967), p. 102.

60. Hermann Herz, "Die Volksbildungsorganisationen in Deutschland: Der Verein vom hl. Karl Borromäus," *Volksbildungsarchiv. Beiträge zur wissenschaftlichen Vertiefung der Volksbildungsbestrebungen* 2, 3/4 (1911): 455 and "Bericht des Borromäusvereins," *Caritas. Zeitschrift für die Werke der Nächstenliebe im katholischen Deutschland* 18 (1912/13): 55.

61. The editor was Hedwig Dransfeld of the *Christliche Frau*, one of the first female deputies of the Catholic Center Party. See her speech given to the sixteenth General Caritastag in Dresden on 26 September

1911 entitled "Die Bekämpfung der Schundliteratur," *Caritas. Zeitschrift für die Werke der Nächstenliebe im katholischen Deutschland* 17, 4 (1912): 126.

62. See Matth. Bretz, *Die Lektüre und ihre erzieherischen Wirkungen auf den Menschen* (Bonn: J. F. Carthaus, 1906), p. 3; Hermann Herz, "Die Massenverbreitung guter Bücher durch volkstümliche Bibliotheken," *Soziale Revue* 7 (1907): 47–8; and the report of the "XXI. Generalversammlung des Verbandes 'Arbeiterwohl' in Düsseldorf am 5. August 1902," *Arbeiterwohl. Organ des Verbandes katholischer Industrieller und Arbeiterfreunde* 22 (1902): 196.

63. The possession of a home library was a hallmark of modern German culture, of which Germans took pains to boast. The contents of such a library were displayed at the 1910 World Exposition in Brussels: see *Das Buch im deutschen Hause. Katalog einer deutschen Familien-Bibliothek auf der Welt-Ausstellung in Brüssel 1910. Zusammengestellt von K. F. Koehler* (Leipzig: Druck von Fr. Richter, G.m.b.H., 1911), p. 3. The only Catholic author, incidentally, to make the list was Enrica von Handel-Mazzetti, whose 1906 novel, *Jesse und Maria*, achieved unheard-of renown among Protestants for being sufficiently "tendenzlos." The works of the unbiased Martin Luther, of course, also made the cut. For an introduction to Handel-Mazzetti and the cultural context in which her work was received, see Jeffrey T. Zalar, "Enrica von Handel-Mazzetti (1871–1955)," in Mary Reichardt (ed.), *Catholic Women Writers: A Bio-Bibliographical Sourcebook* (Westport, CT and London: Greenwood Press, 2001). A monographic study is Bernhard Doppler, *Katholische Literatur und Literaturpolitik. Enrica von Handel-Mazzetti: Eine Fallstudie* (Königstein/Ts: Hain, 1980).

64. For the implications of German *Bildung* for Catholics, see Jeffrey T. Zalar, "'Knowledge is Power': The *Borromäusverein* and Catholic Reading Habits in Imperial Germany," *The Catholic Historical Review* 86, 1 (2000): 20–46.

65. Vernon Lidtke writes: "It is estimated that around 1900 there were in Germany and Austria forty-five thousand book peddlers who were the chief suppliers of reading material to some twenty million people": see Lidtke, *The Alternative Culture. Socialist Labor in Imperial Germany* (New York and Oxford: Oxford University Press, 1985), p. 184. For literacy figures for Germany at this time, see Engelsing, *Analphabetentun und Lektüre*, pp. 96–100.

66. Schenda, *Volk ohne Buch*, pp. 104 and 244–5. See also Blackbourn, *Long Nineteenth Century*, pp. 390–1. As Margaret Stieg (lately Dalton), the prominent historian of German librarianship, puts it,

"Industrialization, urbanization, and universal primary education had created large numbers of readers with no pretensions to high culture, who demanded inexpensive, escapist reading. In response to this demand, publications of all kinds increased dramatically, especially the most noxious and noisome. Yellow journalism flourished. Cheap pornography was readily available and dime novels numerous": see Stieg, "The 1926 German Law to Protect Youth against Trash and Dirt: Moral Protectionism in a Democracy," *Central European History* 23, 1 (1990): 27.

67. See Adam Senger, *Volkslektüre und Volksbibliotheken. Sonderabdruck der Passauer 'theol.-prakt. Monats-Schrift'* (Bamberg: Schmidtsche Buchhandlung, 1907), pp. 6–7 and Rudolf Schenda, *Die Lesestoff der kleinen Leute. Studien zur populären Literatur im 19. und 20. Jahrhundert* (Munich: Verlag C. H. Beck, 1976), pp. 90–1.

68. Herz, "Charitas, Volkslektüre und Borromäusverein," p. 181.

69. Studies that stress clerical reaction include Andrea Asselmann, "Volksbüchereiarbeit im Spiegel der Zeitschrift 'Borromäus-Blätter/ Die Bücherwelt' (1903–1933)," *Bibliothek Forschung und Praxis* 19, 3 (1995): 322–61 and Margaret S. Dalton, "The Borromäus Verein: Catholic Public Librarianship in Germany, 1845–1933," *Libraries & Culture* 31, 2 (1996): 409–21. It is true that there was shared agreement among the clergy that a "good book" was the "most successful and strongest enemy" of a bad one, and members of the German hierarchy wrote pastoral letters denouncing *risqué* literature throughout the Imperial period. Yet the clergy were hardly priggish. In 1909 in the Protestant-Liberal journal *Volksbildung* there were 110 entries on the "Kampf gegen die Schundliteratur." In the first ten years of its Catholic counterpart, the *Borromäus-Blätter/Bücherwelt* (1903–1913), there was all of one. So much for Catholic prudery. See *Volksbildung* 39 (1909): 535–6 and Johannes Braun, "Die Schund- und Schmutzliteratur und ihre Bekämpfung," *Die Bücherwelt* 7 (1910): 105–8 and 124–33. In a delicious bit of irony, Wolfram Siemann notes that the doyen of the Protestant *literati*, Thomas Mann, was a member of the Munich censorship advisory board in 1912/13: see Siemann, "Ideenschmuggel," p. 101. Two examples of pastoral letters are Michael Felix Korum (Trier), "Über die schlechte Lektüre" in Albert Pape (ed.), *Hirtenbriefe des deutschen Episkopats anläßlich der Fastenzeit 1910* (Paderborn: Druck und Verlag der Junfermann-schen Buchhandlung, 1910), pp. 22–37 and Felix von Hartmann (Münster), "Über die schlechten Bücher und Schriften," in Albert Pape (ed.), *Hirtenbriefe des deutschen Episkopats anläßlich der*

Fastenzeit 1912 (Paderborn: Druck und Verlag der Junfermannschen Buchhandlung, 1912), pp. 19–27. Rome, for its part, added a catch-all "lascivious or obscene" category to the normal list of condemned heretical and schismatic books in 1897, imposing frightening penalties on the rule-breaker: "Omnes et singuli scienter legentes, sine auctoritate Sedis Apostolicae, libros apostatarum et haereticorum haeresim propugnantes, nec non libros cuiusuis auctoris per Apostolicas Literas nominatim prohibitos, eosdemque libros retinentes, imprimentes et quomodolibet defendentes, excommunicationem ipso facto incurrent, Romano Pontifici speciali modo reservatam": see the "Decreta Generalia de Prohibitione et Censura Librorum," *Kirchliche Anzeiger für die Erzdiözese Köln* 37, 7 (1897): 48.

70. *Bücherverzeichnis des Vereins vom h. Karl Borromäus in der St. Josephspfarre in Eupen* (Eupen, 1893), p. 3.

71. *Nachrichten für die Vereine vom hl. Karl Borromäus* 4 (1906): p. V. Margaret Anderson has mentioned the ecumenism of the Volksverein's "Index of Social Literature" as evidence of Catholic interdenominationalism: see Anderson, "Interdenominationalism, Clericalism, Pluralism," p. 352. Others interested in assimilation, such as Hermann Herz, the editor of *Die Bücherwelt* in 1910, also recognized the need to develop wide-ranging tastes: "Ein Blick in die heutigen Vereins- und Bibliotheksgabenverzeichnisse zeigt, daß der Borromäusverein in immer größerem Umfang nichtkatholische Autoren berücksichtigt": see Herz, "Die Volksbildungsorganisationen in Deutschland," p. 456.

72. *Nachrichten für die Vereine vom hl. Karl Borromäus in Bonn* 8 (1910): VIII.

73. Hermann von Petersdorff, "Wie das deutsche Reich geworden ist 1848–1871," in *Vaterländische Hausbibliothek* Vol. 1 (Berlin: C. A. Weller, 1904), pp. 6, 34, and 72. I located this book at the Dombibliothek in Cologne.

74. *Bücherverzeichnis Pfarrarchiv St. Walburga in Bornheim-Walberberg* held at the Fernleihbibliothek des Borromäusvereins in Bonn.

75. Ian Kershaw, *Hitler. 1889–1936: Hubris* (New York and London: W. W. Norton & Co., 1998), p. 15. Rudolf Schenda notes that the market for youth books after 1900 was "überschwemmt" by books about the 1870 war. Catholics seemed particularly interested in war reports by, and the first-hand accounts, of priests: Schenda, *Die Lesestoff der kleinen Leute*, pp. 96–7.

76. Marion Kaplan writes similarly of German Jews: "Especially in Jewish families, the collected works of Goethe and Schiller – those mainstays of German middle-class respectability and *Bildung* – had

a vaunted place in the family repertoires. Jews played out, quite literally, their special attachment to what they defined as enlightened German culture. Indeed, their intense engagement with and (possibly conspicuous) display of these classics may be read as an 'overadaptation' reflecting the history as well as actual experiences of discrimination": M. Kaplan, *The Making of the Jewish Middle Class. Women, Family, and Identity in Imperial Germany* (New York and Oxford: Oxford University Press, 1991), p. 120. See also Blackbourn, *Long Nineteenth Century*, p. 392 and Eduard Arens, "Deutsche Lektüre," *Literarischer Handweiser, zunächst für alle Katholiken deutscher Zunge* 52, 6 (1914): 185.

77. Emil Ritter, "Herders Klassikerbibliothek," *Volkskunst. Monatschrift für Theater und verwandte Bestrebungen in den katholischen Vereinen* 1, 1 (1912): 44–5.

78. Ludwig von Hammerstein, S. J., *Ausgewählte Werke*, Vol. 3: *Gottesbeweise und moderner Atheismus, Teil II: Das Christentum und seine Gegner* (Trier: Paulinus Druckerei, 1899), p. 192.

79. After rejecting rationalist theories that did not open themselves to the transcendent, the fathers continued: "Verum etsi fides sit supra rationem, nulla tamen unquam inter fidem et rationem vera dissensio esse potest: cum idem Deus, qui mysteria revelat et fidem infundit, animo humano rationis lumen indiderit; Deus autem negare seipsum non possit, nec verum vero unquam contradicere": Dogmatic Constitution of the Catholic Faith *Dei Filius*, IV in *Acta et Decreta sacrosancti oecumenici concilii vaticani. Cum permultis aliis documentis ad concilium ejusque historiam spectantibus* (Freiburg: Herder, 1892), pp. 253–4.

80. See, for example, the *Nachrichten für die Vereine vom hl. Karl Borromäus* 2 (1904): 7.

81. *Verzeichniß, der von dem Verein vom heil. Karl Borromäus in Bonn empfohlenen Bücher für das Jahr 1890* (Köln, 1890); *Verzeichniß, der von dem Verein empfohlenen Bücher für das Jahr 1900* (Köln, 1900); and *Verein vom heil. Karl Borromäus in Bonn. Bibliotheksgaben-Verzeichnis für das Jahr 1911* (Bonn, 1911). These lists may be found at the Fernleihbibliothek des Borromäusvereins in Bonn.

82. Speech of Msgr. Dr Werthmann, president of the Caritasverband, to the eleventh Caritastag in Danzig on 25 September 1906 entitled "Naturwissenschaft und Volksbildung," *Caritas. Zeitschrift für die Werke der Nächstenliebe in katholischen Deutschland* 12, 4 (1907): 84. One such primer was the greatly successful *Die Kunst, Bücher zu Lesen* (Essen: Verlag u. Druck von Fredebeul & Koenen, 1905)

by Franz Hülskamp, which appeared in five editions over thirteen years.

83. For a differing view, see Smith, *German Nationalism and Religious Conflict*, pp. 20–37 and 80–6. Smith, whose 1995 study of confessional conflict in Imperial Germany has already become a benchmark text, writes that as late as 1887, "nearly a third of all books by Catholic writers in Württemberg were about theology, and more than half of all books written were concerned, in one way or another, with Catholicism" (p. 86). His point is well taken, and no study of German literary engagement in the modern period should ignore the vast popularity – among all German religious groups – of pious reading. Yet I am not convinced that publishing information is a better source for establishing intellectual consumption than evidence of actual reading habits, which I have attempted to assemble here.

84. Frank-Michael Kuhlemann has recommended just such an approach, one that pays attention to the "kleinen, vielfach nur in den Archiven und Spezialbibliotheken zugänglichen Schrifttum . . . Nur so ist ein breiterer, kollektive Mentalitäten widerspiegelnder Kommunikationsraum zu erfassen, und nur auf der Basis eines solchen Materials kann es gelingen, die innerhalb einer religiösen Kultur relevanten und für eine Vielzahl von Individuen und sozialen Gruppen verbindlichen Mentalitätsthemen zu ermitteln:" see Kuhlemann, "Mentalitätsgeschichte. Theoretische und methodische Überlegungen am Beispiel der Religion im 19. und 20. Jahrhundert," in Wolfgang Hardtwig and Hans-Ulrich Wehler (eds), *Kulturgeschichte Heute* (Göttingen: Vandenhoeck & Ruprecht, 1996), p. 192. A good source of such reading material for the Archdiocese of Cologne is the "Gesuche um Erteilung des Imprimatur" files at the AEK Generalia I, 18.1, 1–15 (1825–1914).

85. Arbeitskreis für kirchliche Zeitgeschichte (AKKZG), Münster, "Katholiken zwischen Tradition und Moderne. Das katholische Milieu als Forschungsaufgabe," *Westfälische Forschungen* 43 (1993): 610–11.

86. See the descriptions of *Spirago's Volks-Katechismus* in AEK Generalia I, 18.1, 10, 1893 and *Die Lehrmethode im Katechismus-Unterrichte* by W. H. Meunier in AEK Generalia I, 18.1, 13, 1904. The German Bishops' Conference feared that innovations in the methods of religious education would lead to the "Übertragung des protestantischen Prinzips auf die Katholiken . . . Die Sache ist für die Zukunft sehr gefährlich. Man muß auf die Dozenten der Methodik und auf die Katecheten sehr achtgeben": Gatz, *Akten der Fuldaer Bischofskonferenz* Vol. 3, p. 118.

87. See, for example, the review of Joseph Dahlmann, S.J.'s two-volume *Indische Fahrten* in P. Robert Streit, O.M.I., *Führer durch die deutsche katholische Missionsliteratur* (Freiburg i. Br.: Herdersche Verlagshandlung, 1911), p. 49 and Zalar, "'Knowledge is Power,'" pp. 43–5.
88. J. Kemper (ed.), *Das katholische Kirchenlied in der Volksschule. 72 Kirchenlieder im Anschlusse an die Diözesangesangbücher für Paderborn, Köln, Münster, Osnabrück und Hildesheim* (Hamm: Druck und Verlag von Breer & Thiemann, 1908), pp. 120–1.
89. Barbara Stambolis, "Nationalisierung trotz Ultramontanisierung oder: 'Alles für Deutschland. Deutschland aber für Christus.' Mentalitätsleitende Wertorientierung deutscher Katholiken im 19. und 20. Jahrhundert," *Historische Zeitschrift* 269, 1 (1999): 73.
90. Dr. Kemper, *Neuestes Skapulierbüchlein das ist vollständiger Unterricht über das fünfsache hl. Skapulier nebst den gewöhnlichen Gebeten eines kathol. Christen* (Paderborn: Druck u. Verlag der Bonifacius-Druckerei, 1887).
91. *Andachtsübungen zu Gott dem heiligen Geist bei Ausspendung der heiligen Firmung in Betstunden am Pfingstfeste*, AEK Generalia I, 18.1, 3, 1846 and *Unterricht über das hl. Sakrament der Firmung nebst Gebeten und Liedern beim Empfang desselben. Von einem Priester der Erzdiözese Köln* (Mönchen-Gladbach, 1887) in AEK Generalia I, 18.1, 9.
92. Urs Altermatt, who has probably influenced the field of modern German Catholic history more than any other scholar in the 1990s, understands the "ultramontane" period from 1850–1950 as an *"Ausnahmperiode"*, which saw unprecedented closeness between doctrine and praxis, homogeneity of pious culture, and an "imposed unity" of faith and worldview. The lay takeover of the *Vereine* at the end of the nineteenth century was a revolt against the "backward antimodernism" of their priests and the beginning of their "emancipation": Urs Altermatt, "Katholizismus: Antimodernismus mit modernen Mitteln?" pp. 46–9. His pathbreaking study of Catholic mentality is *Katholizismus und Moderne. Zur Sozial- und Mentalitätsgeschichte der Schweizer Katholiken im 19. und 20. Jahrhundert* (Zurich: Benziger Verlag, 1989). For an indication of how commonplace these views have become in the most recent literature, see Karl-Egon Lönne's comments on the "ultramontane" milieu in his review essay, "Katholizismus-Forschung," *Geschichte und Gesellschaft* 26 (2000): 137–44. Other helpful studies examining recent developments in the historiography of Catholicism include Margaret Lavinia Anderson, "The Kulturkampf and the Course of German History,"

Central European History 19, 1 (1986): 82–3; Michael Klöcker, "Das katholische Milieu. Grundüberlegungen – in besonderer Hinsicht auf das Deutsche Kaiserreich von 1871," *Zeitschrift für Religions- und Geistesgeschichte* 44 (1992): 241–62; and Eric Yonke, "The Catholic Subculture in Modern Germany: Recent Work in the Social History of Religion," *The Catholic Historical Review* 80 (1994): 534–45.

93. Robert Bireley, S.J., *The Refashioning of Catholicism, 1450–1700. A Reassessment of the Counter Reformation* (Washington, DC: The Catholic University of America Press, 1999). If, as Olaf Blaschke has recently postulated, the Counter Reformation and Ultramontanization are to be understood symmetrically, then Bireley's suggestion that the former actually enhanced the cultural integration of Catholics raises intriguing questions about the nature and effect of the latter. A more creative research agenda would ask not only about the defensive strategies of the German Church, but also about, first, how the received set of mental patterns that organized the perceptions of Catholics authorized up-to-date responses to contemporary problems and, second, how these mental patterns were themselves transformed by contact with new ideas. Helmut Walser Smith's work on a Catholic nationalism that appealed to traditions and memories specific to the Catholic experience reflects the first dimension of this agenda. The present study of Catholic reading habits attempts to develop the second. See Olaf Blaschke, "Das 19. Jahrhundert: Ein Zweites konfessionelles Zeitalter?" *Geschichte und Gesellschaft* 26 (2000): 38–75 and Smith's conclusions about Catholic nationalism in *German Nationalism and Religious Conflict*, pp. 237–9.

94. A single parish in Gelsenkirchen before 1914, for example, supported the following pious organizations: Bonifatiusverein, Vinzenz-Verein, Elisabeth-Verein, Missionsvereinigung kath. Frauen und Jungfrauen, Kindheit-Jesu-Verein, Verein der hl. Familie, Männer-Apostolat, Orden des hl. Franciskus, Rosenkranzbruderschaft, Bruderschaft des heiligen und unbefleckten Herzens Mariä zur Bekehrung der Sünder, Bruderschaft der Todesangst unseres Erlösers Jesu Christi, Marianische Jünglingssodalität, Marianische Jungfraukongregation, Marianische Kongregation kaufm. Gehilfinnen u. Beamtinnen, Katholische Gesellenverein, Arbeitsverein St Joseph, Knappenverein St Georg, Hansa-Verein kath. Kaufleute und Beamten, Jung-Hansa-Verein, Volksverein für das katholische Deutschland, Kreuzbündnis-Verein abstinenter Katholiken, Kirchlicher Gesangverein "Cäcilienchor," and Katholischer Fürsorge-Verein für Mädchen, Frauen und Kinder. Its parish library, however, was one of the most "German" in the Rhine-

land, with books by Gustav Freytag, Goethe, the Brothers Grimm, Herder, Heinrich von Kleist, Theodor Körner, Lessing, Schiller, and Raabe, in addition to numerous histories, volumes on natural science, and nationalist "Kriegsliteratur": *Bücherverzeichnis der Borromäus-Bibliothek in Gelsenkirchen* (Gelsenkirchen, 1918) at the Fernleihbibliothek des Borromäusvereins in Bonn. Such evidence as this renders judgments of Catholic piety as indicative of a "depressive, defensive, and anti-modern" mentality severely suspect. See Norbert Busch's conclusions in *Katholische Frömmigkeit und Moderne. Die Sozial- und Mentalitätsgeschichte des Herz-Jesu-Kultus in Deutschland zwischen Kulturkampf und Erstem Weltkrieg* (Gütersloh: Chr. Kaiser/Gütersloher Verlagshaus, 1997), pp. 303–16.

95. Dr. Franz Hermann, *Die Familienbücherei und ihre Auswertung* (Bonn, 1936), pp. 2 and 7.

Anti-Jesuitism in Imperial Germany: The Jesuit as Androgyne

Róisín Healy

One indicator of the extent of Catholic–Protestant antagonism after unification in 1871 was the division of attitudes toward Jesuits along strictly confessional lines. In Imperial Germany, the Jesuits' opponents were, typically, practicing Protestants, and their supporters committed Catholics. The polarization of attitudes to the Jesuits according to confession represented a return to the deep divisions between Protestants and Catholics of earlier centuries. In the eighteenth century, Catholics had themselves been divided in their views of Jesuits, and some, persuaded by the Enlightenment or Jansenism, led campaigns to end Jesuit influence in education and even to expel the order entirely. Protestants were more consistently hostile to the order. Their anger was roused especially by the ultramontane direction of the Catholic Church under Pope Pius IX. The subsequent attack on Catholicism bound Catholics together in the defense of Jesuits. Although some German Catholics continued to be skeptical about Jesuits, Protestant anti-Catholicism ruled out any cross-confessional alliance on the basis of opposition to the order. Jews shared Protestant suspicions of Catholicism, but sympathized with Jesuits as fellow-victims of religious discrimination. Jewish interventions were based on the principle of tolerance. They were rare and of little significance, however. While Catholics occasionally boasted of Jewish support, Protestants ignored it. The Jesuit question remained an internal issue for Christians.

While anti-Jesuitism was a symptom of confessional divisions and its trajectory closely linked to that of anti-Catholicism in nineteenth-century Germany, it also constituted a distinct form of hate discourse.[1] In it, the Jesuit appeared both as the embodiment of the worst qualities of Catholicism and as a peculiar form of bogeyman. Anti-Jesuits associated Jesuits with the elements of contemporary Catholicism that they most despised – internationalism, authoritarianism, and lax moral theology – and held the order responsible for the character of contemporary mainstream Catholicism. According to their enemies, since the order's foundation in 1540, Jesuits had stood in the way of an accommodation of Catholicism with modernity, specifically the nation-state, the autonomy of the individual, and genuine moral responsibility. Jesuits had, so anti-Jesuits maintained, contaminated Catholicism with alien traditions.

The fact that most Catholics in Imperial Germany did not find Jesuit traditions alien at all, however, suggests that anti-Jesuits were not primarily interested in the integrity of Catholicism. The demonization of Jesuits provided anti-Jesuits with a conceit to disguise their general contempt for fundamental elements of Catholicism, such as the authority of the papacy, the intermediary role of the priest, and the formalism of Catholic moral teaching. If anything, anti-Jesuits wanted to remold Catholicism to resemble Protestantism. Such a project was impossibly ambitious, of course. Anti-Jesuits did not conceive of Catholicism as simply a set of theological principles or religious practices, but an entire cultural system that affected all aspects of life. At the very least, anti-Jesuitism served to highlight an alternative system of values that might prevail in the Protestant community.

The precise character of the anti-Jesuit alternative to the Jesuit or Catholic worldview is not immediately apparent from anti-Jesuits' writings, however. For the most part, the anti-Jesuits of Imperial Germany simply reformulated charges that had been made against Jesuits for centuries. The French Jansenist, Blaise Pascal, provided the most frequently cited source in his *Provincial Letters,* first published in 1656. German anti-Jesuits borrowed liberally from more recent works, too, making anti-Jesuit discourse highly formulaic. The context in which anti-Jesuits operated provides the key to understanding the meaning of these charges in Imperial Germany. Understanding the world of these Protestants and how they felt about the society in which they lived helps us decode anti-Jesuitism and, in turn, provides a greater understanding of the precise concerns and desires that this constituency chose to express indirectly.

This chapter investigates the role of ideas about gender for this particular constituency, and argues that they were an important factor in the antipathy to Jesuits expressed by many Protestants. The beliefs and practices of the Jesuits concerning the authority of men over women and the limitations of a man's authority over other men in particular disturbed their critics. The significance of gender issues is immediately apparent from anti-Jesuit writings. Anti-Jesuits maintained that Jesuits had inappropriate levels of intimacy with women, both spiritually and sexually. Jesuits allegedly sought out women as the weaker sex and turned them into their agents. Occasionally, Jesuits took advantage of women for their own sexual pleasure, too, according to their critics. While charges of sexual misconduct are a common trope in anti-clerical discourse, the distinct profile of Jesuits seems to have lent them credibility. As experts on moral theology, Jesuits were linked with the confessional, and it was easy to conclude that they exploited the opportunities for sexual fulfillment afforded by such an intimate space.

Gender forms only one part of a broader political, social, and cultural context in which anti-Jesuitism was embedded, however. To emphasize the role of gender is not to deny the relevance of other factors, but to add another dimension to the existing picture of anti-Catholicism. Anti-Jesuitism became a political issue very soon after the establishment of the German Empire in 1871. In 1872 the *Reichstag* passed a law that expelled the order from Germany. Known as the "Jesuit Law," it was one of the first measures of the *Kulturkampf*, a series of anti-clerical and anti-Catholic laws passed in the 1870s, and unusual in that it applied to the whole empire rather than any one state. While Bismarck was tradition-ally credited with the campaign to expand the state's authority at the expense of the Churches and to suppress Catholicism in particular, he played little role in the Jesuit Law. In this case, the state was facilitative rather than instrumental.

The initiative for the expulsion of the Jesuits came from extra-parliamentary associations, primarily liberal Protestants organized in the Protestant Association and, to a lesser extent, Masonic lodges. Liberal parties were at the forefront of the campaign in the *Reichstag*.[2] Enraged by the Syllabus of Errors of 1864 and the Declaration of Papal Infallibility of 1870, liberal Protestants in particular believed that the Catholic Church was launching a war on the modern nation-state. Specifically, they believed the Church was demanding that Catholics obey the pope rather than their temporal leaders. The Prussian-led unification of Germany in the following year through successive victories over two Catholic powers, Austria and France, intensified Protestants' suspicions of Catholic dis-loyalty, and prepared the ground for the *Kulturkampf*. The fact that the Catholic community included French and Polish members made German Protestants especially doubtful of Catholic loyalty. It was no coincidence that government ministers imposed restrictions on Jesuits in the Polish provinces, out of fears that Jesuits were in league with Polish nationalists, even before the bill for the order's expulsion came before the *Reichstag*.[3] Inspired by their triumph in 1871, German nationalists proclaimed the essentially Protestant character of the German nation, a view that dominated the literary canon and the historiography of the Empire.[4] Resistance to demands for repeal by the Catholic Center Party after 1890 came from the same constituency. Seeing the end of the *Kulturkampf*, necessitated by Catholic resistance, as an erosion of the Protestant character of German nationalism, liberal Protestants formed the more popular Protestant League for the Defense of German-Protestant Interests in 1886.[5]

The struggle against Jesuits went beyond questions of political loyalty, however. Anti-Jesuits found Catholicism as a whole problematic, and attributed the many deficiencies they found in the Catholic community to religion. David Blackbourn has explained how real disparities of education and differences in economic activity between Catholics and Protestants encouraged mutual misunderstanding. Protestants interpreted Catholics' "backwardness" as a product of religion rather than of structural inequalities, believing superstition impeded education and Church holidays took time away from labor.[6] Jesuits were blamed especially for the Catholics' apparent intellectual deficit. According to anti-Jesuits, they encouraged superstitious practices, stunted the intellectual growth of their students by rote learning, and compromised their scholarship by adherence to papal orthodoxy.

The role of gender in fueling Protestant hostility to Catholicism has received minimal attention from historians, despite the frequency of charges of excessive clerical influence over women and of sexual misbehavior in anti-clerical discourse generally. Theodore Zeldin and Ralph Gibson have emphasized the ubiquity of such charges in French anti-clerical writings of the nineteenth century in particular, and offer some fruitful interpretations. They remind us that the private world of the family and sexuality could be just as significant as the public world of diplomacy, business and scholarship in promoting anti-clericalism among bourgeois men. They suggest that charges of unscrupulous clerics reflected concern for paternal authority within the family at a time when it seemed to be under threat. Gibson attributes charges of sexual misbehavior to discomfort with the idea of celibacy in the context of rigorous enforcement since the eighteenth century.[7] While the validity of their conclusions for anti-Jesuitism in Imperial Germany must be tested, the attention they draw to the general context of gender relations and attitudes to sexuality in interpreting anti-clerical literature is instructive.

Recent interest in the history of gender and sexuality has yielded valuable work that suggests some reasons for the seeming obsession with gender themes in anti-clerical discourse in the nineteenth century and provides insights into their meaning. Historians of sexuality, most notably

Thomas Laqueur and Michel Foucault, posit a shift in the conceptualization of gender in Europe around 1800.[8] While differences between the sexes were long recognized, only at this time did these differences come to be viewed as incommensurable. Laqueur describes a shift from a one-sex model, where women were deemed an inferior version of man, to a two-sex model, where women became a sex all of their own. Women's sexual organs were no longer viewed as inversions of male organs but as peculiarly female. Greater scientific knowledge, about the functioning of ovaries, for instance, helped to justify the theory of women's difference; but epistemological and political developments were responsible for the new model. The Enlightenment emphasis on reason led to an insistence that gender be determined according to objective categories, and thus privileged biology over behavior. Where once a person's role in sexual acts, active or passive, determined the sex of awkward cases such as hermaphrodites and homosexuals, genitalia were determinant in the nineteenth century.[9] The opening of the public sphere at the time of the French Revolution prompted calls for women's participation, and in turn, for their exclusion. Defenders of patriarchy seized on women's biology as ammunition, disqualifying women from public life on the basis of physical weakness or incapacitation through pregnancy.[10]

German thinkers were as much responsible for this reformulation of sexual difference as others. Ute Frevert and Isabel Hull have demonstrated how several prominent intellectuals at the turn of the nineteenth century used biology to elaborate a theory of sexual difference that justified women's exclusion from public life on biological grounds. Despite commitment to freedom and equality as rights based on humanity, Kant excluded women from full citizenship. He argued against equality in marriage, insisting that only one person could make decisions and that this should be the man by virtue of his greater physical strength and courage.[11] Fichte made the same point with an argument based on a new view of women's sexuality, which became dominant in the second half of the century.[12] He rejected the traditional view that emphasized women's sensual nature, evident in Rousseau's writings, and redefined women as lacking in sexual drive. Concluding that women engaged in sex out of love, and believing that love was an innate inclination rather than the result of rational decision, Fichte confirmed women's lack of independence. By sacrificing her own wishes for the sake of her husband's pleasure through love, a woman was no longer independent, and hence incapable of participation in public life.[13] The most important theologian of German Protestantism in the nineteenth century and a favorite of liberal Protestants in particular, Friedrich Schleiermacher, endorsed the exclusion of women from public life in his *Katechismus der Vernunft für edle Frauen* of 1798, where he described men as the stronger and more thinking sex, women as more sensitive and noble in thought.[14] Together with Laqueur's medical writers, these thinkers and their followers helped legitimize and popularize the notion of women as a breed apart, although not all men and women lived up to the emerging ideal.[15]

Biology provided new reasons for associating certain characteristics with each sex and ordering gender roles to limit women to the private sphere, the complement to the public sphere that emerged in the revolutionary period. Karin Hausen's analysis of German dictionaries and encyclopedias of the nineteenth century reveals a whole host of gender-specific characteristics, which she divides into male and female categories of activity/passivity, doing/being, rationality/emotionality respectively.[16] These characteristics provided the foundation for the "separation of spheres" model, whereby men devoted themselves to their careers and public life, while their wives took care of the upbringing of their children and their domestic arrangements. As Hausen puts it in her comparative model, men were assigned a "social destiny," while women were assigned a "private destiny." In terms of their public role, men were at a biological advantage. Men were associated in these sources with words such as steadfast, brave, force, ambitious, intellect, and knowledge. The words associated with women, such as devotion, modesty, protective, love, intuition, were not negative ones, and women enjoyed far more virtues than men. Some feminists even exploited such associations to argue that women should represent themselves in public life. The common thread among those who promoted these gender-specific characteristics, however, was an assumption that women existed to help men reach perfection.[17] Ultimately, this model justified patriarchy, both in terms of men's monopoly on public life and women's obedience to men in the home.

This model of sexual difference, expressed in terms of the mutual dependency of the male career and female domesticity, was particularly plausible for anti-Jesuits on account of their social profile. The membership lists of the Protestant Association and Protestant League indicate that anti-Jesuit activists came virtually exclusively from the bourgeoisie, and predominantly from the educated bourgeoisie *(Bildungsbürgertum)*. The Protestant Association had a high proportion of schoolteachers.[18] Pastors and theologians accounted for by far the greatest category in the Protestant League, with teachers of all levels in second place. Affiliated workers' organizations accounted for 11 per cent of the membership in 1910. Signatories on an anti-Jesuit petition to the Kaiser in 1892 reflect a similar class profile, with most professionals being involved in either the Church or education, and a smaller group being owners of factories or shops.[19] The same separation of spheres model so favored by the bourgeoisie and the nobility, and enshrined in law, limited women's role in associational life, so that anti-Jesuit activists were all male. Women were associate members of the Protestant League from the start, but became full members only in 1906. By 1914, they accounted for 20 per cent of the total membership.[20] They do not seem to have taken part in anti-Jesuit campaigns, beyond signing local petitions, however, and none signed the petition to the Kaiser mentioned above.

The patriarchal views of bourgeois men permeated the religious discourse of Imperial Germany, although it is only recently gaining attention from historians.[21] Anti-Catholics complained that the Catholic Church violated the separation of spheres model and also denigrated Catholicism by associating it with femininity. They were responding, in part, to the increasing role of women within the Catholic community, whether as lay worshipers or as nuns, in the nineteenth century. They were disturbed by the predominance of women in public settings, as in Catholic demonstrations against *Kulturkampf* legislation or at religious ceremonies at the site of Marian apparitions in Marpingen, finding it inappropriate and distasteful.[22] Anti-Catholics also objected to the sentimentalization of religious practice that took place at the same time, especially because it required the conformity of men as well as women. Like later historians, they interpreted this process as a feminization of Catholicism. Devotional forms that emphasized emotion rather than intellect came in for extensive criticism. Anti-Catholics dismissed the apparition of Mary at Marpingen as impossible and condemned the Church for encouraging it.[23] They were also uncomfortable with the Sacred Heart cult because of its graphic physicality, which they found sensational.[24] While all clergy were implicated in the feminization of Catholicism, as sponsors of the Sacred Heart cult, Jesuits attracted particular criticism. And in so far as they were active in the devotional revolution of mid-century, Jesuits were associated with the sentimental form that religious worship took.

The significance of gender in anti-Jesuit discourse can be seen in a broader context, however. Anti-Jesuits believed that the very structures of Jesuitism violated the model of gender relations preferred by bourgeois men. Convinced of their own masculinity, anti-Jesuits saw Jesuits as having a more ambiguous sexual identity. The characteristics associated with Jesuits placed them in both male and female camps. Jesuits were unique among Catholic clerics, anti-Jesuits believed, in the premium that they placed on obedience. Jesuits allegedly insisted that their authority was absolute in all matters, and denied their Catholic flock the basic right to make decisions in accordance with reason, conscience and their own interests. At the same time, anti-Jesuits depicted Jesuits themselves as slaves to their superiors within the order. They also pointed to the fourth vow of obedience that Jesuits made to the pope as evidence of the "slave-like obedience" *(Kadavergehorsam)* demanded of them. Jesuits were oppressors, but they were also victims of a kind, anti-Jesuits believed. In the eyes of devotees of the two-sex model of gender, the Jesuits' domination of the Catholic population made them the most masculine of men; their submission to another man made them the most feminine of men.

Anti-Jesuits did not term Jesuits excessively masculine or feminine. Nor did they attempt to coin an intermediary gender category for Jesuits. In anti-Jesuit discourse, Jesuits remained men, albeit in frocks. Yet in their writings, anti-Jesuits reveal how disturbing they found the position of Jesuits in the middle of a chain of command that demanded absolute obedience to those above and from those below, and hence both feminine and masculine attributes. The anti-Jesuits' failure to identify this phenomenon should not preclude us from doing so. In purely gender terms, the image of the Jesuit found in anti-Jesuit literature was that of the androgyne. According to the literary critic A. J. L. Busst, the androgyne is as "a person who unites certain of the essential characteristics of both sexes and who, consequently, may be considered as both a man and a woman or as neither a man nor a woman, as bisexual or asexual."[25] Anti-Jesuit discourse implied that the Jesuit was of the first kind, that is, bisexual.

The "Jesuit androgyne" is visible in the combination of two different but complementary images of the Jesuit. In the first the Jesuit appears as the fulfillment of the bourgeois ideal of masculinity, but in exaggerated form. The following explanation of the distinction between Jesuits and other clerics is full of words associated with Hausen's categories for men – activity, doing, and rationality: "They [other clerics] lack, in particular, the ruthless decisiveness of action, the ice-cold calculation that is free from hide-bound pangs of conscience, the leadership that is equally smooth and sleek as it is focused and logically consistent, the untiring inventiveness in method . . ."[26] The active dimension is unmistakable, with Jesuits engaged in "action" and "leadership." Creativity is suggested in "inventiveness." Their energy is attested to in "untiring." The ambition and force Hausen categorizes under "doing" is evident in the Jesuits' "decisiveness." Several words indicate rationality – "ice-cold calculation," "focused and logically consistent." In the second image, the Jesuit appears very differently, as a person purged of these masculine attributes. As described by one newspaper, Jesuitism "created slaves, it wears the person down to a ball, which rolls around without a will of its own, wherever the foot of the superior lies."[27] The Jesuit suffers the ultimate form of dependence – slavery. He continues to act, but only at the behest of another. The only direction shown is the foot of the superior. The Jesuit is no longer focused, as above, but "rolls around." The intellect displayed above has no outlet in this state of slavery. The Jesuit is feminized by association with the female characteristics of dependence and self-denial, perhaps even devotion.

The significance of the androgynous image of the Jesuit requires an understanding of the androgyne itself. Busst offers one interpretation of the preoccupation with androgyny in the nineteenth century. Focusing on French intellectuals in particular, he describes androgyny as a symbolic vehicle for the general intellectual mood, which shifted in mid-century from utopian beliefs in progress, perfection, and solidarity to disillusionment, despair, and decadence.[28] In the first half of the nineteenth century utopianisim and Romanticism encouraged an optimistic view of the androgyne as healthy. The androgyne was idolized as a model of perfection, combining the best of both sexes. Ganneau made God himself androgynous, coining the composite Mapah from mater and pater. By the second half of the century much of the optimism that had made the androgyne an ideal had faded. Industrialization had not brought universal prosperity, for instance, and progress itself no longer seemed endless. The androgyne became a symbol of pessimism. The result was that sexual ambiguity became associated with moral ambiguity. The androgyne acquired largely negative associations: lechery of the mind, onanism, homosexuality, sadism and masochism.[29]

Busst's insights into the role of the androgyne as a conduit for views about sexuality and broader social and political agendas are of limited value in explaining the Jesuit androgyne, however. Certainly, the latter sentiments were popular in Imperial Germany. Busst suggests that the German Romantics anticipated this shift in France and the phenomenon of "cultural despair" in Germany is well known from the work of Fritz Stern.[30] Anti-Jesuits were indeed concerned about moral standards, and the association of the androgyne with homosexuality and sadism could only exacerbate suspicions of Jesuits. The cultural pessimism described by Stern was not particularly strong among anti-Jesuits, however. While they despaired of the direction in which Germany was going, towards confessional tolerance, they did not embrace cultural despair. Indeed, as liberals, they remained committed to economic progress, and were targets of criticism for the advocates of despair, Langbehn, Lagarde, and Moeller van der Bruck. As an object of study, the androgyne was not of any great interest to anti-Jesuits. The figure exerted a particular fascination in the nineteenth century, but largely among scholars of oriental mysticism, occultists, and Freemasons. Only the latter played any significant role in anti-Jesuitism.[31]

Despite this profile, the contradictory character of the androgyne seems to have provoked particular concern among liberal Protestants in Imperial Germany, however. More plausible than Busst's line of argument is an explanation rooted in the social and political debates of the day. The androgyne was less a vehicle for the articulation of intellectual fashions than a weapon in political struggles, specifically over gender issues. The decades before the First World War witnessed an intense discussion of sexual difference and sexuality, evident in feminist demands for greater access to education and even suffrage campaigns to combat prostitution and venerial disease, and academic fascination with sexuality, and especially with supposed perversions, such as promiscuity, masturbation and homosexuality. John Fout identifies a "gender crisis" in Imperial Germany as feminist and homosexual assertions provoked a restatement of traditional gender roles by conservatives.[32] The system of gendered roles that had allowed Jesuits to be defined as both male and female was coming under threat by the last third of the nineteenth century. Never achieved by the working class, it was now the object of attack by some members of the bourgeoisie. Challenges to traditional gender roles threatened to dismantle the separation of spheres that guaranteed men privileged access to positions of power.

By transgressing gender boundaries in asserting the same rights as heterosexual men, feminists and homosexuals seemed to their enemies to be rehabilitating the androgyne after it had fallen out of favor in mid-century. Critics of feminism suggested that assertive women were not even female, but belonged to an intermediary gender. They used the label, "Amazon," denoting the warrior tribe who cut off one breast for ease of movement in firing arrows, and left their men at home to take care of the domestic duties, to describe women who rejected the roles traditionally assigned them. A more obvious androgyny was implied in the label, "Mannweib," or man-woman. Max Wolff, the medical expert, described feminists as hermaphrodites.[33] The association of homosexuality and androgyny, indicated by the emergence of the "queen," seemed so self-evident that the sexologist and advocate of the homosexual movement, Max Hirschfeld, adopted it. He argued that homosexuals formed a third sex. The androgynous character of the Jesuit was less obvious, and anti-Jesuits made few attempts to condemn Jesuits by association with other androgynes. Anti-Jesuits did not link them to feminists. Jesuits were feminist only in so far as they offered women a social and spiritual outlet outside the home, and thus at best an extension of the private sphere. Certainly, anti-Jesuits accused Jesuits of homosexuality; but the constancy of sexual deviance as a trope in hate discourse allows little interpretative scope.

The androgynous character of Jesuits was no less disturbing, however, for operating at an abstract level – in the fulfilling of two stereotypes at once, the authoritarian male and the submissive female. The profile of anti-Jesuits demonstrates that they, like the moral purity associations, were preoccupied by issues with strong implications for male identity and gender relations. Anti-Jesuit discourse provided a vehicle for expressing such concerns. As Protestants intent on proving the superiority of their faith, they emphasized their distance from the submissive female type that, they believed, characterized lay Catholics. They themselves occupied an intermediary position in the spectrum of authority relations, neither exerting control over other men, nor being submissive to them. Rather they were committed to the principle of independence in moral decisions.

The liberal Protestants who dominated the organizations active in campaigning against the Jesuits were particularly protective of their independence. Although the division of Protestantism into Lutheran and Calvinist traditions had been largely overcome by official Church unions, for instance in Prussia in 1817, theological divisions remained in the form of a conservative/liberal conflict. Conservative and liberal constituencies formed in response to controversial questions such as the source of religious truth, authority structures within the Church, and the Church's relationship to the state. Scholarly works, such as David Friedrich Strauss's *Life of Jesus* (1835), relativized revelation as a source of knowledge and suggested that interpretations of the Bible needed to be revised in the light of historical discoveries. The adoption of this alternative source of religious truth by some pastors prompted a re-examination of the notion of orthodoxy and its enforcement in the Protestant tradition, with conservatives recommending disciplinary measures and liberals insisting on the right of the individual to decide what he preached. The relationship of the Church to the state was also a bone of contention, with conservatives objecting to the secularization of education that took place in the *Kulturkampf*, and liberals upholding the virtues of non-denominational education.

Anti-Jesuitism became a vehicle for liberal concerns about the manliness of Protestantism. The anti-Jesuit resolutions of the Protestant League frequently called on German Protestants to be manly and forthright in their resistance to Jesuits. A Protestant synod in the Palatinate included in its appeal the injunction of St. Paul to the Corinthians (I Cor. 16,13): "Awake, stand up for your faith, be manly (*mannhaft*) and be strong." The image of the androgyne allowed anti-Jesuits to express the two sides of manliness that they wished to preserve – dominance over women and individual independence of mind. As a man enjoying dominance over the lay community, and women especially, the Jesuit represented what liberal Protestants aspired to – the authoritarian male. As a man subordinating himself to another man, the general of the order, the Jesuit represented what anti-Jesuits feared they might become – the submissive female. Anti-Jesuits were no anarchists, however. They continued to believe in traditional gender hierarchies. Demanding obedience from women came naturally to them. They were also prepared to submit to authority under certain circumstances, for instance as in the military. Hierarchy itself was not at issue.

The two figures of the authoritarian Jesuit and the submissive Jesuit help us understand the precise attitude toward authority that liberal and nationalist Protestants espoused. The image of the authoritarian Jesuit was evident in all anti-Jesuit writings. Particular attention focused on sites of Jesuit authority, such as schools and churches, especially confessionals, where Jesuits were depicted as brainwashing the Catholic population. Jesuit interventions in the family and home, especially in so far as they involved women, were also of great concern to anti-Jesuits. In many such places, Jesuits appeared as agents of their superior. To this extent, they were adopting the role of the submissive female. But the Jesuit house itself was the site of the most extreme instance of submission. There the Jesuit was molded into a loyal servant of the superior.

The Authoritarian Jesuit

As the quotation above demonstrated, anti-Jesuits believed that Jesuits exhibited exclusively male attributes in their relations with lay Catholics. In the writings of their enemies, Jesuits exhibited most of the masculine characteristics outlined by Hausen. The very appearance of Jesuits in satirical cartoons emphasized their characteristic drive. Jesuits had thin, supple bodies, honed from their constant activity.[34] Franciscans, by contrast, were small and fat. Jesuits were driven by ambition, according to their critics. Not satisfied with half-measures, Jesuits allegedly sought not merely to dominate in religious affairs but in political ones too. They operated on a global scale and roamed the world in the service of the Church. They apparently commanded great willpower, never slackening or deviating from the task at hand. Paying scant attention to morality, Jesuits were consistently clever in the plans they created to realize their goals, according to their critics. Jesuits were not easily intimidated, either. World domination required considerable bravery as well as energy. Jesuits were supposedly engaged in conspiring against national governments, even consorting with socialists. In the popular cartoon story by Wihelm Busch, the eponymous Jesuit, Pater Filuzius, allies with a socialist and a Frenchman.[35]

The exaggerated masculinity of the Jesuits was unsettling, rather than ridiculous. There was no suggestion of Jesuit bravado. The threat from Jesuits was deadly serious, because they exemplified the attributes that made for success in the professional and political world. Given their personality profile, Jesuits might have blossomed in the world of the bourgeois Protestants to whom they were such anathema. Jesuits had adopted the essential elements of the male career, and, perhaps more impressively, without the support of a loving wife at home. The Protestant historian, Friedrich Paulsen, acknowledged the cool determination of the Jesuits, but hinted that it was unnatural. Jesuits fulfilled their masculine role so fully, they no longer seemed human:

> I believe there has never been a group of people, who have consistently developed the mastery of natural drives and the suppression of individual inclinations and desires more than the Jesuits. There is something of the quiet but persistent working of natural forces in their activity; without passion and the din of war, without agitation and hurry, they push forwards step by step, hardly ever having to take one backwards. Confidence and superiority characterize all their movements. Certainly there are not qualities that make them lovable; no one, who is without human weakness, is lovable.[36]

Their masculine character, already evident in their "mastery," is confirmed by the energy, force, and steadfastness of their movements. Not worthy of love in Paulsen's eyes, they become the opposite of women, whom contemporary works described as lovable.[37]

In another sense, Jesuits violated this model in that they went too far, according to Pauslen and others. Their critics made a fundamental distinction between themselves and Jesuits in arguing that the latter lacked the sense of honor that restrained men from abusing their power as men. Anti-Jesuit literature depicted Jesuits as unashamedly patriarchal in relations with their lay congregation. Not immune from the temptations of patriarchy themselves, anti-Jesuits felt that the Jesuits exercised it in inappropriate situations. Jesuits allegedly adopted a patriarchal position in relation to women who were not their wives and to the Catholic community as a whole, which included men. Jesuits encouraged the sentimentalization and hence feminization of Catholicism, according to their critics. They also took advantage of women's natural weakness and preyed on them sexually. Both of these charges reflected concerns that anti-Jesuits themselves had about women and Protestantism, principally the rise of feminism and its consequences for the home and the Church.

Anti-Jesuits accused Jesuits of exacerbating the feminine character of Catholicism and hence further distancing it from manly Protestantism. If Jesuits were characterized as especially masculine, the corollary was an excessively feminine congregation, characterized by weakness, dependence, and emotion.[38] Just as men encouraged their wives to adopt feminine attributes that complemented their own, so Jesuits allegedly cultivated a feminization of Catholicism. In their moral theology, Jesuits reputedly allowed Catholics to be weak, by making excuses for sinners. By emphasizing the importance of the clergy as a moral guide, especially through the confessional, Jesuits supposedly deepened the dependence of Catholics on them. Catholics had to defer to their priests, just as women deferred to their husbands. Finally, Jesuits allegedly encouraged an emotional form of worship that undermined rationality. The relationship between Protestant pastors and their clergy was quite different, according to anti-Jesuits. Anti-Jesuits boasted that their pastors did not demand submission from their congregations and treated all, men and women, as the guardians of their own consciences. They prided themselves, too, on the sincerity and rationality of Protestant belief and practice.

Numerous anti-Jesuit writings dealt with the complexities of Jesuit moral theology. The most popular theme was whether the order defended the principle that the ends justify the means. Invariably, anti-Jesuits claimed that Jesuits preached a lax moral code, for fear of alienating followers. Jesuits encouraged Catholics to be weak and fickle, feminine characteristics, rather than bold and steadfast, as men should be. Whereas Protestantism rested on a sincere confrontation with one's conscience, Jesuits reduced moral decisions to rules. In the words of one anti-Jesuit, Jesuit moral teaching was a "cleverly thought out accommodation to human weakness."[39] Another, Herrmann of Saxony-Weimar, compared Jesuits to the Pharisees in the formalism of their moral teaching. They outdid the Pharisees, however, in their permissiveness, with rules that were easier to follow.[40] Others went so far as to claim that Jesuits deliberately facilitated sin. One author titled his chapter on Jesuit morality: "How to sin without committing a sin."[41]

By insisting on a corpus of moral rules, Jesuits precluded the development of an individual conscience, according to their enemies. Unlike Protestants, Catholics did not apparently exercise the typically masculine gifts of rationality and judgment. Jesuits allegedly made themselves indispensable in Catholics' basic moral decisions, and thus prevented the development of a responsible conscience. In the case of children, this was most serious. The product of a Jesuit education was "a child's mind that was undeveloped and neglected in every way, which could never, his whole life long, outgrow the paternal guidance of Jesuitism."[42] Jesuits supposedly trained generations that were completely dependent on Jesuits for their moral decision-making. The example of the Jesuit colony in Paraguay was often cited in this context. Such dependence had alarming consequences for the nation as a whole, however, according to anti-Jesuits. Conceding the possibility that the Jesuits were doing some good in Paraguay, one author, Herrmann, complained: "Where a people wishes to advance and is successfully developing, then it requires as large a number as possible of morally autonomous men in its midst."[43] To apply the same treatment to the German Catholic laity as the Indians of Paraguay was unthinkable, however.[44] The intellectual heights that Germany had reached threatened to collapse in the face of Jesuit plans to convert the country into a colony of slaves.

Jesuit scholarship presented a similar problem for liberal Protestants. An anonymous anti-Jesuit author berated the Jesuits for keeping their congregations in "intellectual serfdom and immaturity, in superstition and medieval bonds." He pointed to the Jesuit opposition to modernism, the movement in favor of historical approaches to biblical scholarship that was condemned by Pope Pius X in 1907.[45] The tragedy, for anti-Jesuits, consisted in the threat to Germany's reputation as a nation of culture and an economic powerhouse. The same author indicted Jesuits for opposing "all that has made Germany great and that not only the 40 million Protestants must hold dear as a holy inheritance from their ancestors."[46]

If Jesuits exercised patriarchy in their authority over their feminized flock, made up of people of both genders, they also took advantage of women in a more direct way, according to their critics. Jesuits inveigled themselves into the confidence of women and used them to advance the order's plans, and sometimes for their own sexual pleasure as well. Implicit in such charges was the assumption that Jesuits were overstepping the boundaries of acceptable male behavior. Anti-Jesuits believed that Jesuits broke the traditional contract between the sexes, whereby men recognized their superior strength and intellect but did not use it at the expense of women. Men restrained themselves because women were naturally weak. The Jesuits' predatory behavior affronted men indirectly, because the women with whom Jesuits consorted were often the wives of other men. A class bias was implicit in this critique, in so far as the cult of honor, which moved men to restraint in their relations with women, was peculiar to the bourgeoisie and the aristocracy.[47] Whatever their social background, Jesuits apparently associated themselves with the lower ranks in their treatment of women.

Anti-Jesuits framed their criticisms of Jesuit relations with women in terms of female gullibility and Jesuit guile, but the strength of protest indicates a concern that women were making decisions for themselves. One anti-Jesuit author, the occultist Jörg Lanz-Liebenfels, warned:

> One group must be on all accounts guarded from the Jesuits – women! The Jesuit never attacks the dissenter directly, he goes through his wife! Again, German men, guard your women from them, there is no devout Protestant woman, not even a pastor's wife, whom they cannot get around! If we lose the German woman, everything is lost, then the children belong to them as well, whom they then can model according to their own wishes.[48]

The consequences of independent thinking by women were so dire, but the idea so incredible, that the author assumed an outside influence was at work. The attempts by Jesuits to reconvert the nation to Catholicism became an explanation for women's decisions not to follow their husbands in all matters. Women's abandonment of their husbands' beds was also explained by Jesuit interference. Anti-Jesuits devoted much attention to proving that Jesuits defended breaches of the commandment against adultery, and thus allowed women to betray their husbands.[49] Interestingly, the case that they most liked to cite was that of a woman who had already betrayed her husband. An extract from the moral theologian, Jean-Baptiste Gury, was used to claim that Jesuits allowed women to lie about adultery. The moral equivocation of Jesuits justified retrospectively the independence that women themselves were already claiming. In the context of the Kaiserreichs' "gender crisis," anti-Jesuitism functioned as an attack on feminists, both radicals who endorsed extramarital sexuality, and moderates who demanded more independence of women from their husbands, whether in financial, legal or political matters.

Jesuits posed the most immediate threat when they went beyond providing women with spiritual guidance to engaging in sexual relations with them. The confessional as a site of sin seemed plausible to anti-clericals everywhere, in that it, like the cinema in later years, seemed ideally suited to sexual misconduct. It was dark and enclosed, penetrated only by an attentive ear, and it was the site of intimate revelations. Karl Weiss claimed that Jesuit confessors sought out women's weaknesses in the confessional with a view to seducing them.[50] The sexual relationship between a French Jesuit, Jean-Baptiste Girard, and his young penitent,

Catherine Cordière, in early eighteenth-century France was popular enough to merit numerous recountings, often sensational. In Imperial Germany alone three authors described the affair: Johannes Jühling, a member of the *Protestantenverein*, a pornographer, Carl Felix von Schlichtegroll, and an anonymous author.[51]

There was no implication that Jesuits were particularly adept lovers. The energy of Jesuits was not explicitly sexual. The sublimation of their sexual desires, as a consequence of their vow of celibacy, suggested that Jesuits were constantly on the look-out for opportunities for fulfillment, however. The consensus among Catholics in favor of celibacy in Imperial Germany was overwhelming, and observance probably greater than at any time, a fact that may have fueled expectations that the release of sexual desires might be extreme.[52] Narratives of sexual deviance by clerics also provided titillation for an audience with few public outlets for the exploration of sexual themes.[53] Even Protestant pastors, who set strict limits on their own inquiries of their female parishioners, may have been tempted to hear more.[54] The "gender crisis" may have encouraged male fantasies of sexual domination, too. Jesuits were always the initiators of each sexual drama and exerted spiritual as well as physical control over their victims, as in the case of Father Girard's relationship with the young Cordière.

Explanations might be more innocent, however. Accusations of inappropriate intimacy between Jesuits and women reflected fears about female autonomy beyond the realm of sexuality. Fout argues that the moral purity organizations that complained about deviant sexuality were primarily concerned about the infiltration of the male professional world by women, and not about moral standards. Their members came from the occupations most threatened by women – medicine and education. Fout's observation warns us against making too sharp a distinction among the charges made against Jesuits between those of sexual deviance and others, such as those of blind obedience. The appeal of deviant sexuality as a focus of attack lay in the moral indignation it provoked and the titillation it provided; but it also expressed a broader range of concerns about men's and women's social roles.

Such an interpretation is especially plausible in the light of the threat faced by Protestants from feminists who sought to stretch the bounds of the Protestant commitment to the "priesthood of all believers." The Protestant Church placed strict limits on women. The most influential position was reserved for the pastor's wife; but this itself was strictly limited. Advice books for pastors insisted that wives offer practical rather than spiritual help to parishioners. Women could read out prayers at a patient's bedside, but they should not pray freely. This was "improper because unfeminine."[55] Feminists within the Protestant Church were demanding a greater voice in Church affairs, however, and the anti-Jesuit constituency was not enthusiastic. In 1890 and 1891 Elizabeth Malo campaigned for the admission of women to the Protestant League as full members. The League's members were opposed, and relented only in 1906.[56] With the exception of one article in its newsletter on women's access to education, the League steered clear of the woman question, for fear of splitting its members.[57] In 1896, Malo called for equality for women in Church structures.[58] The German Protestant Women's League *(Deutscher Evangelischer Frauenbund)* took up the issue with repeated petitions to the Protestant Upper Church Council *(Evangelischer Ober-kirchenrat)* for the right to vote at communal level and to elect pastors from 1903 on. Equality came only in 1919, in the aftermath of the granting of electoral suffrage.[59]

The submissive Jesuit

In the face of the feminist assault from within, the Jesuit provided a model of masculinity, if exaggerated, that Protestant men could emulate. For those uncomfortable about the implications of feminist demands for male authority within the Church and the home, playing the authoritarian male might help reinforce the traditional gendered model of authority. At the same time, the Jesuit also provided a model that anti-Jesuits found most objectionable – the submissive female. This second image was useful, too, however, as a means of working against the threatened feminization of Protestantism from another source. As liberals within the Protestant Church, anti-Jesuits were engaged in a campaign against authoritarian males to make sure they themselves did not end up in submissive roles. While anti-Jesuits were content to have men make decisions on behalf of women, they objected to Church leaders imposing doctrinal orthodoxy on ordinary pastors. They rejected the attempts of their own hierarchy to discipline heterodox pastors and thus turn all Protestants into submissive beings. (There were several such cases in Imperial Germany. Adolf Sydow was disciplined in 1872, for instance, for questioning the virgin birth.)[60] Anti-Jesuits feared that Catholic norms seemed to be invading the Pro-testant Church and diluting its commitment to the independence of the individual. The essentially male character of Protestantism was under threat.

Liberal Protestants felt that, as educated men, they had the right to make such decisions and should be accountable only to their own congregations. This principle was central to the platform of the Protestant Association. In an effort to strengthen this argument, one member, Schenkel, wrote an account of Jesus's life, *Das Charakterbild Jesu,* in which, in the words of Douglas Hatfield, he depicted Jesus as "a kind of first-century *Protestantvereinler* [member of the Protestant Association] who inveighs against the conservative hierarchy of the day and condemns those who would attempt to impose the letter of the law."[61] The Progressive Party, which supported the expulsion of the Jesuits in 1872, rejected a Protestant church constitution proposed by Culture Minister Adalbert Falk in 1873 because it required pastors to swear belief in scripture and official doctrines, and thus reminded them of Catholicism.[62] The dominance of conservatives in Church government after 1879 meant that such disciplinary actions continued.[63] While a compromise constitution published in 1876 allowed for devolution in theory, authoritarian habits died hard. The Protestant hierarchy disciplined several pastors during this time, such as Carl Jatho of Cologne. Another, Gottfried Traub, was a brother of an anti-Jesuit author, Theodor.[64] Implicit in anti-Jesuitism was a critique of the authoritarianism of conservative Protestants. As August-Hermann Leugers has argued, attacks on Catholicism often served as a means of undermining opponents within Protestantism.[65]

The worst fears of liberal Protestants in their struggle for doctrinal freedom found expression in the image of the submissive Jesuit. While the Jesuit never appeared in a passive role in his relations with the laity, in his relationship with his superior he was completely subordinate. Anti-Jesuits were convinced that Jesuits demanded a greater level of obedience than any other order. As a subordinate, the Jesuit was thus associated with typically feminine attributes – self-denial, dependency and resignation.[66] Just as the Jesuits' emulation of masculine attributes was exaggerated, so too was their adoption of feminine characteristics. Jesuits were not the subjects but the slaves of their superior, according to their critics. Order members owed the general the same level of obedience as Christ himself, according to one writer.[67] In his semi-pornographic account, Assmus claimed that Jesuits were the tools of the general and characterized discipline within the order as "serfdom of the spirit as opposed to the freedom of reason."[68]

Anti-Jesuits suggested that Jesuit superiors dehumanized their underlings. Jesuits appeared as inanimate objects, principally corpses and machines, in anti-Jesuit literature. An Old Catholic, Johannes Heldwein, described Jesuits as "corpses" *(Leichen)* in the hands of their superiors.[69] Their obedience was often described as "cadaver-like."[70] In a particularly evocative image, Gustav Mix described the Jesuits as "victims of an evil system, in which the individual is only a pathetic, dead cog in a powerful machine."[71] The industrial image of Jesuits as robots was not that far removed from more traditional ones. "Robot" was originally a Czech word for the compulsory labor services owed by serfs to their masters. Anti-Jesuits did not wish this fate, in new or old form, on anyone; but especially not on other men.

Anti-Jesuits devoted considerable attention to the creation of the submissive Jesuit, arguing that he was the product of the Jesuit novitiate, where discipline was enforced even more strictly than in school. According to Deym, Jesuits passed over the most intelligent Catholics when recruiting novices, preferring to select those most likely to submit to authority.[72] The object of the novitiate was not to encourage study of the faith, but to inculcate habits of obedience and religious practice.[73] Jesuit superiors allegedly brainwashed their novices. Deym alleged that the outlook of novices was so distorted that they believed the fantastic tales of their superiors. When told by a Jesuit priest that an alliance of Prussian and Austrian Freemasons had plotted the defeat of Austria, a Catholic power, in the war of 1866, not one novice batted an eyelid, he claimed.[74] Anti-Jesuits imagined that the Jesuit general was unscrupulous in his methods and would not shrink from obliging Jesuits to commit sin.[75]

Once he had taken his vows, the Jesuit pledged absolute obedience. The process of emasculation was apparently complete. And yet, despite their adoption of feminine attributes, Jesuits were supposed to lead the Catholic community. Most bourgeois men rejected feminism because they believed women's lack of independence disqualified them from political participation. Anti-Jesuits rebutted arguments by Catholics for the importance of Jesuits in public life. The Protestant League noted the unsuitability of Jesuits for any public role, on the basis of their repudiation of free will, and responded with incredulity to Catholic claims that Jesuits were necessary to combat irreligious trends: "Priests, teachers, caretakers, who deny the first principle of all true piety and morality, the responsibility of the conscience, for the sake of a cadaver-like obedience to their superior, are the chosen saviors of a society threatened by atheism and Social Democracy?"[76]

Provoked by Catholic boasts about the intellectual heights attained by Jesuits, anti-Jesuits dismissed Jesuit scholarship entirely as compromised by the command of absolute obedience. Critics believed that such scholarship was inevitably tainted because it followed the dictates of the general or pope as opposed to reason. As one author, Doctor Georg Lomer, put it, Jesuits had no interest in the truth, only in "the truth according to the order."[77] Several authors suggested that Jesuit scholarship was superficial, and that Jesuits satisfied themselves with the mundane rather than the ethereal. One Protestant League writer drew a contrast between Jesuit and Protestant scholarship, the former being: "mountain scrub, whose thin branches lean toward the ground, but not the fresh, majestic tree that grows up towards the open sky."[78]

The fact that Protestant men obeyed authority with enthusiasm in other spheres, notably the military, did not however elude anti-Jesuits. In this sense, Protestants might be guilty of adopting a feminine position in an authority structure. Arthur Böhtlingk maintained there was an important distinction between the obedience owed in the army and in the Jesuit order:

> The Jesuit is not supposed to, like a servant or even an ordinary soldier, obey just externally, by carrying out the task or order of his superior; the kind of obedience that does not exclude one's own thought processes, is not sufficient; rather he is not allowed rest, until he has extinguished his own free will for the sake of the superior, that he owns feels and thinks as his master, and his will has been absorbed so completely in that of the superior, that he no longer has any independent wishes.[79]

The difference lay not in the fact of submission but its extent. Anti-Jesuits conceded that a chain of command was necessary, certainly in military affairs. The problem Jesuits posed was that they demanded a level of obedience from men that was acceptable only from women, if at all.

The duty of absolute obedience was disturbing, too, because of the purpose towards which it was directed. Anti-Jesuits viewed women's obedience to their husbands as part of a broader system of gender relations, the separation of spheres, that guaranteed practical and emotional support for each spouse and a nurturing environment for children, The obedience of soldiers to their superiors could be seen in positive terms too, in that it was directed towards the security of the state. The same claim could not be made about Jesuit obedience, however. The purpose of Jesuit obedience was entirely selfish, in the eyes of anti-Jesuits, in that it served the Jesuit general's political ambitions.

Conclusion

The image of the Jesuit evident in anti-Jesuit writings was a caricature. Both the authoritarian male and the submissive female exaggerated the level of obedience demanded by the Jesuit order. Each caricature was unsettling, the authoritarian male because apparently so committed to an ultramontane agenda, the submissive female because apparently so effective in the implementation of Jesuit plans. Such caricatures also helped to account for inadequacies on the part of anti-Jesuits themselves. Through the exaggeration of the masculinity of Jesuits, anti-Jesuit claims that a mere 737 men, the number present at the time of the expulsion in 1872, could destroy the state and nation became more plausible. These were not ordinary men but supermen, possessed of an unnaturally strong drive and remarkable, if misdirected, cleverness. By emphasizing the feminine qualities of Jesuits, anti-Jesuits accounted for the ease with which these men carried out their plans. As robots, they were immune from the restraining force of conscience that limited other kinds of underlings.

The combination of these images in what one might call the "Jesuit androgyne" added an extra element of discomfort for the Jesuits' enemies. As historians are increasingly realizing, confessional conflict took place within a specific context of gender relations as well as ethnic, political and socio-economic relations. The androgyne transgressed the boundaries between men and women as accepted by most of the bourgeoisie. The Jesuit did so in a more subtle way than feminists and homosexuals, who were also labeled androgynes. The effect was the same. The Jesuit androgyne challenged the assumption that people were either masculine or feminine, or at least were either authoritarian or submissive. The Jesuits were both at the one time. Of course, anti-Jesuits occupied intermediate positions in other hierarchies, such as the army or the workplace; but they liked to think that they preserved a part of themselves in all such relationships. Committed patriots, anti-Jesuits were proud of the fact that their nationalist activity, even if limited to attacks on Jesuit internationalism, was voluntary and not imposed from above. In reacting so strongly against this transgression of gender boundaries, anti-Jesuits suggested that they were conscious of challenges to the established order and wished to protect it.

If the anti-Jesuit preoccupation with authority and its gender dimensions was part of a gender crisis, this was an experience shared by contemporary Catholicism and Judaism as well. The question of authority was instrumental in the increasingly female face of the active Catholic congregation. Hugh McLeod points out that Catholicism became feminized not because women flocked to the Church, but because men deserted it. Catholic laymen resented the claims of other men to hold authority over them.[80] The difference with Protestantism was that its theology seemed to promise respect for individual autonomy. The Protestant pastor was never the same threat to lay men as the Catholic priest. The same could be said of the Jewish rabbi. Indeed, the model of devolved authority found in Judaism was closer to Protestantism than

Catholicism, and especially to the ideal of liberal Protestants, and accommodated itself more easily to the separation of spheres model. It helped that the majority of German Jews were middle-class. Judaism envisaged women's religious practice primarily in terms of the observance of Jewish law in the domestic sphere. Marion Kaplan has shown that, despite claims to the contrary, women took their religious duties seriously, so that Judaism did not become less feminine in this period.[81] The move from orthodox to reform Judaism that most German Jews made in the nineteenth century helped fulfill liberal Protestant wishes for a nation in their own image. Reform Judaism employed the vernacular in religious worship and dispensed with traditional dress, for instance. Committed to the Enlightenment and, as a minority, anxious to be accepted into German society, Jews were more cooperative than Catholics, who persisted with their traditions, such as Latin as a language of worship, and remained loyal to the Jesuits.

The fact that the gap in gender roles between Judaism and Jesuitism, as seen by its critics, was even greater than that between Protestantism and Jesuitism did not give rise to any particular antagonism between Jews and Jesuits. Jews certainly shared the distaste of many Protestants for Catholicism. They saw contemporary Catholicism as a repudiation of the Enlightenment, liberalism, and the national principle, and thus supported the legislation of the *Kulturkampf*.[82] At the same time, Jews were sympathetic to Catholics as fellow-victims of religious discrimination. Michael Gross has shown that, of the four Jewish deputies in the *Reichstag*, three voted against the expulsion of the Jesuits in 1872, and one abstained.[83] An article by the well-known Jewish journalist, Maximilian Harden, mocking the fears of anti-Jesuits as vastly out of proportion to the threat, reflected Jews' skepticism about anti-Jesuitism.[84]

The Jesuit question did not offer a sufficient basis for a coalition of Protestants and Jews or, for that matter, Catholics and Jews. Jesuitism was primarily an issue for Christians. The figure of the Jesuit androgyne, with its links to conflicts over gender roles, reminds us that inter-confessional conflict must be seen in the light of intra-confessional conflict, too. The feud between liberal and conservative Protestants in Imperial Germany was intense. While the Jesuit question encouraged Protestants to combine during the *Kulturkampf*, doubts about the state's secularizing agenda in the *Kulturkampf* and the growing threat from atheism and socialism caused conservative Protestants to rethink their position on Jesuits. After the *Kulturkampf* ended the Jesuit question demonstrated ecumenical potential, as conservative Protestants, under attack from their liberal co-religionists, wondered if Jesuits were not the lesser of two evils. While in the eighteenth century Enlightenment concerns about education had brought liberal Catholics and Protestants together, by the turn of the twentieth century opposition to liberals rather than Jesuits brought conservative Protestants and mainstream Catholics together. Only after the traumas of the Nazi period did a common Christian cause gain strength.

Notes

1. For a more complete account of anti-Jesuitism see my dissertation, "The Jesuit as Enemy: Anti-Jesuitism and the Protestant Bourgeoisie in Imperial Germany, 1890–1917," Georgetown University, 1999 or the book based on it, to be published by Brill, 2002.
2. Michael Gross, "Kulturkampf and Unification: German Liberalism and the War Against the Jesuits," *Central European History* 30 (1999): 545–66.
3. Lech Trzeciakowski, *The Kulturkampf in Prussian Poland* (New York: East European Monographs, distributed by Columbia University Press, 1990). On Jesuits, see pp. 50–2 and 89–91.
4. On the Protestant character of the German nation, see the discussion of the literary canon and historiography of Imperial Germany in Helmut Walser Smith, *German Nationalism and Religious Conflict: Culture, Ideology, Politics, 1870–1914* (Princeton, NJ: Princeton University Press, 1995).
5. For a full account of the Protestant League see Armin Müller–Dreier, *Konfession in Politik, Gesellschaft und Kultur des Kaiserreichs: der Evangelische Bund 1886–1914*, Religiöse Kulturen der Moderne, Vol. 7 (Gütersloh: Chr. Kaiser, 1998).
6. David Blackbourn, "Progress and Piety: Liberalism, Catholicism, and the State in Imperial Germany," *History Workshop Journal* 26 (1988): 57–78.
7. Theodore Zeldin, "The Conflict of Moralities: Confession, Sin and Pleasure in the Nineteenth Century," in T. Zeldin (ed.), *Conflicts in French Society: Anticlericalism, Education and Morals in the Nineteenth Century* (London: Allen and Unwin, 1970), p. 50; Ralph Gibson, *A Social History of French Catholicism* (London: Routledge, 1989), p. 45.
8. Thomas Laqueur, *Making Sex: Body and Gender from the Greeks to Freud* (Cambridge, MA: Harvard University Press, 1990); Michel Foucault, *The History of Sexuality* (New York : Pantheon, 1978).
9. Laqueur, *Making Sex*, pp. 134–6.

10. Ibid., esp. pp. 149–92.
11. Ute Frevert, "Bürgerliche Meisterdenker und das Geschlechterverhältnis: Konzepte, Erfahrungen, Visionen an der Wende vom 18. zum 19. Jahrhundert," in U. Frevert (ed.), *Bürger und Bürgerinnen: Geschlechterverhältnisse im 19. Jahrhundert* (Göttingen: Vandenhoeck and Ruprecht, 1988), pp. 21–3.
12. Isabel V. Hull, "Sexualität und bürgerliche Gesellschaft," in U. Frevert (ed.), *Bürger und Bürgerinnen*, p. 61.
13. Frevert, "Bürgerliche Meisterdenker," pp. 23–4.
14. Frevert, "Bürgerliche Meisterdenker," pp. 27–8.
15. See Anne-Charlotte Trepp, *Sanfte Männlichkeit und selbständige Weiblichkeit: Frauen und Männer im Hamburger Bürgertum zwischen 1770 und 1840* (Göttingen: Vandenhoek & Ruprecht, 1996). I am indebted to Julia Brüggeman for this reference.
16. Karin Hausen, "Family and role-division: the polarisation of sexual stereotypes in the nineteenth century – an aspect of the dissociation of work and family life," in Richard Evans and W. R. Lee (eds), *The German Family: essays on the social history of the family in nineteenth- and twentieth-century Germany* (London: Croom Helm, 1981), pp. 51–79.
17. Frevert, "Bürgerliche Meisterdenker," p. 31.
18. Gangolf Hübinger, *Kulturprotestantismus und Politik: Zum Verhältnis von Liberalismus und Protestantismus im wilhelminischen Deutschland* (Tübingen: Mohr Siebeck, 1995), pp. 61–2.
19. Schlechtendahl, Kirschstein, Superintendent and President of the Rhenish Provincial Synod, Wiemann for Inner Committee for Defense against the Readmission of the Jesuits to the Kaiser, 1 June 1892, Konfesssionskundliches Institut des Evangelischen Bundes, Bensheim, S500.009.106b.
20. For an analysis of the membership of the League see Müller-Dreier, *Konfession in Politik*, pp. 106–21.
21. See Manuel Borutta, "Das Andere der Moderne: Geschlecht, Sexualität und Krankheit in anti-Katholischen Diskursen Deutschlands und Italiens (1850–1900)," in Werner Rammart (ed.), *Kollektive Identitäten und Kulturelle Innovationen. Historische, soziologische und ethnologische Studien* (Leipzig: Akademie Verlag, forthcoming), which compares anti-Catholic discourse in Italy and Germany in the late nineteenth century.
22. David Blackbourn, "Progress and Piety," p. 63 and *The Marpingen Visions: Rationalism, Religion and the Rise of Modern Germany* (London: Fontana, 1995), p. 293.

23. Blackbourn, *Marpingen*.
24. Norbert Busch, *Katholische Frömmigkeit und Moderne: die Sozial- und Mentalitätsgeschichte des Herz Jesu-Kultes in Deutschland* (Gütersloh: Chr. Kaiser, 1997).
25. A. J. L. Busst, "The Image of the Androgyne in the Nineteenth Century," in *Romantic Anthologies* (London: Routledge and Kegan Paul, 1967), p. 1.
26. A. Krantz, *Der sittliche Charakter der Jesuiten, eine nothwendige Folge ihrer ersten Erziehung*, Flugschrift 39 (Leipzig: C. Braun, 1890), p. 3.
27. *Der Tag*, 9 Jan. 1913.
28. Busst, "Image of the Androgyne," p. 38.
29. Ibid., p. 39.
30. Fritz Stern, *The Politics of Cultural Despair – A Study in the Rise of the Germanic Ideology* (Berkeley, CA: University of California Press, 1961).
31. Busst, "Image of the Androgyne," p. 4.
32. John Fout, "Sexual Politics in Wilhelmine Germany: The Male Gender Crisis, Moral Purity, and Homophobia," *Journal of the History of Sexuality* 2 (1992): 419.
33. David Ehrenpreis, "Cyclists and Amazons: the New Woman," *Women's Art Journal* 20 (1999): 25.
34. *Simplicissimus 6*, no. 48 and 17, no. 4. Six of seven Jesuits drawn in these cartoons are tall and thin. The exception seems to be the superior.
35. Wilhelm Busch, "Pater Filuzius. Eine allegorische Geschichte," in Rolf Hochhut (ed.), *Sämtliche Werke* (Gütersloh, 1956).
36. Friedrich Paulsen, *Geschichte des gelehrten Unterrichts auf den deutschen Schulen und Universitäten vom Ausgang des Mittelalters bis zur Gegenwart* (Berlin: Walter de Gruyter, 1965), p. 418.
37. Hausen, "Family and role division," pp. 55–6.
38. Ibid.
39. Zur Linden, *Paskals Kampf wider die Jesuiten. Beitrag zur Jesuiten-frage* (Leipzig: Verlag der Buchhandlung des Evangelischen Bundes von Carl Strien, 1892), p. 18.
40. R. Herrmann, *Die jesuitische Moraltheologie. Ein Wort zur Liguori-Debatte* (Leipzig: Verlag der Buchhandlung des Evangelischen Bundes von C. Braun, 1903), p. 35.
41. Karl Weiss (Sauvain), *Der Jesuit im Beichtstuhle. Dreimal drei Briefe an einem katholischen Prälaten* (Bamberg: Handels. Dr., 1913), p. 70.

42. Franz Graf Deym, *Beiträge zur Aufklärung über die Gemeinschaft-lichkeit des Jesuitenordens,* 2nd edn (Leipzig: Hartknoch, 1872), p. 39. For a fuller critical account of Jesuit pedagogy, see Georg Mertz, *Die Pädagogik der Jesuiten nach den Quellen von der ältesten bis in die neueste Zeit dargestellt* (Heidelberg: C. Winter, 1898).
43. Herrmann, *Jesuitische Moraltheologie,* p. 38.
44. Gustav Mix, *Wir lassen sie nicht herein,* Wartburgheft 64 (Berlin: Evangelischer Bund, 1912), p. 2.
45. Anonymous, *Katechismus der Jesuitenmoral* (Leipzig: Breitkopf and Härtel, 1913), pp. 91–2.
46. Ibid.
47. Kevin McAleer, *Dueling: The Cult of Honor in Fin-de-Siècle Germany* (Princeton, NJ: Princeton University Press, 1994).
48. Jörg Lanz-Liebenfels, *Katholizismus wider Jesuitismus* (Frankfurt am Main: Neuer Frankfurter Verlag, 1903), p. 39.
49. Franz Huber, *Jesuitenmoral. Aus den Quellen dargestellt* (Bern: Haller'sche Verlagshandlung, 1870), pp. 311–47.
50. Weiss, *Jesuit im Beichtstuhle,* p. 14.
51. Hertha Busemann, *Der Jesuit und seine Beichttochter: die Faszination eines Sittenskandals in 3 Jahrhunderten* (Oldenburg: Bibliotheks- und Informationssystem der Universität Oldenburg, 1987). See also Burghard Assmuss (ed.), *Jesuitenspiegel. Interessante Beiträge zur Naturgeschichte der Jesuiten* (Berlin: Berliner Verlag Inst., 1904), p. 180.
52. August Franzen, "Die Zöllibatsfrage im 19. Jahrhundert: Der 'Badische Zolibatssturm' (1828) und das Problem der Priesterehe im Urteile Johann Adam Moehlers und Johann Baptist Hirschers," *Historisches Jahrbuch* 91 (1971): 383.
53. Philip Ingram, "Protestant Patriarchy and the Catholic Priesthood in nineteenth-century Britain," *Journal of Social History* 24 (1991): 787. In Britain, interest in clerical sexual transgressions was so great that pornographers seized upon anti-clerical literature as a source for their work.
54. Oliver Janz, *Bürger besonderer Art: Evangelische Pfarrer in Preussen 1850–1914* (Berlin: de Gruyter, 1994), pp. 409–10.
55. Ibid.
56. Ursula Baumann, *Protestantismus und Frauenemanzipation in Deutschland 1850 bis 1920* (Frankfurt: Campus, 1992), p. 71. Baumann claims that the members used the excuse that the League was classified as a political association, and thus not open to women until 1908. This was true only for certain provinces and regions, however. Müller-Dreier, "Konfessionelle 'Selbstbehauptung,'" p. 152.

57. Baumann, *Protestantismus,* p. 72.
58. Ursula Baumann, "Religion und Emanzipation: Konfessionelle Frauenbewegung in Deutschland, 1900–1933," in *Tel Aviver Jahrbuch für deutsche Geschichte* (1992): 188.
59. Baumann, "Religion," pp. 188–9.
60. Douglas W. Hatfield, "Reform in the Prussian Evangelical Church and the Concept of the Landesherr," *Journal of Church and State* 24 (1982): 563.
61. Ibid., p. 558.
62. Ibid., p. 565. Only half the Progressive deputies in the Reichstag voted for the Jesuit Law, but the others seem to have been dissatisfied because the restrictions were insufficiently strong: Michael Gross, "Anti-Catholicism, Liberalism and German National Identity, 1848–1880," (Ph.D. diss., Brown University, 1997), p. 235.
63. The compromise constitution published in 1876 allowed for devolution in theory, but authoritarian habits died hard.
64. Th. Traub, *Die Jesuiten. Material zur Jesuitenfrage* (Berlin: Evangelischer Bund, 1912).
65. August-Hermann Leugers, "Latente Kulturkampfstimmung im wilhelminischen Kaiserreich," in Johannes Horstmann (ed.), *Die Verschränkung von Innen-, Konfessions- und Kolonialpolitik im Deutschen Reich vor 1914* (Schwerte: Katholische Akademie, 1987), p. 23.
66. Hausen, "Family and role division," pp. 55–6.
67. *Die Wahrheit über die Jesuiten,* (Berlin: Carl Habel, 1900), pp. 11–16.
68. Assmus, *Jesuitenspiegel,* p. 44.
69. Johannes Heldwein, *Die Jesuiten und das deutsche Volk* (Munich: P. Müller, 1913), p. 7.
70. Heinrich Boehmer, *Die Jesuiten. Eine historische Skizze.* 2nd extended and rev. edn (Leipzig: Teubner, 1904), pp. 41–2.
71. Mix, *Wir lassen sie nicht herein,* p. 2.
72. Deym, *Beiträge zur Aufklärung,* pp. 18–19.
73. Ibid., pp. 20–21.
74. Ibid., p. 22.
75. Bishop von Ketteler challenged this assumption in *Kann ein Jesuit von seinem Oberen zu einer Sünde verpflichtet werden: Correspondenz mit dem Freihrn. v. Starck* (Mainz: Kirchheim, 1874).
76. Appeal to Protestant Germany, Central Committee of the Protestant League, cited in *Leipziger Tageblatt,* Jan. 4 1894.

77. Georg Lomer, *Ignatius von Loyola, vom Erotiker zum Heiligen: eine pathographische Geschichtsstudie* (Leipzig: J. A. Barth, 1913), p. 1.

78. Christian Friedrich Meyer, *Der Jesuitenorden und die deutsche Volksseele,* Wartburgheft 64 (Berlin: Verlag des Evangelischen Bundes), 1913, p. 15.

79. Arthur Bohtlingk, *Die Jesuiten und das deutsche Reich; Zeitgemässes* (Frankfurt a.M.: Neuer Frankfurter Verlag, 1903), p. 8.

80. Hugh McLeod, "Weibliche Frömmigkeit – männlicher Unglaube? Religion und Kirche im 19. Jahrhundert," in Frevert (ed.), *Bürger und Bürgerinnen,* pp. 34–56.

81. Marion Kaplan, *The Making of the Jewish Middle Class: Women, Family and Identity* (New York: Oxford University Press, 1991).

82. Uriel Tal, *Christians and Jews in Germany: Religion, Politics and Ideology in the Second Reich, 1870–1914* (Ithaca, NY: Cornell University Press, 1975), p. 98.

83. Gross, "Anti-Catholicism," p. 239

84. *Die Zukunft,* 52, 1912.

Part IV
Religious Difference, Local Politics, and Pluralism

The Rise of the Religious Right and the Recasting of the "Jewish Question": Baden in the 1840s*

Dagmar Herzog

Although some scholars who have investigated the relationship between German liberalism and Jewish emancipation have noted the phenomenon of liberal ambivalence about emancipation, the prevailing view in German history and Jewish studies circles is that liberals were the most important and dependable political allies of the Jews.[1] What has not been explained is precisely how reluctant liberals became the staunch defenders of emancipation they were subsequently celebrated to be. By analyzing debates over Jewish rights in Baden, well known as nineteenth-century Germany's most liberal state, this chapter explores this apparent contradiction.

The contention here is that debates over Jewish rights can be more fully understood when we grasp how these debates were interwoven in complex ways with a variety of intra-Christian conflicts over sex, love and marriage, and over the relationship between individual subjectivity and religious authority. For Baden, in the 1830s and 1840s, was not only home to some of Germany's greatest liberal luminaries, but was also the seedbed for politically effective conservative Catholicism. Disputes over priestly celibacy, over mixed marriages between Protestants and Catholics, and over the rights of Christian dissenters increasingly pitted political liberals against this rising religious Right led by ultramontanes. It was really, at base, a long-standing fight over male sexual and romantic rights that ultimately caused the most admired and respected of German liberals to become the defenders of Jewish rights that most historians have assumed they were all along. This was so because the intensification of conflict over the content and meaning of Christianity caused a fundamental recasting of the terms in which the "Jewish Question" was understood and debated.

The Grand Duchy of Baden was formed between 1803 and 1806 as part of the Napoleonic reorganization of Europe. A Protestant monarch ruled over a population that was two-thirds Catholic and only one-third Protestant. Nonetheless, there were initially few conflicts between the state and the Catholic leadership, for, in the early decades of the nineteenth century, much of Baden's Catholic hierarchy and many clergy were Enlightenment-inspired and sought out reconciliation with Protestants and distance from Rome. The great drama of the 1830s and 1840s involved the displacement of these more reformist Catholics by activist ultramontanes. Contemporaneously with the rise of ultramontanism came the rise of self-conscious, self-confident political liberalism. Although the Baden Diet had been established in 1819, it was only after the accession to the throne in 1830 of Grand Duke Leopold, more open-minded than his predecessor, that the Lower Chamber of the Diet acquired the freedom to discuss any and all political matters that made it the envy of the rest of Germany, and the leading forum for the airing of liberal views in the pre-1848 era.

The year 1831 was considered a year of triumph for liberal agendas as such as free elections, a freer press and expanded communal self-government; but when discussion turned to the issue of Jewish emancipation, liberals joined conservatives in rejecting the Jewish community's petitions for full equality. Thus, in 1831, the 18,000 Jews in a population of more than one million Badeners (by 1846 there would be approximately 21,000 Jews in a population of 1.3 million Badeners) were still denied four fundamental rights: the right to be a delegate to the Lower Chamber, the right to all military and state offices, the right to be a mayor or town councilor, and the right to move from one community into another, where no Jews had as yet lived, without permission from that community.

On the issue of Jewish emancipation, the self-identified liberals in Baden's Lower Chamber tended to divide into two general camps. A majority of liberals (and herein they concurred with the majority of those who saw themselves as government loyalists) insisted that emancipation could not be granted until Jews had proved themselves worthy by becoming more assimilated into Christian society. Nonetheless, except for a dogged few who expressed doubt that Jews were capable of, or interested in, such moral self-improvement, this group continually averred that it favored emancipation as an ultimate goal. A minority of liberals, by contrast, pressed for immediate emancipation, arguing that only the granting of emancipation would cause Jews to assimilate in the desired ways.

The majority resistant to emancipation included some of the most illustrious liberals in Baden: men roundly esteemed for their consistent commitment to securing all manner of free institutions and expansions of civic rights; men like Karl von Rotteck, Adam von Itzstein, Adolf

Sander, Ignaz Rindeschwender and Friedrich Hecker. They perceived Jews to be the ones who were peculiarly illiberal, resistant to modernity, uncompromising towards Christians. Sander even went so far as to declare that "if we were to change positions, and to trade places with them, if we 18,000 Christians placed ourselves *vis-à-vis* one million Jews, I ask you, would they emancipate us? No, they would devour us, as the hated children of Noab [*sic*], with fire and the sword. Don't think that these are empty words."[2]

The majority of liberals found three dimensions of Jewish distinctiveness objectionable – they referred to them as religious, national and social peculiarities – and tended to see these three dimensions as inextricably fused with one another. Thus, for example, in response to those leaders of the Jewish community who stressed that it was unconscionable for the delegates to demand that Jews change any of their religious practices – that no human being should be asked to trade his faith for political advantage – these delegates vehemently denied that they had any religious prejudice against Jews, even as they continually referred to Baden as a Christian state. But because they saw the three dimensions of Jewish difference as interconnected, they then typically proceeded either to argue that the problem with the Jewish religion was that it was "theocratic" – that the longing of the Jews for their Messiah made them incapable of genuine obedience to the laws of a non-Jewish state – and/or that rabbinical teachings caused Jews to behave in socially offensive ways, and thus that it was the national or social difference of Jews that was the "real" problem.

Within this circular method of argumentation, the national dimension of Jewish difference was also emphasized by constant reference to the notion that Jews constituted a separate nation, that they were foreigners, not Germans, not Badeners: a homeless, displaced people that refused to mingle with any other peoples, that clung rigidly to the faith of its fathers. Arguments about the social dimension also circled back to religious matters. Here the two main complaints had to do with Jewish self-segregation – believed to be expressed in such elements of Jewish religious practice as dietary laws or the observation of the Sabbath on Saturdays – and with the perception that Jews were dishonest in their economic dealings with non-Jews: that the petty trading and money-lending on which the majority of Baden's Jewish community subsisted was necessarily usurious and exploitative, and that this "unproductive" behavior took its justification from the Talmud.

In short, despite the disclaimers about religious prejudice, these liberal delegates tended to portray Judaism as a religion vastly inferior to

Christianity, and to stress a causal connection between this religion and the Jews' much-maligned economic roles. As self-perceived represent-atives of "the people," the majority of liberals used popular hostility towards Jews as the justification for their own hesitancy to extend emancipation. They did so without bothering to analyze how the transition from a feudal to a market economy had forced rural Christians into a dependent relationship with Jews as the social group responsible for exporting and importing goods out of and into the rural economy, and the group most willing to offer small credit. They also failed to consider how the ongoing restrictions on Jews' residence rights limited the feasibility for Jews of taking up their only recently acquired right to enter the trades or agriculture, for in most villages all occupational niches were filled.

The more progressive minority of liberals sought to counter these arguments in a variety of ways. They tended to emphasize that the major difference between Jews and Christians was a religious one, and that religious difference should be no excuse for political inequality. But they also stressed the ways in which Baden's Jews were modernizing their religion: how they were replacing the Hebrew language with German in their synagogue services; or how the new books for religious education of their children contained only the purest moral principles. They insisted that Baden's Jews were indeed Germans and Badeners, that they had lived in the land for centuries, that they were loyal to the monarch and that they had fought impressively in the recent Wars of Liberation. They reeled off statistics about the number of Jews who were taking up respectable trades and entering the professions. They reminded their colleagues that there were Christian usurers as well as Jewish ones; that by no means all Jewish money-lenders were usurious; that the operative moral distinction should be between usurers and non-usurers, not between Jews and Christians. Finally, they stressed that they, too, were faith-filled Christians, and many (though not all) also said they valued the notion of a Christian state; but they pointed out that Christianity was a religion based on love and equality, not hatred and hierarchy.

Yet these counter-arguments were almost invariably embedded in a more problematic line of reasoning, which turned on the notion that the granting of equality would lead to the dilution of difference, and that such dilution was eminently desirable. No matter how militant their defense of the principle that "by nature every human being has equal rights," they routinely coupled this insight with the notion that "emanci-pation should not be . . . the reward for enlightenment, but rather the means by which that enlightenment will be achieved."[3] As one avid pro-emancipationist put it in a classic formulation: "It is my conviction that nothing remains but to throw the Israelites, with equal rights, into the mass of the Christian population, so that, ripped along by the torrent, they will, like the pebbles rolling along in a riverbed, round themselves off and fit themselves in."[4] Another fervent pro-emancipationist declared:

> "I want to give them freedom . . . because I want to better them, and because I am convinced that only in freedom . . . can one truly thrive . . . We should seek justice, and *then* all else will be given unto us. *Then* also the Jews will be given unto us, that means they will no longer hesitate . . . to accommodate themselves more fully to our conditions."[5]

Although (in response to petitions submitted by leaders of Baden's Jewish community) Jewish emancipation was debated in Baden's Lower Chamber in 1831, 1833, 1835, 1837, 1840, 1842 and 1845, nothing much changed either in the terms of debate or in the proportion of delegates supporting equality. From a high of nineteen men (out of a total of sixty-three) in 1835, the number of pro-emancipationists in the Chamber tumbled back down to fifteen in February 1845, even as the number of self-identified liberals in the Chamber had climbed in the 1840s to more than half the delegates. However, only a brief eighteen months later, in August 1846, there was a dramatic reversal of opinion: fully two-thirds of the delegates, in a triumphant landslide, voted in favor of full Jewish emancipation. This sudden shift in liberal attitudes cannot be understood until we see that the 1830s and 1840s were times of intensifying ideological polarization in Baden, in which the liberal majority in the Lower Chamber became increasingly distressed about the growth of a religious Right outside the Chamber.

The polarization first took shape in the late 1820s and early 1830s around a conflict over priestly celibacy. In two widely-publicized campaigns, reform-minded Catholic laypeople and priests (led by prominent professors at Freiburg University) solicited the Lower Chamber's assistance in convincing the Grand Duke to induce the archbishop to abolish enforced priestly celibacy within Baden's borders. The reformers called celibacy "unnatural, illegal and immoral," an "unnecessary coercion," which robbed the individual of his "personal freedom" and of the "enjoyment" of "one of the most essential natural rights".[6] Because of the enlightened tendencies of much of Baden's Catholic clergy in the early nineteenth century; because in the wake of the French Revolution Rome's power was at a nadir; and especially because of the Baden state government's commitment to keeping the Catholic Church in check with

189

the principle of *Staatskirchentum,* the anti-celibacy activists' hope of success was actually plausible.

Although the intimidated Chamber of 1828 did not feel competent to take a stand on religious matters, the famous liberal Chamber of 1831 enthusiastically supported the reformers' demands. Calling celibacy "unnatural" and "inhumane," and decrying the "exclusion of a whole class from the greatest of life's pleasures," one delegate after another voted in favor of urging the Grand Duke to plan for a Catholic synod at which the matter of priestly celibacy could be discussed and appropriately resolved.[7] The reformers had miscalculated, however, when they tried to play two authorities off against each other; for despite its resistance to Catholic autonomy, the state felt itself far too dependent on the Catholic Church as a guardian of order and morality even to consider intervening in the Church's handling of celibacy, and therefore rejected the reformers' request out of hand. The reformers had clearly failed to achieve the desired result.

More significantly, the long-term effect of the anti-celibacy campaign was that the leaders of the campaign lost their jobs. Though initially the state government was reluctant to accede to Rome's wishes, eventually all the progressive Catholic professors at Freiburg were replaced by men who had, as one historian put it, "overcome . . . the Enlightenment."[8] Young men studying for the priesthood in Baden were now exposed primarily to conservative teachers, and this tremendously alarmed political liberals. From this point on, men's rights to sexual expression and freedom from Church coercion would be a major plank in the liberal platform and liberals would identify the now increasingly confident ultramontanes as their most formidable ideological opponents. The liberals' sense of threat intensified in the 1840s as a conservative renewal indisputably took place within Badenese Catholicism. A group of leading laypeople, with the immensely influential professor and publicist Franz Josef Buß foremost among them, had founded a new Catholic newspaper, the *Süddeutsche Zeitung für Kirche and Staat,* which tried to spread ultramontane ideas and soon established itself as the most conservative newspaper in Baden. It succeeded dramatically in expanding the terms of debate on a wide range of issues, and continually forced papers of all other persuasions to engage with its perspectives. Another prominent conservative and director of the *Collegium Theologicum* in Freiburg, Alban Stolz, had begun to produce the *Kalender für Zeit und Ewigkeit,* an annual almanac with explicitly ultramontane tendencies, written in an accessible, earthy style, which rapidly became one of the few texts typically read in Baden's impoverished rural areas. The new archbishop Hermann von Vicari also contributed to the conservative revival through his many travels and visits to parishes throughout Baden, and through his establishment of new church-run seminaries. Liberals were especially worried about these new educational institutions, in which they feared that young boys would be trained in obscurantist anti-rationalism.

Just how much the hostility between liberals and conservative Catholics had grown became apparent particularly when a growing conflict over mixed marriages between Catholics and Protestants came to a head early in 1845. The conflict had already been initiated by Rome in 1836, but for a while it remained largely confined to negotiations between representatives of the state and the Church. In Baden at that time, many hundreds of couples lived in mixed marriages – more, in proportion to the size of the population, than in any other German state.

The state government, deeply concerned to maintain confessional peace and believing mixed marriages to be the major site at which the Catholic and Protestant populations of the Grand Duchy could be harmoniously unified, strenuously sought to protect the rights of mixed couples to choose each other and to choose how to raise their children. Thus, for example, Baden's liberal Minister of the Interior, Karl Friedrich Nebenius, earnestly discoursed on "the reconciling power of marriage," and elaborated that mixed marriages had helped to "overcome the damaging mutual prejudices, antipathies and hesitations, interweave the physical and spiritual interests of families of different confessions in the most intimate way, and therefore in all these ways like almost no other thing worked towards the inner unity and strengthening of the life of the state and the life of the *Volk*."[9] The state therefore insisted on maintaining the long-established practice (which was also ensconced in the law of the land) that both the Catholic and the Protestant clergyman should refrain from pressuring mixed couples in any way and that both should participate in blessing the marriage.

However, the state once again also felt itself to be dependent on the churches, for it wanted marriage to be not just a civil act, but rather for "its higher nature also to be brought to light through the consecration of the Church."[10] In short, it was precisely because of this ambivalence on the part of the state that Catholic conservatives could promote their own perspectives ever more successfully. This became apparent in January 1845, when the new archbishop Vicari, with Rome's support, circumvented the state authorities and secretly circulated a directive to his clergymen with the goal of encouraging them either to dissuade mixed couples from marrying at all or at least to insist on the Catholic upbringing of their children. Baden's Catholic clergymen were now faced with two competing authorities: the state demanding that they maintain the old and more relaxed practice, and the church hierarchy insisting that they initiate a stricter practice.

This state–church stand-off (which, incidentally, the church would win) was soon publicized and rapidly spiraled into a much larger public debate with far-reaching effects.[11] From the pulpit, in the daily press, in polemical tracts and in scholarly reference works, mixed marriages became the subject of the most heated outpourings. Liberals in the Lower Chamber and the press, wielding the slogan "Love unites what faith divided," continually stressed individual freedom of choice and the socially trans-formative power of love, and pounced on every countervailing perspective presented by the conservatives. For liberals, the controversy over mixed marriages was another incarnation of the earlier controversy over celibacy. In both, their anti-authoritarianism and preoccupation with individual freedom of choice was conjoined with a programmatic insistence on the joys of married life, in which they continually conflated insistence on every man's right to sexual expression with paeans to domestic bliss.[12]

Conservative Catholics, by contrast, voiced a deep distrust of love and sexual attraction as the basis for a marriage: "What?," a member of the archbishop's staff had asked, "The conscience of the couple . . . bribed by the most powerful sensual attraction, should *decide* – decide in . . . their own case?! What? The defendant should also be the judge?"[13] Similarly, the *Süddeutsche Zeitung für Kirche und Staat* asserted that "in marriage a brutal, powerful sensuality must be combated. If marriage becomes debased, then the spouses, the children, the family, and the state . . . are *all* endangered."[14] And one of the newly-installed conservative Freiburg professors declared that it was (Catholic) Christianity that saved sexual relations within marriage from being purely "animalistic."[15] In mixed marriages, on the other hand, as one conservative priest intoned, there was "only love of the flesh."[16]

It was right in the midst of this battle, in the summer of 1845, that the religious landscape of Baden changed. Just as elsewhere across the German lands, so also in Baden, a protest movement emerged specifically in reaction to the rise of Catholic ultramontanism in general and Rome's new authoritarianism in marital matters in particular (although the most immediate catalyst was outrage over a mass pilgrimage organized in 1844 to the Holy Robe of Trier, supposedly worn by Jesus at his death). The Catholic dissenters, led by Johannes Ronge, a former Catholic chaplain from Silesia who had been excommunicated because of a letter of dissent he wrote about the Robe, were joined by Protestants disaffected by neo-orthodox trends in their own church. Together, they split from the established churches and founded democratically-run congregations, dedicated to individual freedom of belief and the separation of church and state. In Baden, there were ten congregations, encompassing 700 official members, though there were many more sympathizers.

The dissenters particularly welcomed priests who wanted to marry as their spiritual leaders, and especially encouraged mixed Protestant–Catholic couples to join their fold, thus directly snubbing the Catholic hierarchy in its stances on sex and marriage. The dissenters developed the liberal defense of sex even further, insisting that sex was not only natural, but also divine – a "sacred yearning" – and they rhapsodized about "sexual love, that divine and deifying love between man and woman."[17] The dissenters called themselves *Deutschkatholiken,* as opposed to Roman Catholics. Though a number of historians have analyzed the nationalist, anti-Rome impulses reflected in the movement's chosen name, and others have studied its important role in launching the first organized German women's movement, the movement's central preoccupation with men's sexual and romantic rights has received no attention.[18] Yet because of the evolving tension between liberals and ultramontanes over these rights, it was precisely this element of the movement's vision that was to have important consequences for how liberals came to reconceptualize the "Jewish Question". Because of their own indignation at conservative Catholic views on individual freedom and on sex and marriage, political liberals were thrilled with the emergence of dissent and rushed vociferously to the dissenters' defense when these dissenters, by stepping out of the traditional Christian churches, lost the political rights they had previously held and became similar in status to Jews. Simultaneously, livid about how brazenly the dissenters were taking on the Catholic hierarchy, Catholic conservatives vied with each other to defame them in the most lurid terms.

It was in this context of liberal delight in dissent and concern about rising ultramontanism that the liberal delegate Karl Zittel, on 15 December 1845, advanced before his colleagues in the Lower Chamber the principle that every citizen in Baden ought to be able to profess his faith without thereby forfeiting any rights of citizenship. He introduced a motion that would implement this principle, yet he also included a clause that would limit it to avowed Christians. Although the realization of complete religious freedom was his genuine goal (Zittel, a recent convert to emancipation, had already expressed strong support for it in the last debate on that topic ten months earlier), he added this limiting clause because his most immediate goal was to secure the right of *Deutschkatholiken* to organize themselves as a church. He was well aware that his motion could face severe objections even with this clause, but given the continuing hostility to Jewish emancipation among the majority of his colleagues, the motion had almost no chance of passing without it.

Therefore, in the speech introducing his motion for universal religious freedom, Zittel went to great lengths not to mention Jews by name, in an obvious attempt to strengthen the motion's chances. He did, however, albeit in a convoluted fashion, refer to the implications the motion inevitably held for Baden's Jews:

> "I would be unfaithful to my own principles if I were to limit my motion from the outset through the exclusion of any one religious party. But – I cannot say this without a certain shame – I cannot insist on this, for I can have no hope that my motion, phrased so generally, will receive the approval of the House. The majority of you feels itself more accountable to the general antipathy against a religious party which lives among us, an antipathy which it has of course primarily incurred through the way of life of its lower classes, than to justice . . . In order therefore not to cause the motion for religious freedom itself to fail, [a freedom] which has recently become so very important because of the movement in the Christian population, I at this point of course see myself forced possibly to limit the motion in the second instance to those who profess the Christian religion."[19]

Recognizing that this willingness to limit the motion only to Christians necessarily called attention to the question of whether the dissenters were in fact Christians, Zittel knew he had to counter the new strict definitions of Christianity increasingly being advanced by conservative Catholics in the contentious debates surrounding priestly celibacy and mixed marriages. These conservatives insisted that the Catholic Church, under the guidance of Rome, was the only true expression of Christianity. They continually asserted that without obedience to the church hierarchy and uniformity of belief within the church, disintegration of the social fabric and the spread of immorality were inevitable.

Against this conception, Zittel stressed the sacred inviolability of the individual's understanding of spiritual matters. He also argued that the drive for community was fundamental to human nature, and that each individual should be free to join with others of like mind to satisfy his or her spiritual needs; and he insisted that society as a whole benefited from such freedom of spiritual expression. In summary, Zittel wished to "let truth everywhere cut its own path, and give the spirit freedom; true religiosity is rooted only in this freedom. Even if this may seem problematic for the church, religion is more important than the church; better no church than no religion."[20]

It was clear that it was the growth of ultramontanism that was motivating Zittel to attempt to ensconce religious freedom in the law of the land, for he offered his colleagues an extended summary of the whole rise of the religious Right over the preceding years, replete with references to the battles over mixed marriages in Prussia and Baden, and to the Trier pilgrimage that had been the catalyst for the dissenting movement. "Worse things yet are being silently planned," he warned, "the dark spirit of fanaticism has almost everywhere moved in to the educational institutions for future religious teachers . . . a dark mysterious force has arisen from the grave and has spread itself over our fatherland . . . Jesuitism is marching forwards with giant steps, trampling under its feet our century's budding seeds of freedom and Enlightenment."[21]

Acutely aware that the *Deutschkatholiken* were not considered Christians by conservative Catholics, Zittel addressed this point directly:

> "Gentlemen, recognize well what question lies here before us: Are the *Deutschkatholiken* Christians? Is their statement of faith Christian? Is their church Christian? Now, who will answer? Who should decide? . . . Look around, gentlemen, in the whole realm of the state you find no tribunal of faith; the nineteenth century no longer tolerates one. For the state, it must be enough that a religious corporation declares, *that it wants* to be *Christian*. The *deutschkatholische* community has done this; it has declared that it wants to develop a community in the sense and the spirit of Jesus the Christ, and that it seeks nourishment in His gospel for its religious meaning and life. The state must see to it that the spirit of immorality does not gain ground within it and that it does not nurture principles dangerous to the state; but as long as that is not the case, the state cannot deny it the label and recognition as a *Christian* community."[22]

In his concluding remarks, Zittel reiterated the Christian identity of the dissenters when he stressed that the movement for religious freedom they represented would lead to the reconciliation of all Christian Germans that had for so painfully long eluded the German people.

Similar tendencies appeared in the remarks made by other liberal delegates in the brief discussion following Zittel's statement. Liberals who favored Jewish emancipation extolled the virtues of dissent, continually reinforced the idea that dissenters were Christians, and made only indirect gestures in favor of Jewish equality by applauding the inclusion of "all religions" in Zittel's motion.[23] The fervently pro-dissent but anti-emancipationist Friedrich Hecker, prominent liberal and later revolutionary, however, made the distinction he saw between dissenters and Jews explicit. Hecker, who hated ultramontanes – "nobody lusts for power like the priest", he wrote in a book defending dissent – also here in the Chamber described in glowing terms the "great moment in our history" signaled by the emergence of dissent, and declared that it would be "blasphemy," "slander of that which is most sacred, if one were to try to prevent a human being from worshipping the Eternal in his own way".[24] Yet he failed to connect such sentiments with his attitudes towards Jews; the allusion was indirect, but Hecker's meaning was unmistakable: "In the interest of freedom, I do not support the motion for one part of the population of this land. I do not want the priests' state, and I also do not want the theocratic state."[25]

Less liberal delegates lamented the assaults on Catholicism and/or indicated that they were not in agreement with Zittel on all points, but they acknowledged that the motion was "maybe the most important matter that will be discussed in this session of the Diet," and they were willing to let the motion be debated further at a later date.[26] In fact, the discussion that day was only supposed to decide one thing: whether Zittel's motion should be printed and sent to committee, so that a report could be prepared and then the matter could be discussed substantively at a future point by the full house. At the end of the discussion, the sixty delegates present unanimously decided that this would indeed happen.

The relaxed attitude of the conservatives in the Lower Chamber incensed conservatives elsewhere in Baden. While the *Süddeutsche Zeitung für Kirche und Staat* had been fiercely criticizing the *Deutschkatholiken* since their emergence, it was specifically the unanimous vote to send Zittel's motion to committee that turned its single-handed effort into a broad-based protest.[27] A rash of tracts censuring the *Deutschkatholiken* appeared, stirring up public opinion, alerting Grand Duke Leopold's government to the dangers of religious freedom, and castigating the conservative delegates for their inattention. [28]

In stark contrast to the vague allusions to Jews made by Zittel and his liberal supporters in their endorsement of the dissenters, critics of the motion for religious freedom constantly worked to link dissenters and Jews. The pamphleteer Ludwig Castorph, for instance, articulated clearly what he saw as the logical implication of granting full equality to the dissenters: "The requested religious freedom, in the way *they* mean it, is unacceptable, because then, to be fair, the *other sects* and *the Jews* would also have to be granted equal rights and privileges."[29] The prominent conservative Catholic professor Johann Baptist Hirscher similarly warned that "immorality . . . is decisively encouraged when good and bad are treated equally in social life. Thereby the worth of morality sinks in the eyes of the public. Likewise, the worth of religion must sink in the eyes of the people, when the law . . . treats Christians, Jews and pagans as equals."[30] Franz Josef Buß, in his *Das Rongethum in der badischen Abgeordnetenkammer* (1846), exposed the implications of Zittel's reasoning most pointedly:

> But you, Mr. Friend of Light, believe that as long as the spirit of morality finds its place in your protégé congregation, and as long as no principles are nurtured there that threaten the state, then the state could not refuse it recognition as a *Christian* community. But according to this logic, a Jew, a pagan, and a Turk would also be a Christian.[31]

Aside from Buß, the other most influential anti-dissent activist was Alban Stolz, who wrote three tracts against the dissenters. His *Landwehr gegen den badischen Landstand* (1845) was sent into every Catholic community in Baden and was read aloud to the townspeople by priests and mayors.[32] It explicitly urged the readers and listeners both to pray daily that God might rescue Baden from the dissenting movement and the faithlessness, sin and sexual corruption it represented, and to send petitions to the Grand Duke requesting that the Lower Chamber be dissolved for having let Zittel's motion go to committee. (This dissolution of the Chamber had been Buß's express goal as well.)

Furthermore, in a striking parallel with the way religious and economic arguments had long been intertwined in attacks on Jews, Stolz used a similar combination of arguments against dissenters. He accused the Diet delegates of using the dissenting movement to destroy Catholicism, and he claimed that if Zittel's motion was passed, the townspeople would be forced to pay heavily for dissenters' churches, pastors and schoolteachers. Like other pamphleteers, Stolz stressed that the dissenters were just as un-Christian as Jews or Turks. [33]

Stolz's two other anti-*Deutschkatholiken* tracts, also consciously geared to a partially literate rural audience, were even more graphic in the way they both sexualized and "judaized" the dissenters. Both these tactics served to undermine dissenters' claims to be Christians. The sexualization was a logical rhetorical tactic because of the genuine significance of sexual matters for the movement and its supporters – sex was very much at the heart of liberal–ultramontane hostilities – but it also served as a more general signifier of the all-too-human and thus not properly spiritual concerns of the dissenters. The "judaizing" of dissenters was obviously a way to undermine their self-perception as Christians; throwing in references to Turks for good measure served to exoticize both Jews and dissenters, reinforcing the implication that these were foreign elements. In *Amulett gegen die jungkatholische Sucht* (1845), Stolz repeatedly associated dissent with lust and adultery, and slyly suggested that dissenters were offering Catholic priests a trade: the "priests of the flesh" could have women, if the parishioners no longer had to go to confession.[34] Furthermore, after having established that "God destroyed the Jews' temple and rejected their worship," he declared that "now the *Rongeaner* want to become like the Jews, they want . . . only rabbis who will sing for them and make pretty speeches".[35] In criticizing the dissenters' rationalist rejection of the notion that Christ was literally present in the communion wafer, he declared that "if Christ were not in the Host, then we Catholics would be idol worshippers, we would thus be more wicked than Jews and Turks."[36]

Merging these two rhetorical maneuvers in *Der neue Kometstern mit seinem Schweif, oder Johannes Ronge und seine Briefträger* (1846), Stolz described those Catholics who would be attracted to such a "religion of the flesh" as he claimed the dissenters were promoting: those who "grew up lasciviously in arrogance and licentiousness, whose synagogue is the tavern, whose gospel is newspapers with rotten principles."[37] Among the dangerous newspapers he named was also "that Jew-paper, the *Frankfurter Journal.*"[38] Equating Christianity with Catholicism, he also argued that "the most precious thing the human being can possess is the Christian religion, the secure, solid Catholic faith, the Holy Sacraments. But now there are peddling Jews [*Schacherjuden*] at the door, traders in souls . . . who want to swindle you, Catholic folk, out of your precious faith . . . Whoever has good sense and love of religion will be filled with nausea at . . . this carnal lust and haughtiness."[39]

Buß made similar connections between sex, dissent and Jews. For example, this is how Buß described the entry of the *Deutschkatholiken* into the Lower Chamber's agenda: "A few dissolute chaplains begin the business. A debauched press, usually led by Jews, seizes upon the inflammatory subject-matter. Political radicalism, having exhausted its formal constitutional questions, throws the material onto its dying embers."[40] Buß mocked the concessions to anti-Judaism evident in Zittel's willingness to limit his motion solely to the dissenters – "because you fear the consequences of Jew-hatred in the Chamber and among the people for your miserable little bit of popular appeal"[41] – but also contributed to anti-Jewish sentiments with his own remarks, taking swipes at "Young Israel's" role in the "crusade against Catholicism," and telling Zittel that his comments in his speech about the archbishop's handling of mixed marriages showed the speech could just as well have been delivered by "a Jew, a Turk."[42] Buß also called dissenting groups "these untested suddenly-surfacing sects, germinated in the lasciviousness of radical rabble-rousing," and declared that "it is not rationalism which confronts us here, it is a disgraceful sensualism, the wretchedness of which is glued together with a few rags of humanitarianism of the sort which all lewd people appeal to, bedizened with a few glitters of nationalism . . . They have done all frivolous and sensuous people a favor by offering them a religion of convenience, because it is still somewhat a part of good manners to be religious."[43]

Banking on popular animosity towards Jews (but obviously also dignifying it as an article of faith); casting aspersions on the dissenters' characters and motivations; playing on the economic fears of a predominantly agricultural population whose financial security was frequently shaky, the anti-dissent activists successfully convinced thousands of Baden Catholics that dissent was a mortal danger. Archbishop von Vicari, too, had thrown his weight behind the anti-dissent campaign, releasing an "emergency call" to his flock that "they are trying to steal your faith!"[44] Already in January 1846, petitions against Zittel's motion started arriving in the Lower Chamber and, in keeping with Stolz's suggestions, the petitions stressed the religious and economic dangers dissent presented.[45] Defenders of the motion tried to organize petitions as well, but the opponents were in the overwhelming majority.

The Right was not only more in touch with grassroots sentiment on religious and economic matters than the Left, but also in a better position to organize petitions. Priests across the Catholic areas of Baden announced from the pulpit that their parishioners should sign petitions against the motion and these were laid out for signing immediately after church. Liberals had no forum like the church in which to display petitions or solicit signatures, with the exception of newspapers, and (according to liberal delegates) censors saw to it that every announcement about petitions in the newspapers was excised.

Already by the middle of January 1846, liberal delegates were becoming worried by the preponderance of anti-*Deutschkatholiken* petitions. This was so not least because the petitions often demanded that the Lower Chamber be dissolved by the Grand Duke for having allowed Zittel's motion to go to committee in the first place. But it was also because the liberals saw whatever hopes they had had for religious liberalization in Baden slip away under the impact of an unforeseen radicalization and organization of the Right.

Also within the Chamber, conservatives now started to mobilize. Countering demands for religious freedom became a matter of principle for conservative delegates, who had been silent only a few weeks earlier, and had voted with the liberals to send Zittel's motion to committee. The same tracts detailing the dangers of *Deutschkatholizismus* that had convinced local priests to organize petition drives, had also persuaded them. Now conservative delegates began to argue, as Johann Baptist Karl Junghanns did, that passage of the motion would lead to "the disintegration of Christianity in the Grand Duchy of Baden". [46]

Conservatives took the pamphleteers' cue to expose how the liberals' humanist redefinition of Christianity, taken to its logical conclusion, made religious differences uncomfortably difficult to pinpoint. Gideon Weizel expressed the conservative view clearly when he said:

> "How can you hold it against a Catholic if he resists with all his strength this motion, which in its first sentence requests that *every* religious association, no matter of what name, whether it is a *Christian* one *or not,* should be granted already through the fact of its emergence alone *full* and *equal rights* with both of the existing Christian churches in our land, whereby the delegate who made the motion sets up no other precondition except that the members of that society should only fulfill the *state-citizen* duties, for the rest it could be Christian or Mohammedan. Gentlemen, against such a motion I would vote as a *Christian,* not as a Catholic or Protestant . . . After all, they are not only requesting religious freedom for Christian associations, but also for *un-Christian* ones." [47]

Ultimately, the "petition storm" organized by conservatives brought 347 petitions (with close to 50,000 signatures) against the *Deutschkatholiken* into the Lower Chamber. (Only 31 petitions had been sent in support of Zittel's motion.) [48] It was the first mass petitioning campaign in German history, and the moment historians rightly cite as the birthdate of political Catholicism in Germany. [49] The general state of uproar in the land convinced Grand Duke Leopold's ministerial advisers that the Lower Chamber should indeed be dissolved, and the Grand Duke did so on 9 February 1846.

Thinking that the petition storm also reflected a politically conservative trend in the population, the Grand Duke and his advisors assumed that in the new elections set for 3 April 1846 a majority of conservative candidates would win. But confessional tensions within the conservative camp hampered campaigning – traditional Protestant government loyalists, for example, were quite uncomfortable making common cause with upstart ultramontane Catholics; meanwhile, the emerging tension between radical and moderate liberals was temporarily put aside in the interests of combating the religious Right. Furthermore, as liberals later analyzed it, it is also likely that although rural Catholics would mobilize to defend their faith and economic interests in a petition campaign, they saw their political interests as best guaranteed by liberals, who were not so tainted by association with the often detested local government administrators as the conservatives were. Conservative observers, by contrast, called attention to the peculiarities of Baden's indirect voting system, which favored the persistence of a "politics of notables," in which well-known individuals routinely got voted into public office regardless of their ideological affiliation. For all these reasons, an even larger liberal majority was returned to the Lower Chamber than before.[50] Thirty-six liberals faced twenty-seven conservatives when the Lower Chamber reopened on 1 May. In fact, the only new conservative to win a seat was Franz Josef Buß himself.

On 26 June 1846, the liberal delegate Ignaz Rindeschwender delivered the report of the petition committee on the *Deutschkatholiken's* request for revocation of the Grand Duke's decree, which had deprived them of political rights and restricted their ability to worship and organize. The committee was very favorably disposed to the petitioners. The major thrust of Rindeschwender's argument was that:

> "It would offend healthy common sense and moral feeling alike, if a citizen who previously enjoyed *all* state-citizen rights, should now find himself . . . robbed of . . . the most important of these, because on a few points he is changing his religious opinion – to be more exact, because he is honest enough to speak openly, that which thousands and thousands think of as he does, but do not profess loudly."[51]

Thus Rindeschwender not only placed the *Deutschkatholiken* firmly among the Christians from whom they had emerged, but also portrayed them as even better Christians than those who remained in the traditional churches.

Rindeschwender, who as a long-standing fierce opponent of Jewish emancipation had once been a pioneering articulator of the "Christian state" concept, now also used arguments that fundamentally undermined that ideal. He noted that many feared "an atomistic disintegration of the existing great churches"; but said that this was not the concern of the state, whose only purpose was to guarantee justice (which included full freedom of conscience) and whose justification only derived from its capacity for "satisfaction of the general needs of human nature."[52] He further redefined both Christianity and the purpose of state when he argued:

> If it lies in the course of the development of humanity that from time to time the Christian religion creates other forms for itself . . . if periodically there emerges . . . a dissatisfaction with the old structure, *the state should let it be;*

the movement will either, in league with the *truth,* safely break ground for itself and bear good fruit, or it will – if its foundation is *frivolous* – silently seep into the sand like undammed water, without leaving a trace . . . A government . . . does not comprehend its position, its well-being, if it, with intensified heart-pounding, tightens the reins of domination ever more, instead of letting go freely that which has outgrown its minority and can control itself in a manly, prudent manner. Let religious life take care of itself."[53]

It was a fact not lost on any of the men in the liberal majority that it was the issue of religious freedom that had caused the Chamber to be dissolved in the first place, and that religious conservatism was their most immediate enemy. As one newly-elected liberal put it, "let's admit it, the Chamber was dissolved . . . as a result of a *monstrous priestly lie,* the petition storm, or if you prefer, as a result of the religious upheaval in the land.[54] Buß and Stolz and their cohorts had made opposition to the *Deutschkatholiken* a matter of principle for the Right; in response, the *Deutschkatholiken* became even more of a *cause célèbre* for the Left. No longer was it only the promise of national unity and an end to the religious divisions that rent Germany; no longer was it only the appeal of a democratic experiment in brotherly love that inspired the *Deutschkatholiken*'s defenders. Despite their electoral triumph, they had also had to confront the political effect-uality of conservative Catholicism; its ability to expose the liberals' distance from "the people," in whose name they pronounced their views on matters great and small; its ability, indeed, to rob them (however temporarily) of their exalted status and identity as members of a Diet that had the eyes of all Germany on it. Religious freedom, once a matter of ambivalence for liberals, became their rallying cry. And – especially given the comparisons between dissenters and Jews that their opponents were pressing – this could not help but affect their stand on the "Jewish Question" as well.

The liberal delegates' overriding concern, however, was to resist the ways in which the religious Right was trying to define the content of Christianity. In the two days of debates about Rindeschwender's report, on 12 and 13 August 1846, liberal after liberal certainly called for relig-ious freedom, but the bulk of most liberals' statements was given over to an elaborate defense of the *Deutschkatholiken's* identity as Christians. Some delegates even went so far as to compare the dissenters with the early disciples of Christ, taunting those who opposed dissent that if they had lived 1,800 years earlier, they would have, "in the name of peace, order, unity," opposed Christ himself.[55] As the Grand Duke's decree limiting dissenters' rights had implicitly acknowledged that the dissenters were Christians, giving liberals a wedge with which to argue that the decree itself was unconstitutional, the focus on the dissenters' Christian identity was a logical strategy to pursue. [56]

Yet the insistence on the dissenters' Christianity was not purely strategic, but also the result of a deeply-felt revulsion at those who would arrogate to themselves the right to determine the value of another person's faith. As Friedrich Hecker put it to those of his colleagues who denigrated dissent: "How can you be so presumptuous as to present yourself, as it were, as identical with God and say: these alone are the true paths that lead to temporal and eternal happiness?"[57] Others criticized Buß and everything he stood for directly, either declaring that "not one Badener out of a thousand wants a Catholicism like Buß's," or trying to point out that "we all stand on the ground of subjectivity, Representative Buß just as much as we."[58] The general message of most of the liberals' statements was that Baden was in grave danger because of "jesuitical" and "ultramontane" machinations, and that supporting dissenters' rights was an excellent way to resist such trends.[59] Thus, given the preponderance of liberals in the Chamber, it was no great surprise that when the vote was held on whether the dissenters' petitions should be forwarded to the Grand Duke's government with the "urgent recommendation" that the petitioners' requests be satisfied, this recommendation passed by a vote of thirty-six to twenty-six.[60]

Significantly, in this debate on the dissenters it had been left to the Lower Chamber's conservatives to point out that liberals had caught themselves in a contradiction when they demanded freedom of religion for those who left the Christian churches, even though they had not been particularly eager to work for the equality of non-Christians. Franz Christoph Trefurt, one of the very few pro-emancipationists who was also a government loyalist, specifically asked Hecker how he could reconcile his previous opposition to equality of Jewish rights with his indignant demands for an equal status for the *Deutschkatholiken*. It was this challenge which prompted Hecker to declare:

"I must admit that this religious persecution, this repression for the sake of faith, makes quite clear to me what sort of oppression has weighed on the Jews, and from the moment I saw the oppression of our *Deutschkatholiken, I* vowed to vote for the emancipation of the Jews. (Many voices cry bravo.) . . . I was caught in the prejudice of youth, of custom, and now I have returned to freedom . . . I would not be able to justify it before God and the people to put someone in a worse or lower position, because he cannot worship God as I do, but rather wants to serve Him in his own way."[61]

Both the liberal and the conservative press recognized the significance of Hecker's public change of heart, because of the important leadership role he played among his fellow liberals. The progressive *Mannheimer Abendzeitung* notified its readers that:

> Many previous opponents of emancipation among our delegates have changed their opinion on this matter, and particularly the delegate Hecker has publicly declared in the midst of the debates on the *Deutschkatholiken* that with respect to Jewish emancipation he has changed his previous views; and so it cannot be doubted that an imposing majority will be for emancipation.[62]

The conservative *Mannheimer Morgenblatt,* however mockingly, conveyed the same message: "Now various of the most bitter opponents of emancipation have converted; Mr. Hecker has transformed himself from a Christian Paul into a Jewish Saul; without fail, the great man will carry away the little ones with him."[63]

And indeed, so it was. One week after the debate on the dissenters, on 21 August 1846, when debates were reopened on Jewish emancipation, it quickly became evident that the terms in which the debates had for so long been cast had been fundamentally transformed. Previously, the debate had centered on whether equality would cause the dilution of difference or whether it should be the reward for such dilution. In the most recent debate on the subject in February 1845, for example, one anti-emancipationist had summarized the delegates' choices thus:

> "The giving-up of nationality is either the prerequisite or the result of so-called emancipation . . . We, and all Diet decisions since 1831, demand certain concessions, the clearing-away of the obstacles inhibiting equalization; we attach to emancipation *conditions that must be fulfilled beforehand,* but the petitioners and their Christian friends say: emancipate us *first,* and then the fulfillment of your demands will come of its own accord; for this is the necessary effect of emancipation." [64]

In August 1846, the operative question had changed entirely. Now, what was at stake was deciding between the realization of the principle of religious freedom on the one hand, or the maintenance of a Christian state on the other. As the pro-emancipationist Anton Christ put it:

> "Choose one or the other of the two opposing possibilities, either take a stand for emancipation or against it. In both cases, what is at stake is the principle of religious freedom; and here everyone is consistent if he says, I demand sameness [*Gleichheit*] of religion in a state, or if he says, in relation to the state it is not necessary for all members to have the same religion . . . If one

starts from the principle [that the religion of the individual should be irrelevant to the state], then one can with respect to the Jews no longer be in doubt even for a moment, that one must also declare them to have equal rights in relation to the state." [65]

In short, Christ urged consistency from those who a week earlier had propounded the notion that there was more than one acceptable way to be a person of faith. Newly fervent for the cause of emancipation, Friedrich Hecker similarly called attention to the way the emergence of dissent and the conservative attack on it had changed the ways Jewish emancipation needed to be conceptualized. He, too, as his colleagues well knew, had once been ambivalent about Jewish rights. "But in the meantime," he said, "an event has intervened that challenged everyone to think more closely about persecution for the sake of faith."[66]

Other liberal pro-emancipationists sought to provoke those liberals who were still reluctant in similar ways, particularly by focusing on the concept of the "Christian state," which had in previous years so successfully been used to justify the maintenance of the Jews' political inequality. Some pro-emancipationist liberals had already in earlier debates argued that a truly Christian state was one in which everyone was treated in accordance with the Christian values of love and justice, not one in which everyone had to be Christian, and this kind of argument recurred in 1846 as well. But now that religious conservatives had given the idea of the Christian state a new, and for most liberals, quite frightening meaning, there was a greater pugnacity in liberal comments on the term.[67] One expressed gratitude that his opponents' concept of a Christian state did not exist, for, he charged, "it would necessarily lead to an inquisition or to hypocrisy." Another delegate compared the idea of the Christian state to the Ottoman Islamic state – where Christians were being persecuted.[68] Yet others provocatively equated the Christian state with the notion of the "theocratic state" more typically evoked in standard criticisms of the Jews, pleading instead for a "state of law" *(Rechtsstaat)* in which the state "has no right to demand of its citizens . . . that they belong to a particular faith."[69]

A newly elected radical liberal delegate, Johann Georg Christian Kapp, played out the comparison between the new conservative Roman Catholicism and the old stereotypes against Judaism with particular wit and rage. Reminding his listeners that German Jews had modernized their faith over the centuries just as most German Christians had, Kapp responded to the venomously anti-emancipationist liberal Ludwig Weller – who had just warmed up all the hoary clichés about the Jews' rigidity, self-segregation and arrogance *vis-à-vis* Christians – by contending that the Roman Catholic Church was just as separatist as Weller claimed the Jews were, and that conservative Catholics also thought themselves to be the chosen people of God. "According to this theory of exclusivism the state government would, to be *consistent,* finally also have to take away the rights of all who belong to the Roman Church, in so far as it wants to be exclusive." But Kapp went on to note that "the humorous side of such consistency harbors a tragic seriousness."[70]

Another effect of the reconfiguration of Baden's religious landscape was that liberals came to feel differently about "public opinion." The petition storm had driven home for the liberals their distance from "the people," and this had clearly created an awkwardness for many liberals about the old tactic of wrapping themselves in the cloak of "public opinion" when they sought to justify their resistance to Jewish emancipation. Furthermore, the entire conservative mobilization against dissent had revealed that the strategic deployment of anti-Jewish rhetoric in general was a gambit that was now being used more effectively by the Right – not just against dissent, but also against liberalism itself, and the issues dear to its heart. (Typical devices designed to excite public opinion against liberalism and its values, for example, were to call liberal newspapers "Jew-papers," and to portray mixed Catholic–Protestant marriages as just as "unacceptable" as a Christian–Jewish marriage.)[71]

As a result, liberals were suddenly theorizing the gaps in their relationship to the populace as never before, and commenting on the phenomenon of mass politics and its vulnerability to demagogic manipulation. Alexander von Soiron, for example, suggested that "there is also a sort of public opinion that one shouldn't really recognize."[72] Lorenz Brentano called on his colleagues to "have the courage to resist public opinion when it wants something unjust . . . especially when public opinion has been led astray. For who represents public opinion? Surely not those who consider themselves justified when they persecute another because of his faith."[73] And Kapp announced that Jews "are almost only hated in those places where one *fanaticizes the people against them,*" and reported that the conservatives were already plotting how to use the pro-emancipationist stand the Chamber was to take that day to embitter public opinion against the liberals.[74]

In the end, it was the way in which the "Jewish Question" had been recast that caused the answer to that question to be new and different as well. Characteristically, it was again the conservative Catholic Buß who articulated more clearly than any other the new division between defenders and opponents of emancipation: The choice no longer revolved around whether *Gleichheit* (sameness, equality) would be the precondition or the reward for overcoming difference. Now the choice was: support for complete religious freedom or support for the hierarchical Christian state. Thus the anti-emancipationist Buß echoed the pro-emancipationist Christ's remarks, but from the opposite perspective. Both sides were aware how much the terms of debate had shifted. Buß said:

> "The question of emancipation, which is a source of embarrassment for many a political character, is not so for me. Someone who starts from the principle that our states are Christian states, and that Baden, too, is still a Christian state; who strives to restore the quality of a Christian state, which has in recent times become completely weakened under the impact of legal religious indifference, cannot be for emancipation. But all who are for this religious indifference, all who advocated the civic recognition of *Rongethum,* must, if they are to be consistent, vote for the emancipation of the Jews."[75]

Though they disagreed with Buß, many delegates agreed with his summary of the choices facing them. A number of previous opponents of equal rights for Baden's Jewish community indicated clearly that – although they retained deep ambivalence about Jews – the changed context was leading them to support emancipation for the first time. Other long-standing anti-emancipationists simply voted quietly in favor of it, without making any speech at all. Thus, for the first time in its history, on 21 August 1846, the Lower Chamber voted for Jewish emancipation by a margin of thirty-six to eighteen.[76]

Jewish observers across the German lands were absolutely delighted, and expected that Jewish emancipation would soon become law in Baden.[77] But as it turned out, these observers were wrong, for precisely at this moment when Baden's famed liberals were most visionary, their hands were tied. The Grand Duke, his ministers and the Upper Chamber stalled and failed to accept the Lower Chamber's recommendation.[78] Although emancipation was partially implemented in the revolutionary year of 1849 (indicatively, it was understood as part of a larger move to make political rights independent of religious affiliation and to ensure that churches should have no influence on the state), there were many post-revolutionary set-backs, and it was not until 1862 that Jews were given complete equality with Christians in Baden. Indeed, the most immediate effect of the vote was to inspire outbreaks of anti-Jewish violence in a number of Baden communities.[79] And, as Kapp had predicted, conservative Catholics tried to turn this popular hostility to their own advantage. The *Süddeutsche Zeitung für Kirche and Staat* reported smugly that "the vote on the issue of Jewish emancipation has generated a great deal of hostility among the people, something that can be excused by anyone who is familiar with the situation in places where Christians and Jews live beside each other and therefore knows how much the domestic welfare of the latter is ever increasing at the expense of the former."[80] The paper noted with glee how, in the wake of the vote, "the popular halo of certain people has been severely tarnished" and how "every now and then one of our parliamentary men-of-the-people trembles in fear of losing his popular glory."[81] Increasingly, liberals returned the favor – comments about how conservative or "jesuitical" forces were fanaticizing the masses against Jews became standard elements in liberals' arguments.[82]

Thus essentially it was not the emergence of the *Deutschkatholiken* themselves that made religious freedom a matter of principle for liberals and led them to change their minds about Jewish rights. Rather, it was the conservative counter-attack on liberalizing tendencies within Christianity; the conservative assault on free choice in matters of faith and love, culminating in the stricter handling of mixed marriages and in the petition storm; and the rhetoric in and around the dissolution of the Chamber, that had confronted liberals with the reality of conservative Catholicism's increasing political effectiveness. It was this that provoked Baden's leading liberals into taking an emancipatory stand. In short, it was above all liberals' hatred of conservative Catholicism, and not a commitment to universal equality, that led them to reframe how they understood the "Jewish Question," and to revise their previous stance on it.

Notes

* Dagmar Herzog, "The Rise of the Religious Right and the Recasting of the 'Jewish Question': Baden in the 1840s", was previously published in slightly altered form, in Leo Baeck *Institute Yearbook XL* (1995): 185–208.

1. Groundbreaking early efforts to document liberal ambivalence and/ or hostility towards Jews can be found in Eleonore Sterling, *Judenhaß. Die Anfänge des politischen Antisemitismus in Deutschland, 1815–1850* (Frankfurt a. Main: Europäische Verlagsanstalt, 1969); Reinhard Rürup, "German Liberalism and the Emancipation of the Jews," in *LBI Year Book XX* (1975), pp. 59–68. But in a recent collection of essays on the relationship between German liberalism and Jewish emancipation, although various authors mention the problems in liberals' attitudes, the overall message once again reflects the scholarly consensus that "Liberals were the staunchest, indeed the only allies of Jews in their

struggle for emancipation and equal rights", and "Liberals regarded Jewish emancipation as an integral part of their political programme". Werner E. Mosse, "Introduction. German Jewry and Liberalism," in Friedrich-Naumann-Stiftung (ed.), *Das deutsche Judentum und der Liberalismus* (Sankt Augustin: Comdok-Verlagsabteilung, 1986), pp. 22–3.

2. Adolf Sander, in *Verhandlungen der Stände-Versammlung des Grossherzogthums Baden* (hereafter *Verhandlungen*) (II. Kammer), 27 September 1833, 14. Protokollheft, p. 305.
3. Johann Baptist Bekk, ibid., p. 293; cf. also p. 295. Emphasis, here as elsewhere in this chapter, was in the original quote.
4. Josef Merk, ibid., p. 281.
5. Karl Christian Mez, in *Verhandlungen* (II. Kammer), 18 February 1845, 12. Protokollheft, p. 78.
6. See the oft-repeated slogan of Professor Heinrich Schreiber, cited in Heinrich Maas, *Geschichte der katholischen Kirche im Grossherzogthum Baden* (Freiburg i. Br.: Herder, 1891), p. 52; and the petition by Professors Heinrich Amann and Karl Zell, signed by twenty-three Catholic laypeople, reprinted in *Verhandlungen* (II. Kammer), 9 May 1828, 4. Protokollheft, pp. 59–75, especially pp. 64 and 69.
7. Johann Sebastian Bader, *Verhandlungen* (II. Kammer), 16 December 1831, 35. Protokollheft, p. 22.
8. Josef Becker, *Liberaler Staat und Kirche in der Ära von Reichsgründung und Kulturkampf. Geschichte and Strukturen ihres Verhältnisses in Baden, 1860–1876* (Mainz: Matthias Grünewald Verlag, 1973), p. 20.
9. [Karl Friedrich Nebenius], *Der Streit über gemischte Ehen und das Kirchenhoheitsrecht im Grossherzogthum Baden* (G. Braun: Karlsruhe, 1847), p. xvii.
10. Ibid., p. xxix.
11. The prospect of priests suddenly refusing to play their dual role as servants of both church and state – in other words, the specter of potentially massive civil disobedience from a sector of its employees – finally forced the state to promulgate a new law in November 1846; this a law that provided for the possibility of secular civil marriage in the event of the non-cooperation of religious authorities. Thus it seemed as though the liberal premise of equality between the confessions and every individual's right to marry whomever he or she chose, had emerged victorious. However, the outcome of the dispute was far more ambiguous. Not until 1862 did the first couple in Baden get married in a purely civil ceremony, so that the

promulgation of the new law had nothing to do with actually opening up new freedom for mixed couples. Rather, the real and immediate effect of the November 1846 law was that the state had implicitly given up its legal right to intervene in the Catholic Church's handling of marriage; and, with very few exceptions, priests immediately began to follow Vicari's directives and thus to intervene more forcefully in the private lives of their parishioners.

12. For a classic articulation of this combination of views, see Karl Theodor Welcker's opening statement in "Verbotene Ehen, insbesondere Priester-Cölibat," in Welcker and Karl von Rotteck (eds), *Das Staats-Lexikon,* 1st edn, vol. XV (Altona: Hammerich, 1843), p. 665.

13. Ludwig Buchegger's memorandum of 1839, repr. in [Adolf Strehle], *Die gemischten Ehen in der Erzdiöcese Freiburg* (Regensburg, 1846), p. 79.

14. *Süddeutsche Zeitung für Kirche and Staat,* Freiburg (29 November 1846), p. 1077.

15. See Johann Baptist Hirscher, *Die Christliche Moral als Lehre von der Verwirklichung des göttlichen Reiches in der Menschheit,* 5th edn, Vol. 3 (Tübingen: H. Laupp, 1851), pp. 513 and 516.

16. Anon., *Die Musterehe und die Nothwendigkeit einer Wiederherstellung der Ehe nach der Musterehe* (Freiburg i. Br., 1850), p. 17.

17. "Die Ehe, vom bürgerlichen und kirchlichen Standpunkte aus betrachtet," in *Katholische Kirchenreform,* Berlin (June 1845), p. 165; and J. Kinorhc, "Über die Ehe zwischen Juden und Christen," in *Kirchliche Reform,* Halle (October 1846), p. 1.

18. See especially Sylvia Paletschek, *Frauen und Dissens. Frauen im Deutschkatholizismus und in den freien Gemeinden, 1841–1852* (Göttingen: Vandenhoeck and Ruprecht, 1990); and Catherine M. Prelinger, *Charity, Challenge and Change. Religious Dimensions of the Mid-Nineteenth-Century Women's Movement in Germany* (New York: Greenwood Press, 1987).

19. Karl Zittel, *Verhandlungen* (II. Kammer), 15 December 1845, 6. Beilagenheft, p. 42.

20. Ibid., p. 39.

21. Ibid., p. 37.

22. Ibid., p. 43.

23. Friedrich Daniel Bassermann, *Verhandlungen* (II. Kammer), 15 December 1845, 1. Protokollheft, p. 140; cf. Welcker's call for "the whole motion," followed by a "general bravo," ibid., p. 145.

24. Karl Friedrich Hecker, *Die staatsrechtlichen Verhältnisse der Deutsch-katholiken mit besonderem Hinblick auf Baden* (Heidelberg: Groos, 1845), p. 28; and idem, *Verhandlungen* (II. Kammer), 15 December 1845, 1. Protokollheft, p. 147.
25. Hecker, *Verhandlungen* (II. Kammer), 15 December 1845, 1. Protokollheft, p. 147.
26. Cf. Franz Christoph Trefurt, ibid., p. 143; Bader and Christian Friedrich Platz, ibid., p. 146; Friedrich Theodor Schaaff, ibid., p. 148.
27. For an overview of its attacks on the *Deutschkatholiken,* see Wilhelm Hubert Ganser, *Die Süddeutsche Zeitung für Kirche and Staat* (Berlin: E. Eberling, 1936), pp. 24–46.
28. Aside from the ones to be quoted below, typical examples include Wilhelm Stern, *Antrag auf Glaubensfreiheit (*Karlsruhe: Macklot, 1846); Franz Anton Staudenmaier, *Das Wesen der katholischen Kirche. Mit Rücksicht auf ihre Gegner dargestellt* (Freiburg i. Br.: Herder, 1845), esp. pp. 177–93; and Franz Josef Mone, *Beleuchtung der Zittelschen Motion über Religionsfreiheit* (Bonn 1846).
29. Ludwig Castorph, *Sendschreiben als unterthänigste Petition an die Allerhöchste Badische Staatsregierung und Hohe Badische Stän-dekammer. Hervorgerufen durch die Motion des Herrn Abgeordneten Zittel* (Baden: Scotzniovsky, 1846), p. 30.
30. Johann Baptist Hirscher, *Beleuchtung der Motion des Abgeordneten Zittel* (Freiburg i. Br.: Herder, 1846), p. 21.
31. Franz Joseph Buß, *Das Rongethum in der badischen Abgeordneten-kammer* (Freiburg i. Br.: Herder, 1846), p. 70. "Friends of Light" (*Lichtfreunde*) was the sarcastic term formerly applied to Protestant dissenters by their opponents. Soon, however, dissenters proudly adopted the term to describe themselves. "Rongethum" was a reference to Johannes Ronge, the founder of the *deutschkatholische* movement.
32. Alban Stolz, *Landwehr gegen den badischen Landstand* (1845), repr. in Alban Stolz, *Gesammelte Werke,* ed. Julius Mayer, 3rd edn, Vol. VIII (Freiburg i. Br.: Herder, 1913/1914), pp. 7–14. The information about the public readings comes from the editor Julius Mayer's introduction (p. vii) and his editorial footnote on p. 14.
33. "In many towns two churches would have to be built . . . For the *Rongeaner* fit just as poorly into a Catholic church as Jews or Turks, probably because the majority of them, and especially their main founders, believe just as little in Jesus Christ, the Son of God, even though they won't admit it." Stolz, *Landwehr*, p. 9.

34. Alban Stolz, *Amulett gegen die jungkatholische Sucht* (1845), repr. in *Gesammelte Werke*, pp. 30 and 43.

35. Ibid., pp. 32–3.

36. Ibid., p. 30.

37. Alban Stolz, *Der neue Kometstern mit seinem Schweif, oder Johannes Ronge und seine Briefträger* (1846), repr. in *Gesammelte Werke*, pp. 56 and 60.

38. Ibid., p. 58.

39. Ibid., pp. 57–8.

40. Buß, *Rongethum*, p. 75.

41. Ibid.

42. Ibid., pp. 8–9, 63.

43. Ibid., pp. 21,72.

44. Quoted in Karl Zittel, "Die politischen Partheiungen in Baden," in *Jahrbücher der Gegenwart,* ed. Albert Schwegler (Tübingen: Fues, 1847), p. 358.

45. The petition from the city of Konstanz, for example, argued that the *Deutschkatholiken's* "divergence in matters of faith will logically not encourage the unity of the German people, but rather will paralyze its strength through internal divisiveness, because it consumes its life-marrow, which is the Christian principle" (see Generallandesarchiv Karlsruhe, 231/1436, petition of 8 January 1846). The petition from the town of Wiesloch, however, was most concerned that the *Deutschkatholiken* should be denied "those same state-citizen rights which the members of the Roman Catholic and Evangelical Protestant Church are allowed, that they should thereby not be granted . . . the right to state financial support of their potential future parsonages and schools etc." (quoted by Johann Baptist Karl Junghaans in *Verhandlungen* (II. Kammer), 23 January 1846, 2. Protokollheft, p. 74).

46. Ibid., p. 75.

47. Franz Gideon Weizel, *Verhandlungen* (II. Kammer), 3 February 1846, 2. Protokollheft, pp. 207–8.

48. See Generallandesarchiv Karlsruhe, 231/1436.

49. Becker, *Liberaler Staat,* p. 21; Kurt Kluxen, "Religion und National-staat im 19. Jahrhundert," in Julius H. Schoeps (ed.), *Religion und Zeitgeist im 19. Jahrhundert* (Stuttgart–Bonn: Burg, 1982), p. 41.

50. Cf. Norbert Deuchert, *Vom Hambacher Fest zur badischen Revolution. Politische Presse und Anfänge deutscher Demokratie, 1832–1848/ 49* (Stuttgart: K. Theiss, 1983), p. 201; and Manfred Hörner, *Die Wahlen zur badischen zweiten Kammer im Vormärz, 1819–1847*

(Göttingen: Vandenhoeck and Ruprecht, 1987), pp. 454–68. For the contemporaries' contrasting views, see Zittel, "Die politischen Partheiungen," pp. 352–3 and 358–61; and *Süddeutsche Zeitung für Kirche and Staat* (9 April 1846), p. 292; ibid. (15 April 1846), pp. 308; ibid. (24 June 1846), pp. 542–3.

51. Ignaz Rindeschwender, *Verhandlungen* (II. Kammer), 26 June 1846, 7. Beilagenheft, p. 135.

52. Ibid., p. 149.

53. Ibid., p. 150.

54. Johann Georg Christian Kapp, *Verhandlungen* (II. Kammer), 13 August 1846, 8. Protokollheft, p. 63.

55. Rindeschwender, ibid., p. 155; cf. Karl Mathy, ibid., p. 118; and Bassermann, *Verhandlungen* (II. Kammer), 12 August 1846, 8. Protokollheft, p. 50.

56. The Evangelical-Reformed and Lutheran Churches in Baden were not united with each other until 1821, and thus in 1818, when the constitution was formulated, it had been necessary to say that members of all three Christian Churches in the state (the two Protestant ones and the Catholic church) would be guaranteed equal political rights. The original recognition that there were three fully legitimate forms of Christianity gave liberals the opening for arguing that newly emergent forms of Christianity should also be legitimated.

57. Hecker, *Verhandlungen* (II. Kammer), 13 August 1846, 8. Protokollheft, p. 103.

58. Welcker, ibid., p. 139; Zittel, ibid., p. 148.

59. For example, cf. Kapp, ibid., pp. 74–5; and Ludwig Weller, ibid., p. 141.

60. Ibid., p. 160.

61. Hecker, ibid., p. 106.

62. *Mannheimer Abendzeitung* (20 August 1846), p. 898.

63. *Mannheimer Morgenblatt* (14 April 1847), p. 491.

64. Franz Burckhard Fauth, *Verhandlungen* (II. Kammer), 19 February 1845, 13. Beilagenheft, p. 362.

65. Anton Christ, *Verhandlungen* (II. Kammer), 21 August 1846, 9. Protokollheft, pp. 47–8.

66. Hecker, ibid., p. 63.

67. Lorenz Peter Brentano, in his report to the Chamber, in *Verhandlungen* (II. Kammer), 7 August 1846, 7. Beilagenheft, p. 341. This report served as the basis for the 21st August discussion.

68. Bassermann, *Verhandlungen* (II. Kammer), 21 August 1846, 9. Protokollheft, p. 61.

69. Alexander von Soiron, ibid., p. 62.
70. Kapp, ibid., p. 67.
71. For examples, see notes 38 and 40; Franz Josef Buß, "Aufgabe der Zeitschrift," in *Capistran. Zeitschrift für die Rechte und Interessen des katholischen Teutschlands,* Vol. 1, No. 1 (Schaffhausen: Hurter, 1847), pp. 15–16; and Franz Rosshirt, *Beleuchtung und actenmässige Ergänzung der Karlsruher Schrift "Der Streit über gemischte Ehen und das Kirchenhoheitsrecht im Grossherzogthum Baden"* (Schaffhausen: Hurter, 1847), p. 19. Also cf. Amts-Assessor Herterich, "Die Judenemancipation und ihre beiden Geschwister, der Deutschkatholicismus und der Radicalismus," in *Mannheimer Morgenblatt* (26 February 1847), p. 269.
72. Soiron, *Verhandlungen* (II. Kammer), 21 August 1846, 9. Protokollheft, p. 62.
73. Brentano, *Verhandlungen* (II. Kammer), 7 August 1846, 7. Beilagenheft, p. 342.
74. Kapp, *Verhandlungen* (II. Kammer), 21 August 1846, 9. Protokollheft, pp. 66 and 69.
75. Buß, ibid., pp. 69–70.
76. The Lower Chamber protocols only listed thirty-five proponents of emancipation (see ibid., p. 74). But contemporary newspaper reports said the vote was thirty-six to eighteen; see, for example, *Seeblätter,* Konstanz (25 August 1846) – apparently Trefurt belatedly added his name to the pro-emancipation side. *Die Reform des Judenthums,* Mannheim (26 August 1846), p. 176, reported that of the delegates missing on the day of the vote, "five as well as the president of the Chamber had already earlier expressed their support for [Jewish] equalization; thus, forty-two members, i.e. exactly two-thirds of the Chamber, have voted for emancipation, surely a happy outcome."
77. For example, see the *Allgemeine Zeitung des Judenthums,* Leipzig (14 September 1846), p. 549, which argued that "it is true that the vote has as yet no immediate practical result; . . . [and] that until its realization it must still pass through three authorities . . . But let us not forget, that in Baden it is *usually* a matter of *principle* rights, less of material [rights] . . . Restrictions, reservations, clauses may therefore become popular, but the principle has been decided, it has conquered, and after a short time it will also conquer them." Also compare *Die Reform des Judenthums* (26 August 1846), p. 176; *Zeitschrift für die religiösen Interessen des Judenthums,* Leipzig 1846, p. 389; *Reform-Zeitung,* Berlin (April 1847), p. 30; and the enthusiastic report on the Baden vote squeezed into the index of Isaak

Markus Jost's about-to-be-published *Culturgeschichte zur neueren Geschichte der Israeliten von 1815 bis 1845* (Berlin: Schlesinger, 1847), p. 283.

78. On the Ministry of State's and the Upper Chamber's deliberate obstructionism, see the detailed report in Berthold Rosenthal, *Heimatgeschichte der badischen Juden seit ihrem geschichtlichen Auftreten bis zur Gegenwart* (Bühl/Baden: Konkordia, 1927), pp. 285–8.

79. See Franz Hundsnurscher and Gerhard Taddey, *Die jüdischen Gemeinden in Baden. Denkmale, Geschichte, Schicksale* (Stuttgart: W. Kohlhammer, 1968), p. 16; and Adolf Lewin, *Geschichte der badischen Juden seit der Regierung Karl Friedrichs, 1738–1909* (Karlsruhe: G. Braun, 1909), p. 277.

80. *Süddeutsche Zeitung für Kirche and Staat* (16 September 1846), p. 822.

81. *Süddeutsche Zeitung für Kirche and Staat* (13 September 1846), p. 815; ibid. (16 September 1846), p. 822.

82. For examples, see *Mannheimer Abendzeitung* (25 December 1846), p. 1405; ibid. (8 March 1847), p. 259; ibid. (14 October 1847), pp. 1118–19; ibid. (9 March 1848), p. 271; Brentano, in *Verhandlungen* (II. Kammer), 9 March 1848, 3. Protokollheft, p. 108; Hecker, in *Verhandlungen* (II. Kammer), 7 April 1848, 4. Protokollheft, p. 45; and *Deutschkatholisches Sonntags-Blatt,* Wiesbaden (7 August 1853), p. 125.

Unity, Diversity, and Difference: Jews, Protestants, and Catholics in Breslau Schools During the *Kulturkampf*

Till van Rahden

Schools loomed large in the political culture of Imperial Germany and played an important role in many ideological conflicts. Schools, the left liberal *Breslauer Zeitung* believed, were "sanctuaries of cultural progress dedicated to our nation's future."[1] Furthermore, secondary schools, especially the *Gymnasien*, belonged to those institutions that reflected the bourgeois ideal of *Bildung*.[2] An analysis of Jewish–Gentile relations in Breslau schools is therefore especially fruitful in the context of recent debates about the concept of *Bildung*'s ambivalent nature and about the tension between equality and difference within the liberal tradition.[3] By distinguishing a Christian from an abstract form of universalism, I would like to show that liberalism's inability to accept a right to be different reflected the strength of Christian universalism rather than dilemmas embedded in the general tension between the universal and the particular, as Dagmar Herzog or Zygmunt Bauman have argued.[4] Although many Protestant liberals invoked liberalism's universalistic principles, they turned their own Protestant cultural particularism into a universal principle. Any tensions between the universal and the particular they resolved in favor of their Protestant particularity and at the expense of abstract universalism. The latter, in contrast, rested on the idea of universal ethics conceived of as neither Jewish nor Christian but as universally "human." Although it could also lead to moral dilemmas, individual legal equality was never questioned.

Within a history of relations between Jews and other Breslauers the *Johannesgymnasium* holds a special place. The school, which was opened in 1872, embodied the pluralist school policies of the liberal majority in the city council and the magistracy. Jewish, Catholic and Protestant students and teachers should enjoy the same rights and the same recognition.[5]

As a consequence of this pluralism, the city entered a struggle with the conservative Prussian state, which supported the Protestant character of the school system, and with politically organized Catholics, who envisioned a segregated Catholic school system. The conflict began in 1863 and lasted until the early 1880s. The struggle's length and bitterness, and the liberal magistracy's endurance and sense of mission have to be understood within the context of the *Kulturkampf*.[6] Remarkably, Jewish liberals played an active role in this struggle. Co-operating with liberal Protestants, Catholics, and Freethinkers, they succeeded in turning the *Johannesgymnasium* into a pluralist school and hoped that it would serve as a model.

The Local Conflict and the Formation of the Catholic Milieu

Because secondary schools in Breslau had been crowded since mid-century, the municipal authorities decided in 1863 to found three new schools, including one *Gymnasium*.[7] The debate about the religious character of the schools was initiated by a Catholic citizens' movement that included both ultramontane and liberal Catholics. Its speaker was Peter Elvenich, a professor of philosophy in the Department of Theology at Breslau University, who had been a leader of the Hermesian movement and was soon to become a prominent Old Catholic. Equally interested in the conflict was Joseph Hubert Reinkens, who became Germany's first Old Catholic bishop in 1873.[8] This broad Catholic coalition petitioned the magistracy to open one of the schools as a Catholic *Realgymnasium*. Although one of Breslau's oldest *Gymnasien*, the *königliche Matthias-gymnasium*, was Catholic, all the secondary schools the city had opened since 1800 had a Protestant character.[9] The city's leading Catholic paper, the *Breslauer Hausblätter*, had good reason to lament that the predominantly Protestant character of Breslau's secondary schools constituted "a glaring violation of the basic principles of parity the city was obliged to observe." [10]

In contrast to the Catholic citizens' movement led by Elvenich, the *Breslauer Hausblätter* raised the more far-reaching demand of building a separate Catholic school system. While the voice of Breslau Ultramontanism complained about the "Protestantization" of Breslau secondary schools and emphasized that the Catholics of Breslau were entitled to their own secondary schools, the *Hausblätter* also subscribed to a volatile mixture of anti-Semitism and anti-liberalism. According to the paper, the conflict over the *Johanneum* was symptomatic of the "Judaization" of Breslau politics. The municipal authorities wanted new "non-denominational" schools, "in which Jews, Turks, and primarily, of course, dissenters and atheists were allowed to instruct Christian adolescents and to maintain the glow of Enlightenment." Eventually, the *Hausblätter* warned, "primarily Jewish and anti-Christian elements would occupy the chairs in order to corrupt the youth with the magic potion of progress."[11]

Whatever we make of the paper's anti-Semitism, its charge of secularization was justified. The magistracy and especially the city council did indeed want all new schools to be "non-denominational." "Non-denominational," of course, should not be confused with secular or anti-religious.[12] All students, including Jews and dissidents, had to attend religious instruction. That all other subjects should no longer be informed by Christian doctrine, however, raised the ire of ultramontane Catholics. A secularized history or science instruction, the *Hausblätter* argued in 1865, was nothing but "a machine of destruction against the Church, faith, and Christian ethics."[13] Six years later, when the bitter struggle about the *Johannesgymnasium* was still going on, the *Hausblätter* further explained the Catholic position: "Religion must, as a factor shaping educational activity, pervade the whole essence of school instruction." Education's principal aim was "to strengthen the children's religious convictions," and this could only be achieved, if "children [were] . . . segregated along denominational lines, and if their teachers bore witness to the same faith as their students."[14] "Christian discipline," the paper elaborated, "primarily seeks to enrich and to bend the human will, whereas non-denominational schools aim to strengthen cognitive capacities."[15] As early as the mid-1860s, Breslau Catholics opposed pluralist schools, criticized the allegedly secular *Gymnasien*, and supported a religiously segregated school system as part of a Catholic milieu.[16]

As late as 1869 – four years into the conflict when the differences had long become irreconcilable – a liberal Protestant commentator acknowledged that moderate Catholic demands were justified. The anonymous author, who considered himself an "independent freethinker . . . fully agreed with the 'separation of Church and state,' or more precisely: the division of their respective administrative concerns." Most school subjects "had absolutely nothing to do with religion"; there was "no Catholic, Protestant, or Jewish mathematics, chemistry, or natural history etc." Yet whereas radical secularizers were convinced that only religious instruction was moulded by denomination, the "independent freethinker" argued that it was also true that within the realm of history "one could not cast off one's 'denomination'." In contrast to "pure and free science," historical instruction "should not be combined with the spirit of critique and doubt," offering something "positive, concrete and grounded" instead. This positive historical knowledge always contained a denominational bias, because Catholicism and Protestantism, just like spiritualism, materialism, and idealism were "not just an affiliation, but "a philosophy of life and a *Weltanschauung*."

No less important than these more general considerations was the local situation in the Silesian capital, a city in which Protestants were "not just by themselves." Breslau Catholics had demanded that at least one of the new municipal schools should be given a Catholic charter. "One can wish that this were not the case, that they would gladly send their children to Protestant or parity schools; all this was wishful thinking, because that is simply not the way things are." By rejecting the Catholic demand, the city was inviting Breslau Catholics to create "their own denominational school." Instead of supporting moderate Catholics, the city was playing into the hands of "radical agitators." An "institution produced by confessional agitation, and consecrated with anger and frustration, and standing by itself" will sharpen confessional antagonism more than a school "amicably presented and watched over by the community."[17]

Within the city itself the Catholics could hardly hope to realize their goals, because a broad liberal coalition supported the municipal authorities' pluralist school policy. In the city council meeting of 26 October 1865 – which was attended by almost all councillors, the Mayor, and "an unusually numerous audience" – this liberal alliance demonstrated its determination for the first time.[18] The magistracy had proposed that the "institutions of higher learning" the city was planning to build "should have no specific denominational character" and that one of the new middle schools should be staffed with Protestant, the other with Catholic teachers."[19] Almost unanimously, the city council's school commission recommended accepting the magistracy's proposal. The commission's speaker, the well-respected veteran of the revolution of 1848, Moritz Elsner, criticized the Catholics' demand to maintain the Christian nature of secondary education. The natural sciences, history and languages, he argued, should be taught "objectively, without a religious bias." He explicitly rejected the reproach of being anti-Catholic. Had the city's Protestants or Jews put forward a similar request the school commission would have also rejected it.[20]

The Catholic spokesman was no ultramontane radical close to the *Hausblätter*, but a good friend of Reinkens, Commissioner (*Generallandschaftssyndikus*) von Görtz.[21] He declared that he was not "opposed to the principle of non-denominational schools but to its immediate implementation." As long as all municipal secondary schools were

Protestant it was perfectly reasonable to demand another Catholic school. Görtz therefore introduced a motion "in accordance with the principle of non-denominational schools to first erect a Catholic *Realschule* of the highest quality to satisfy Breslau's system of parity, which for Görtz excluded the Jews, and therefore to lend to the decrees the consecration of justice."[22]

While Görtz was still trying to win support for the Catholic position, a group of liberal councillors had taken a more radical position than had the magistracy. Whereas the magistracy wanted to implement fully its pluralist school policies only in the new *Gymnasium*, the city council wanted to secularize all new secondary schools. The group's speaker was Richard Roepell, a historian who had been an active member of the liberal movement since 1848 and a Breslau city councillor since 1859.[23] "The modern era," the Protestant Roepell argued, "calls for the non-denominational character of schools . . . We should not force the middle schools . . . into the bounds of the past, i.e. denominations, or provide the Churches with new means to interfere with municipal affairs."[24]

Explicitly, the city wanted to secularize the schools in order to allow the hiring of Jewish teachers, as David Honigmann, a Jewish city councillor who unlike Elsner and Roepell did not indulge in anti-Catholicism, emphasized. "It would be advisable to divest the administration of its Protestant character, particularly since the building of a parity school does not mean the banishing of religion from the school." Not only did the city plan to extend the same recognition to Judaism, Catholicism and Protestantism; it also intended to "do away with all barriers regarding the hiring of teachers because of their religion."[25] For some years, German Jews such as the Breslau philologist Wilhelm Freund had grown increasingly bitter because Jewish candidates were still being denied tenure at secondary schools.[26] In order to call this issue to mind, Honigmann had proposed to emphasize explicitly that these schools could hire Jewish as well as Protestant and Catholic teachers.

In October 1865, the liberals carried the day. Among Breslau city councillors Görtz found little support, and they decided instead that the new schools should have no confessional character and explicitly stated that Jewish teachers could be hired at all of them. The councillors recognized Catholic demands only in so far as they asked the magistracy to "uphold more than in the past the integrated (*simultane[n]*) character of the *Realschule zum Zwinger* with regard to the hiring of teachers."[27] The Jewish press enthusiastically supported the school policies of the Breslau municipal authorities. In April 1869, the *Allgemeine Zeitung des Judenthums*, the voice of German Reform Jews, agreed with a liberal Catholic who had just argued that mixed schools "neither neglect religious education nor endanger religious life, but only prevent the abuse of schools for secular purposes."[28] Little surprise, then, that in August 1869 *the Allgemeine Zeitung des Judenthums* praised Breslau school policies as an "example of steadfast independence well worth imitating."[29]

The *Breslauer Schulstreit* – A Conflict Between the City and the State

Although the vast majority in the Breslau city council had supported the pluralist school policies, the Catholics did not give up. In November 1865, the *Hausblätter* announced that Breslau Catholics, who had been treated as "white slaves," would "try to ascertain whether the city was entitled to put religious communities recognized by the state on the same level as tolerated sects."[30] Successfully, Breslau Catholics turned to the Provincial School board and the Department of Religious and Educational Affairs.[31] From now on, this was no longer a local conflict. Instead, the so-called Breslau School Struggle (*Breslauer Schulstreit*) attracted attention all over Germany.[32] An assorted crowd of liberals who held influential positions in the magistracy and the city council now faced both the ultramontane movement and the conservative Prussian state bureaucracy.

Prussia rejected Breslau's liberal school policies and refused to allow the opening of the new schools. In particular the *Johanneum*, the only *Gymnasium* among the new schools, had to have a "Christian character," the conservative Secretary of Religious and Educational Affairs, Heinrich von Mühler, announced in 1867.[33] Carl Gottfried Scheibert, who had been head of the Silesian school board since 1855, considered the school to be a "threat to the German mind." According to Scheibert, Christian faith would have to inform all aspects of education. Jews could never teach subjects which "touch upon religious matters or could only be taught truthfully and fruitfully from a religious point of view." That list of subjects included, he added, mathematics and grammar because here too a teacher was forced to rely on "the motivating will inside of him."[34]

The municipal authorities, however, did not cave in, and instead, in 1868, petitioned the Prussian *Landtag* that the state should accept the pluralist character of at least the *Johanneum*. Because the *Landtag* refused to consider the petition, the magistracy was willing to give way, especially as the need for new secondary schools had become even more dire since 1863. The new school buildings, moreover, had been very costly. The bill for the *Johannesgymnasium* alone, which had been ready to open its doors since October 1866, amounted to 60,000 *Taler*.[35] Owing to the ongoing conflict, the *Johanneum*, just like the other new school buildings, had since stood empty, although, as the *Schlesische Zeitung* noted, the need for new schools had grown with every term.[36] In June 1868, the magistracy proposed to the city council, "to open the *Johannes-Gymnasium* on October 1 as a denominational school."[37]

The city council's liberal majority, however, did not want to sacrifice rashly their vision of a pluralist school policy to the constraints of *Realpolitik*. On their meeting of 9 July 1868, the city councillors rejected the magistracy's suggestion and almost unanimously voted for a counter-motion introduced by its chairman, Karl Gustav Stetter, that both the magistracy and the city council should petition the *Landtag* again.[38] Now the petition was again with the Prussian *Landtag*.

In late February 1869, the *Landtag* saw a bitter debate about the religious character of Breslau secondary schools. Here, ultramontane Catholics and liberals opposed each other as irreconcilably as in the Silesian capital. What the liberals considered model school policies, Catholic deputies saw as a nightmare. Hermann von Mallinckrodt, for instance, urged the parliament "to imagine what a non-denominational school in Breslau would look like in practice." Such schools would educate a "race that has lost a sense for the highest goals and amble through life without faith." Only denominational schools could educate students "who are faithful to God . . . [and] loyal to their fellow humans." Only within a confessionally segregated school system should Jews be granted equality. If Breslau Jews wanted their own secondary school, the city had to build one. Yet Jews had no right to demand that Christian schools should give way to pluralist schools. It did not correspond to Mallinckrodt's idea of parity, "that one blend all the confessions into one, but rather one must revere and respect each in their particularity and individuality."[39] Two liberal deputies defended the position of the municipal authorities. Both knew Breslau local politics well. The Progressive deputy, the merchant Carl Wilhelm Laßwitz, had been city councillor since 1860; the National Liberal deputy, the lawyer Wilhelm Lent, since 1862. After a heated five-hour debate, the liberals carried the day. The majority of Prussian deputies supported the liberal motion urging the state to allow the city to open the secular schools.[40]

After the debate in the Prussian diet the municipal authorities hoped that a compromise was possible, especially as the city had tried to accommodate Breslau Catholic demands by opening a Catholic *Realschule* in 1868.[41] In the course of the city council meeting of 26 April 1869, frictions within the broad liberal coalition surfaced. Again the meeting drew considerable attention. As in October 1865 almost all city councillors showed up and "the gallery was crowded, especially with women."[42] The minority envisioned a state fully neutral in religious matters. Its speaker was Wilhelm Bouneß, who had been city council chairman in 1864 and 1865 and represented Breslau in the Constituent *Reichstag* of 1867.[43] He reminded the city council that David Honigmann's motion, which the council had passed almost unanimously in 1865, "undoubtedly excluded any religious character for the schools in question." Now the majority of liberal councillors seemed to be opting for a different policy, namely to give the *Johanneum* a Christian character. Such a step would leave the city at the mercy of the state, which strictly opposed the hiring of Jewish teachers at Christian schools. "What Christian means with respect to these institutions," Bouneß warned, "can be learned from the well-known case of Jutrosinky, who was denied a position at a Christian school because he is Jewish."[44]

In contrast to 1865, the majority of liberal councillors now wanted the schools to maintain a diffusely Christian character. This, in essence, was the liberal-Protestant paradigm of cultural homogeneity that denied Jews a right to be different. Breslau's Mayor, Arthur Hobrecht, had already suggested bestowing a Protestant character on the *Johannesgymnasium* in order to end the conflict as early as June 1868. Now he reminded his audience that a complete separation of Church and State was inconsistent with the Prussian constitution. He therefore warned "not to claim rights for non-Christian Confessions that did not exist, and whose denial is ameliorated by the fact that the great majority of Breslau inhabitants are Christian."[45] Remarkably, Richard Roepell, who had introduced the most far-reaching motion in 1865, now spoke for the Christian-liberal majority. Naturally, the *Johanneum* had to be a Christian school. "We call these schools Christian because the *Bildung* they preserve and spread is Christian in nature. No one hesitates to call Prussia a Christian state, [and] the Germans a Christian nation. Were we not convinced that Jewish teachers inculcated Christian *Bildung,* we would not hire them at our schools." Yes, Roepell seemed to be saying, to the hiring of Jewish teachers in general, that is "Christian" schools; no, to granting Jews a right to be different. The majority of councillors supported Roepell's viewpoint, although the margin of 51 to 44 votes was unusually narrow. The city council decided to inform the Provincial School Board that the city of Breslau wanted the schools "to have a Christian but not narrowly denominational character" and demanded "that members of no Christian or non-Christian religious communities should be barred from teaching solely because of their religious affiliation."[46]

The voice of Church-affiliated, liberal Protestants, the *Schlesisches Protestantenblatt*, articulated even more clearly the liberal-Protestant paradigm of cultural homogeneity. In June 1875, it derided the demand of Jewish parents to exempt their children from writing in school on the Sabbath as a symbols of "the whole superficiality of Judaism." German Jewry, "which sees itself as contemporary with the spirit of our age and the ideals of modern culture," one of the *Schlesischen Protestantenblatt*'s four editors, the pastor Julius Decke argued, "is in fact powerfully pervaded by religious superstition and one encounters in its circles a narrow-mindedness that is in glaring contrast to its lofty claims." Moreover, Decke added, "Any true understanding of the truly human religious and moral ideal presupposes a radical reform of the average Jewish character." Until then "the German people" will consider "Jews generally as alien and disagreeable."[47]

The struggle over the *Johannesgymnasium* had attracted considerable attention among the liberal and Catholic public in the Silesian capital. On 3 June 1869, at a meeting of the *Katholische Volksverein*, which had been founded two years earlier, 2,500 Breslauer Catholics voted to petition the Prussian King urging him to support the Catholic demand for a *Realschule* of the first order. Remarkably, Peter Elvenich, a subsequent Old Catholic who was still a board member of the *Volksverein*, led the meeting.[48] The ultramontane *Breslauer Hausblätter* happily reported in 1869 that Catholic leaders had "chosen Breslau as a testing ground for their powers" and their "energy . . . in this matter was incredible."[49] The liberal public was outraged that Breslau Catholics had criticized municipal authorities *vis-à-vis* the King. Within two weeks, liberal city councillors collected more than 12,000 signatures for a statement of support for the magistracy in order to counter the "ultramontanes' passionate attacks on the Mayor" – as the semi-official Chronicle of the City of Breslau recalled twenty years later. On 20 June 1869, a deputation of Breslau citizens – two prominent Jews, the dentist Moritz Fränkel and the printer Moritz Spiegel among them – formed a "solemn procession" to present the address to the Mayor. The deputation's speaker, Professor Christlieb Julius Braniss, and the Mayor both used the occasion to reiterate that it was hard to exaggerate the significance of the conflict.[50]

Although the city was willing to give the school a vaguely Christian character, the Provincial School Board and the Department of Religious and Educational affairs refused to allow the opening of the school. According to the state, a school's religious character found its clearest expression in the make-up of the teaching staff. The Prussian bureaucracy was outraged by the fact that the municipal authorities were claiming an area of authority for themselves that according to the Provincial School Board belonged to the state alone. "Only specific circumstances," the Board argued, permitted the hiring of Jewish teachers. Whatever those circumstances might be, each of those cases had to "evaluated and decided" by the state. In no uncertain terms, the Provincial School Board defended the traditional concept of Prussia as a Christian state: "To call Christian an institution free to hire (. . .) Jews and Dissidents," as the municipal authorities had done, "was an empty play with words inappropriate to the gravity of the matter at hand."[51]

This curt rejection left little room for compromise. In September 1869, the municipal authorities announced that they "no longer hoped for an unbiased assessment of our motives and intentions by the Provincial School Board." In response, the magistracy and the city council decided to rent out the *Johannesgymnasium*'s building. The city was playing for time, hoping that the conservative Secretary of Religious and Educational Affairs Mühler would resign soon.[52] Yet Breslau schools continued to be jam-packed. Whereas the city could limit its financial losses by renting out the school building, such a measure could not alleviate the over-crowding of the city's secondary schools.

In the summer of 1870, a group of Breslau liberals close to the *Schlesische Zeitung* once again tried to dilute the municipal authorities' pluralist school policies. They were responding to the Provincial School Board's offer that the Department of Religious and Educational Affairs would be willing to allow the schools' opening if the city "recognized that the Christian nature of schools had to guide the hiring process of teachers."[53] The *Schlesische Zeitung*, which had reported favorably on municipal school policies, now entered the struggle with an editorial that was reprinted by numerous other leading liberal German papers, perhaps because it represented National Liberal opinion on school policies more generally.[54] Because the Secretary of Education had met the city half-way, Breslau should accept his offer. It went without saying that "the inner nature of the new schools would be based on the generally Christian foundation of our nation's cultural life." The editorial only touched upon the question of Jewish teachers, which was central for the city council. It was desirable if the city could prevent the state from denying "the confirmation of teachers the municipal authorities had chosen by invoking the schools' denominational charter." In order to end the over-crowding of Breslau schools, the magistracy should accept a Protestant school charter for the *Johannesgymnasium*, because the spirit of religious tolerance would prevail in the end.[55]

The Jewish press was alarmed by the *Schlesische Zeitung's* editorial. In July 1870, the *Israelitische Wochenschrift* published a lengthy analysis of the Breslau School Struggle. Much of the blame for the current confusion lay with the city's magistracy and on liberals like Roepell who had told the Prussian state bureaucracy in 1869 that the new schools should have a generally "Christian character." Now the *Schlesische Zeitung* had argued that "the inner nature of the new schools" would have to be "based on the generally Christian foundation of our nation's cultural life." If that were correct, the *Wochenschrift* pointed out, the Prussian Secretary of Education's argument would be justified that "schools grounded in such a spirit had no place for Jewish teachers." Naturally, this was not what the magistracy had had in mind. Instead, it had wanted to emphasize that the schools "had to be founded on the basis of a common human morality," a morality the magistracy had called "'generally Christian.'" Thus the magistracy had "followed a commonly held, but nonetheless false opinion according to which Christianity is identical with humanity, an opinion based on the spirit of intolerance and exclusion." "Our cultural life and our educational institutions," the *Wochenschrift* argued instead, "have nothing to do with either Christianity or Judaism. The study of ancient and contemporary languages, . . . history and geography, . . . mathematics and the natural sciences is neither Christian nor Jewish, except for that part that is grounded in specifically Christian or Jewish ideas of faith, points of view, or duties."[56]

Unlike the *Schlesische Zeitung*, the magistracy did not want to rely on the state bureaucracy's goodwill, especially as long as von Mühler headed it. When the Prussian Secretary of Education stipulated on 24 June 1870 that the hiring process of teachers should be based on the premise "that the institution should be Christian," the magistracy answered on 6 July 1870 that this amounted to an "explicit statutory fixing." Although the city had been willing to accept a "generally Christian character" of the school, it was unwilling to establish it in the school's statute because it did not want to dilute the pluralist character of its municipal school policy. As long as the state bureaucracy demanded a statutory fixing of the Christian character of Breslau's secondary schools, the city felt obliged to leave the school building empty.[57]

"A Welcome Precedent" – The *Johannesgymnasium*'s Opening

Only when the national-liberal Adalbert Falk took office in 1872 could the city authorities recover their hopes of realizing their pluralist school policies. When von Mühler's dismissal became public in late January 1872, the *Allgemeine Zeitung des Judenthums* expressed its hopes that his successor would break with von Mühler's "clinging to formalism, his petty-minded holding on to the wording and the letter of the law."[58] As soon as Falk had taken office, the Breslau city council chairman, Georg Friedrich Lewald, received a letter from Adolph Wohlauer. The Jewish salesman asked the city council, "to take any appropriate steps regarding the opening of the non-denominational schools . . . as soon as possible. Motives: the change of personnel and the currently liberal mood in the Department of Religious and Educational Affairs."[59] The magistracy sent the superintendent of schools to Berlin to explain the city's position and to ask for the permission the city had been denied for seven years. On 1 April 1872, Falk instructed the provincial school board that when confirming the hiring the teachers for the *Johanneum* it should "not consider abstract criteria" such as religious background but only look at professional qualifications.[60] The municipal authorities now selected the teachers, including two Catholics and one Jewish candidate.[61] In August 1872 the *Allgemeine Zeitung des Judenthums* and the *Israelitische Wochenschrift* carried the sensational piece of news that "one of our co-religionists," Dr. Hermann Warschauer, was "indeed among the teachers chosen" for the *Johanneum.*[62]

The *Johannesgymnasium*'s opening in 1872 represented a triumph for Breslau's liberal municipal government as well as a major step toward tangible Jewish equality. The school hired two Jewish teachers, who were also entitled to teach ethics (*Gesinnungsunterricht*) and, at least initially, Jewish religious instruction was compulsory for Jewish students and therefore part of their final exams – something formerly unheard of in Germany.[63] At least symbolically, the city therefore accepted a right to be different.

Whereas, as the director of the *Realgymnasium am Zwinger* had explained in 1865, the city's other secondary schools were dominated by a "spirit of Christian love and compassion" that respected "Judaism" only as a "historical prerequisite for Christianity," Jewish religious instruction and Judaism generally now had the same status as Catholic and Protestant instruction at the newly founded school.[64] "In the *Johannesgymnasium*'s latest Baccalaureate exams (*Abiturientenexamen*), the subject of Jewish religion was part of the public examinations" the *Israelitische Wochenschrift* proudly reported in October 1874. Not surprisingly, the weekly paper lauded the school as "a welcome precedent for many successors."[65]

In order to do justice to the significance of 14 October 1872, the magistracy had decided to open the school with a "solemn celebration." "Today" the *Israelitische Wochenschrift* wrote, is a day of "significance not only for Breslau, but for the whole German *Vaterland.*"[66] Max von

Forckenbeck, Breslau's newly elected mayor, emphasized in his address given at the school's inauguration, "that the opening of this *Gymnasium* signaled that a right the city had long been denied had indeed been granted, to establish institutions of higher learning that grant citizens who are given the same duties the same rights as well."[67] Forckenbeck expressed two hopes for the future: that the school would disprove the reproach that "non-denominationalism, i.e. the principle that no denomination should receive preferential treatment" was "identical with lack of religion," and that "this institution would educate its students to become independent citizens true to their own convictions and impervious to the spirit of religious persecution."[68]

Although the municipal authorities and the school's headmaster repeatedly emphasized the principle of religious pluralism and of tolerance, the "general Christian," and in particular the Protestant character of the school was unmistakable. Even the school's opening ceremony, where Forckenbeck and Müller proclaimed the pluralist policies of Breslau's schools, was framed by two Protestant church songs: "Lord, your goodness reaches so far," and "Praise the Lord, my soul."[69] When in the academic year 1883–1884, the usual school celebration of the birthday of Wilhelm I was cancelled, because it fell during vacation, the school administrators and city officials celebrated the 400th anniversary of Luther's birthday, because of the preponderance of Protestant students.[70] Moreover, even if it were true that the name of the school primarily expressed civic pride – Johannes der Täufer (John the Baptist) was the patron of the metropolis on the Oder – the appellation was also in the Christian tradition. The courage, in any case, to name the school after Humboldt or Lessing, as the Berlin city council had done in 1875 and 1882, and as the Frankfurt city council would do in 1887, was lacking among the Breslau liberals.[71]

Where liberal-protestant tolerance dominated, Old Catholicism was not far away. The city did appoint one Roman Catholic teacher, Robert Gregor Depène. But with the agreement of the city council, the city assembly and the Provincial School Board, the Breslau school board and the superintendent of schools appointed an Old Catholic, a former priest named Jakob Buchmann, to the position of Catholic religion teacher.[72] The appointment was no accident. Born in 1807, Buchmann had received his ordination in 1834 and since 1837 had served as a priest in the small town of Kanth some twenty kilometers southwest of Breslau. He became well known in 1850 with the publication of his book, *Populärsymbolik*.[73] Starting in the summer of 1864, Buchmann had close contacts with Reinkens, with whom he had commiserated in June about the disastrous administration of the Archbishop of Breslau, Heinrich von Förster.[74] In May 1871, Buchmann refused to sign a petition supporting the curatorial clergy of Munich.[75] In the summer of 1871, he advanced to become one of the best-known martyrs of the Silesian Old Catholics. In June 1871, Reinkens reported that "one cannot imagine" how much Buchmann suffers "from his chaplains." They refuse to eat with him, because he is an apostate; they turn their back on him, supposedly on the instructions of the Apostles; and they preach sermons against him, and so on."[76] In July 1871, Reinkens reported in the *Kölnischer Zeitung* on the Buchmann case; in October he also wrote in the *Breslauer Zeitung* on Buchmann's being relieved of his post. Then, in December 1871, Buchmann published a series of articles in the *Rheinischer Merkur* against the Jesuits, which Reinkens thought to be excellent and had published in 1872 as a brochure.[77]

In the city assembly of 15 November 1872 the Catholics protested in vain against the appointment of Buchmann as the Catholic religion teacher in the *Johanneum*. "It is a public affront to the Catholic pupils," the *Schlesische Volkszeitung* commented, to appoint "an excommunicated priest as their religion teacher." One of the leaders of the Liberals, the Jewish city council member Sigismund Asch, emphasized that the city could hardly get involved in an inter-Catholic conflict by now firing Buchmann.

The *Schlesische Volkszeitung* retorted sharply that Asch tosses "Old Catholics, that is non-Catholics, a sect, together in the same pot" as the Catholic Church. The paper did however concede that this position was consistent in so far as one followed a "certain principle . . . mainly that of recognizing the equal rights of all religions." But even if the city Magistracy was of Asch's opinion, it is unclear why the decision for an Old Catholic came about without consulting the parents of Catholic students. "We haven't heard," the newspaper of Breslau's Catholics reported, "that the students, as once were the Polish soldiers in Prussia, were asked if they wanted to be Old Catholics or Roman Catholics."[78] But almost unanimously, the city assembly rejected the resolution of its Catholic colleague Rockel, which called for a Roman Catholic rather than an Old Catholic to be hired. Consequently, in the winter semester of 1872–1873, and in the summer semester of 1873, Buchmann taught Catholic religion at the upper levels (*Prima, Sekunda and Tertia*) of the *Johanneum*.[79] In September 1873, Buchmann gave up his position, officially "because of his health and his advanced age." His teaching duties were picked up by Benno Hirschwälder, also an Old Catholic, a regular teacher at the *Johanneum* who had already taught Catholic religion at the lower levels.[80]

When the waves died down the school director and the school committee found a pragmatic solution to the problem. Since Buchmann and Hirschwälder "are affiliated with the Old Catholics," the *Gymnasium*'s chronicle stated, the parents of seven of altogether thirty-four pupils allowed their children to be exempt from religious instruction. Even though the parents wanted to have their children taught "privately by a priest," the city magistracy ordered on 4 April 1873 that Catholic pupils who did not want to be taught by an Old Catholic religion teacher were to report to Catholic religious instruction at the nearby *Realschule* of the Holy Spirit.[81]

Thus the conflict about the pluralistic character of the *Johanneum* and the limits of tolerance seemed to be at an end. The city conceded to the Catholics, and the Jewish public in and around Breslau had every right to praise the *Johanneum* and the city's school policies. Yet the Prussian state strongly objected to this manifestation of parity for Judaism with Christianity. In February 1876, the Department of Education and Religious Affairs ordered the municipal school board to end the obligatory character of Jewish religious instruction, thereby reinforcing the second-class status of Judaism under the Prussian constitution.[82] The magistracy asked the Breslau Jewish Community Board for an expert opinion "on the value of the obligatory character of the Jewish religion class." "If this class is given an elective character from the administration, it will have received in the eyes of the pupils and the parents the stamp of an irrelevant, unimportant, and indeed superfluous class," the executive of the Breslau Jewish Community Board warned, and "the result must necessarily be a nearly unanimous self-exemption from this class." If one were to do away with the obligatory character of the Jewish religion class one would also "give the Christian pupils the idea of an objective and justifiable inferiority of the Jewish religion against other religions" and thereby sharpen "the consciousness of religious difference."[83]

Although the magistracy armed itself with the arguments of the Jewish community, the provincial school administration rejected the Magistracy's request to make Jewish religious instruction obligatory at all higher school levels and not just at the *Johannesgymnasium*.[84] In its session of 23 April 1877, the city assembly reacted. The Jewish city councillor, Julius Hainauer, spoke for the liberal majority. Born in Glogau in 1827, a bookseller, music vendor, and publisher, Hainauer was as the director of "the Society of Friends" one of the most prominent figures in Jewish associational life and in the cultural life of Breslau. As a friend of Abraham Geiger, whose *Jewish Prayer Book* of 1854 he had published, Hainauer was also connected to the Jewish reform movement.[85] His voice therefore carried weight when he emphasized in the city council that the Minister's decree "revoked the principle of equality of the confessions, announced at the school's inauguration." Yet the character of the *Johanneum* demanded that it be an "inter-confessional institution in which no single confession received preference." But now that Jewish religious instruction had lost its obligatory character, the school "has become a Christian school." But this was precisely what "the city of Breslau had once challenged." "Nearly unanimously," the City Assembly passed Hainauer's motion that "the Assembly should seek of the Magistracy that it should, with respect to the *Johanneum*, attempt again to request that the Ministry reinstate the old relationships between Jewish religious instruction and the Christian confessions, that is, to make the class obligatory again."[86]

Although the magistracy agreed with the city councillors in principle, it demurred from petitioning the Department of Religious and Educational Affairs. Informal talks had revealed that the chances of the requests being approved were "quite hopeless." The intervention of the "Association of Jewish Religion Teachers in Silesia and Posen" did not change matters. Consequently, Jewish religious instruction at the *Johannesgymnasium* remained elective and Judaism *de facto* a second-class religion.[87] Nevertheless, Hainauer used the session of the city council in November 1877 to again underscore the cardinal importance of the school. "Has the idea, which we associated with the founding of the *Johanneum*, really come to the fore? Has the phrase, which the Lord Mayor spoke at the opening of the school, that in its rooms all faiths should come to air and light equally, become reality? And may we congratulate ourselves and still see in the *Johanneum* an inter-confessional *Gymnasium*?"[88]

Conclusion

The struggle over the *Johannesgymnasium* exemplifies the position of Jews in Breslau schools. Although the *Johanneum* remained an exception even in Breslau, it served as a symbol within the city and beyond. Until the end of the Weimar Republic, one of Breslau's most respected schools served as a reminder that it was possible to reconcile humanist ideals of *Bildung*, Jewish equality and a large degree of pluralism. The municipal authorities' endurance and determination had to do with multiple facets of the conflict. To the city it was first a struggle about the power of municipal authorities. Although the city did not question the view that educational affairs, such as curricular questions, were matters of state policy, it tried to use and expand the remaining room to maneuver. In 1908, the Mayor of Halle and former Breslau city councillor Richard

Robert Rive proudly emphasized to the Prussian conference of mayors that the cities had upheld "idealistic enthusiasm in order to make urban education into the finest creation of civilization, notwithstanding all formal limitations" imposed by the state.[89]

There were also considerable frictions among Breslau liberals, even if both sides supported the hiring of Jewish teachers. Two varieties of liberalism, which dealt differently with the tension between the universal and the particular, conflicted. City Councillors close to National Liberalism opted for a Christian form of liberalism. For them, Christian entailed not a system of values, which gave their own way of life a higher value than others, but rather a normative model that claimed to be valid for the whole of society. The state, the nation, the society, and consequently also the school could not, as a consequence, be "neutral," but must, in the end, be Christian.[90] In 1869, Abraham Geiger had accused one of the most prominent representatives of the Progressive Party, Rudolf Virchow, that "when it came to Christianity, even he could not free himself from prejudice." During a debate on Prussian school policy, Virchow had argued that "the whole of our modern education" rested "on the basis of Christianity, not on its dogmatic foundation, but on the ground of a decisively Christian ethics."[91] Although these liberals supported the inclusion of Jewish teachers and students into public schools, they did not embrace a politics of recognition. In their view, Jews should be tolerated, but not accepted. Whereas cultural Protestants like Heinrich von Treitschke rejected the reproach of "confessional hypocrisy," as applying to them, they nevertheless became all the more angry at those who demanded "the literal parity in all things for everyone" and "no longer wanted to see" that "we Germans are in fact a Christian nation and the Jews are only a minority among us."[92] The inability of these liberals to embrace a universal right to be different reflected the strength of Christian universalism rather than dilemmas embedded in tensions between the universal and the particular.[93] Many Protestant liberals could invoke liberalism's universalist principles only in so far as they raised the particularism of their own cultural Protestantism to the only true universalism. They thus dissolved the tension between particularism and universalism in favor of a cultural-Protestant particularism at the cost of an abstract universalism

Universalism in a Christian key competed with an abstract form of universalism shared by the Jewish press, Jewish city councillors and other Breslau left liberals. It rested on the idea of universal ethics, which were conceived of as neither Jewish nor Christian but universally "human." In their view, the state should be neutral and the role of religion in schools, as well as in public life, should be narrowly defined. Only within religious instruction should religious difference and diversity be recognized. The position of Jewish students should not differ from that of Protestant or Catholic students, the place of Jewish teachers should be the same as that of Christian teachers. Although abstract universalism could also lead to moral dilemmas, individual legal equality was never questioned.

The tension between particularism and universalism remained in place, and confessional particularism was not restricted to religious instruction. As long as multiplicity and difference, and the plurality of perspectives did not become the theme of religious instruction, and as long as ethical subjects (*Gesinnungsfächer*) were supposed to communicate objective knowledge and homogeneous historical narratives, everything depended on which particular culture could win out at the cost of others. We should not, however, interpret the demands of Breslau Catholics as anti-modern or anti-liberal, because many Catholic critics of the city later became Old Catholics and because Catholic concerns about the Protestant character of Breslau's secondary schools and about liberal anti-Catholicism were justified. Breslau Catholics, however, made it easy for the city to disregard their more far-reaching demands. Thomas Nipperdey's observation that Catholics proved unable "to translate their right to be different into universal principle" holds true for Breslau too.[94] In the end, even moderate Catholics were convinced that in a Christian state parity and pluralism was in the first order a privilege of Protestants and Catholics. Beyond this, many Catholics demanded that the school's task was not to "develop cognitive abilities" but to sharpen "the religious consciousness of the children." Such polemics awoke, to borrow Carl Schmitt's phrase, "deep-seated anti-Roman emotions" among Protestant liberals and confirmed their Manichean world view.[95]

Notes

1. "Hier steht der Liberalismus, er kann nicht anders!" *Breslauer Zeitung* (hereafter: BZ), 4 October 1879, No. 463.
2. Reinhart Koselleck, "Zur anthropologischen u. semantischen Struktur der Bildung," in idem (ed.), *Bildungsbürgertum im 19. Jahrhundert*, Vol. 2 (Stuttgart: Klett Cotta,1990), pp. 11–46; Margret Kraul, "Bildung und Bürgerlichkeit," in Jürgen Kocka and Ute Frevert (eds), *Bürgertum im 19. Jahrhundert: Deutschland im europäischen Vergleich*, Vol. 3 (Munich, 1988), pp. 56–73.
3. See especially: Shulamith Volkov, "The Ambivalence of *Bildung*: Jews and Other Germans," in Klaus L. Berghahn (ed.), *The German–Jewish*

Dialogue Reconsidered: Essays in Honor of George L. Mosse (New York: Peter Lang, 1996), pp. 81–98, 267–74; George L. Mosse, *German Jews Beyond Judaism* (Bloomington, IN: University of Indiana Press, 1985); Stefan-Ludwig Hoffmann, *Die Politik der Geselligkeit: Freimaurerlogen in der deutschen Bürgergesellschaft 1840–1918* (Göttingen: Vandenhoeck and Ruprecht, 2000).

4. Dagmar Herzog, *Intimacy and Exclusion: Religious Politics in Pre-Revolutionary Baden* (Princeton, NJ: Princeton University Press, 1996); Zygmunt Bauman, *Modernity and Ambivalence* (Cambridge: Polity, 1991).

5. For a study that suggests numerous parallels to school policies in Frankfurt see Jan Palmowski, *Urban Liberalism in Imperial Germany: Frankfurt am Main, 1866–1914* (Oxford: Oxford University Press, 1999), pp. 189–99.

6. To this day many interpretations of the *Kulturkampf* continue to reflect the spirit of the *Kulturkampf* itself; for studies that suggest more fruitful methods of analysis see: Margaret L. Anderson, *Windthorst: A Political Biography* (Oxford: Oxford University Press, 1981); David Blackbourn, *Fontana History of Germany 1780–1918: The Long 19th Century* (London: Fontana, 1997), pp. 261–3; Thomas Mergel, *Zwischen Klasse und Konfession: Katholisches Bürgertum im Rheinland im 19. Jahrhundert* (Göttingen: Vandenhoeck and Ruprecht, 1994), pp. 253–307; Marjorie Lamberti, *State, Society, and the Elementary School in Imperial Germany* (New York: Oxford University Press, 1989), pp. 40–87; Thomas Nipperdey, *Deutsche Geschichte, 1866–1918*, Vol. 2: *Machtstaat vor der Demokratie* (Munich: C. H. Beck, 1992), pp. 364–81; on liberal anti-Catholicism see: Michael Gross, "Kulturkampf and Unification: German Liberals and the War Against the Jesuits," in *Central European History* 30 (1997): 545–66, and Róisín Healy, "Religion and Civil Society: Catholics, Jesuits, and Protestants in Imperial Germany," in Frank Trentmann (ed.), *Paradoxes of Civil Society: New Perspectives on Modern German and British Society* (Oxford: Berghahn, 2000), pp. 244–62.

7. [C. F. W. Müller], "Die Eröffnung des Johannesgymnasiums," in *Programm des städtischen Johannes-Gymnasiums zu Breslau für die Zeit von Michaelis 1872 bis Ostern 1874* (Breslau, 1874), pp. 1–10, here p. 1.

8. On Elvenich see "Elvenich (Peter Josef)," in *Allgemeine deutsche Real-Encyklopädie für die gebildeten Stände (Conversations-Lexikon)*, 9th edition, Vol. 14 (Leipzig: Brockhaus, 1847), pp. 682–3, Heinrich Bacht SJ, *Die Tragödie einer Freundschaft: Fürstbischof Heinrich Förster*

und Professor Joseph Hubert Reinkens (Cologne: Böhlau, 1985), p. 9, n. 36; Kurt Engelbert, *Die Geschichte des Breslauer Domkapitels im Rahmen der Diözesangeschichte vom Beginn des 19. Jahrhunderts bis zum Ende des Zweiten Weltkriegs* (Hildesheim: A. Lax, 1964); "Joseph Hubert Reinkens to Wilhelm Reinkens, Breslau, 11 May 1866," in *Joseph Hubert Reinkens: Briefe an seinen Bruder Wilhelm (1840–1873)*, ed. Hermann Josef Sieben (Cologne: Böhlau, 1979), Vol. 3, p. 1435.

9. For a summary of the Catholic petition see: "Communales," in *Schlesische Zeitung* (hereafter: *SZ*), 24 October 1865, No. 497; the *Realgymnasium am Zwinger*'s director responded to the Catholic criticism immediately; see: "Schlesischer Nouvellen-Courier," in *SZ*, 26 October 1865, No. 501. See also: "Breslau," in *Schlesisches Kirchenblatt* 29 (1863): 285–7, and Ulrich Seng, *Schulpolitik des Bistums Breslau im 19. Jahrhundert* (Wiesbaden: Harrassowitz, 1989), pp. 233–4.

10. See "Das höhere städtische Schulwesen in Breslau," in *Breslauer Hausblätter* (hereafter: BHB), 28 October 1865, No. 86, pp. 681–3, quotation on p. 681.

11. See "Die Väter der Stadt," in *BHB*, 1 November 1865, No. 87, pp. 689–91.

12. In this regard, the terminology was itself an object of contention. The *Schlesische Zeitung* explicitly emphasized that this was "a school that with regards to confession followed legal parity" and not "as some have called it with an unfortunate turn of phrase – without confession." See "Die neueste Eröffnung der Regierung in Sachen der projectirten Lehranstalten," in *SZ*, 1 July 1870, No. 299, p. 1. Supplement. The liberal-protestant *Schlesische Morgenblatt* argued in November 1872 that one should call the *Johanneum* not *inter-confessionell* but rather "non-denominational." See: "Der evangelische Religionsunterricht an dem confessionslosen Gymnasium zu Breslau," in *Schlesisches Protestantenblatt*, 2 (1872): 85–6.

13. See "Die Väter der Stadt," in *BHB*, 1 November 1865, No. 87, pp. 689–691, quotation on p. 690; for a short summary of the diametrically opposed position see: "Confessionelle oder confes-sionslose Schulen?" in *Allgemeine Zeitung des Judenthums* (hereafter *AZJ*), 33 (1869): 285–9, especially p. 287.

14. See "Schulbriefe II," in *BHB*, 1 June 1871, No. 134, pp. 1039–40.

15. See "Schulbriefe III," in *BHB*, 2 June 1871, No. 135, pp. 1046–47.

16. Lamberti, *State*, pp. 40–87; Geoffrey G. Field, "Religion in the German Volksschule, 1890–1908," in *Year Book of the Leo Baeck*

Institute 25 (1980), pp. 41–71, especially 46, 50–2, and 66; Mergel, *Klasse*, pp. 371–3.

17. See *Die Weisheit der Braminen in der confessionslosen Schule: Ungehaltene Rede eines unabhängigen Freidenkers* (2nd edn, Breslau, 1869), pp. 4–8. The pamphlet had originally appeared as an article in the periodical *Rübezahl: Schlesische Provinzialblätter* (1869, No. 1); see: *Weisheit der Braminen*, p. 8.

18. See "Stadtverordnetenversammlung," in *SZ*, 27 October 1865, No. 503.

19. See Protokollbücher der Stadtverordnetenversammlung, Archiwum Państwowe we Wrocławiu (hereafter: APW), Akta miasta Wrocławia (hereafter: AMW), H 120, Vol. 62, council meeting of 26 October 1865, submission No. 1133.

20. See "Confessioneller Charakter der höheren städtischen Schulen," in *SZ*, 27 October 1865, No. 503.

21. Bacht, *Tragödie*, pp. 124, 57, 203–4 and 206; *Reinkens: Briefe an seinen Bruder Wilhelm*, Vol. 2, p. 1108.

22. "Confessioneller Charakter der höheren städtischen Schulen," in *SZ*, 27 October 1865, No. 503.

23. Eduard Reimann, "Geh. Regierungsrath Roepell: Ein Nekrolog," in *Zeitschrift des Vereins für Geschichte und Altertum Schlesiens* 28 (1894): 461–71; and Manfred Hettling, *Politische Bürgerlichkeit: Der Bürger zwischen Individualität und Vergesellschaftung in Deutschland und der Schweiz von 1860 bis 1918* (Göttingen: Vandenhoeck and Ruprecht, 1999), pp. 103 and 161; *Biographisches Handbuch für das Preußische Abgeordnetenhaus 1849–1867*, ed. Bernd Haunfelder (Düsseldorf: Droste, 1994), p. 214.

24. "Confessioneller Charakter der höheren städtischen Schulen," in *SZ*, 27 October 1865, No. 503, and "Nochmals Stadtväterliches," in *BHB*, 11 November 1865, No. 90, p. 713.

25. "Confessioneller Charakter der höheren städtischen Schulen," in *SZ*, 27 October 1865, No. 503; on Honigmann see: "Nekrolog David Honigmann 1821–1885," in *Mittheilungen des Deutsch-Israelitischen Gemeindebundes* 16 (1886): 1–4, and the obituary in *Allgemeine Zeitung des Judenthums* (*AZJ*) 49 (1885): 518, and the Breslau magistracy's appreciation in APW, AMW, III, 2189, f. 265.

26. [Wilhelm Freund], *Die Anstellung israelitischer Lehrer an Preußischen Gymnasien und Realschulen: Ein Wort zur Aufhellung der Sachlage von einem praktischen Fachmann* (Berlin, 1860).

27. Protokollbücher der Stadtverordnetenversammlung APW, AMW, H 120, Bd. 62, council meeting of 26 October 1865, submission No. 1133.

28. "Confessionelle oder confessionslose Schulen?" in *AZJ* 33 (1869): 285–9, especially 287.
29. "Privatmittheilung, Breslau, 19. August," in *AZJ* 33 (1869): 744.
30. "Stand der Welthändel," in *BHB*, 8 November 1865, No. 89, pp. 705–6.
31. Seng, *Schulpolitik*, pp. 233–4.
32. *Das höhere Schulwesen in Preussen*, ed. Ludwig Wiese, Vol. 1 (Berlin: Wiegand and Grieben, 1863), 165; ibid., Vol. 2 (Berlin: Wiegand and Grieben, 1869), p. 173.
33. Even the name of the Ministry stood for the close connection between Church and school. See Franz Schnabel, *Deutsche Geschichte im neunzehnten Jahrhundert*, Vol. 2 (first published Freiburg: Herder, 1929–1937; reprinted Munich: Deutscher Taschenbuch Verlag, 1987), p. 342.
34. Quoted in *Schulwesen*, ed. Wiese, Vol. 2, pp. 19–20. Carl Gottfried Scheibert, *Die Confessionalität der höheren Schulen* (Stettin, 1869) quoted in *Pädagogisches Archiv* 11 (1869): 185–93, quotation: p. 192, and in Hugo Preuß, *Die Maßregelung jüdischer Lehrerinnen in den Berliner Gemeindeschulen* (Berlin, 1898), pp. 22–3.
35. [Müller], "Eröffnung," p. 1.
36. "Die neueste Eröffnung der Regierung in Sachen der projectirten Lehranstalten," in *SZ*, 1 July 1870, No. 299, 1. supplement.
37. "Die Errichtung des Johannesgymnasiums," APW, AMW, III, 26365, fos. 23–24; Protokollbücher der Stadtverordnetenversammlung APW, AMW, H 120, Vol. 73, council meeting of 9 July 1868, No. 623.
38. Protokollbücher der Stadtverordnetenversammlung APW, AMW, H 120, Vol. 73, council meeting of 9 July 1868, No. 623.
39. *Stenographische Berichte über die Verhandlungen der durch die allerhöchste Verordnung vom . . . einberufenen beiden Häuser des Landtages. Vol. 1868/69,2, Von der neunundzwanzigsten Sitzung am 7. Januar 1869 bis zur Schluß-Sitzung der vereinigten beiden Häuser des Landtages am 6. März 1869* (Berlin 1869), pp. 1983–2009, quotation on pp. 1984–5; on Mallinckrodt see: Anderson, *Windthorst*, pp. 108–10.
40. *Stenographische Berichte über die Verhandlungen . . .*, Vol. 2, 1994–1997 (Laßwitz), pp. 1999–2003 (Lent), p. 2008; on Lent see *Biographisches Handbuch für das preußische Abgeordnetenhaus* (Düsseldorf: Droste, 1988), p. 242; "Zu Ehren der Abgeordneten Lent u. Röpell," in: *BZ*, 24 February 1870, No. 91, 652–3.
41. See: *Kalender für das höhere Schulwesen Preußens*, ed. Emil Toeplitz and Paul Malberg, 5 (1898): 70.

42. "Stadtverordnetenversammlung," in *SZ*, 27 April 1869, No. 191, 1. Supplement, pp. 1–2.

43. Hermann Markgraf, *Geschichte Breslaus, 2nd ed.* (Breslau: J. U. Kern, 1913), pp. 99 and 116.

44. "Stadtverordnetenversammlung," in *SZ*, 27 April 1869, No. 191, 1. supplement, pp. 1–2.

45. Ibid.

46. Ibid.

47. "Etwas vom Judenthum," in *Schlesisches Protestantenblatt*, 5 (1875): 93; for a rejoinder see: "Breslau," in *AZJ*, 39 (1875): 429–30.

48. "Breslau," in *Katholisches Schulblatt* 15 (1869): 221–2; Seng, *Schulpolitik*, pp. 234 and 250; Paul Mazura, *Die Entwicklung des politischen Katholizismus in Schlesien* (Breslau: Marcus, 1925), p. 66.

49. *BHB*, 1869, No. 116, p. 286, quoted in: Mazura, *Entwicklung*, p. 83.

50. F. G. Adolf Weiß, *Chronik der Stadt Breslau* (Breslau, 1889), p. 1160. See also: "Die Ueberreicherung der Adresse an Oberbürgermeister Hobrecht," in *SZ*, 21 June 1869.

51. "Zur Schulfrage," in *SZ*, 12 August 1869, No. 371, 1. supplement.

52. "Stadtverordnetenversammlung," in *SZ*, 3 September 1869, No. 409, 1. supplement.

53. "Schreiben des Schulprovinzialkollegiums an Magistrat, 24. Juni 1870," in *SZ*, 21 July 1870, No. 333.

54. In any case, many newspapers, including the *Kölnische Zeitung*, the *Magdeburger Zeitung* and the *Weser Zeitung* published the editorial. See "Zur Breslauer Schulfrage," in *SZ*, 6 July 1870, No. 307, 1.

55. "Die neueste Eröffnung der Regierung in Sachen der projectirten Lehranstalten," in *SZ*, 1 July 1870, No. 299.

56. "Der Breslauer Schulstreit," in *Israelitische Wochenschrift* (hereafter: *IW*) 1 (1870): 247–8.

57. "In Sachen Eröffnung der beiden höheren Lehranstalten," in *SZ*, 21 July 1870, No. 333, 1. supplement, 1–2.

58. "Was erwarten wir von dem neuen preussischen Cultus- und Unterrichtsminister?" in *AZJ* 36 (1872): 97–100, quotation: pp. 98–9.

59. "Adolph Wohlauer, Reuschestr. 48 an Herrn Lewald, Stadtverordnetenvorsteher, 25. Feb. 1872," in APW, AMW III, 26365, fo. 95a.

60. "Magistrat an Stadtverordnetenversammlung, 11. April 1872" and "Stadtverordnetenversammlung an Magistrat, 25. April 1872," in APW,. AMW III, 26365, fos. 99–102; Müller, "Eröffnung," p. 3.

61. [Müller], "Eröffnung," pp. 4–5.

62. "Breslau, im August," in *AZJ*, 36 (1872): 690; "Breslau. Anfang August," in *IW*, 3 (1872): 268–9.

63. *Schulwesen*, ed. Wiese, Vol., p. 185; *AZJ*, 36 (1872): 690.

64. The director made his comment in the early days of the Breslau School Struggle; quoted in "Schlesischer Nouvellen-Courier," in *SZ*, 26 October 1865, No. 501.

65. "Breslau, im Oktober," in *IW* 5 (1874): 352.

66. "Breslau, 14. Oktober," in *IW* 3 (1872): 353–4.

67. [Müller], "Eröffnung," 6–7.

68. "Breslau, 14. Oktober," in *IW* 3 (1872): 353–4.

69. [Müller], "Eröffnung," pp. 7 and 10.

70. *Jahresbericht des städtischen Johannes-Gymnasiums für das Schuljahr von Ostern 1883 bis Ostern 1884*, ed. C. F. W. Müller (Breslau, 1884), p. 10.

71. Palmowski, *Urban Liberalism*, pp. 257–8; the Berlin municipal *Humboldtgymnasium* was founded in 1875, the municipal *Lessinggymnasium* in 1882; see: *Kalender für das höhere Schulwesen Preußens und einiger anderer deutscher Staaten*, ed. Emil Toeplitz and Paul Malberg, Vol. 17 (1910), p. 437.

72. See: "Personalbogen Robert Gregor Depène," Pädagogisches Zentrum, Berlin, and "Personalakte Robert Gregor Depène," APW, Oberpräsidium Breslau, 17/II, 3936.

73. Jakob Buchmann, *Populärsymbolik, oder vergleichende Darstellung der Glaubensgegensätze zwischen Katholiken und Protestanten*, 2 Vols, 3rd edn (Mainz: Kirchheim, Schott and Thielmann, 1850).

74. *Reinkens: Briefe an seinen Bruder Wilhelm*, Vol. 2, p. 1301.

75. *Reinkens: Briefe an seinen Bruder Wilhelm*, Vol. 3, p. 1762.

76. *Reinkens: Briefe an seinen Bruder Wilhelm*, Vol. 3, p. 1770; see also p. 1772.

77. *Reinkens: Briefe an seinen Bruder Wilhelm*, Vol. 3, p. 1775 and 1785; "Ueber die Amtsentsetzung des Pfarrers Buchmann," in *BZ*, 9 October 1871, No. 472, p. 3572; Jakob Buchmann, *Über und gegen den Jesuitismus* (Breslau: Gosohorsky, 1872).

78. "Die Stadtverordnetenversammlung," in *Schlesische Volkszeitung*, 19 November 1872, No. 269; generally see: Ernst-Rudolf Huber, *Deutsche Verfassungsgeschichte seit 1789, Vol. 3: Bismarck und das Reich* (Stuttgart: Deutsche Verlagsanstalt, 1963), pp. 687–8.

79. *Programm des städtischen Johannes-Gymnasiums zu Breslau für die Zeit von Michaelis 1872 bis Ostern 1874* (Breslau, 1874), pp. 11–14 and 17–21.

80. Ibid., pp. 11–14, 17–21 and 28.
81. Ibid., p. 29.
82. For details see: "Der jüdische Religionsunterricht an den höheren Schulen," in *AZJ* 40 (1876): 218–19 and 561–5, see also *AZJ* 41 (1877), p. 280.
83. "Ein Gutachten über den obligatorischen jüdischen Religionsunterricht," in *IW* 8 (1877), pp. 12–13 and 19–21, quotations on pp. 13 and 19.
84. "Breslau, 24. April," in *IW* 8 (1877): 139.
85. On Julius Hainauer see: Maciej Lagiewski, *Wroclawscy Zydzi 1850–1944* (Wrocław: Muzeum Historyczne, 1994), Pictures Nos. 334–6; Willy Cohn, *Verwehte Spuren: Erinnerungen an das Breslauer Judentum vor seinem Untergang*, ed. Norbert Conrads (Cologne: Böhlau, 1995), pp. 26–9, quotation: p. 26; Emil Bohn, *Festschrift zur Feier des 25jährigen Bestehens des Breslauer Orchester-Vereins* (Breslau: Hainauer, 1887), p. 11; "Rede zum Gedächtnis von Freund Julius Hainauer am 9. Januar 1898," in *Gesellschaft der Freunde, Verwaltungsbericht pro 1897/1898 und 1898/1899* (Breslau, 1899), pp. 11–13.
86. "Breslau, 24. April," in *IW* 8 (1877): 139.
87. See the reports in *IW* 8 (1877): 367 and 392.
88. See the report in *IW* 8 (1877): p. 392.
89. Richard Robert Rive, "Die Entwicklung der preußischen Städte sei dem Erlaß der Städteordnung von 1808," in *Verhandlungen des sechsten preußischen Städtetages am 5. und 6. Oktober 1908 zu Königsberg* (Konigsberg, 1908), pp. 29–36, quotation: pp. 34–5.
90. Generally see: Blackbourn, *Fontana History*, 293–4; Nipperdey, *Deutsche Geschichte, 1866–1918*, Vol. 2, 316 and 322; Gangolf Hübinger, *Kulturprotestantismus und Politik: Zum Verhältnis von Liberalismus und Protestantismus im wilhelminischen Deutschland* (Tübingen: Mohr Siebeck, 1994); Helmut Walser Smith, *German Nationalism and Religious Conflict* (Princeton, NJ: Princeton University Press, 1995).
91. Abraham Geiger, "Die Schulfrage im preußischen Abgeordnetenhaus," in *Jüdische Zeitung für Wissenschaft und Leben* 7 (1869): 216–19.
92. Heinrich von Treitschke, "Unsere Aussichten," quoted in *Der Berliner Antisemitismusstreit*, ed. Walter Boehlich (Frankfurt: Insel-Verlag, 1965), pp. 12–13; for a similar argument see: Theodor Mommsen, "Auch ein Wort über unser Judenthum," ibid., p. 226.

93. Bauman, *Modernity*; Herzog, *Intimacy*.
94. Nipperdey, *Deutsche Geschichte, 1866–1918*, Vol. 2, p. 369.
95. Carl Schmitt, *Römischer Katholizismus und politische Form* (Munich: Theatiner-Verlag, 1925), p. 5.

Part V
From Conflict to Coexistence

–10–

The Catholic Missionary Crusade and the Protestant Revival in Nineteenth-Century Germany
Michael B. Gross

At the height of the 1848 Revolution, liberal and democratic delegates met at the National Assembly in Frankfurt to plan the political reform and national unification of Germany. In the fall of that year, their work was interrupted when angry crowds stormed the Assembly in an effort to oust conservatives and radicalize the revolution. When Prussian troops intervened to restore order, radical-democrats threw up barricades throughout the city. Fighting raged in the streets until the radicals were subdued with artillery barrages and infantry assaults. The street battles in Frankfurt were only part of the wave of democratic demonstrations and radical movements breaking out all over western Germany. Short-lived insurrections erupted in Cologne, the largest city of the Rhineland, and then again in the Grand Duchy of Baden.[1]

Meanwhile, not much farther up the Main River in Würzburg, a wholly different kind of meeting was taking place. Here the bishops and arch-bishops of the dioceses of the Catholic Church in Germany assembled to assess the tumultuous events erupting across Germany and to plan the counter-revolution. They believed that the revolutions were not fundamentally the result of political movements and social unrest. The revolutions were both cause and effect of a deeper erosion of religion, morality and obedience among the people that threatened religious as much as secular authority. The bishops agreed that the Church could not stand idly to one side and watch Germany descend into chaos. They agreed, therefore, to commit the Church to an extraordinary measure: a full-fledged campaign of popular missions (*Volksmissionen*) to restore faith, obedience and order among Catholics all across Germany. In a pastoral letter to the priests of his diocese the bishop of Münster explained "There has never been a time more than our own when such extraordinary means have been necessary, a time of religious indifference and immorality in which more than ever before divine and human laws are being trampled under foot."[2] Later in a letter to the king of Prussia justifying the missions, the clergy of the diocese of Münster cataloged a host of sins they believed characterized the spirit of the age: "Indifference, depravity, an undermined sense of right, irresolute faith, indecision, treason and fraud, insolence, a spineless anything-goes and an almost thorough self-interest and selfishness in religious and political matters is the signature of our time which we clergy encounter among the masses."[3]

Catholic Church authorities all over Germany agreed that the erosion of faith and obedience was due not just to the normal wear and tear of daily life. The people had been "bewildered" and "bewitched" by the fashionable and "false philosophies" (*Trugphilosophien*) of the modern age, including materialism, rationalism, liberalism and democracy, all propagated, church leaders claimed, by an endless number of anti-Christian and antisocial newspapers.[4] The depravity of the *Zeitgeist*, one bishop explained, could be judged by the fact that it was "a mark of enlightenment to eschew religion, to embrace unholy indifference, to deny God and the immortality of the soul as absolute in the life hereafter, and to limit the entire destiny of man to a possible earthly life of pleasures."[5] Local clergy confirmed such sentiments. In 1850 a priest in Bonn, a stronghold of liberalism, complained to his bishop that "a significant part of the population has unfortunately . . . not been spared by the spirit of the age, which characterizes itself as the enemy of religion, right and morals."[6]

In July 1849 members of the Society of Jesus, the Jesuits, gathered in Cologne, agreed to take up the call of the bishops and organized a missionary campaign. They were joined by additional Jesuits from America, Australia, England, France and Belgium. Other religious orders including the Redemptorists and Franciscans and to a lesser extent the Capuchins and Lazarists joined the crusade and organized their own popular missions.[7] Catholic authorities might have condemned the radicalization of the revolution, but they enjoyed the new constitution (the "decree constitution") imposed by the reactionary Brandenburg ministry in the fall of 1848 and then the new Prussian Constitution of 1850, both of which ended the state interference in ecclesiastical affairs of the *Vormärz*. The new constitutional guarantees granted to the Church included the right of the Catholic religious orders to settle freely in Prussian territory and to hold their missions.

The missions held by the Catholic religious orders across Germany not only revived and reshaped popular German Catholicism.[8] Jonathan

Sperber has shown that the missions also formed a counter-revolutionary, antiliberal, anti-Enlightenment mass movement that served both the Church and the interests of the monarchical state in the conservative decade of reaction.[9] The Catholic missionary crusade, however, also had a profound but surprisingly overlooked impact on Protestants and Catholic–Protestant relations in Germany. Protestant Church leaders believed the missions threatened to convert the Protestant population and to destroy their religion. In fact, however, the Catholic missions initiated a popular Protestant revival during the third quarter of the nineteenth century.

With the banning of the Jesuit Order by papal decree in 1773 the popular missions had disappeared in Central Europe. When the Order was restored in 1814 with the defeat of Napoleon and the restoration of the monarchical regimes of Europe, state authorities within the German Confederation looked upon the Jesuits with deep suspicion, and the Prussian government did not allow the Order to enter its territory. Secular clergymen in Westphalia, therefore, attempted themselves to revive the missions shortly before the breakout of revolution. It was, however, only with the social and political crisis of 1848, the new freedoms guaranteed in the Prussian constitution to the Church and the leadership of the Jesuits and the other religious orders that the missions proceeded in earnest.

Church authorities did not impose the popular missions on an unwilling population. Already during the *Vormärz* many German lay Catholics had crossed from Baden into Alsace and from the western Rhineland into Belgium to observe the missions held near the borders. Catholics were eager now for the missions to be held on German territory. When the Catholic deputy to the National Assembly, Franz Joseph Buss, left the Assembly and finally returned to Baden in the late summer of 1850, hundreds of Catholic men asked him to add his voice to the call for missions to restore faith and morality among the people.[10] Starting in 1849 and for the next twenty-three years teams of missionaries during all seasons of the year swept across Germany visiting hundreds of villages and towns and major cities. During this period the number of missions did not abate. They were more numerous, better organized and better attended in the late 1860s than they were during the post-revolutionary period of reaction. The accompanying table gives an estimation of the level of Jesuit, Franciscan and Redemptorist mission activity between 1849 and 1872, when the missions were finally brought to a halt by *Kulturkampf* legislation. The Redemptorists held an additional 700 missions in Bavaria between 1848 and 1872. The Lazarists held an average of eight to ten missions each year during this period.[11] Meanwhile, the

Capuchins added at least 152 missions between 1853 and 1872.[12] On the basis of these statistics and excluding hundreds of shorter follow-up missions (*Missionserneuerungen*), the total number of missions held throughout Germany between 1848 and 1872 reached at the very least 4,000. Not surprisingly, the missionaries concentrated on areas of dense Catholic population.

Franciscan, Jesuit and Redemptorist Missions, 1849–1872

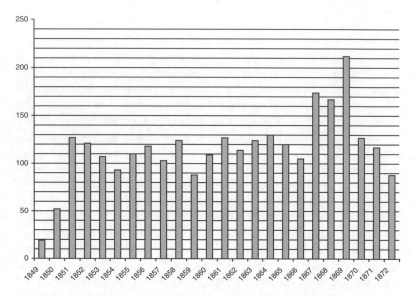

Sources: Autbert Groeteken, *Die Volksmissionen der norddeutschen Franziskaner vor dem Kulturkampf (1849–1871)* (Münster: Alphonsus Buchhandlung, 1909), pp. 110–33; Bernhard Scholten, *Die Volksmission der Redemptoristen vor dem Kulturkampf im Raum der Niederdeutschen Ordensprovinz* (Bonn: Hofbauer Verlag, 1976), pp. 103, fn. 9; 151. The table indicates the number of Jesuit missions held throughout Germany; the number of Franciscan missions in the Prussian dioceses of Breslau, Cologne, Münster and Osnabrück as well as missions held in the Austrian dioceses of Königsgrätz and Olmütz; and the number of Redemptorist missions in the dioceses of Cologne, Limburg, Münster, Paderborn and Trier. Between 1850 and 1872 the Redemptorists held an additional fifteen missions in the diocese of Osnabrück. The Franciscans held twenty additional missions in Paderborn and thirty missions in both Trier and Lüttich dioceses between 1849 and 1872.

The Redemptorists and Franciscan missionaries moved throughout Germany concentrating on the towns and villages of the countryside, where in 1850 two-thirds of the population still lived. The Jesuits, however, also brought the Catholic revival to large, secularizing cities, including those with slim Catholic minorities such as Hamburg, Bremen and even Berlin. Typically the missionaries worked together in groups of three, but they also often formed teams of as many as eight. Missions lasted usually two weeks. Not only missionaries but also the Catholic laity were on the move all over Germany. From the surrounding areas and from neighboring towns and villages hundreds or thousands of Catholics led in processions by their parish priests journeyed to the mission sites. Towns bulged to four or five times their normal population. When the Jesuit missionaries came to the small town of Gabsheim in the Rhineland in 1851, over 3,000 people converged on a population of 600. "All the houses and huts were filled with lodgers."[13]

Wherever the missions were held, they were unprecedented, all-consuming events. Factories, businesses, shops, theaters and schools shut down; housework and fieldwork were suspended.[14] Catholic and Protestant factory owners encouraged and even ordered their workers to go to the missions. Full wages were often paid to those who attended. When the Redemptorist mission came to the industrial town of Bottrop near Bochum in 1868, mine and factory managers were delighted. In an age requiring a new industrial discipline, employers recognized the value of sermons that extolled the virtues of authority and obedience.[15] On the other hand, when unsympathetic Protestant factory owners in Aachen refused to suspend or to shorten the workday, workers simply reset the clocks to make time to attend the sermons.[16]

The missionary campaign was a well-organized, systematic effort involving coordination at all levels of the church hierarchy. Bishops plotted the movement of the missions throughout their dioceses, and parish priests prepared their congregations weeks in advance. Carpenters were hired to build additional confessionals; churches were emptied of their pews to allow for the maximum amount of room. When the doors were opened, people flooded into the churches at four or five in the morning and they remained until far into the night. During the sermons they stood shoulder to shoulder from the portals to the altar. The overflow stood outside in the churchyard, straining to hear the sermons and trying to find a way to enter. According to parish reports to bishops and state surveillance reports, men and women from all social strata participated: peasants, factory workers, servants, artisans, and aristocrats and in the cities students, soldiers, professionals, civil servants and university professors.[17]

The sermons, offered three times a day at dawn, in the afternoon and in the evening, lasted two hours each. According to a report from the Ruhr region, Jesuits may have delivered sermons that "appealed to understanding and sound reason and took great pains to avoid exciting the mind."[18] Where local priests, however, encouraged the Jesuits to give "not especially learned, scientific, but on the contrary more powerful, forceful sermons emphasizing sin and repentance,"[19] the missionaries captured their audiences with dramatic orations that looked like tantrums. According to one troubled witness, "The preacher breaks the staff of God's wrath over everyone. He shouts with his hands balled into fists. He violently swings his body, working on one side of the pulpit then the other. He stamps his feet, smacks his hands together, stretches his arms high over his head then out over the rails."[20]

The secular priest Joseph Hillebrand, the indefatigable director of missions in the diocese of Paderborn, has left a rich collection of mission sermons.[21] They indicate that the missionaries concentrated on the major aspects of church doctrine: the origins of man, sin and repentance, the judgment after death and the threat of damnation, the need for confession, the incarnation of Christ, and the incontestable authority of the Church. In addition, the sermons introduced powerful, new forms of popular veneration, including the crucifix and the Virgin Mother of Christ (whose immaculate conception became dogma in 1854). Sermons also railed against basic features of popular culture: drinking and dancing (*the* forms of working-class entertainment), gambling, foul language and sexual permissiveness.[22]

It was, however, the sermons delivered on the theme of hell that brought men and women back to the Church. The missionaries terrorized their audiences with furious and graphic depictions of hell and the promise of eternal damnation for unrepentant sinners. Here is a typical example of the way the missionaries repeatedly hammered their audiences with the reality of hell:

> Hell is a gruesome dungeon in which sinners languish for all eternity. Hell is the state of excommunication, where horror and misery reign. Hell is the place where fire and brimstone burn forever. Hell is the place of constant despair and everlasting damnation. Hell is the place of wailing and darkness, the shadow of death and chaos, confusion and terror.[23]

The number of sermons in Hillebrand's collection on the theme of hell attests to the power the missionaries believed the threat of damnation had over their audiences. The sermon titles include "The Judgment of Damnation," "There is a Hell," "What Does it Mean to be Damned?"

"Hell," "The Sinner in Hell and the Sinner on Earth," "The Sorrow of the Damned," "The Fear of Hell," "The Eternal Fires," "The Rich Man in Hell," "The Gradations of Punishment in Hell," "Eternal Punishment in Hell," "The Danger of Going to Hell," "The Fruits of Considering Hell" and "The Belief in Hell and the Behavior of Christians." Fire and brimstone were invoked so often in the sermons that the missionaries found themselves dubbed the hell-preachers. As one disgusted critic complained, "What do the Jesuits preach? – Hell and damnation and damnation and hell!"[24] Hillebrand himself became popularly known as "Höllebrand" ("Hellfire"). The missionaries warned their listeners not to seek solace in the hope that the fires of hell were a mere metaphor without real consequences. "Everything endures pain in the flames: the evil tongue, the lusting eyes, the imprudent ear, the unchaste body, the impure heart. All suffer. The entire body is gripped and consumed with fire."[25] "Hell is an eternity of pain. Endless burning in the fire pits, hearing without end the howls and shrieks of the damned, enduring forever the worm burrowing into the breast, eternally suffering the scorn of the all-powerful and just God, that is the horrible, hopeless condition. . . . Forever! Eternity without end!"[26] Hillebrand admonished "Sinners!" to "Leave the path of ruin!" and confront the choice "Repent or hell!"[27]

Men and women panted, wailed in anguish, "wept like children" and dropped to their knees.[28] Those who fainted under the weight of the bombardment or collapsed for lack of oxygen were dragged to the first-aid stations located at the church portals. Liberal and Protestant critics were aghast by what they believed was psychological coercion, and they argued that the sermons contributed to mental illness and distress that might lead to suicide.[29] They charged that the Jesuits preyed especially on emotionally more susceptible and religiously-inclined women. Church authorities argued that the reports of hysteria and psychological malaise prominent in liberal newspapers were merely attempts to discredit the missons. But it is telling that the Jesuits themselves began to warn at the opening of their missions that anyone prone to anxiety and depression should avoid the sermons.[30]

The missionaries scheduled the themes of the sermons in order to maximize their impact. During the first three days they prepared their audiences by preaching first on the themes of sin, then on judgment upon death and punishment in hell and finally on the need for repentance and confession.[31] By the fourth day men and women were eager to enter the confessionals, and they gathered before dawn in front of the church. They continued to wait as long as twelve to fifteen hours in seemingly endless lines for their turn in the confessional. Teams of priests, gathered from the neighboring parishes demanded complete, detailed "life confessions" of every penitent, each of which lasted about twenty minutes.[32] One Redemptorist could not find words adequate to describe the desperation before the confessionals when the missions came to the diocese of Limburg.[33] Men and women burst into tears if they missed the chance to confess their sins and had, therefore, to return to the lines the following day. After exiting the confessional, some headed back to the end of the line to confess all over again. On the final day the missions culminated with a large festive procession led by the missionaries, the local priests and maidens dressed in white to erect the mission cross. Crowds then accompanied the missionaries, throwing flowers in their paths on the way to the train station. They left to repeat their work at the next site.

The hundreds of reports by parish priests effusively singing the praises of the missionaries no doubt pleased the bishops who had called for and organized the missionary campaign; but many local priests, in fact, resented being overshadowed in their own parishes by the younger, dynamic and zealous missionaries. Even the *Landrat* at Malmedy in the district of Cologne recognized "The local clergy is in general no friend of the Jesuits and does not like their visits;" parish priests were offended by the Jesuits' "far-reaching ambitions that don't agree with their comfortable, quiet lives."[34] Nor were the missionaries greeted everywhere with open arms by the laity. In the village of Öfft, hard on the French border, the congregation broke out into a riot of protest when the parish priest announced that the Redemptorist missionaries were coming.[35]

An overwhelming number of parish reports indicate, however, that even despite initial opposition the missionary crusade was an enormous success in the towns and villages of the countryside. According to reports from the parish priests at Warburg to their bishop of Paderborn in 1851, the arrival of the missions marked "a new epoch." The parish priest at Niederembt reported to the archbishop at Cologne in 1858 that "a new life for the Church" had begun.[36] According to the priest at Cochem in the diocese of Trier, after the mission only ten of the 500 parishioners who had stopped attending mass refused to return to the fold.[37] The priest at Neunburg vorm Wald in the diocese of Regensburg explained to his bishop that the Jesuits had been irresistible. By 1869 they could, he believed, declare in the immortal words of Caesar, "Veni. Vidi. Vici."[38] Men and women who had not confessed or taken the Eucharist for fifteen or twenty years received the sacraments in the confessional and at the altar. "The indifference that ran like a thread through the so-called educated strata and also stuck the working class many times," according to the priest at Worbis in the diocese of Paderborn in 1859, was transformed into religious conviction.[39] According to the report of a parish priest, even a year after the missionaries had come to Offenstetten in the diocese of Regensburg in 1867, his congregation was still attending his masses with more intense and heartfelt attention.[40] The priest at Darfeld told his bishop at Münster in 1851 that during the year following the mission the morality of the community had also significantly improved. There was no longer any boozing and nightly romping. Girls were even wearing their hats more modestly, without bands and flowers.[41] Prussian state authorities may have been unsettled by the power of the missions, the Catholic popular revival and particularly the Jesuits' popularity; but they also welcomed the missionaries' attack on rampant alcoholism, demand for social discipline and call for obedience to the monarchy.[42]

Among villagers and peasants accustomed to the traditional and quiet routines of rural life, the missions had a powerful impact. The melodrama of the sermons, the psychological purgation of life confession and the relief, if not euphoria, of forgiveness were intense individual and collective religious and emotional experiences not readily imaginable today. Participants remembered the mission as the date of reconciliation with feuding family members and neighbors, recovery from alcoholism, their return to the Church and salvation. For years the experience of religious renewal was recycled whenever people talked about the mission that came to their community. In Sunday sermons parish priests often reminded their congregations of their common dedication at the mission to religious life and moral sobriety.

In the secularizing cities the success of the Jesuit missions was more qualified. The percentage of the Catholic urban population attending them remained lower than in the countryside, where entire villages and small towns participated. At the height of the missionary campaign, in Aachen 20,000 of the total Catholic population of 73,000 attended the mission in 1868. When the mission came to Cologne in the same year 30,000 of a population of 100,000 attended.[43] On the other hand, by nineteenth-century standards crowds of 20,000 and 30,000 were spectacular and confirmed the new, mass power of Catholicism. Even so, the *Rheinisches Kirchenblatt* noted that in Cologne the "affluent part" of the population stayed away from the mission or came only to see enough to be able to join the current conversations about it.[44] Missions in cities were less well attended than those in rural areas, partly because cities were often hotbeds of agitation by democratic radicals who decried the missions as instruments of counter-revolution. For example, when the Jesuits came to Düsseldorf in 1851, democrats greeted them with defamatory posters and threatening letters.[45] More importantly, city missions proved less successful because educated, relatively secularized, urban Catholics resented the missionaries' antiliberal, antirational, antimaterialist message that struck at the heart of their social-cultural identity as members of the *Bürgertum*. Middle-class Catholics may have appreciated the Jesuits' campaign for social order and moral sobriety among the lower classes, but they distrusted their heavy-handed manner and winced at the unseemly spectacle of women at the sermons moaning, swooning and pressing their lips to the Jesuits' robes. Throughout the 1850s and 1860s Catholic liberals, as Thomas Mergel has argued, found themselves increasingly torn between their membership in the middle class on the one hand and their loyalty to the Catholic Church on the other.[46] They were wary of militant ultramontane Catholicism that was especially influential among "ignorant" peasants and "privileged" aristocrats. The prominent role of the Jesuits placed a further strain on their relationship with the Church. In 1858, to cite one example, Cologne's liberal-Catholic patrician Eberhard von Groote railed against the Jesuit "parasites in the ecclesiastical hierarchy."[47] By the 1870s liberal Catholics – like secular and Protestant liberals – had become fervently anti-Jesuit. During the *Kulturkampf* all the liberal Catholics in the National Liberal party and in the *Liberale Reichspartei* in the Reichstag threw their votes behind the anti-Jesuit legislation that brought a halt to the missionary campaign in 1872. It was, in fact, Eduard Windthorst, a Catholic progressive from Berlin and nephew of the Catholic Center Party leader, Ludwig Windthorst, who led the attack against the Jesuits in the *Reichstag*.[48] Even Ludwig Windthorst had never made a secret of his personal distaste for the Jesuits, although he believed the anti-Jesuit law was an abusive use of state power and an intolerable attack on the autonomy of the Catholic Church.[49]

Catholics were not the only ones to experience the missions. Although the missions did not intend to attract and convert non-Catholics, hundreds and thousands of Protestants were nonetheless drawn to the missions all over Germany. In towns like Lüdenscheidt in the diocese of Paderborn half those attending the Franciscan sermons were Protestants. The parish priest thought that "their attitude showed that they were deeply moved."[50] In predominantly Protestant, more secularized cities the number of Protestant participants was also relatively high. For example, despite the barrage of anti-mission and anti-Jesuit articles in the local newspapers, when the mission came to Bremen the Protestant churches stood empty while their congregations flocked to the sermons.[51] A Protestant layman enthusiastically defended the Jesuit mission when it came to Danzig in 1852.[52] Protestant interest in the missions reached up to the highest levels of the monarchy. Among the attentive participants at the mission in Bonn in 1851 was no less than Prince Friedrich Wilhelm, student at the university and heir to the Prussian throne. He was especially impressed by the power and the eloquence of the Jesuit sermons. His father Wilhelm, future king of Prussia and as such "supreme bishop" of the Protestant Church and later *Kaiser* of the German people, publicly sanctioned his attendance.[53] Numerous parish reports, Catholic newspapers and state surveillance reports indicate that not just Protestants but Jews often attended the missions.[54] The parish priest at Neheim in the diocese of Paderborn reported that both all the Protestants and all the Jews in the town listened to the sermons.[55] The spectacle of the missions, their excitement and their religious fervor cut across confessional lines.[56]

Protestants who attended the Catholic missions were, however, not interested in leaving their Church. There were instances of Protestants converting to Catholicism or attending confession in response to the sermons, but these were relatively rare. Many Protestants instead wanted only to participate in the experience of religious revival. They were, in fact, eager for a revival of their own. One parish priest reported with self-satisfaction that Protestants in Hüpstedt in the diocese of Paderborn confessed, "If only we were so lucky. If only we could have such a mission!"[57] In the absence of an organized missionary campaign for Protestant revival, many Protestants looked to the Catholic missions for Christian instruction. The liberal-Protestant *Bremer Bürgerfreund* did not disapprove: it was better that secularized Protestants be brought back into the Christian fold by Catholic missionaries than not at all.[58] The mission at Nordhausen in the diocese of Paderborn "wasn't just a mission for Catholics; it was a mission for thousands of Protestants too," according to the local priest.[59]

Protestants participated without offense since the sermons predominantly offered general Christian instruction common to both confessions (the immortality of the soul, the trinity, the Ten Commandments, the divinity of Christ), not specifically Catholic doctrine and dogma. "Even we Protestants," the *Evangelisches Kirchen-und Schulblatt für Schlesien* argued, "have no reason to be angry about them [the Jesuit missions]; most of their sermons were without confessional impurities" (*ohne confessionelle Beimischung*).[60] District officials and provincial authorities in the Rhineland, many of whom had anticipated that the sermons would disrupt confessional peace, were impressed by the relative (though not complete) absence of confessional polemics.[61] The missionaries steered clear of topics that would alienate Protestants, and the Catholic bishops quickly disciplined missionaries who provoked controversy.[62] Almost everywhere, in fact, the missionaries encountered popular Protestant support. When the Jesuits came to Damsdorf in the diocese of Kulm,

Protestants decorated the church and pulpit with garlands and oleanders.[63] At the Franciscan mission in Neheim the Protestant factory owner contributed to the missionaries' travel-expense account.[64]

Of course, not all Protestants who attended the sermons did so because they wanted to be part of a religious revival. The director of a *Gymnasium* in Danzig took his Protestant pupils to the mission sermons not for Christian instruction but because they served as models for his class of eloquent and persuasive rhetoric.[65] Many others no doubt went to the missions simply because they were curious. One Protestant author argued that the Jesuits in Hildesheim were mistaken to imagine that Protestants had come to them to listen with any sincere reverence. They went, he argued, merely to find out for themselves whether all the fuss about the missions in the newspapers was true and to make their own judgment. At the same time, however, Protestant pastors were now working harder to educate their congregations about the difference between the Protestant and Catholic faith:

> And so Protestants have drawn a profit from the Jesuit missions. Many Protestant Christians are now better informed about the doctrinal differences and show more interest in Church matters than they did before. In a word, their indifference, which was the result of a long period of peace in Church affairs, has come to an end."[66]

Already in 1852, the Prussian state authorities in Berlin were taking measures to restrict the holding of the missions. In May of that year, the Minister of Interior Ferdinand von Westphalen and the Minister of Educational and Religious Affairs Karl Otto von Raumer issued a decree (the "*Raumer Erlass*") prohibiting missions in Catholic parishes in predominantly Protestant areas. They believed that the missions were trying to convert Protestants. While a caucus of Catholic deputies in the Prussian parliament ultimately forced the state to back down from enforcing the decree, many Protestants also recognized that prohibiting the missions did not necessarily serve their own best interests. At the fifth annual Conference of the German Evangelical Church in September 1852, Ernst Wilhelm Hengstenberg, a prominent leader of the Protestant orthodox movement, the editor of the *Evangelische Kirchenzeitung* and no friend of the Jesuits, frankly explained to the Protestant Church leadership that their Church benefited from the missions. The challenge presented by the missions and the temptation they posed to Protestants, he argued, ultimately awakened the Protestant Church from its lethargy.[67] In response to the flow of Protestants to the missions, Protestant religious leaders now worked feverishly throughout the 1850s and 1860s to inculcate Protestant consciousness and preserve Protestant identity. Pastors, theologians and religious leaders unleashed a deluge of anti-Catholic and hysterically anti-Jesuit literature that drew a sharp theological and moral line between Catholicism and Protestantism and polarized the two confessions.[68] Protestant religious authorities believed the period of interconfessional peace of the *Vormärz* was over and found themselves now in the middle of a new "state of war" (*Kriegszustand*). They imagined the Catholic missionaries were invading Vatican armies that planned to destroy the Protestant Church and envisioned a rising tide of Catholicism threatening to wash over Germany. Protestant religious leaders called for an end to divisive intraconfessional rivalry among Lutherans, Calvinists and Pietists and between liberal and orthodox Protestants and for a united effort against the Roman enemy.[69]

The feverish anti-Catholicism and anti-Jesuitism of Protestant Church authorities in the 1850s and 1860s helped prepare the *Kulturkampf* of the 1870s and early 1880s, the liberal- and state-sponsored attack on Catholicism and the Catholic Church. *Kulturkampf* legislation expelled the Jesuits, closed the religious orders, ended the missions, arrested thousands of priests and created a Catholic pariah community within the new, predominantly Protestant German Empire. According to the *Kölnische Zeitung*, the anti-Jesuit law of 1872 abrogating the residence rights of Jesuits shot through the Catholic population like "a bolt of lightning."[70] When police authorities in Essen moved to enforce the law closing down the local Jesuits, the Catholic population of the city stormed into the streets in defiant rebellion. Two battalions of fusiliers were required to suppress the Catholic insurrection and restore order in the city. Even those Catholics who were otherwise no friends of the Jesuits found the law an outrageous attack on the autonomy of their Church.[71]

The Catholic missionary crusade that swept across Germany between the 1848 Revolution and the *Kulturkampf* was an ambitious and dramatic effort to repietize the Catholic population. Though less thorough among the more secularized middle-class Catholic population in the cities, the campaign was enormously successful, especially in the towns, villages and peasant communities of the countryside. Though this has been passed over by historians, there are also equally significant indications of a Protestant revival under way in the 1850s and 1860s, incited quite unintentionally by the Catholic Church and the Catholic missions. Ironically, the rechristianization of Protestants took place in Catholic churches and church yards where Protestants and Catholics stood literally side by side participating in the missions and listening to the sermons.

The Protestant revival was unplanned, reactive and more muted than its confessional rival. The meaning of Protestant attendance at the missions is also admittedly more ambiguous than Catholic participation, and the Protestant revival, like the Catholic revival, was a highly complex process with variations according to class, region and gender that still remain to be better understood. This episode of Protestant revival also gave way to the currents of secularization that only increased after the 1870s with, as historians have argued, continuing migration, urbanization, industrialization, the shortage of churches in large cities, the spreading culture of science and progress among the middle class, and the development of a large social-democratic working-class subculture.[72] But the eager participation of Protestants at the missions and the campaign by Protestant religious elites to reawaken Protestant identity during the third quarter of the century nonetheless refutes the assumption of an uninterrupted linear decline of religiosity among Protestants throughout the nineteenth century.

Acknowledgement

I would like to thank Charles Calhoun, Bodo Nischan and Carl Swanson for their meticulous reading of and constructive comments on earlier versions of this article.

Notes

1. Jonathan Sperber, *The European Revolutions, 1848–1851* (Cambridge: Cambridge University Press, 1994), pp. 212–15.
2. "Rundschreiben des Bischofs Johann Georg (Müller) von Münster an sämtliche Herren Pfarrer des Bistums Münster, 4 Feb. 1850," in *Aktenstücke zur Geschichte der Jesuiten-Missionen in Deutschland, 1848–1872*, ed. Bernhard Duhr (Freiburg im Breisgau: Herdersche Verlag, 1903), p. 8. See also Karin Jaeger, "Die Revolution von 1848 und die Stellung des Katholizismus zum Problem der Revolution," in *Kirche zwischen Krieg und Frieden. Studien zur Geschichte den deutschen Protestantismus*, ed. Wolfgang Huber and Johannes Schwerdtfeger, (Stuttgart: Ernst Klett Verlag, 1976), pp. 243–91.
3. "Immediatvorstellung der zehn Landkapital des Diözese Münster an den König von Preussen für die Jesuiten. Münster, 16 Okt. 1852," in *Aktenstücke*, p. 167.
4. See, for example, "Bischof Nikolaus v. Weis an den König Max von Bayern, 24 Juli 1851," in *Aktenstücke*, pp. 72–9; "Rundschreiben des

Bischofs Johann Georg von Münster an die Geistlichkeit über die Missionsvereine, 31 Dez. 1852," ibid., p. 181; "Bischof Nikolaus v. Weis an den König Max von Bayern, 3 März 1865," ibid., p. 337.

5. "Bischof Nikolaus von Weis an den König von Bayern, 3 März 1865," ibid., p. 337.

6. "Pfarrer von Bonn an den Erzbischof Johannes von Geissel, 28 Aug. 1850," ibid., p. 34.

7. Accounts of the Jesuit Order and its missionary activities include the work by the Jesuit Bartholomew J. Murphy, *Der Wiederaufbau der Gesellschaft Jesu in Deutschland im 19. Jahrhundert. Jesuiten in Deutschland, 1849–1872* (Frankfurt am Main and New York: Peter Lang, 1985). Enno Kopperschmidt's *Jesuiten Arbeiten. Zur Geschichte der Jesuitenorden in Deutschland von 1866 bis 1872* (Munich: Ludendorff Verlag, 1940) is a biased account published by the notorious Ludendorff publishing house during the Nazi period. The accounts of the Redemptorist missions by the Redemptorist Bernhard Scholten, *Die Volksmission der Redemptoristen vor dem Kulturkampf im Raum der Niederdeutschen Ordensprovinz* (Bonn: Hofbauer-Verlag, 1976) and *Die Volksmission der Niederdeutschen Redemptoristen und Oblaten während des Kaiserreichs (1873–1918)* (Bonn: Hofbauer-Verlag, 1978) are narrow and institutional studies. For a more interesting study of the Redemptortist popular missions in Bavaria see the thematically broader, richly-detailed and more critical work by Otto Weis, *Die Redemptoristen in Bayern (1790–1909). Ein Beitrag zur Geschichte des Ultramontanismus* (St. Ottlien: EOS Verlag, 1983) For the missions see pp. 977–1017. See also the valuable work by Jockwig Klemens, *Die Volksmission der Redemptoristen in Bayern von 1843 bis 1873. Dargestellt am Erzbistum München und Freising und an den Bistümern Passau und Regensburg* (Regensburg: Verlag des Vereins für Regensburger Bistumsgeschichte, 1967). The single source concerning the activities of the Lazarists is Leonhard Dautzenberg, *Geschichte der Kongregationen der Mission in der deutschen Provinz* (Graz, n.p., 1911). For the popular missions in the Rhineland see Erwin Gatz, *Rheinische Volksmission im 19. Jahrhundert. Dargestellt am Beispiel des Erzbistums Köln* (Düsseldorf: L. Schwann, 1963).

For a rich and indispensable collection of clerical letters, missionary reports, Catholic and Protestant eyewitness accounts, liberal and conservative newspaper articles, government and miscellaneous documents see *Aktenstücke*. Also valuable, though much less extensive for the Franciscan missions are the documents collected in *Die Volksmissionen der norddeutschen Franziskaner vor dem Kulturkampf*

(1848–1872), ed. Autbert Groeteken (Münster: Alphonsus Buchhandlung, 1909). A compilation of Protestant declarations attacking the missions and Catholic popular petitions in defense of the Jesuits compiled by a Jesuit can be found in *Aktenstücke betreffend die Jesuiten in Deutschland*, ed. Christoph Moufang (Mainz: Verlag von Franz Kirchheim, 1872). For the perspective of a Jesuit active in the missionary campaign see the biography by Johannes Mundwiler, *Georg von Waldburg-Ziel. Ein Volksmissionar des 19. Jahrhunderts* (Freiburg im Breisgau: Herdersche Verlagshandlung, 1906). This includes extensive use of Waldburg-Ziel's diary.

8. For the revival of popular Catholicism in Germany after 1850 see Jonathan Sperber, *Popular Catholicism in Nineteenth-Century Germany* (Princeton, NJ: Princeton University Press, 1984). For the popular missions see pp. 56–63. For recent debates on the periodization and interpretation of the Catholic revival see Margaret Lavinia Anderson, "Piety and Politics: Recent Work on German Catholicism," *Journal of Modern History*, 63 (1991): 681–716.

9. Jonathan Sperber, "Competing Counterrevolutions: Prussian State and Catholic Church in Westphalia during the 1850s," *Central European History*, 19 (1986): 45–62.

10. Franz Joseph Buss, *Die Volksmissionen. Ein Bedürfnis unserer Zeit* (Schaffhausen, 1850), p. 152.

11. Scholten, *Volksmission der Redemptoristen*, p. 108.

12. Ibid., p. 112.

13. *Katholisches Sonntagsblatt*, 16 Feb. 1851; *Aktenstücke*, p. 44.

14. "Mission Pfarrer Nieters an den Bischof Paulus Melchers von Osnabrück, Emden, 5 April 1864," *Aktenstücke*, p. 318; "Pfarrer Koester an das Bischöfl. General Vikarat Münster. Ölde, 20 Feb. 1850," ibid., p. 10; Die Missionen im Münsterlände, Oldenburg, 10 Nov. 1850," ibid., p. 95; Scholten, *Volksmission der Redemptoristen*, pp. 143, 155.

15. Ibid., p. 129.

16. Ibid., p. 140.

17. Landeshauptarchiv Koblenz [hereafter LHAK], Bestand 403, Oberpräsidium der Rheinprovinz, Nr. 7511, "Die Jesuiten, 1855–1865," Coblenz, 28 Feb. 1856. Polizei Direktor Junker an Regierungs Präsident [hereafter R.], Coblenz. Bl. 99–106; 13–17 Feb. 1853; Bericht der Zeitschrift "Sion," *Aktenstücke*, p. 197.

18. Hauptstaatsarchiv Düsseldorf [hereafter HSTAD], Regierungsbezirk Düsseldorf, Präsidium, Nr. 1252, "Katholische Orden und Missionen. Betr. vor allem Niederlassungen und Missionsveranstaltungen des Jesuitenordens, Bd. 1, 1852–1887," Bürgermeister Hüls an Landrat

zu Kempen, 17 Jan. 1872. Bl. 15; Bürgermeister Schwartz, Brügger an Landratsamt zu Kempen, 19 März, 1857. Bl. 10.

19. "Pf. Cruse an Bischof Konrad Martin, 24 April 1868," *Aktenstücke*, p. 377.

20. *Die Jesuitensiedlung in Westfalen und das Westfälische Junkerthum. Beiträge zur Geschichte der Volksverdummung in Preussen* (Bremen: A.D. Giesler, 1850), p. 14.

21. Joseph Hillebrand, *Missionsvorträge*, 2 vols. (Paderborn: Ferdinand Schöningh, 1870). From 1846 to 1856, Hillebrand reportedly held 155 missions, gave 3,852 sermons and (incredibly?) heard 194,634 "life confessions" – each of which would have taken about twenty minutes. In addition, he was credited with enrolling 109,656 people in alcohol abstinence sodalities and registering 26,679 young women in religious associations. It came as a surprise to no one perhaps when he finally collapsed from exhaustion in 1863.

22. For a list of forty-two sermons delivered at a mission at Danzig, see *Über die von Missions-Priestern aus dem Orden der Gesellschaft Jesu in Danzig gehaltenen Missionen* (Paderborn: Ferd. Schöningh, 1852), pp. 7–12. See also the list in K. A. Leibbrand, *Die Missionen der Jesuiten und Redemptoristen in Deutschland und die evangelische Wahrheit und Kirche* (Stuttgart, 1851), pp. 30–4.

23. Hillebrand, *Vorträge*, Vol. 2, "Was ist ein Verdammter," p. 267.

24. *Jesuitensiedlung in Westfalen*, p. 14.

25. Hillebrand, *Vorträge*, Vol. 2, "Was ist ein Verdammter," p. 272.

26. Quoted in Scholten, *Volksmission der Redemptoristen*, p. 172, note 34.

27. Hillebrand, *Vorträge*, Vol. 2, "Die Furcht vor der Hölle und die Bewahrung vor der Hölle," p. 288. For a psychological study of the centrality of the threat of damnation in hell in Catholic life and moral behavior see Andreas Heller, "'Du kommst in die Hölle . . .'. Katholizismus als Weltanschauung in lebensgeschichtlichen Aufzeichnungen," in *Religion und Alltag. Interdisziplinäre Beiträge zu einer Sozialgeschichte des Katholizismus in lebensgeschichtlichen Aufzeichnungen*, eds. Andreas Heller, Therese Weber, and Olivia Wiebel-Fanderl (Vienna, Cologne: Böhlau Verlag, 1990), pp. 28–55.

28. *Allgemeine Zeitung*, Nr. 316, 1852, *Aktenstücke*, p. 174; "Bericht eines Augenzeugen, Münnerstadt, 29 Feb. 1852," ibid., p. 114; *Volksmissionen der norddeutschen Franziskaner*, p.11.

29. K. A. Leibbrand, *Die Missionen der Jesuiten und Redemptoristen in Deutschland und die evangelische Wahrheit und Kirche* (Stuttgart: Schweizerbart'sche Verlagshandlung, 1851), pp. 30–1.

30. See "Mission Bericht des katholischen Pfarramt, Thennenbronn, 9 Dez. 1862," *Aktenstücke*, p. 304. For one examination of the larger context of gender and religious madness, which cannot be explored here, see Ann Goldberg, *Sex, Religion, and the Making of Modern Madness: The Eberbach Asylum and German Society, 1815–1849* (Oxford: Oxford University Press, 1999).

31. See the order of sermons recorded with brief summaries in *Gesellschaft Jesu in Danzig*, pp. 7–12.

32. At the Jesuit mission in Heiligenstadt in the diocese of Paderborn in 1859, thirty to forty priests heard the confessions of 8,000: "Pfarrer Zehrt an Bischof Konrad Martin, 15 Mai, 1859, Heiligenstadt," *Aktenstücke*, p. 277. To ensure anonymity and encourage attendance, local priests did not hear confession during the missions.

33. Scholten, *Volksmission der Redemptoristen*, p. 214.

34. HSTAD, Regierung Aachen, Präsidialbüro, Nr. 1239, "Missionare, Jesuiten, Lazaristen. Ordenstätigkeit derselben in Kirche und Schule, 1835–1916," Landrat an R. Kühlwetter. Aachen, 13 Aug. 1859. Bl. 156.

35. Scholten, *Volksmission der Redemptoristen*, p. 119, note 48. For popular opposition to the missions see Sperber, *Popular Catholicism*, pp. 62–3.

36. "Die Pf. Willmes und Pees an den Bischof Drepper von Paderborn, Warburg, 27 Dez. 1852," Aktenstücke, 180; "Pfarrer an das Erzbischöfl. Generalvikariat Köln, 8 Nov. 1858," ibid., p. 272.

37. "Dechant Schnorfeil an das Generalvikariat in Trier, Cochem, 18 April 1864," ibid., p. 319.

38. "Pf. Fell an den Bischof Ignatius vom Regensburg, Neunburg vorm Wald, Juli? 1869," ibid., p. 396.

39. "Pf. Huschenbett an Bischof Konrad Martin, Worbis, 20 Jan. 1859," ibid., p. 276.

40. "Pf. Rosmann an den Bischof von Regensburg, 8 Nov. 1867," ibid., p. 363.

41. "Pf. Fenslage an den Bischof von Münster über den Segen der im März 1850 gehaltenen Mission, Darfeld, 16 April 1851," ibid., p. 63.

42. LHAK, Bestand 403, Nr. 7511, R. an der Oberpräsident [hereafter O.] der Rheinprovinz, Pommer-Esche zu Coblenz. Aachen, 13. Sept. 1859. Bl. 367–77.

43. Scholten, *Volksmission der Redemptoristen*, p. 241.

44. Ibid., p. 242.

45. Mundwiler, *Georg von Waldburg-Ziel*, p. 85.

46. Thomas Mergel, *Zwischen Klasse und Konfession. Katholisches Bürgertum im Rheinland 1794–1914* (Göttingen: Vandenhoeck & Ruprecht, 1994); Thomas Mergel, "Ultramontanism, Liberalism, Moderation: Political Mentalities and Political Behavior of the German Catholic Bürgertum, 1848–1914," *Central European History*, 29(1996): 151–74.

47. Mergel, *Zwischen Klasse und Konfession*, p. 399.

48. Michael B. Gross, "Kulturkampf and Unification: German Liberalism and the War against the Jesuits," *Central European History*, 30(1997): 545–66.

49. Margaret Lavinia Anderson, *Windthorst: A Political Biography* (Oxford: Claredon Press, 1981), pp. 128, 166.

50. "Pfarrer Baumhöer an Bischof Conrad Martin, Lüdenscheid, 26 April 1860," in *Volksmissionen der norddeutschen Franziskaner*, p. 62.

51. *Bremer Bürgerfreund*, 28 May 1863, *Aktenstücke*, p. 306.

52. *Gesellschaft Jesu in Danzig.*

53. Murphy, *Wiederaufbau der Gesellschaft Jesu*, pp. 108–9; *Aktenstücke*, p. 57, note 1; Gatz, *Rheinische Volksmission*, p. 97.

54. LHAK, Bestand 403, Oberpräsidium der Rheinprovinz, Nr. 7511, Coblenz, 28 Feb. 1856. Polizei Direktor Junker an R., Coblenz, Bl. 99–106; "Westf. Kirchenblatt für Katholiken," 31 May 1851; *Volksmission der norddeutschen Franziskaner*, p. 35; "Kathol. Missionsblatt," 4 July 1858, ibid., p. 49; pf. Klütsch an Bischof Wilhelm (Arnoldi) von Trier über die vom 17 Feb. bis 2 März abgehaltene Mission, Oberwesel, März 1856 *Aktenstücke*, p. 248; "Pfarrer Wiemann an Bischof Drepper von Paderborn, Dortmund, 20 März 1853," ibid., p. 203. See also Gatz, *Rheinische Volksmission*, pp. 99, 104, 108.

55. "Pfarrer Münstermann an Bischof Conrad Martin. Neheim, 20 März 1868," *Volksmission der norddeutschen Franziskaner*, p. 94.

56. The parish priest at the mission at Allenstein reported that Catholics, Protestants and Jews knelt together and wept at the sermons: "Erzpriester Pruss an den Bischof Josef Ambrosius von Ermland, Allenstein, 29 Sept. 1857," *Aktenstücke*, p. 264.

57. "Pfarrer Sittel an Bischof Conrad Martin. Hüpstedt, 19 März 1864," *Volksmissionen der norddeutschen Franziskaner*, p. 85.

58. *Bremer Bürgerfreund*, 28 Mai 1863, *Aktenstücke*, p. 306.

59. "Pf. Baumhörer an den Bischof Konrad Martin. Nordhausen, 24 April, 1860," *Aktenstücke*, 283.

60. *Evangelisches Kirchen- und Schulblatt für Schlesien und Posen*, Nr. 20, 13 May 1852. *Aktenstücke*, p. 126.

61. HSTAD, Regierungsbezirk Düsseldorf, Präsidium., Nr. 1252, "Katholische Orden und Missionen. Betr. vor allem Niederlassungen und Missionsveranstaltungen des Jesuitenordens," Bd. 1, 1852–1887; Bürgermeister Schwartz, Brügger an Landratsamt zu Kempen, 19 März 1857. Bl. 10; HSTAD, Bestand Regierung Aachen, Präsidium. Nr. 1239, "Missionare, Jesuiten, Lazaristen. Ordenstätigkeit derselben in Kirche und Schule, 1835–1916," Landrath, Düren, an R., Kühlwetter, Aachen, 31 Aug. 1859. Bl. 164; LHAK, Bestand 422, Regierungsbezirk Trier, Nr. 3963, "Wirken und Verhalten der katholischen Missionen und der Jesuiten, 1850–1900," Landrath, Wittlich zu R. Gärtner zu Trier, 20 Nov. 1866. Bl. 385–86; LHAK, Bestand 403, Oberpräsidium der Rheinprovinz, Nr. 7511, "Die Jesuiten, 1855–1865," R., Aachen an O. der Rheinprovinz, Pommer-Esche zu Coblenz, 13 Sept. 1859. Bl. 367–77; Polizei Direktor Tilligen, Trier, 24 Juni, 1856. Bl. 147–8; R., Aachen an O. der Rheinprovinz Kleist-Retzow, Coblenz, 26 Juli, 1856. Bl. 157–9. But for an attack on Luther's translation of the Bible see HSTAD, Bestand Regierung Düsseldorf, Präsidium, Nr. 1252, Duisberg, 1 Juni 1856, Bürgermeister an Landrath Keshler. Bl. 72.

62. When a Jesuit missionary exclaimed before Protestant listeners that Catholic parents in mixed (Catholic-Protestant) marriages who did not baptize their children faced damnation, he was reprimanded by the bishop of Breslau. The bishop argued that the missionaries must work for the respect and trust of Protestants as well as Catholics: see "Pf. Plütschke an Fürstbischof Förster in Breslau, Neufalz, 31 Mai 1855," *Aktenstücke*, p. 238; "Fürstbischof Förster an Pf. Plütschke, Breslau, 11 Juni 1855, ibid., p. 240.

63. "Dekan Kammer(?) an den Bischof von der Marwitz in Pelpin, Darmsdorf, 26 Aug. 1861," *Aktenstücke*, p. 283.

64. "Pfarrer Münstermann an Bischof Conrad Martin, 20 März 1868," *Volksmissionen der norddeutschen Franziskaner*, p. 94.

65. "Bericht des Protestanten Richard Wulckow," *Aktenstücke*, p. 140.

66. *Die Jesuitenmissionen in Hildesheim und damit Zusammenhängendes. Worte der Belehrung und Mahnung an den protestantischen Bürger und Landmann* (n., n.d.), p. 15.

67. "Verhandlung des Fünften deutschen evangelischen Kirchentages in Bremen, 15 Sept. 1852," *Aktenstücke*, pp. 157–61.

68. See for example Hermann Reuter, *Ueber die Eigenthümlichkeit der sittlichen Tendenz des Protestantismus im Verhältnis zum Katholicismus* (Greifswald: König. Univ.-Buchdruckerei, [1859]); Erich Stiller, *Grundzüge der Geschichte und der Unterscheidungslehren*

der evangelisch-protestantischen und römisch-katholischen Kirche (Hamburg: Robert Kittler, 1855); Adolf Stöber, *Evangelische Abwehr, katholischer Angriffe* (Strassburg: J. Kräuter, 1859); J. F. E. Sander, *Der Beruf der Protestanten, Rom gegenüber, in dieser Zeit. Sendschreiben an die evangelischen Gemeinden* (Leipzig: Gebhardt und Reisland, 1853) and G. Vintzelberg, *Protestantismus und Katholicismus oder: Die Werthschätzung des evangelischen Glaubens* (Fehrbellin: Im Selbstverlage des Verfassers, 1862).

69. See for example Th[eodor] Kleifoth, *Wider Rom! Ein Zeugniss in Predigten* (Schwerin und Rostock: Stiller'sche Hofbuchhandlung, 1852); Heinrich Wiskemann, *Die Lehre und Praxis der Jesuiten in religiöser, moralischer und politischer Beziehung* (Cassel: J. Georg Luckhardt, 1858); Daniel Schenkel, *Das gegenwärtige aggressive Verfahren der römisch-katholischen Kirche in ihrem Verhältnisse zum Protestantismus* (Darmstadt: C. W. Leske's Separat-Conto, 1857) and *Deutschlands Erb- und Erzfeind. Mahnruf an das deutsche Volk* (Coburg: F. Streit's Verlagsbuchhandlung, 1862).

70. HSTAD, Regierung Düsseldorf, Nr. 20111, "Jesuiten," Bd. 1, newspaper clip, 6 Aug. 1872.

71. HSTAD, Riegurung Düsseldorf, Nr. 20111, Bd. 1, Essen, 14 Aug. 1872. Bürgermeister, Gustav Adolf Waldthausen; newspaper clip from *Essener Zeitung*, 25 Aug. 1872; newspaper clip from *Essener Blätter* 25 Aug. 1872; *Vossische Zeitung*, 7 Sept. 1872.

72. See, for example Hugh McLeod, *Piety and Poverty: Working-Class Religion in Berlin, London and New York, 1870–1914* (New York: Holmes & Meier, 1996).

Building Religious Community: Worship Space and Experience in Strasbourg after the Franco-Prussian War

Anthony J. Steinhoff

Introduction

By the end of the nineteenth century, Friedrich Nietzsche and many other critics of organized religion had declared God dead. Recently, however, scholars have begun to demonstrate that, in fact, religious factors critically shaped culture, society, and politics throughout the Second German Empire (*Kaiserreich*).[1] While this research has fittingly highlighted religion's influence in Imperial Germany, it has largely avoided inquiry into the actual forms and meanings of religious life. We know little about how individuals experienced and practiced religion. Similarly, our understanding of how or why people affiliated themselves with a religious community is sketchy. Yet, these are precisely the kinds of issues we must address if we are to answer the larger question opened up by this recent work: *why* could confessional affiliation function as a powerful social category in late-nineteenth-century Germany? Moreover, examining the structures and practices of religious communities will help us grasp more fully religion's ongoing sociological and psychological relevance in modern European society.

Several historians have begun to investigate aspects of the organization and content of religious life in German Europe, particularly for Roman Catholicism.[2] Wolfgang Schieder, Jonathan Sperber, and David Blackbourn, for example, have shed invaluable light on such topics as Catholic popular devotion and religious associations.[3] Other scholars have started to examine the secular and regular clergy and their respective roles in parish and community activities.[4] Finally, research into the impact of social and cultural change on formal religious belief and practical theology has advanced.[5] Taken together, this work portrays the last half of the nineteenth century as a time of religious revival and an era when many religious groups strove to overcome the many challenges the modern world presented to religious belief and community.[6] Nevertheless, even this research overlooks the forms of ordinary religious experience and practice, especially that which most contemporaries regarded as fundamental: public worship.[7]

In the final decades of the nineteenth century, Christian clergy and laity experimented with many ways to instill and express religious identity, for example through religious associations and newspapers. Yet they continued to accord worship – particularly on Sunday and feast days – special importance. The special weight attached to this type of experience even in the late nineteenth century stemmed from several factors, but above all, from worship's capacity to build and express religious community. The act of congregating at a particular time and place explicitly created and made visible the religious community. At a time when the parish's role as a center of sociability was steadily declining, gathering for religious services – claiming specific time and space as religious – provided a rare instance when the sense of membership in the community became tangible. Moreover, from a Christian perspective, coming together not only carried out a Gospel commendation but also brought Christ himself into the presence of the group.

From the clerical standpoint, a second consideration added to worship's import. The very organization of the service (its liturgy) permitted the elaboration of a distinct notion of religious community. Through the selection and organization of texts, the liturgy crafted a story about what it meant and means to belong to a particular religious community. Furthermore, the ritual activity during the service emplotted the members of the congregation directly into this narrative, so that they became actively involved in this process of community building.[8]

Finally, liturgy's inherent plasticity allowed worship to be a very distinctive type of religious event. The choice (and rejection) of specific ritual elements and their arrangement into a whole produced an experience that was unique to each faith community. Worship, thus, built religious community by creating a shared experience for the members, which thereby distinguished them from non-members. Hence, worship functioned as powerful means by which to articulate and maintain the boundaries between religious groups.[9] When inter- (and even intra-) confessional religious tension rose in the late nineteenth century, not surprisingly, one of its most vigorous expressions was heated discussions of worship theory and practice.[10] For example, Protestant theologians regularly explained and justified their own positions by pointing out (perceived) errors in Catholic ritual belief and practice.

In short, worship brought individuals together and provided them a significant, shared and distinctive religious experience. It is this type of activity that established and gave meaning to membership in a religious community. This, in turn, permits confessional affiliation to have wider social, cultural, and political resonance. To examine more concretely this relationship between public worship and religious community, this chapter concentrates on the two primary aspects of this type of religious experience: the space in which it unfolds and the organization of the event itself. It works through the prism of a local study, namely two events in the life of Strasbourg's Lutheran New Church immediately following the annexation of Alsace–Lorraine (the *Reichsland*) to the German Empire. The first section examines the reconstruction of the New Church; the second analyzes the ceremony held to dedicate the completed church in 1877. This tack permits a more thorough appreciation of Protestant religious experience than currently exists in the literature. And, because of the long history of tensions between Strasbourg's almost equally-sized Protestant and Catholic communities, it also illuminates the impact of interconfessional competition on the process of religious community-building in the final decades of the nineteenth century.[11]

Rebuilding the New Church: Worship Space in Strasbourg

By mid-August 1870, the Franco-Prussian War had reached the Alsatian capital of Strasbourg. German forces surrounded the city and commenced bombing to force its capitulation. On the night of 24–25 August 1870 the Lutheran New Church (*Temple Neuf*) caught fire during a particularly intense period of bombardment. When day broke on the 25th, all that remained of the immense former church of the Dominicans was "four blackened walls topped by an enormous gable."[12] The destruction of the New Church afflicted the members of New Church parish as well as the entire Protestant community of Strasbourg. Since the restoration of the cathedral to Catholic worship in 1681, the New Church hosted the Lutheran congregation that had worshiped at the cathedral, making it the most prominent of the city's Lutheran churches and the unofficial center of the French Lutheran Church.[13] By destroying the church, the Germans had laid waste to this symbol of local Protestant pride, decimated the treasures stored there, and humbled the community itself (which was the most bourgeois and, arguably, francophile in Strasbourg) by forcing it to worship in another church at times that were often inconvenient.[14]

Yet, the cloud produced by the demise of the New Church turned out to have a silver lining. For the first time since the Reformation, Lutherans could construct a space for worship and fellowship in accord with Protestant liturgical needs and theological perspectives.[15] The New Church parish would no longer have to contend with the "un-Protestant" features of a church originally built for Catholic worship. Throughout the seven years of planning and building, the New Church's Consistory (a lay-dominated parish council) articulated its visions of Protestant ritual environment and community space, above all by rejecting design elements and architectural styles it regarded as "Catholic." The formal process for erecting the New Church also drew attention to institutional differences between the Lutheran and Catholic Churches. Thus, both the process and the final product clearly marked the new New Church as a home for a Protestant religious community.

At its session of 17 April 1871, the New Church Consistory began the rebuilding process: it appointed a building commission, composed of two pastors and four elders, to supervise the project. At its first meeting, the commission decided to select the design for the new church through a public competition. Shortly thereafter, the Consistory approved the guide-lines for this *concours*, which enumerated the concerns that every project had to address. In effect, this document stated both the parish's ideal of Protestant church architecture and its estimation of the building's principal functional and representational requirements.[16] From the first to the last paragraph of this document, the Consistory reminded all prospective architects that the new structure would be a Protestant church. The first two criteria presented the most important indications of what this meant:

> Because the edifice to be reconstructed is a Protestant church, it is necessary above all that the needs of Protestant worship be completely satisfied and that, in particular, its [interior] organization be such that when the pastor speaks, either from the pulpit or the altar, he may be seen and understood in every part of the building.

> The altar should have a central position [in the church] and also be close to the pulpit; however, it shall not be placed in a chancel, which is unnecessary for Protestant worship.

The guidelines thereby established the pulpit and altar as the two focal points of religious activity in a Protestant church, the places where the community heard the word of God and commemorated the Last Supper. The centrality of the Word in Protestant worship – in the sense of Scripture reading and exegesis as well as spoken prayer and song – emerges here in that the position of the altar is defined almost exclusively in relation to

the location of the pulpit. Moreover, the guidelines intended the organization of the church's interior space to represent physically Protestant
teaching about the close relationship between Word and Sacrament by
requiring that the altar and pulpit be placed near each other. Nevertheless,
while the guidelines prescribed a "pulpit–altar" unit, the architects could
define "central" as they saw fit.

The guidelines' first paragraphs mostly outlined the characteristics
that made a church Protestant, but they also contained phrases that
contemporaries would have recognized as renunciations of Catholic
architectural practices. One was the stricture that all members of the
congregation should be able to see and understand the pastor at all times.
This demand reflected the importance of the Word in Protestant worship.
In addition, it reflected a desire to counter a popular belief, dating back
to the Middle Ages, that the clergy conducted "magic" at the altar, especially during the Communion service. Thus, the Consistory wanted the
architects to eschew columns and pillars, common in most of Strasbourg's
churches, for they reduced the usable space in the nave by obstructing
the view.[17] The Catholic Church in Alsace also recognized this problem,
but only required architects "to avoid when possible any structural
elements that would hinder the faithful from seeing the altar or understanding the preacher."[18]

More directly, the competition rules stipulated that the chancel, or
choir, area was "unnecessary" for Protestant worship. Although the word
"Catholic" never appeared in the text, this was the intended referent. For
Catholics, the chancel was the area where the clergy performed the liturgy;
therefore, the primary altar of a Catholic church had to be placed there,
either in the far end or towards the front near the nave. Indeed canon law
and local custom also required that the priest pay particular attention
to the location and decoration of the altar, because this "holy site of
the sacrifice of the new covenant and the dwelling place of God" stood
at the center of the Catholic religion and, therefore, each Catholic
church.[19] Finally, the chancel was "priestly" space, in contrast to the nave
(a "lay" space). From a Protestant perspective, however, the Reformation's
reconceptualization of the priesthood and the communion sacrament made
the chancel area "dead space"; thereafter, it found use only during
communion services, for communicants could assemble there around the
altar.

The remaining items in the announcement stated requirements that
revealed the Consistory's understanding of how the church would be used.
Here we see the parish leadership trying to accommodate two, somewhat
contradictory, goals. On the one hand, the new New Church would be a

parish church. It had to contain spaces for the types of worship held in the parish and meeting rooms for the Consistory and parish associations. On the other hand, the reconstructed church had to fulfill the representative functions of being the "first among equals" among Strasbourg's Lutheran churches. That is, the New Church had to be able to serve as a "Lutheran Cathedral," in which the comparison to the Catholic Cathedral, begun in 1681, would remain active.[20] These considerations strongly affected the interior design and outfitting of the church as well as its exterior appearance.

Above all, the church had to be large enough for the New Church congregation and also sufficiently spacious to accommodate larger assemblies of Protestants at special services (e.g. city-wide services for the Emperor's birthday). The guidelines thus required that the plans provide for occupancy of at least two thousand people on the main floor and, as necessary, in galleries, with a space for at least eighty people directly in front of the altar. This space before the altar was intended for communion services. Its size reflects the pastors' estimation of the normal rate of communion, Easter excepted, when it would be too small and the pastors would have to adopt another method of commemorating the Last Supper.

The mention of a minimum capacity of two thousand is especially illuminating, for it represents a compromise between the church's two roles. In the strictest sense, even two thousand seats was inadequate to seat everyone at the principal service (the *Amtpredigt* or *Hauptgottesdienst*). Between 1866 and 1914, the size of the New Church parish fluctuated between 4,400 and 5,000 souls, making a church with the stated capacity too small by half for the parish. But the Consistory acknowledged that on most Sundays the prescribed capacity vastly exceeded the needs of the parish: only on feast days (e.g. Christmas, Easter, Pentecost) would the church truly be full. Nonetheless, because of the New Church's representative role, it required a larger interior space.

Indeed, one could argue that the proposal called for a church that would be too large, especially from the perspective of how the parish would most frequently use the church. The issue of size was far from trivial, for it directly affected perception of community within the church. Sitting with a handful of others in an expansive space tended to produce a sense of isolation rather than community and warmth, which worship aimed to generate. Thus, regardless of how the architects ultimately organized the interior of the new edifice, the need to have a large New Church ensured that the difficulties posed by falling levels of church attendance would be present in the new structure, just as in Strasbourg's other (large) Protestant churches.

In this respect, too, the relationship between worship space and liturgical experience was distinctively Protestant, albeit in a more negative fashion. The "empty church" phenomenon plagued Strasbourg's Protestant churches to a much higher degree than the Catholic ones because the Protestant churches had no requirements for attendance or communion reception.[21] Indeed, several of Alsace's pastors complained that churches were emptiest at the time they should have been most full: at communion. In Alsace, at least, when communion would be part of the service, all those who did not intend to receive normally left the church before the communion liturgy began, extenuating the communal context of the rite. Catholic priests also complained about poor attendance, but the centrality of communion in the Catholic mass altered the relationship between ritual space and collective sentiment. As the central, rather than a peripheral event of Catholic worship, communion formed the primary means by which the bonds of community were expressed in a Catholic service. That a lesser or greater number of people were present at communion did not alter this association.[22]

The Sunday *Amtpredigt*, however, was not the only event in the life of the New Church community. Hence, every project for the new church had to create special spaces for other congregational activities: a chapel and a sacristy. On the one hand, this accorded with the pastors' convictions that the activities of the parish should, as much as possible, take place within the church, the meeting place of the parish. On the other hand, in parishes such as the New Church, where significant theological differences among the pastors existed, the church figured as a neutral space that did not favor any of the pastors or their congregations as a rectory would.[23]

The primary function of the proposed chapel was to provide a smaller location for liturgical activity. That is, it served as a miniature church where pastors held weekday prayer services, preparation for communion, and rites that only a relatively small number of people attended (e.g. baptisms and some weddings). In the smaller confines of the chapel, the structural and social divisions of the nave vanished. During the Reichsland period, the notion of chapel as "substitute church" gained additional weight, for at one time or another, all Strasbourg's Protestant churches underwent renovation and repair. Once the chapel was again usable, it was pressed into service. Thus, after the New Church's chapel was completed in late 1876, the pastors started to use it even though the main church was not yet finished.[24]

Whereas parishes used chapels primarily for religious gatherings, sacristies functioned as meeting places for organs of parish government and religious associations. Protestant consistories and parish councils met in these rooms to regulate the parish's business.[25] Most of Strasbourg's Protestant churches held parish elections in the sacristy. The Directory also required that each church secure its electoral registers, parish council minutes, and records of the rites performed by each pastor in this room. Finally, parish associations, for example women's charity groups and diaconates, regularly held their meetings in the sacristy. In these respects, the church was not simply a place for worship but, in a very real sense, the heart of the parish community.

The one major design element that the New Church Consistory did not fix in advance was the overall architectural style of the church. On this point the competition text stated simply: "the competitors must not lose sight of the fact that the building is a Protestant, Christian church." In other words, the Consistory did not feel that any particular style was inherently Protestant or Lutheran. What mattered most was the degree to which the design satisfied the New Church's liturgical and fellowship needs. The silence on this matter is particularly curious because the outward form of a church powerfully affected how Strasbourg's residents, whether Protestant or not, would "read" it. The Catholic Diocese of Strasbourg, for its part, strongly recommended the Gothic and Romanesque styles for new churches.[26] Similarly, beyond the Rhine, many Protestant church authorities encouraged constructing new churches in a Gothic or Renaissance style.[27]

Just before the jury announced the results of the competition, the Consistory took the unusual step of displaying the thirty-four entries in Strasbourg's City Hall for public viewing. Although none of the concerned parties left any explanation for this decision, two considerations may well have made it necessary. First, the members of the parish needed to be able to view the projects; they had a specific and legitimate interest in the results. The New Church did not have a suitable space to display them at its disposal in February 1872, thereby necessitating the use of another locale, like the nearby City Hall. Second, by choosing City Hall as the site, the New Church effectively declared the future form of the reconstructed New Church to be a matter of public (municipal) and not just parochial interest. It also reasserted the traditional link between civic pride and Protestant identity in Strasbourg.

The characteristics of the submitted projects as well as the jury's awards aroused the impression that the new New Church itself represented a protest against the German annexation of Alsace–Lorraine. French firms dominated the competition. As the reviewer "(E.L.)" of the exhibition in the admittedly francophile (and religiously rationalist) *Progrès Religieux* of 24 February noted, 24 of the 34 entries were French (including 6 Alsatian projects!); these were the most polished designs. E.L. also observed a marked correspondence between nationality and style: French architects preferred Romanesque and Byzantine styles; German firms utilized Gothic or Renaissance forms.[28] Moreover, the jury awarded all five prizes to "French" firms. However, the Consistory eventually decided that none of the designs, as submitted, could be executed. It then contracted Emile Salomon, the head of the one Alsatian firm honored by the jury (fourth place), to draw up new plans using the first-place Romanesque project (of a Parisian firm) as his starting-point.[29]

In 1876 Jules Sengenwald, a member of the jury and member of the Consistory, explained that proper consideration of the New Church's representative functions eventually prejudiced the jury in favor of the "French," Romanesque projects:

> Many people were inclined in favor of the Gothic, which seems to be native to our region and predisposes the soul to religious sentiment.[30] However, apart from the fact that that style satisfies few of the needs of Protestant worship, the proximity of the admirable [Catholic] cathedral to the New Church made it unthinkable to build a monumental Protestant church in the same style. In addition, several of the projects used the [Romanesque] basilica form of the fifth century. These structures originally served as courtrooms and were then converted to Christian churches as soon as public worship was authorized; therefore, this style is contemporaneous to the origin of Christianity and easily adaptable to the simple and austere forms of Protestant worship.[31]

In other words, the awareness that the public would compare the new New Church and the Catholic Cathedral encouraged the jury and the Consistory to favor a plan for a "monumental" Lutheran church whose exterior clearly distinguished it from the Cathedral.

Between 1872 and 1877 Salomon planned and carried out the final project for the "Lutheran Cathedral." Constructed out of red sandstone from the Vosges, the church took the form of a Romanesque basilica with the nave divided into a central and two side sections. The pulpit was placed on the east wall of the church, at the end of the central axis, with the altar situated immediately in front of the pulpit. To either side of the pulpit–altar group stood special pews for the officials of the church: the pastors and the members of the Consistory. Although this practice, observed in all of Strasbourg's Protestant churches, seemed to violate Protestant notions of Christian equality (most pastors and elders generally belonged to the upper and middle classes), the custom derived from the men's roles in the parish, not their social status.[32]

Each of the side areas of the nave had balconies with seating to complement that available on the main floor. Yet this space was not entirely unstructured. Despite efforts to abolish the customs, the Consistory voted in May 1877 to re-establish separate seating for men and women and to allow parishioners to rent seats on an annual basis. In this manner, the organization of the church's interior constrained how people would participate in the liturgies and, consequently, how they related to the sense and message of community developed by the pastor's ritual actions.[33]

Finally, the entire process for reconstructing the New Church set the church off as Protestant, for something entirely different would have occurred had the New Church been Catholic. The New Church Consistory essentially had a free hand in all phases of the project; therefore, we can make a strong case for stating that the finished building faithfully represented the parish's desires and needs. Legally, all consistorial resolutions required the Directory's approval to be binding, but the Consistory did not have to work through the Directory to obtain, for example, the requisite building permits. Indeed, in reviewing a Consistory's resolutions, the Directory focused on the financial and legal aspects of the project.[34] In this particular case, the Directory had little to worry about: the vast majority of the building costs would be underwritten by the *Reichsland*'s government; the New Church, the richest of Strasbourg's seven Lutheran parishes, was fully capable of raising what might remain.[35]

By contrast, the strictly hierarchical nature of the Catholic Church, especially in the Diocese of Strasbourg, meant that a parish had a very limited degree of autonomy when it came to constructing a new church.[36] The bishop had to determine that a new church was necessary; he chose its future location. The parish or local community would then present to the bishop its wishes, including the choice of building style; but a lengthy list of regulations governed the development of each proposal, so that even at this level the parish's actions were checked. Moreover, these regulations emphasized that no parish could begin discussions with civil authorities until the bishop approved the blueprints and the parish's cost estimates for the church.[37]

Both in process and outcome, the construction of the New Church after 1870 emerged as a distinctively Protestant, or at least Lutheran, enterprise. The building was new and stood out architecturally from Strasbourg's other churches. Yet, as long as the bell tower remained unbuilt, the New Church bore a certain resemblance to the Calvinist temple on *rue Bouclier*. Above all, the interior space – the position of the altar directly in front of the pulpit; the open nave, free of pillars and columns; and the absence of a chancel area – set it off as a Protestant place of worship. As we have seen, the ability of this structure to take on a Protestant character also resulted from the ongoing comparisons with its Catholic other, the Cathedral. In the end, however, the architectural distinctions aimed to promote another type of difference: the creation of an unmistakably Protestant worship experience.

Dedicating the New Church: Protestant and Catholic Approaches to Worship

On 4 October 1877 the New Church formally dedicated its new place of worship with a festive service. For this day's liturgy, the New Church's four pastors constructed an elaborate version of a normal Sunday morning service (*Amtpredigt*) to endow the dedication with a celebratory character. This ceremony exemplifies how Strasbourg's Protestants used ritual and liturgy to shape the worship experience. The service developed a clear narrative about the New Church community, its past, present and future, which the congregation endorsed through its presence at and participation in the service. Yet, all who participated in, saw, or read about the dedication would also have understood it as a Protestant event. Not only did the service take place in a Lutheran church, and one designed for Lutheran worship at that, but it differed notably from its Catholic analog. Hence, the dedication service illuminates how worship itself helped to maintain awareness of interconfessional difference in the final decades of the nineteenth century.

At the end of May 1877 the New Church Consistory commenced preparations for the dedication service. It named a committee to plan the service and decided to hold the dedication, not on a Sunday, but rather on a Thursday.[38] These two initial steps contributed to establishing this event as unique. First, the creation of a committee meant that no one pastor would organize the service. The four pastors decided collectively what prayers and scripture passages to use, which hymns to sing, and who would officiate at which part of the service.[39] Moreover, the committee included five lay elders, who would handle the non-liturgical aspects of the event, but could also resolve any differences of opinion that might arise among the pastors. This too figured as exceptional, for the laity normally played no role in preparing a worship service; this was the pastor's responsibility.[40] Finally, the choice of Thursday for the service betrays the Consistory's view that the ceremony was not a special occasion for the parish alone. Rather, the restoration of the Lutheran Cathedral, this symbol of Protestant pride and identity in Strasbourg, was a banner event for the entire city and territory.

The appointment of a planning committee also set the New Church dedication apart from a Catholic service. On the one hand, Catholic parishes would have had no need for such a committee. Catholic church law required that the bishop consecrate new Catholic churches; therefore, he would preside over the ceremony. Moreover, whereas the Alsatian Lutheran Church had no fixed order of service for a dedication, the diocesan *Ritualium* already established the liturgy for consecrations. It specified the ritual gestures employed, listed most of the prayers, songs and scriptures to be used, and allotted tasks to the concelebrating priests.[41] On the other hand, canon law defined liturgical activity as exclusive to the clergy, thereby prohibiting any lay participation in the planning of a Catholic service.

Most significantly, though, the decisions of the planning committee established the New Church's ceremony as a Protestant experience. Although the pastors had considerable freedom in selecting and organizing ritual elements into a complete liturgy, the service did have to begin with a formal rite of dedication and benediction. The remainder of the celebration was then modeled on a typical Sunday morning service. Both of these parts differed profoundly from their Catholic correlates, which helped reinforce the message about Protestant community developed by the pastors and the liturgy in the course of the service.

At nine o'clock on 4 October 1877, the doors to the completed church opened and the members of the congregation and invited guests quickly filled the pews. Thirty minutes later, representatives of the ecclesiastical and political establishments in Strasbourg and Alsace–Lorraine walked the short distance from the Protestant Gymnasium to the plaza in front of the church, led by the clerical and lay members of the New Church Consistory.[42] Thus began the dedication portion of the New Church service. But it was highly unusual. On the one hand, Protestants did not hold religious processions and rarely paraded in their official dress, so this prelude would have stood out to all who saw (or read about) it. On the other hand, the display probably piqued the Catholics, for they were forbidden to hold religious processions of any sort in Strasbourg. Not only did the Protestants march on this occasion, but the territory's most important political leaders (all old-German and Protestant) joined them.[43]

Once the procession had arrived, Emile Salomon presented the keys of the rebuilt church to Pastor Louis Leblois, the president of the Consistory. At that point, the main doors of the church opened and the procession continued into the building, while a hired orchestra played a march. After everyone had taken their seats, a men's chorus sang an anthem of praise and Pastor Gustav Ungerer, who was also the religious inspector for the New Church Inspection, approached the altar. He read the Eighty-Fourth Psalm and then pronounced his address, using 1 Corinthians 3:9–23 as his text.[44] Ungerer next blessed and dedicated the church – its altar, the pulpit and pews, the bells and organ – and then closed this portion of the service by reading the popular Alsatian hymn of praise, "Jehovah," as a concluding prayer.

As with any introduction, this first part of this service established the tone for the rest of the ceremony. But it did so largely by elaborating on the distinctive features of Lutheran worship in Alsace. Most Protestant religious services began with the playing of an organ and a congregational hymn. In honor of this special occasion, however, the Consistory engaged an orchestra to provide the processional music and hired a choir to perform the opening song.[45] The text of this "Halleluja" also fostered a festive mood, by praising the Lord, His miracles, power, and glory as well as His "gift" of Christ, who brings salvation to the world.

Ungerer's actions reinforced the celebratory quality of this service. But, more importantly, they commenced the spinning of the narrative thread about the day and the New Church community. In typical Lutheran fashion, this narrative was developed primarily through texts: hymns, prayers, scripture passages, and commentary on the latter. The key to constructing a meaningful liturgy thus lay in the careful choice and arrangement of these texts to create the desired plot. Ungerer's reading of scripture constituted the first stage of this narrative generation; two aspects of his choices deserve attention. First, he opted to read two lengthy passages (Psalm 84 and 1 Corinthians 3: 9–23), instead of a short verse on which he would preach. This decision, with its heavy emphasis on scripture (the Word), imbued the dedication with the character of a Protestant feast day, for normally only on a day like Easter would such a long scripture reading occur. Second, these passages presented many of the central themes for the day's narrative, which subsequent texts and actors would develop.

The overall message for the day was that the New Church should rejoice now that, after seven years, it again had its home for worship. Furthermore, the community should view the building's reconstruction as a type of rebirth. Therefore, it should seek to renew its own faith and devotion to both Christ and God. The first two scripture passages introduced this idea by presenting two accounts of the relationship between a people and a religious building: first, Israel and the Temple in Jerusalem; then the early Christian church as a "House of God." By reading these texts, particularly the Psalm, which seemed to recount the recent history of the New Church itself, Ungerer located the story of the New Church community in the larger story of Christianity. He thereby implied that the congregation could also turn to these stories to make sense of its present situation.[46]

Just as the high point of any Protestant service in Alsace was the sermon, so too did the first part of the dedication ceremony reach its climax with the inspector's address.[47] Here, Ungerer used New Testament references to articulate a more explicit message about the new New Church. In 1 Corinthians, St Paul equates the Christian community to a temple, built and inhabited by Christ. Ungerer wanted the congregation to understand that rebuilding the New Church served as a sort of profession of faith in Christ. He was the builder; "they were the essence and vitality of the Protestant, evangelical Church, founded on a unique and unchangeable base – the Word of Jesus Christ." This emphasis on the Word as the cornerstone of Christian community restated one of the basic tenets of Protestantism and may also have explained Ungerer's decision to read so much of it. But it also accorded with Ungerer's religious liberalism. In closing his speech, the Inspector not only wished that the New Church community would not divide itself, but rather that it should focus on the one Lord, Spirit and God. And, he hoped that the Church would allow "everyone the liberty and independence to interpret and practice the scripture according to their own conscience."

The first part of the New Church's service thus celebrated the community as much as it did the new space and its future. It also highlighted the Protestant attention to the Word, inasmuch as Ungerer's address, and not the formal benediction of the temple that followed, occupied the greatest amount of time. This contrasts greatly to what would have occurred had the New Church been Catholic. To be sure, there would have been a difference in personnel. The head of the Catholic Church, the bishop, would have presided, assisted by the parish's clergy. But the very structure of the Catholic liturgy developed another story, emphasizing instead the sacralization of space. In the place of scripture readings and a formal speech in the vernacular, the Catholic consecration liturgy employed a series of ritual gestures (e.g. sprinkling of holy water, incensing of the exterior and interior of the church) and Latin prayers and hymns, the latter chanted by a special men's choir. Thus, whereas Ungerer's remarks introduced elements of the present (and future) into the New Church service, the rituals in a Catholic consecration emphasized tradition. Indeed, they sought to make the present dissolve into the past and the unchangeable.[48]

After the blessing of the church, both the Protestant and Catholic service would continue with its version of the main Sunday service, respectively, the *Amtpredigt* and *Hochamt*. At this level, too, the contrast between the two ceremonies remained sharp. The New Church service had a simpler and freer liturgical structure, elaborated a different kind of narrative, and gave all four of the pastors as well as the laity meaningful roles in the celebration. Moreover, the essential absence of liturgical prescriptions for the event enabled the New Church liturgy to express in a positive manner the theological and linguistic diversity within the parish.

Thus, on this day, a long, improvised prelude on the new organ signaled the start of the "main" service, which took the traditional form of a dialogue between pastors and congregation. The congregation would sing a hymn, then the pastor would lead a brief service at the altar. Next the congregation would sing a second hymn, followed by the sermon and a third hymn. The service would end with a final set of petitions and prayers, the recitation of the Lord's Prayer and an organ postlude. The New Church's service followed this basic plan. Each of the three pastors who had not yet spoken led one the three parts: Leblois spoke the opening prayer and greeting, Gustav Kopp gave the formal sermon, and Gustav Haerter pronounced the final blessing. The decision to have each of the pastors give, in effect, a sermon, required the exclusion of most other ritual elements regularly used on Sundays and feast days from this liturgy. Otherwise, the service would have become excessively lengthy.

The ability of the New Church's pastors to simplify and tailor this liturgy to meet their needs raises one of the ways in which Lutheran worship varied from Catholic worship in Strasbourg. Particularly on this day, the Lutheran celebration made use of very few elements: organ playing, hymns, prayers, and speeches. Its apex was the sermon. The liturgy for the Catholic high mass, though, like the consecration itself, followed an established script: that for the particular day in the church year or for the church's patron saint. This would determine the service's scriptural readings and special prayers as well as most of the texts for the service music (the Proper, e.g. gradual, offertory). The mass would probably contain some sort of address, but it would be rather short, since the highpoint was the communion sacrifice with its rich ritual activity.[49]

Although all worship services constructed plots, three features distinguished the narrative of a Protestant service, especially this dedication, from its Catholic other. First, what held the various elements of the New Church's service together was not an established order of service, but rather reliance on a common repertoire of images. The prayers, hymns, and speeches all referred to temples and churches. They discussed the communities who worshiped there. They praised the divinity for His majesty and works. For example, the benediction was linked to the main service through the congregation's singing of the Alsatian hymn that Ungerer had used for his final prayer: "Jehovah." Each of the pastors also discussed aspects of the New Church's past and related it to the community's present and future.

This brings up the second important aspect of the narrative structure of this Protestant service. While it made use of elements that were products of the past (Scripture, traditional prayers, hymns) to place the community in the larger context of Christian history, the liturgy and the narrative concerned themselves, above all, with the present and future. Singing the hymns enabled the congregation to repeat and actualize these statements of belief and community from the past. They made the past part of the present. This orientation towards the present also explains the seminal importance of the sermon in Protestant worship.[50] Not only is it a product of the present, but its primary purpose consists in helping the congregation understand the contemporary meaning of the Word and Christianity. On the other hand, the preordained order in the Catholic service, the use of the Latin language, even the repetition of the mass sacrifice sought to contextualize the present as a continuation of a long, abiding tradition.

Finally, the Protestant narrative took the form of a dialogue between pastor and congregation. Not only did the congregation at the New Church have a significant and more active role in this ceremony than a Catholic congregation would have, but the "concelebrating" pastors also contributed more substantially to the service than would their Catholic counterparts. In this liturgy, as in most Protestant services, singing served as the principal way in which the assembled men and women actively participated in the service. The worship committee included three hymns in the program, two in German and one in French. Of the three instances, the first had particular importance, for it transformed the individuals gathered in the church into a collectivity through the act of singing the same words to the same text. This is why, for the opening hymn, pastors generally selected hymns, like "Jehovah," which expressed religious sentiments using the first person plural rather than the singular (we vs. I/me).[51]

Moreover, the words of the hymns played a powerful role in the elaboration of the liturgical narrative. By singing them, the congregation not only repeated the sentiments of the hymn, but endorsed and interiorized the liturgical narrative. For example, the references in "Jehovah" to the Hebrew Temple echoed Ungerer's remarks. When the congregation intoned this hymn, it affirmed the Inspector's message and, thanks to the hymn's origin, introduced an Alsatian character into the narrative. Congregational singing also helped to re-establish the community as the focus of worship, especially after a pastor emerged to speak on behalf of the community (in prayer) or to the community (in a sermon). For once the pastor joined in the hymn, he ceased to have particular importance as an individual. There now existed only the collectivity of the singing congregation.

To enrich the service, the planning committee had two choirs perform at three points in the service. According to prevailing liturgical practice, the choir functioned as a representative of the congregation. However, in this celebration, a congregational hymn followed every choral moment, except for the first (by the male choir *Union sacré*). Thus, in keeping with the desire to include the assembly in the service, the activity of the choir functioned largely to enrich the festive quality of the event, rather than to silence the voice of the people.

Protestant and Catholic liturgical practices diverged most clearly on this point of lay participation and music. The Catholic mass did create a type of dialogue, but between the priests, not between the priests and the laity. Indeed, in the high mass a cleric, not the congregation, sang (or spoke) most of the liturgical responses. The mass took place in Latin, because the vernacular was permitted only for the sermon and the hymns immediately preceding or following the sermon.[52]

The Catholic church valued music highly; in fact, a consecration service would be almost entirely sung. But the dominant form of Catholic service music was not the popular hymn but the Latin chorale, sung by a special, male, church choir, which also chanted the other parts of the service. The relegation of a chorale to a mixed choir (like *Chant sacré*) would have been unthinkable. Hence, in most high masses, the congregation had an extremely limited, passive role in the service: at most it would respond to prayers with "Amen" and, occasionally, sing the better-known hymns (e.g. "Ave Maria").[53]

The other aspect of participation in the service that requires attention concerns the role of the ministers. Previously, we noted that in a Catholic service, the bishop would serve as celebrant, assisted by the parish priest and, in a larger parish, vicars and/or visiting clergy. While the parish priest would have a significant role in the liturgy – he might greet the congregation and perhaps even lead the communion rite – the other priests (vicars, visiting clerics) participated primarily by singing parts of the service (as a choir), distributing communion, or reciting part of the Eucharistic prayers (canon).

Because each of the four pastors at the New Church were equal, however, the liturgy provided for each of them to have a comparable equal part in the service. Namely, each would give an address. This enabled each pastor to contribute to advancing the day's narrative and shape it in keeping with his own personal religious views. Louis Leblois, the pastor for the French community at the New Church and Consistory president, officiated over the second portion of the service. Thus, this entire section – the greeting, opening prayer, invocation, choral anthem, and congregational hymn – took place in French (the main language for the day was German).[54] In the invocation, Leblois encouraged the congregation to bring "a new spirit to the sanctuary; to forget the past and march towards the great goal placed ahead of them . . . namely, to realize not the unity of faith but rather the unity of hearts in the spirit of freedom and diversity." Here we see Leblois expanding on Ungerer's message about the New Church community. But he also gives it a rationalist twist. In this quotation, he stresses notions of liberty and diversity. And in other passages he adds "principles of humanity" to the list of religious ideas, avoiding any significant reference to Christ or dogma.

Gustav Kopp had received the honor of delivering the sermon. Like Ungerer, he turned to the writings of St Paul for his sermon text, this time a verse from 2 Corinthians (5:17).[55] The verse itself expressed what had happened to the New Church: the old one was gone and a new one stood in its place. Moreover, it set the stage for Kopp's pietist version of the day's message, especially evident in the sermon's Christocentrism. For example, instead of dwelling on the church as building, he focused on it as a people united and made new by Christ. Thus, Kopp called on his listeners to use the New Church's restoration as a chance to renew their faith and devotion to Christ. Indeed, they should make themselves, as individuals and as a group, a (new) dwelling place for God.

The task of bringing the service to its end fell to Gustav Haerter. He drew inspiration for his petitions and prayers from Revelations 21: 5–7, which aptly recalled several of the liturgy's main narrative themes. The minister brought closure to the day's narrative, by praying that God would be proclaimed from the new church's pulpit and altar. And he thanked the Lord for "bestowing upon them a new church." Haerter's own brand of Pietism also shaped the remarks, evident in the reference not only to Christ but also to more somber notions like sin and repentance as well as Jesus' death and suffering. Just before twelve-thirty, the pastor called on the Lord to bless, protect, and give peace to the congregation. And three and a half hours after the doors of the church first opened, the service ended and the congregation, over two thousand strong, departed from the church.[56]

Although the extraordinary length of the dedication service and the use of special liturgical elements betray its uniqueness, in its basic features this service was little more than a festive *Amtpredigt*, one of the fundamental means of building religious community among Alsatian Protestants. Indeed, the ability of the service as a whole to create and foster a message of *Protestant* community and identity ultimately rested on its faithfulness to prevailing liturgical practices and forms. But, the freedom with which these pastors could structure the service enabled them to make each ritual element fit the occasion and establish a narrative that embraced and expressed the diversity within the community while also promoting a sense of Christian unity.

From the perspective of the structure of the dialogue and the allocation of roles, the New Church dedication service was itself fairly simple. Hence, instead of making the dedication service special by introducing new liturgical forms that would have the congregation and pastors interact in a new fashion, the planners simply multiplied the use of the same elements (singing and preaching) and assigned them to distinct (and new) groups. This faithfulness to tradition, the active participation of the congregation in worship, and the avoidance of elements (e.g. communion) that would be used in the Catholic Church also created a religious experience that was unambiguously Protestant. Consequently, the service not only celebrated the reconstitution of a specific Lutheran community but, through its implied contrasts to the Catholic other, rearticulated the boundaries that gave meaning to Protestantism as a social identity in late-nineteenth-century Strasbourg.

Conclusion

Interconfessional competition and conflict strongly influenced the cultural, social, and political development of the Second German Empire. In effect, all of these actions can be regarded as efforts to maintain and reinforce the boundaries demarcating religious community, whose relevance itself was challenged by modern types of social organization. Although there are several ways in which one could build or attach oneself to a religious community, this chapter has argued that participation in worship remained one of the most fundamental in the eyes of both clergy and laity. Indeed, while the final decades of the nineteenth century witnessed the development of new types of piety and devotion, the fact that many of them promoted private religious action (reading religious newspapers or pamphlets) meant that activities that developed a group identity, like public worship, continued to have great importance.

Worship built religious community by bringing together individuals into a specific place at a given time to share a common experience. But, as the analysis of the rebuilding of Strasbourg's New Church and the ceremony for its dedication has demonstrated, the very nature of the worship space and the selection of ritual elements in worship also permitted the articulation of a distinct experience for the members of that community. The New Church Consistory capitalized on the tragedy of 1870 to establish a liturgical and ritual space that satisfied Protestant needs of worship and fellowship, even if the building also had to fulfill broader representative functions within Strasbourgeois and Alsatian Protestantism. From beginning to end, the Consistory elaborated its understanding of what was "Protestant" or "Lutheran" about a liturgical space not only by stating what was "Protestant" about it, but also what was not. And, in many respects, the "negative definition," that is the rejection of Catholic features, appeared to be the strongest.

The service for dedicating the New Church similarly operated on a set of comparisons with Catholic liturgical practices. While the service itself did not directly refer to Catholics or Catholicism, the ritual devices used in the service as well as the freedom with which the pastors could combine and organize them produced a liturgy that was unmistakably Protestant. While these and other differences marked the New Church's dedication as a Lutheran or Protestant event, the real power of worship as a device for building religious community lay in its organization and content. On the one hand, the wording of the songs and the action of singing and praying together transformed the assembly of individuals into a collectivity. On the other hand, the language of the hymns, prayers, scripture passages and pastoral remarks developed a story about the congregation and its relationship with God, Jesus, and the contemporary world. Rather than passively hearing this story, the congregation actively participated in its construction and affirmed it as their own. Careful choice of ritual elements also enabled the liturgical narrative to embrace and make sense of the theological and linguistic diversity present in a parish such as the New Church.

Finally, this service, despite its special features, relied on a repertoire of liturgical and ritual forms that were traditional and already established as Protestant. Even if a Protestant attended services infrequently, perhaps only at the baptism of his/her child or the marriage of a friend, use of these same elements and their organization into a specific narrative still permitted him/her to identify with and claim membership in a Protestant religious community. And, ultimately, it is this sense of belonging to a religious community, established by participating in religious events, that made it possible for confessional affiliation to have such significance in the political and social life of the *Kaiserreich*.

Notes

1. A general overview of this development appears in the introduction to this volume.
2. Good introductions to the overall contours of religious life in late-nineteenth-century Germany appear in Thomas Nipperdey, *Religion im Umbruch: Deutschland 1870–1918* (Munich: Beck Verlag, 1988); Gerhard Besier, *Religion–Nation–Kultur: Die Geschichte der christlichen Kirchen in den gesellschaftlichen Umbrüchen des 19. Jahrhunderts* (Neukirchen-Vluyn: Neukirchner Verlag, 1992); and Kurt Nowak, *Geschichte des Christentums in Deutschland: Religion, Politik und Gesellschaft vom Ende der Aufklärung bis zur Mitte des 20. Jahrhunderts* (Munich: Verlag C. H. Beck, 1995). Research into German Catholicism has become somewhat of a scholarly growth industry as of late. See Margaret L. Anderson, "Piety and Politics: Recent Work on German Catholicism," *Journal of Modern History* (hereafter, *JMH*) 63 (1991): 681–716; and Wilfried Loth (ed.), *Deutscher Katholizismus im Umbruch zur Moderne* (Stuttgart: Kohlhammer, 1991). Michael A. Meyer (ed.), *German-Jewish History in Modern Times*, Vol. 3, *Integration in Dispute: 1871–1918* (New York: Columbia University Press, 1997), presents the current state of research into Jewish religious life. Curiously, there remain very few recent works devoted to nineteenth-century German Protestantism. See, however, Lucian Hölscher, "Die Religion des Bürgers. Bürgerliche Frömmigkeit und protestantische Kirche im 19. Jahrhundert," *Historische Zeitschrift* 250 (1990): 595–630; and Friedrich Wilhelm Graf and Hans Martin Müller (eds), *Der deutsche Protestantismus um 1900* (Gütersloh: Chr. Kaiser/Gütersloher Verlagshaus, 1996).
3. Wolfgang Schieder (ed.), *Volksreligiosität in der modernen Sozialgeschichte* (Göttingen: Vandenhoeck & Ruprecht, 1986); idem, *Religion und Gesellschaft im 19. Jahrhundert* (Stuttgart: Klett-Cotta, 1993); Jonathan Sperber, *Popular Catholicism in Nineteenth-Century Germany* (Princeton, NJ: Princeton University Press, 1984); and David Blackbourn, *Marpingen: Apparitions of the Virgin Mary in Nineteenth-Century Germany* (New York: Knopf, 1994).

4. See, in particular, Irmtraud Götz von Olenhusen, "Die Ultramonta-nisierung des Klerus. Das Beispiel der Erzdiözese Freiburg," in W. Loth (ed.), *Deutscher Katholizismus*, pp. 20–45; and Oliver Janz, *Bürger besonderer Art: evangelische Pfarrer in Preussen 1850–1914* (Berlin: de Gruyter, 1994).

5. Many of the recent articles and monographs on Protestantism during the *Kaiserreich* have dealt with this topic, especially Hans Martin Müller (ed.), *Kulturprotestantismus: Beiträge zu einer Gestalt des modernen Christentums* (Gütersloh: Gütersloher Verlagshaus Gerd Mohn, 1992); and Gangolf Hübinger, *Kulturprotestantismus und Politik. Zum Verhältnis von Liberalismus und Protestantismus im wilhelminischen Deutschland* (Tübingen: J. C. B. Mohr, 1994). See also the older work of Klaus-Erich Pollmann, *Landesherrliches Kirchenregiment und soziale Frage* (Berlin: de Gruyter, 1973).

6. W. Schieder, "Säkularisierung und Sakralisierung der religiösen Kultur in der europäischen Neuzeit. Versuch einer Bilanz," in *Säkularisierung, Dechristianisierung, Rechristianisierung im neuzeitlichen Europa,* ed. Hartmut Lehmann (Göttingen: Vandenhoeck & Ruprecht, 1997), here, pp. 311–12. Indeed, Schieder suggests regarding the nineteenth century as a second period of confessionalization, above all in the sense of confession-building. On the concept of confessionalization, see Joel F. Harrington and Helmut W. Smith, "Confessionalization, Community, and State Building in Germany, 1555–1870," *JMH* 69 (1997): 77–101.

7. Margaret Anderson noted this lacuna ten years ago in her review of works on Catholicism: Anderson, "Piety and Politics," pp. 694–5. While the lack of attention to the religious dimension of community life is especially notable in German historiography (see W. Schieder, "Religion in der Sozialgeschichte," in *Sozialgeschichte in Deutschland* ed., Wolfgang Schieder and Volker Sellin [Göttingen: Vandenhoeck & Ruprecht, 1987], pp. 9–31), scholarly neglect of such aspects of religious experience as worship and ritual in modern Europe is fairly widespread: Catherine Bell, *Ritual: Perspectives and Dimensions* (Oxford: Oxford University Press, 1997), p. 205.

8. On narrative and identity, see Margaret D. Somers, "The Narrative Constitution of Identity: A Relational and Network Approach," *Theory and Society* 23 (1994): 605–49.

9. Fredrik Barth, "Introduction," in *Ethnic Groups and Boundaries: The Social Organization of Culture Difference*, ed. Fredrik Barth (Boston: Little, Brown and Company, 1969), pp. 9–38.

10. Helmut W. Smith, *German Nationalism and Religious Conflict* (Princeton, NJ: Princeton University Press, 1995) provides the most recent account of the rise of interconfessional religious tension in Imperial Germany.
11. In 1866, roughly 55% of Strasbourg's population was Catholic; 40% Protestant, and 5% Jewish. Within the Protestant fold, perhaps as many as 85% were Lutheran, with the remainder Calvinist. Although significant differences existed between Lutherans and Calvinists, by 1870 these paled in comparison to what divided each Protestant group from Catholicism. For this reason, and in view of the relatively harmonious relations between the two Protestant faiths in Strasbourg, this chapter generally uses the word "Protestant," except when discussing features or practices peculiar to the Lutheran Church in Alsace. See Anthony J. Steinhoff, "Protestants in Strasbourg, 1870–1914: Religion and Society in the Late Nineteenth-Century Europe," (Ph.D. dissertation, University of Chicago, 1996).
12. Théodore Gérold, "Le Temple-Neuf," *Le Progrès Religieux* 3 (29 October 1870): 277–9.
13. Between 1802 and 1871, the French Lutheran Church had its seat in Strasbourg (not Paris). Thus, the Church's highest organs of government – the Directory (an executive council headed by a lay president) and Superior Consistory (a deliberative body) – convened in Strasbourg. On the organization of Protestantism in Strasbourg prior to 1870, see Steinhoff, "Protestants in Strasbourg," pp. 11–106.
14. Despite the prominence of German language and culture in nineteenth-century Strasbourg, its residents were committed French citizens who fought to keep Strasbourg out of German hands and hoped that Alsace would remain in French hands in 1871. Yet throughout the nineteenth century French language and culture gained ground in the city, especially among the commercial and educated classes. In 1851 this situation prompted the appointment of a French-speaking pastor at the New Church. Compare Bernard Vogler, *Histoire culturelle de l'Alsace* (Strasbourg: Éditions La Nuée Bleue, 1993), pp. 286–91.
15. Until the new New Church was completed in 1877, the Reformed Temple (built in 1790) represented the only new church built in Strasbourg since 1517. However, even in this case, the Calvinists had not had full freedom of action with respect to design. French officials decreed that, outwardly, the structure should not resemble a church; therefore, it could have neither bells nor a tower: *Zur Erinnerung an das Jubelfest der reformierten Kirche zu Straßburg am 15. Juni 1890* (Strasbourg: J. H. Ed. Heitz, 1890), p. 14. The new

New Church commenced an important period of church building in Strasbourg, lasting until 1914, which resulted in the construction of two military churches (one Protestant, one Catholic), a Catholic parish church (Young St. Peter), two independent Protestant churches, and the Jewish synagogue.

16. Notes of 17 April 1871 and "Programme du Concours ouvert pour la reconstruction du Temple-Neuf à Strasbourg (n.d.)," in *Faits du Temple-Neuf*, Archives of the New Church. The *Faits* are a sort of diary and scrapbook of the church kept by Gustav Kopp, one of its pastors and a member of the building commission.

17. This is precisely the point that Ernst R. Eichler, pastor at the New Church 1898–1919, expressed in "Sind unsere Kirchen noch zeitgemäß?" *Monatschrift für Gottesdienst und kirchliche Kunst* (hereafter *MGkK*) 3 (1898): 68–81.

18. "Instruction über den Kirchenbau" of Bishop Adolf Fritzen, 20 December 1894, published in *Straßburger Diözesanblätter* (hereafter *SDB*) 13 (1894): 268. This instruction repeated and gave additional clarifications of existing practices in the Diocese of Strasbourg.

19. "Vom Gotteshaus," in *Das Meßbuch der heiligen Kirche*, ed. Anselm Schott and Pius Bihlmeyer (Freiburg im Breisgau: Herder & Co., 1925). Indeed, the Catholic Church wished that the altar be so located as to hinder most access to it: "so ist doch zu wünschen, damit . . . das Betreten der Altarplatte möglichst verhindert werde"; "Liturgische Fragen. II: Der Altar," *SDB* 13 (1894): 130.

20. See, for example, Franklin L. Ford, *Strasbourg in Transition, 1648–1789* (New York: W. W. Norton, 1958), pp. 129–30 and 203.

21. For an "Alsatian" perspective on this issue, see Friedrich Curtius, "Über die Pflicht zur Teilnahme am Gottesdienste," *MGkK* 6 (1901): 153–5. An old-German civil servant at the time, Curtius became President of the *Reichsland*'s Lutheran church in 1903.

22. Nevertheless, regulations on Catholic church construction stated clearly that the size of the congregation should determine the seating capacity of a church. Therefore, the possibility that now and again a larger gathering might be held at the church, would not be allowed to affect the size of the finished Catholic church: "Liturgische Fragen: I. Die Kirche," *SDB* 13 (1894): 79.

23. In an ecclesiastical sense, Strasbourg was very unique during the nineteenth and early twentieth centuries. Instead of having geographically-defined parishes, which were served by one or more pastors working in collaboration with one another, each Lutheran church in Strasbourg was home to one or more personal congregations, communities of

Lutherans who had selected a particular pastor to be their minister. In the truest sense of the word, therefore, Strasbourg had no "parishes." The parish existed only in the form of the parish council or consistory, composed of members of the personal congregations of the church, which was legally responsible for the church's property and finances. Because each pastor could organize his services and ministry in accord with his own theological convictions, tension between pastors of different views was not uncommon, especially after the onset of the Pietist and Orthodox Revivals in the 1830s and 1840s. By 1870, two of the New Church's pastors were liberal-rationalist and two pietist: Steinhoff, "Protestants in Strasbourg," pp. 77–89.

24. Most notably, the parish held its confirmation services there in the Spring of 1877. *Faits du Temple-Neuf*, entries for 1876–7; announcements to the New Church congregation in 1877: Archives Departmentales du Bas-Rhin (hereafter, ADBR) 2G 482 A 75.

25. On the functions of the Protestant parish council and consistory, see Steinhoff, "Of Pastors and Laity, The Organization and Administration of Protestantism in German Strasbourg," in "Protestants in Strasbourg," esp. pp. 285–330. Although they are beyond the scope of this chapter, the lay-dominated Protestant parish councils had significantly more power than their Catholic counterparts, which functioned almost exclusively as financial advisors to the priest.

26. Renaissance and Baroque styles were also possible, but the regulations on church construction as well as discussions concerning the nature of Catholic churches concentrated almost exclusively on the Romanesque and Gothic styles: "Instruction über den Kirchenbau," *SDB* 13 (1894): 268.

27. These suggestions are summarized in the regulations formulated by the Eisenacher conference in 1861. By 1890 protagonists of a new approach to practical theology and church architecture in Germany would criticize the neo-Gothic as a style particularly ill-suited for Protestant worship. One of the most outspoken proponents of reform was the Dresden pastor Emil Sulze: compare Sulze, "Ratschläge für den Bau evangelischer Kirchen," *MGkK* 4 (1899): 335–47. See also Hanns Christof Brennecke, "Zwischen Tradition und Moderne: Protestantischer Kirchenbau an der Wende zum 20. Jahrhundert," in F. W. Graf and H. M. Müller (eds), *Der deutsche Protestantismus*, pp. 173–203.

28. "Le concours pour la reconstruction du Temple-Neuf à Strasbourg," *Progrès Religieux* 5 (24 February 1872): 62.

29. *Faits du Temple-Neuf*, entries for 9 Februay 1872 and 23 May 1874. In addition to four members from the New Church Consistory, the jury included three architects of European renown: the General Inspector of Historical Monuments in Paris (Boeswillwald, a native Alsatian); the Architect of the Palace of Versailles (Questel); and the creator of Vienna's *Ringstrasse*, Semper.

30. Indeed, in a historical study of Strasbourg's architecture, Louis Müller, the architect of the neo-Gothic evangelical garrison church (today, St Paul), described his work as being "in the style of the early Gothic which is native to Strasbourg." With this he implied that the style of his Protestant church (whose design required the approval of the military authorities in Berlin) was more appropriate to Strasbourg than that of the New Church: Architekten- und Ingenieur-Verein für Elsass-Lothringen (ed.), *Strassburg und seine Bauten* (Strasbourg: Verlag Karl J. Trübner, 1894), p. 404.

31. *Faits du Temple Neuf*, entry for 18 January 1876. Sengenwald's remarks appeared as part of the explanation of the building project that accompanied the parish's subscription campaign for additional funds. E. L.'s account of the projects in the *Progrès Religieux* contained similar sentiments. He described the Roman and Byzantine styles as simple and sober, thus, "best suited for a Protestant church," whereas the projects in the Gothic or Renaissance style appeared "cold, solemn and busy, appropriate for modern [Catholic] chuches": *Progrès Religieux* 5 (24 February 1872): 58–9.

32. Nevertheless, since only men could be pastors or elders, these benches were clearly marked as male space. In addition, the fact that the special seats were close to the pulpit also placed the members of the consistory in full view of the congregation, since the pulpit–altar unit was the focus of the congregation's attention in most churches. The congregation would thereby know when the elders were absent from services: Steinhoff, "Protestants in Strasbourg," pp. 439–42.

33. The majority of the reserved seats were for women. Franz Haerter, a pietist pastor at the New Church, opposed both of these practices resolutely, because they harmed the health of the community and its sense of identity. While the pastor preached from the pulpit the biblical and Gospel praise of poverty, humility, and the insignificance of social difference before Christ, the faithful themselves were divided in the church according to contemporary standards of gender and, to a certain degree, class: Archives Municipales de Strasbourg TN 135, 103, 192 and 205 (session of 28 May 1877).

34. This level of autonomy was also unique with respect to most of the German Protestant *Landeskirchen,* in which the central Church authorities exerted significant control over the decisions of the local parishes. This divergence resulted in part because of Napoleon's reorganization of the Protestant Churches in 1802, but also because of the "defeat" of religious liberalism and rationalism in the German Churches, especially between 1830 and 1848: see Nowak, *Geschichte des Christentums,* pp. 77–80 and 137–40.

35. French reparation payments to the Germans provided the source for the German "largesse" (this was how the Germans atoned for their destruction of the church). Nonetheless, by 1876 building costs had exceeded available funds, forcing the parish to launch a subscription drive to raise the needed money. Proclamation book for the New Church, 13 February 1876, ADBR 2G 482 A 74. Yet even then the subscription came up short, forcing the postponement of the bell tower construction until 1888, when a generous gift from Jules Sengenwald removed the financial impediment. The total cost of construction, 1872–88, amounted to 938,000 marks: *Strassburg und seine Bauten,* p. 394.

36. The centralization of authority within the diocese around the bishop reflected Napoleon's reorganization of the French Catholic Church in 1801–2. These measures remained in force in Strasbourg after the German annexation of Alsace–Lorraine.

37. These principles are summarized in "Verordnung betreffend Bau und Ausstattung der Kirchen" and "Instruction über den Kirchenbau," *SDB* 13 (1894): 266–9.

38. *Faits du Temple Neuf,* entry for 28 May 1877.

39. Normally, a Protestant minister would devise a liturgy for a service on his own. On feast days, however, and then alone, a similar division of functions might take place. For example, one pastor might give the sermon, while another led the prayers and/or the altar liturgy. As we will see, the committee resolved the issue of equality among the pastors and their congregations by having each of the pastors deliver a sermon-like address during the service.

40. This is one of the many particularities of Alsatian Lutheranism, especially when compared to the other German *Landeskirchen.* According to the Organic Articles of 1802 and the Decree-Law of 1852, Protestant parish councils and consistories had, at least in principle, wide-ranging authority with respect to worship within the parish. However, this was asserted only rarely, when one or more pastoral positions were vacant, for example, or when the pastors

couldn't agree among themselves. The creation of a liturgy committee, which included lay members, to plan the dedication service at the New Church was indeed rare, but did reflect the strong sense of lay action in this Consistory that had arisen after the annexation as well as in the presence of tension between some of the pastors.

41. "Ritus benedicendi novam Ecclesiam seu oratorium publicum," in *Collectio Rituum in usum cleri dioecesis Argentinensis* (Strasbourg: Le Roux, 1898), pp. 119–24.

42. *Einweihung der Neuen Kirche zu Straßburg am 4. Oktober 1877* (Strasbourg: J. H. Ed. Heitz, 1877). This pamphlet presents the full text of the service's prayers, hymns, and addresses. After the New Church Consistory members followed (in order): the *Oberpräsident* of Alsace–Lorraine, the President of the Directory (Kratz, a former member of the New Church Consistory); the *Bezirkspräsident* of Lower Alsace; the acting Mayor of Strasbourg; the members of the Directory and Superior Consistory; the Professors of Strasbourg's Theological Faculty; the members of the St Thomas Foundation; the directors of the Protestant Gymnasium and the *Studienstift*; the pastors and lay members of the four other consistories in the New Church inspection; the members of Strasbourg's other Lutheran parishes; and Strasbourg's members in the Reformed Consistory of Strasbourg.

43. Article 45 of the Organic Articles for the Catholic Church (1802) prohibited Catholics from holding religious ceremonies outside the church in cities where Protestant consistories (later expanded to include all recognized Protestant parishes) existed.

44. *Einweihung der Neuen Kirche*. In the Alsatian Lutheran Church, the religious inspector (and not the president of the Alsatian Church, who was a layman) had to participate in (if not actually lead) the worship service at the dedication of a church. Thus, among all the New Church's four pastors, only Ungerer's role in the service was fixed in advance.

45. In 1877, none of the Protestant churches had standing church choirs, although they would develop in the 1880s. The two choirs hired for the dedication, the male *Union musicale* and the mixed-voice *Chant sacré*, were two of many Strasbourg associations in the 1870s that were staunchly francophile, opposing the annexation and presence of the German immigrants (old-Germans). Again, we can see why old-Germans viewed the history of the New Church in the 1870s with some suspicion.

46. That ritual objects saved from the old New Church stood on the altar during this reading only strengthened these associations. Nonetheless, we should point out that, from the outset, many Protestants cast the demise of the New Church in biblical terms, since the New Church community, like the Israelites, had been deprived of their temple. Compare Théodore Gérold's "obituary" for the New Church, *Progrès Religieux* 3 (29 October 1870): 279. (Gérold had been named pastor at Strasbourg's German-language parish at St Nicholas in 1872.)

47. According to Protestant tradition, the pastor acts as God's representative not only in reading scripture, but also in interpreting it. Thus, to a certain degree he embodies the relationship that scripture establishes between Christians and God. Julius Smend (professor of practical theology at the University of Strasbourg from 1893 to 1914), "Die Predigt als gottesdienstliche Rede," in Smend, *Der evangelische Gottesdienst. Eine Liturgik nach evangelischen Grundsätzen* (Göttingen: Vandenhoeck & Ruprecht, 1904), pp. 18–40.

48. Thus, Catholics called the dedication a "consecration," a view of religious space that Protestants renounced during the Reformation. "Ritus benedicendi novam Ecclesiam"; "Liturgische Fragen: I. Die Kirche. 2. Consecration und Benediction der Kirche," *SDB* 13 (1894): 81–2.

49. "Die heilige Messe (Ordo Missae)," in *Das Meßbuch der heiligen Kirche*, pp. 2–36.

50. Hence the common appellation of the main service as the *Amtpredigt*. Smend, *Der evangelische Gottesdienst*, p. 24; see also the papers and the discussions on preaching at the 1905 Alsatian Pastoral Conference: Karl Braun (*Referat*) and Karl Hackenschmidt (*Korreferat*), "Schwierigkeiten und Erfordernisse der modernen Predigt," *Archiv der Straßburger Pastoral Conferenz* (1905): 114–51.

51. On singing and Protestant concepts of liturgy, see Smend, *Der evangelische Gottesdienst*; and Rainer Volp, *Liturgik: Die Kunst, Gott zu feiern* (Gütersloh: Gütersloher Verlagshaus, 1994), pp. 818 and 1036–8.

52. However, the texts and music for these hymns had to adhere to rigid standards (re-released and explained by the Congregation of Rites in 1894) so that all would understand them as sacred music. For example, texts for hymns had to come from Scripture, official Church prayers, or approved devotional and other religious literature. The Congregation also "strongly prohibited the use of all secular vocal or instrumental music, especially when it is influenced by theatrical

motives, variations, and reminders": "Anordnung für die Kirchen-musik," 7 and 12 June 1894, published in *SDB* 13 (1894): 176–80.

53. Only towards the end of the nineteenth century did this situation begin to change, thanks to the efforts of Bishop Adolf Fritzen (1891–1918). For example, he encouraged congregations to sing the Ordinary of the Mass when possible. The bishop's promotion of hymn-singing in smaller devotional services, pilgrimages, and processions also resulted in the 1900 release of a new diocesan hymnal, *Psallite*: A. Schmidlin, "Der kirchliche Volksgesang," *SDB* 34 (1915): 150–61 and 232–45.

54. Other liturgical elements, for example a confession of faith or an examination of conscience, could be inserted between the opening prayer and sermon, depending on the theological views of the presider and the type of service. Many Alsatian parishes went directly from prayer to sermon ("interrupted" only by a hymn), especially at the time of such a public ceremony: Volp, *Liturgik*, p. 818. Contrast this to the practice in most of the other German *Landeskirchen*, where pastors were bound to follow the order of service printed in the official *Agenda*. On the problems of "individual choice" in German *Landeskirchen*, the conflicts over the use of the confessions of faith in the final decades of the nineteenth century are particularly enlightening. See, for example, Hans Martin Müller, "Persönliches Glaubenszeugnis und das Bekenntnis der Kirche, 'Der Fall Schrempf'," in F. W. Graf and H. M. Müller (eds), *Der deutsche Protestantismus,* pp. 223–37.

55. Had the dedication taken place on a Sunday, Kopp's choice of sermon text would probably have stood out as unusual. Unlike their Calvinist brethren, the Lutheran Church in Alsace, like the other German *Landeskirchen*, designated particular Biblical passages (*pericopes*) as the sermon text for each Sunday and feast day of the church year. Yet, Alsatian practice did permitted exceptions for special worship services; in any event, even on normal Sundays, the use of the *pericope* was not obligatory.

56. *Faits du Temple-Neuf*, entry for 4 October 1877.

–12–

The Development and Destruction of a Social Institution: How Jews, Catholics and Protestants Lived Together in Rural Baden, 1862–1940

Ulrich Baumann

Until the advent of the Third Reich, Jews and Christians lived as close neighbors in villages and small towns in many regions of southern and western Germany. The religious coexistence of Protestants and Catholics, though it did not occur without conflict, belonged to the rhythms of everyday life. Rooted in informal neighborly contact, such as male youth groups and local voluntary associations, this religious coexistence was also part of the more formal spheres of village, regional and national politics. Although it survived the anti-Semitism in the 1890s, any semblance of religious coexistence found its end in National Socialist persecution and the eventual extermination of the Jewish minority in Germany. The Jews of Baden, the focus of this essay, were deported to the camp of Gurs in the South of France in 1940. Most of those who survived Gurs and the other French camps were transported from August 1942 onwards to the extermination camps of the East to be murdered.

This study sets out to describe the diversity of relationships between Christians and Jews. The sources used mirror the complexity of their coexistence. Details of informal contacts between Christians and Jews may be found in memoirs as well as in Church archives, documents of Jewish communities, papers from communal and governmental archives, and articles in local newspapers. For the last stages of Christian–Jewish relations (1918–1940), I have also drawn on a mixture of autobiographical and oral accounts, including sixty-three interviews with informants.

Christian–Jewish relationships in the countryside have only recently come to be the subject of historical research.[1] This new work belongs to the larger field of German-Jewish history, in particular the history of rural Jewry in Germany.[2]

This study addresses issues raised by the history of rural Jews in Germany, and integrates folklore and ethnology.[3] It is also part of a new regional history that attempts to understand local society within the tensions of wider social developments.[4] Regional history is in this sense a part of the "new history." It attempts to integrate at the regional level categories and concepts that are derived from the approaches and findings of a historical social science otherwise focused on the whole of society and large chronological and geographical spaces. Regional focus allows for questions about the validity of structures within society and about people's ability to influence these structures. Recent regional history also borrows from the history of everyday life (*Alltagsgeschichte*). The historian Alex Flügel argues in favor of calling relationships of everyday life "social institutions," which he defines as "specific combinations of normative regulations, material conditions and meaningful actions of subjects."[5] He thus widens the scope of analysis to include institutions such as monasteries and farms, but also feasts, rituals, or the life of an individual. According to Flügel, the institutional analysis brings out subjective and objective elements, "objectified structures as well as individual perceptions," rules and exceptions for people's actions.[6] "Social institutions" might include the ways in which neighborhoods, associations and communities connect, but above all they constitute the sites of social relationships of Christians and Jews in the countryside.

Neighborhood

I would like to begin with the closest-knit social framework of the traditional European village and small town outside the family and the household: the neighborhood. The question of neighborliness poses a fundamental challenge to an analysis of relationships between Jews and Christians in rural regions. "Neighborliness" involved relations of adjacent farms, and it entailed the mutual help and direct interdependence of farmers. Where did Jewish inhabitants fit in and what did they or did they not share with their neighbors? The interviews provide evidence that people of different religious groups shared personal events in their neighborhood very closely. Mutual help with farming, the most important area of neighborly support, was however very different among Christians than it was between Christians and Jews. Few Jews worked as farmers, as a consequence of medieval bans on the purchase of land. Although many Jewish families had acquired some land in the meantime, most still earned a living from trade with cattle or agricultural products. The consequences for neighborly support was that Jewish families partly depended on the help of Christian neighbors, but were seldom able to offer farming help in turn, as they had to look after their own businesses. Christian neighbors often noticed this asymmetry in their relationships, but nevertheless maintained their support. Jewish families reciprocated with attentiveness and gifts. Thus occupational separation of professions along religious lines had little impact on neighborly helpfulness, but played a large role in the way Christians perceived Jews. The professional and economic difference was less central to this perception than the difference between trade and farming, two areas that were also interconnected. The two following extracts are representative of the evidence found in many of the interviews. However, it is important to note that the interviewees (born in 1914 or 1915) were influenced by National Socialist racial theories and are therefore only partly representative of the adults of the generation of the 1930s. For example, a Christian son of a master saddler stated: "The Jews are simply traders. They are not great with work. But they are good at trading. And in the end trade pays better than work." In a similar vein the daughter of a Christian farmer from another village reported: "Well, I felt sorry for them when they left. I still see them. (. . .) There was a kind of connection between us and them. But they didn't want to work. I mean physical labor. They went in for trade: they were trading Jews, as they used to be in the temple. (. . .) There the Lord had punished them already." [7] In a different part of the interview, she said: "Thus we knew all of them, whether we liked it or not. As I said there was an invisible dividing line, a Jew would have never ever farmed the land or kept a garden "[8] Not only do these one-sided views disregard the fact that individual Jewish families were involved in farming; the source also ignores the stress and exhaustion of the cattle trade, which was often dangerous and could stretch out over an entire week. The farming community did not regard this as work: trade as such was "superfluous" and not "real."

The ethnologist Utz Jeggle attributes the stereotype of the Jewish trader to the Christian farmer's dichotomous world view divided between producer and consumer.[9] One should however not overestimate the significance of this dichotomy. Not only did Jews and Christian farmers trade without problems, but they had a tradition of it, often cutting across personal acquaintances or friendships. Monika Richarz, the foremost historian of German rural Jewry, rightly called the cattle trade a "symbiotic economic relationship."[10] Recently, Helmut Walser Smith has also emphasized those "rural commonalities," the similar economic ethics of Christians and Jews.[11] Perhaps one can find an explanation for the contradiction between this division in their self-images and the relative familiarity of their relationships (e.g. a shared economic ethics) in the farmers' ambivalent attitude. Later works by Utz Jeggle and his colleague Albert Ilien identify ambivalence as the fundamental predisposition of the farmers' mentality, whether *vis-à-vis* neighbors of any denomination or members of their own families, who were both helping hands and hungry mouths in a shared household.[12] The female interviewee quoted above, daughter of a farmer in central Baden, spoke of a "boundary" with regard to the Jewish villagers and explained: "There was a kind of connection between us and them," and went on to raise the delicate subject of work–trade. In retrospect, closeness and distance blend into an ambivalent attitude.

It seems that stereotypes and ideological interpretations had much less impact on religious coexistence between Christians and Jews than on their trade relations (which were, after all, close and effective). This does not mean, however, that the traditional Christian anti-Judaism had no effect on the churchgoing population in the countryside and that campaigns relating to Church policy did not find an audience. But Jewish religious practice was carried out in the public sphere and was considered part of village life. In communities with a significant percentage of Jews, Jewish holidays were as much part of village life as Christian ones. The piety of Jewish men and women was respected. A Jewish woman born in 1840 in Rust wrote in her memoirs that Jewish religion and its customs had been "particularly well regarded in Catholic circles," even where there was "little sympathy for its followers."[13] Similarly, a Christian inhabitant of the predominantly Protestant town of Nonnenweier told a researcher about seeing "Jewish men saying their early morning prayers at home and wearing straps around their arms." "The Jews were Christian," he commented, and religious too.[14] And a Christian woman, born in 1923, from the village of Rust remembers that the "laws" of the Jewish faith had been alien and incomprehensible to the religious Catholics from the village. But ritual celebrations in the synagogue had mesmerized the Catholics.[15] Some types of work in the field had followed the Jewish calendar.[16] It is also important to note at this point that at least until 1918 most clergy encouraged mutual respect between members of different religions and denominations. Catholic and Protestant clergy as well as Christian mayors were frequently present when a newly-built or renovated synagogue was opened or a new scroll of the Torah was to be consecrated.[17]

The problematic side of religious coexistence emerged in other areas. Every now and then the observation of Sunday as a day of rest would cause conflicts. Jews, for example, would not always show appropriate respect, especially because Sunday was for the cattle-traders an ideal day

for trading. Conversely, there were also complaints about occasional dist-
urbances during the Jewish service. In Gailingen, near the Swiss border,
Christian troublemakers played a prank when they taunted Jewish families
who had assembled for the Feast of the Tabernacles by poking them with
long sticks that reached through the hut that stood in front of the house
(a joke that was called "Sikkes-Stupfen"). The female interviewer who
questioned people in Gailingen regards these pranks not as attacks on
the religion of the Jews but on Jews who drew attention to themselves,
"which was more noticed and less tolerated among children and youth
than among adults."[18]

There were of course more substantial confrontations between the
villagers, which the mayor often had to arbitrate. The analysis of 478
conciliatory hearings (*Sühneverhandlungen*) pertaining to insults (*Belei-
digungssachen*) showed that the number of legal proceedings between
Jews and Christians was proportional to their respective populations. The
percentage of Jewish–Jewish complaints was however higher than the
proportion of Jewish members of the population. Jews, one may conclude,
felt sufficiently secure that they could pursue internal arguments in public.
The most astonishing evidence comes from Jewish reports against
Christians. Until the 1930s, the records show hardly any attacks on the
Jewish religion or individual Jews. This does not necessarily mean that
such attacks did not happen. One must instead suspect that Christians
and Jews often avoided crossing certain boundaries – the social institutions
described by Axel Flügel – in their conflicts in order to maintain the
economic, social and cultural balance. One of the interviews revealed
that potentially thoughtless and careless anti-Jewish comments were taken
back when people became aware of what they had said. Jews were also
careful not to attract attention. They used the Yiddish expression – "Mach
kein Risches!" – to say "don't cause Jew hatred." Sometimes this merely
meant urging one's wife not to push the baby carriage down Main Street
because the farmers' wives did not have one. "Mach kein Risches" related
to the material aspects of coexistence, not to those religious practices
that happened in public.

Our analysis of the economic and subsidiary elements of neighborhood
and of the problems of religious coexistence ought not to ignore the
sociable aspect of "leisure" in contemporary villages and small towns.
Despite anti-Jewish sentiment among Christians and occasional reservations among Jews, relations were generally close and warm. This was
especially true for Catholic and Jewish women. Only in two villages did
female Jewish witnesses report a rift. Jewish or Christian sources from
other villages never tired of praising the good relations that existed before

1933. Self-evidently, such sources cannot be read without skepticism. Yet such sources also provide us with a glimpse of the everyday, in which young women had a lot to talk about, particularly when Jewish girls returned home full of stories from their visits to the city. Another important factor was Jewish women's expertise in fashion.[19] Closer friendships were however restricted by the course of peoples' lives and usually ended when they married, moved or followed a different course of education. Unmarried women and widows kept more closely in touch.

These female encounters had their counterpart in the groups of male adolescents who filled the streets of the village in the evening and at night, often consuming alcohol on the sly. Did Jews belong to these groups?

These groups did have Jewish members, but interviews with the generation born around the year 1910 revealed that Christians tended to keep to themselves. In Schmieheim in 1925 there were roughly thirty-five Christian youths in the peer group as against eight Jewish youths. One of the latter recalled, "there was never a Jew who went out with a *gojim*."[20] It is however unclear whether this is true for all villages and for the whole period under consideration. There was a notable case in Breisach of a disturbance on 2 January 1888, where nine men, among them one Jew, were caught in front of the house of a Christian denizen. Five of them, including the Jewish participant in the disturbance, were fined for singing and disturbing the peace.[21]

Once they reached adulthood young men socialized in pubs and clubs. But as pub life leaves few documentary traces, it is difficult to research. Religious coexistence in clubs, organizations and societies can, however, be documented more closely. These were not rural inventions but rather came from the cities at the beginning of the nineteenth century, originally as reading clubs and reading societies. The rural elite, civil servants, merchants, rich farmers and pub owners subscribed to magazines and bought books for the communal library. From time to time they held dances, very honorable occasions, which, however, typically excluded Jews. Jews, in turn, founded their own reading societies. With few exceptions, the Christian and Jewish rural elites remained separate. Yet the exceptions were notable. Jews and Christians, for example, collaborated intensively in the choral movement (*Sängerbewegung*) that became popular in Germany from 1840 onwards. Most of the choral societies of the eighteen "Jewish villages" in southern Baden had Jewish members, sometimes in leading positions. Alongside the clubs in which Christians and Jews were members, there were also exclusively Jewish choral societies as well as other kinds of associations, which maintained vitality until the twenties, when Jews increasingly left the village in significant numbers. The voluntary fire brigade and military societies also became important pillars of Christian–Jewish cooperation in the 1860s and 1870s. Finally, the fire brigades had Jewish members from their beginnings in the 1860s. Ideologically, the military societies were important, for they united war veterans and former conscripts. Jewish membership was self-evident, and nowhere did Jews and Christians enjoy a closer link than in the military societies of the village.[22]

Communal Politics

The mixture of religious groups among members of the voluntary fire brigades and military organizations – the social backbone of the male public in the village – shows relationships that went beyond neighborhood networks. From the 1870s onwards, communal politics constituted a central area of public debate. In what follows, we shall consider aspects of this conflict-ridden, but still functioning political sphere.

It is important to remember that many communities in Baden had fought vehemently against equal Jewish participation in local civic rights. This resistance was expressed in a protest movement much of whose political background still remains unclear. The protest originated in the late winter of 1862, following a draft bill by the Ministry of the Interior regarding the civic equality of the Jews in Baden. Petitions to stop the bill were sent in from all over Baden. Mass protest in the form of petitions had become a form of political pressure since mid-century. As early as 1848/50 more than 79,000 people in Bavaria had successfully protested against the conferral of civic rights on Bavarian Jews.[23]

In the village of Schmieheim near the border of Alsace, the Christian inhabitants also participated in this general movement. They stressed the community's great poverty and feared the freedom of movement that the Jews might expect from the bill. "Wealthier, emancipated Jews," the Christians of Schmieheim argued, would leave their communities and the care for their poorer co-religionists whom they had supported until then – "for which they deserved praise" – in the hands of the Christians. The non-Jews in the community, who made up 55 per cent of the population, were also not willing to share in the decision-making process:

> (. . .) because already now we hear Jews declare publicly that they will tell us what to do as soon as they hold any communal offices and that things in the community cannot continue as they are. (. . .) These threats frighten us as we know the brutality and cunning of the Jews. In these bad circumstances many

a local resident (. . .) if he is able to leave behind the little property he owns would rather leave his home than live under the pressure and force of the Jews.[24]

However genuine these words by the Schmieheimers sound, it is nevertheless difficult to characterize the overall movement. The 235 petitions filed in Baden were of two types. Only fifteen of them were drawn up individually, like the Schmieheim petition. The majority consisted of forms containing exactly the same text but signed by the inhabitants of different villages. These petitions were drawn up centrally and pose a problem for historical scholarship. How important is the fact that local residents rarely wrote these texts themselves and simply signed ready-made forms? And who were the authors of these leaflets, those "friends of the people, the fatherland", as they called themselves in the preface to the petitions?[25] It is certain that they relied on a system of distribution within the different regions of Baden. In the Second Chamber as well as in liberal newspapers, there were indications that the authors were connected to Catholic circles who had been in opposition to the government since the Church–state conflict of the 1850s.[26] In this conflict, as Reinhard Rürup has pointed out, the liberals were convinced that the flood of anti-Semitic petitions was generally directed against the liberal government and thus "intentionally or not served the interests of the Catholic opposition."[27]

Recently, the historian Uwe Schellinger has re-examined the origin of these petitions. He followed a certain hypothesis: If they really originated from a Catholic or ultramontane initiative – for whatever reasons – it was probable that mostly Catholic and ultramontane communities would have used them and this should be visible from the statistics. Schellinger started by looking at the designations of origin on all petitions, and found that two-thirds (66 per cent) of the communities who had sent them had a substantial Catholic majority.[28] This seems to fit in with the overall picture, as 65.5 per cent of Baden men and women belonged to the Catholic Church. But the comparison should not be with the population of Baden as a whole but with those communities in Baden with a Catholic majority, which meant only around 50 per cent of the villages. In this context the contribution of Catholic communities to the petitions is striking. A look at the 220 petitions whose authorship is in question demonstrates the dominance of villages with a Catholic majority (156, or 70.9 per cent). In the end it is impossible to determine the origin of the petitions, although the pattern of distribution suggests ultramontane authorship. It is also important to note that there was an ideological basis for anti-Jewish actions in the ultramontane camp; this is at least suggested by the vehement, if rare, outbursts of anti-Jewish rhetoric in their publications. Dagmar Herzog dates this rhetoric back to the 1840s, and sees the aggressiveness as a central part of a successful Catholic populism. This phenomenon had increased further in the following decades.[29] Although Uwe Schellinger notes, in his analysis of select Catholic publications from the Baden region, that Catholics who sided with political ultramontanism were certainly ideologically predisposed to engage in anti-Jewish actions, rhetoric and action are certainly not one and the same. All in all opinions regarding the Baden petitions remain split. The movement cannot be described as an "organization at the grass roots," which is how James F. Harris characterized the Bavarian initiative.[30] There had been no ready-made forms in Bavaria (although newspapers published suggestions), and Catholic religious circles did participate in the drafting of individual petitions, though not exclusively.

Equality came regardless of the petitions, though it did not necessarily entail real *rapprochement* between Christians and Jews. Rather, coexistence between Christians and Jews had to be shaped further to become a "social institution" characterized by material interdependencies and meaningful relationships between subjects. In the legal domain, the implementation of the law had as a consequence that by 1933 a certain number of Jewish district councillors had been elected. In Gailingen in 1870, local citizens even elected a Jewish mayor, L. H. Guggenheim, with the help of Christian votes as well. Consequently, more and more Jewish citizens became engaged in the renovation of the town. By felling a large number of trees, the community went on to pay its debts, and then used the remaining capital to build a slaughterhouse; to replace water pipes; to build an old age home and an infirmary; and, in 1891, to construct a Jewish hospital. From 1893 onwards two Catholic nurses worked for Christians and Jews on behalf of the municipality. A local Jewish woman remarked on the changing meaning of *Kehilla* (which signifies "holy Jewish community") in the mind of the Jews of Gailingen. It was becoming a community in cooperation with the Christians.

But while things seemed auspicious for Jewish villages in the second half of the nineteenth century, social problems remained and even increased, causing the economic situation of Jews and Christians in some villages to diverge markedly. With conditions in Baden exacerbated by the long-term effects of land shortage, an agricultural crisis struck in the 1870s and 1880s. Those who did not leave the countryside tried to earn an extra income by working in rural factories, as their farms only just covered their basic needs. Money was very tight and the economic situation was difficult, also for the Jews, among whom were people with limited income, as well as for the Christians. Thus, for example, in 1900 three select communities show between 19 per cent and 29 per cent of Jewish taxpayers earning no more than 200 marks a year.[31] But still, a Jewish middle class had worked its way up in rural areas. Some made a modest fortune with cattle, horses, or agricultural products, others opened shops. They wanted the villages to keep up with developments in the cities in order to be able to compete with the competition. Inevitably this led to conflict. Jewish traders were interested in the modernization of the village; Christian notables on the other hand wanted to economize.

Every social situation is interpreted differently according to the perspective of the participants. In the eyes of small-town Christian politicians, the rapid economic success and financial strength of a few Jewish traders reinforced the image of the "all-powerful" Jews. There was a suspicion that "Jewish citizens would put Christians under economic pressure to get their own way or somehow, had them in their pocket."[32] The local magistrate (*Amtsmann*) of Konstanz used a more blatant expression to describe the Christian–Jewish relations during a visit to Gailingen in 1883: He saw the Christians of Gailingen in opposition to an "expanding, liberalizing Jewry," and added "unless they are economically or commercially dependent on the Jews."[33] This suggestion did not entertain the possibility that local Christian citizens might be in mutual agreement with their Jewish counterparts. The magistrate was spurred by current debates relating to Catholic–liberal conflicts. His comments were also provoked by the local accountant (*Gemeinderechner*) moving from the National Liberals to an unspecified party of opposition, most probably the Catholic Center Party. In the previous year he had even been put forward as a candidate against Mayor Guggenheim, though without success. This was a heavy loss for the liberal magistrate, who said that the Gailingen Jews were "rampant" (*überwuchern*), and accused them of perverting liberal thought. Both his choice of words and his suspicions brought the magistrate close to the contemporary anti-Semitic movement, with which he otherwise had no connection.

Anti-Semitism in South Baden

The term "anti-Semitism" dates back to September 1879, when it was first used in connection with an "anti-Semitic Weekly" ("*antisemitisches Wochenblatt*"). In January 1881 the new movement had already caused a stir in South Baden. The senior local magistrate (*Oberamtmann*) of Müllheim reported that the waves of "the anti-Semitic movement created in

North Germany" had reached Müllheim and that in private and public houses people "greedily devoured what was written against the Jews." There was, according to the magistrate, talk in pubs: "'What a stroke of luck it would be if the entire Jewry were forced to leave the town and district of Müllheim.' These and similar utterances must have gradually led to the rumor that this town was bent on harassing the Jews, and a few jokers got quite unwarranted enjoyment out of saying that on the night of the 21st of the month, they're going to go after the Jews." However, official inquiries had revealed that "no sensible person is inclined to violence towards the Jews here. Many however gloated over their fear and did not regret the terror they suffered."[34] Indeed, nothing happened in Müllheim in January 1881. This suggests that the possibility that violence coexisted with a tradition of good neighborly relations. But how do the two go together? If we look at the "dark side" of coexistence it becomes clear that rumors in Müllheim were part of a chain of anti-Jewish aggressions particularly manifest during the Revolution of 1848/9. The knowledge that there might be such outbreaks of violence in their own village was an integral part of the life of rural Jews in the nineteenth century. Yet most of the time, daily life itself was remarkably free of such troubles. In peaceful times people repressed these moments of danger, which had a discrete beginning and end, without easily forgetting them.

After 1880 the anti-Semitic movement managed to establish itself in regional politics. In the 1893 Reichstag elections the party gained between 30 and 40 per cent of the vote in communities within the Müllheim region. For Müllheim, there are a number of explanations. First, it was a wine-growing region and thus prone to crises: a bad harvest, severe winters (as in 1879/80) and its constant need for capital led to property auctions above the regional average. In this situation it was easy to blame Jewish creditors. More important, however, was the generally favorable climate for anti-Semitic parties. Helmut Walser Smith has pointed out that the movement was often attractive because it challenged local elites and questioned the National Liberal system of notable politics.[35] Electoral behavior in Müllheim thus seemed to be directed in the first instance against the National Liberal candidate, Ernst Blankenhorn, who as a winegrower belonged to the most distinguished families in Müllheim. His opponents were equally well respected, which contributed to the success of the anti-Semitic party. It is reported that the anti-Semitic party was particularly successful among the town's tradesmen and artisans. Confession also played a role in electoral behavior. In almost all cases, communities with a Protestant majority proved to be the strongholds for the anti-Semitic movement.

Yet this was not necessarily because of the activity of Protestant pastors, for there is little evidence that they were susceptible to political anti-Semitism. Indeed, the only documented exception for the region of South Baden is Schmieheim, where, in 1893, the local pastor supported an electoral alliance between Conservatives and anti-Semites. Generally, it becomes clear that local Protestants were more susceptible to anti-Semitic candidates because their ties to a political milieu had weakened in the 1890s. When this occurred, frustration with the National Liberals and the resultant protest vote happened among the Protestant population. Conversely, the Catholics of Baden followed a completely different course during the second half of the nineteenth century. As religion increasingly structured their milieu, Catholic voters increasingly supported the newly-formed Center Party; and after the *Kulturkampf* between Church and state, Catholics more and more found themselves in political opposition to Liberalism. This opposition was not bereft of anti-Semitic overtones. At the same time, however, it immunized Catholics against political anti-Semitism.

The Grand Duchy of Baden was still able to contain the anti-Semitic danger. The Badenese electoral reform in the late *Kaiserreich* strengthened the democratic parties and the Grand Duke stood firmly against the anti-Semitic current, thus causing its isolation. The Jews themselves did not remain passive either. Consequently, the anti-Semitic movement, weakened by inner rifts, lost political (but not social) importance around 1900.

The Rise of National Socialism

During the crisis after 1918 many right-wing splinter groups built on the groundwork laid during the *Kaiserreich*. After 1928 the NSDAP managed to focus these forces by specifically targeting a countryside shaken by a serious agricultural crisis. Part of this campaign was an aggressive presence in the villages, as in the case of Gailingen. There the Jews, who represented a quarter of the local population in 1925, concentrated on an intensive defence against National Socialist activities. Jewish men and women attended DVP events and broke up a National Socialist assembly in 1928.[36] But the National Socialists had at least attracted people's attention. During a second assembly they founded a local group, possibly benefiting from a previous conflict between some of the Jewish and Christian inhabitants over the election of a new mayor. The resentment of the defeated might well have turned into votes for the NSDAP. Nevertheless, while political Catholicism had weakened, it was still very influential. The NSDAP came second in the local elections of 1930, but fell back to fourth and then to the last place in two repeat elections in 1931. In her analysis of local politics in Gailingen, Regina Schmid points out that local voters had less sympathy for the NSDAP at the communal than in the Reichstag elections. This lack of enthusiasm suggests that people did not want to ruin the Christian–Jewish relationship by giving the NSDAP too much room locally.

Another example of the local rise of the NSDAP was the development in Ihringen, a mostly Protestant winegrowers' village near Kaiserstuhl with a comparatively small Jewish rural community in 1930. After 1918 Ihringen showed the lack of political direction typical for Protestant communities. At first, *völkisch* activities were unsuccessful. In this situation, the NSDAP started its tactics of agitation. It cleverly played on the despair of many winegrowers, who had lost around 80 per cent of the harvest in the cold winter of 1929 and were later affected by the world economic crisis.[37] In the *Landtag* elections of October 1929 the NSDAP gained 40.4 per cent of the votes, in the 1930 *Reichstag* elections, 50.2 per cent and in July 1932, 77 per cent. In October 1932 a National Socialist became mayor. In Ihringen, the National Socialists had made no secret of their anti-Semitism. The local SA- leader stated as early as June 1930 that "once things got started, the head of the Jewish community would be the first to be attacked."[38] The house of the Jewish leader had been marked with a "1" in chalk – the intended meaning being obvious for everybody. In addition, a rumor was spread about a planned expulsion of the Jews.

The developments in Gailingen and Ihringen are only two variants of the many forms of electoral behavior. According to Utz Jeggle and Martin Liepach the larger question is whether the presence of Jews in the village was a factor governing political behavior. Liepach investigated this in a sociological analysis of elections. He created for Baden a sample of villages with Jewish residents and one of villages without Jews but with a similar social and denominational structure. For both samples Liepach calculated the respective share of the NSDAP. The differences are marginal.[39] In my research I have attempted, though without using quantitative analysis, to supplement Liepach's findings with regard to a few subregions. An overall comparison of villages with significant Jewish minorities and neighboring villages without Jewish minorities shows little difference with respect to NSDAP support, although none of the Protestant villages with a Jewish minority reached the maximum values of some Protestant villages without Jewish minorities (up to 97 per cent). Protestant voters seemed to accept the NSDAP not only because of their weak ties with a political milieu but possibly also as a result of the attitude of the Protestant pastors. According to a survey of the "Kirchliche Vereinigung für positives Christentum" in 1932, seven of the twenty-four pastors and vicars of the Church district of Lahr belonged to the NSDAP. A further six were described as "sympathetic." The followers of the "Evangelischer Volksdienst," a conservative Protestant party, numbered just four. Thus the Protestant National Socialists could base their activities on the support of more than half the Protestant clergy. Given the success of the NSDAP in regions with Protestant majorities, the exceptions stand out. The NSDAP results in Sulzburg, for example, were well below average; there the local pastor opposed the Nazi party, and the town enjoyed a left liberal tradition. Cultivated to a considerable extent by local Jews, this local left liberal tradition also suggests a connection between the presence of Jews in a Christian community and its political behavior. Similar links can be found in the Catholic village of Breisach. The low results of the NSDAP were not only a consequence of the strong Center Party.[40] The SPD and the DDP/Staatspartei were also strong, so that Breisach was known as the "black-red-gold town on the Rhine." Since 1919, the Social Democrats as well as the Liberals also had Jewish support. In cultural affairs as well, there was during the Weimar republic remarkable cooperation in Breisach. Members of both religious groups, for example, founded an amateur theater festival that involved the whole town and shortly afterwards an annual carnival that attracted tourists from throughout the region. Overall, however, electoral results in villages with a Jewish presence differed positively from voting in exclusively Christian villages in only a few cases.

Conclusion

What influences supported the social institution of Christian–Jewish coexistence? How was its brutal destruction made possible? On the one hand, the village in the second half of the nineteenth century was under great inner and outer pressure from agricultural crisis, industrialization, population growth and migration. The social structure of the village changed and efforts at integration increased, not least through the formation of societies and associations. Christians and Jews regarded cooperative coexistence as the ideal norm and as part of this integration. The idea of conflict-free collaboration also conformed to the realization of the Christians that, after Jewish emancipation in 1862, it was in fact necessary politically and socially to work together with the Jews. Perhaps accepting the inevitable encouraged an attitude that favored the rational resolution of conflict in such a way as would advance the interests of the village. Moreover, given the interdenominational mixture, the Grand Duchy of Baden could only continue if peace were maintained between the various denominations. This was particularly urgent because of the clashes between the liberal government and the Catholic Church. Despite this clash, the Baden governments vehemently fought for the maintenance of "inter-denominational peace." By and large they succeeded, helped by large numbers of pastors and priests of both denominations.

If we ask what endangered this fragile social institution of interreligious coexistence, and above all what the effects of political anti-Semitism were, a study of individual cases can again be helpful and can enrich the knowledge of larger processes. The magistrate of Müllheim reported in 1881 that the anti-Semitic publications from North Germany "were devoured avidly" in private and public houses of the region. Yet the public threat of violence was only indirectly connected with the anti-Jewish propaganda that these publications contained. Rather, it originated from the repertory of traditional anti-Jewish actions. The problem of everyday life in Müllheim was less the threat of violence or the distribution of the literature than the "avidness of the reading." And this avidness was mainly caused by local crises, especially among farmers, artisans and petty merchants.

The coexistence of Jews and Christians as a social institution survived the stormy 1890s. This was made possible by local dignitaries who stood up for the continued existence of this social institution as well as for the authoritarian structure of village society and the monarchical state that provided additional security. In 1918 various parameters of the Christian–Jewish cooperation in the countryside changed. The villages became politicized; the old system of dignitaries collapsed; and politics simply mirrored an increasing social differentiation among the rural population that also provoked fear among several groups in the villages. Furthermore, the percentage of Jews declined and with it their influence on rural life. For the Christians this meant that during the Weimar Republic it was now less necessary to cooperate with the Jews than had been the case fifty years earlier. And finally, the idea of interdenominational peace was overshadowed by the success in the countryside of new movements, whether socialist or National Socialist. Thus at the end of the 1920s the integrative forces of the old village society had lost their power and by 1930 the ever-fragile balance between Christians and Jews was already seriously threatened.

Translated by Maike Bohn

Notes

1. Utz Jeggle, *Judendörfer in Württemberg*, 2nd edn (Tübingen: Vereinigung für Volkskunde, 1999); Regina Schmid, *Verlorene Heimat. Gailingen – ein Dorf und seine jüdische Gemeinde in der Weimarer Zeit* (Constance: Arbeitskreis für Regionalgeschichte, 1985); Jacob Borut, "'Bin Ich doch ein Israelit, ehre Ich auch den Bischof mit'– Village and Small-Town Jews within the Social Spheres in Western German Communities during the Weimar Republic, in *Jüdisches Leben in der Weimarer Republik, Jews in the Weimar Republic*, ed. Wolfgang Benz, Arnold Paucker and Peter Pulzer (Tübingen: Mohr Siebeck, 1998), pp. 117–34; Ulrich Baumann, *Zerstörte Nachbarschaften. Christen und Juden in badischen Landgemeinden 1862–1940* (Hamburg: Dölling and Golitz, 2000). For the history of anti-Semitism, see Helmut Berding, *Moderner Antisemitismus in Deutschland* (Frankfurt a.M.: Suhrkamp, 1988). For a more recent survey of the literature, see Till van Rahden, "Ideologie und Gewalt. Neuerscheinungen über den Antisemitismus in der deutschen Geschichte des 19. und frühen 20. Jahrhunderts," *Neue Politische Literatur* 41(1996):11–29.
2. See Hermann Schwab, *Jewish Rural Communities in Germany* (London: Cooper Books, 1956); Werner J. Cahnmann, "Village and Small Town Jews in Germany – A typological study," *Leo Baeck Institute Year Book* 19(1974): 107–30; Emil Schorsch, "'The Rural Jew. Observations on the Paper of Werner J. Cahnmann," ibid., pp. 131ff; Elfie Labsch-Benz, *Die jüdische Gemeinde Nonnenweier. Jüdisches Leben und Brauchtum in einer badischen Landgemeinde* (Freiburg: Mersch, 1981); Monika Richarz, "Die Entdeckung der Landjuden. Stand und Probleme ihrer Erforschung am Beispiel Südwestdeutschlands," in *Landjudentum im süddeutschen- und Bodenseeraum*, ed. Vorarlberger Landesarchiv (Dornbirn: Voralberger Verlagsanstalt, 1992), pp. 11–21; see also *Jüdisches Leben auf dem Lande. Studien zur deutsch-jüdischen Geschichte*, ed. Monika Richarz and Reinhard Rürup (Tübingen: Mohr Siebeck, 1997).
3. Ingeborg Meyer-Palmedo, *Das dörfliche Verwandtschaftssystem: Struktur und Bedeutung. Eine Figurationsanalyse* (Frankfurt: Campus, 1985).
4. Alex Flügel, "Chancen der Regionalgeschichte," in *Regionales Prisma der Vergangenheit. Perspektiven der modernen Regionalgeschichte*, ed. Edwin Dillmann (St. Ingbert: Röhrig, 1996), pp. 27–46, esp. p. 27. On the new regional history more generally, and its place within a wider history of society, see Manfred Hettling *et al.* (eds), *Was ist*

Gesellschaftsgeschichte? Positionen, Themen, Analysen (Munich: C. H. Beck, 1991); Jürgen Kocka, *Sozialgeschichte. Begriff–Entwicklung–Probleme*, 2nd edn (Göttingen: Vandenhoeck & Ruprecht, 1986); Reinhard Rürup, *Historische Sozialwissenschaft. Beiträge zur Einführung in die Forschungspraxis* (Göttingen: Vandenhoeck and Ruprecht, 1977); Hans-Ulrich Wehler, *Deutsche Gesellschaftsgeschichte*, 3 vols. (Munich: C. H. Beck, 1985–1995); Hans-Ulrich Wehler, *Geschichte als Historische Sozialwissenschaft* (Frankfurt: Suhrkamp, 1973).

5. Flügel, "Chancen der Regionalgeschichte," pp. 27–46.
6. Ibid.
7. Interview with Frieda Hauger (the name was changed), Kippenheim. The "temple" the witness refers to is, as she says in her statement (not presented here), the old temple of Jerusalem.
8. Interview with Frieda Hauger (the name was changed), Kippenheim.
9. Jeggle, *Judendörfer*, p. 158.
10. Monika Richarz, "Viehhandel und Landjuden im 19. Jahrhundert. Eine symbiotische Wirtschaftsbeziehung in Südwestdeutschland," *Menora. Jahrbuch für deutsch-jüdische Geschichte* 1(1990): 66–88.
11. Helmut Walser Smith, "The Discourse of Usury. Relations Between Christians and Jews in the German Countryside, 1880–1914," *Central European History* 32,3 (1999): 255–76, esp. 276.
12. Albert Ilien and Utz Jeggle, *Leben auf dem Dorf – zur Sozialgeschichte des Dorfes und zur Sozialpsychologie seiner Bewohner* (Opladen: Westdeutscher Verlag, 1978); Utz Jeggle and Albert Ilien, "Die Dorfgemeinschaft als Not- und Terror-Zusammenhang. Ein Beitrag zur Sozialgeschichte des Dorfes und zur Sozialpsychologie seiner Bewohner," in *Dorfpolitik. Sozialwissenschaftliche Analyse*, ed. Hans-Georg Wehling (Opladen: Westdeutscher Verlag, 1980), pp. 45ff.
13. Labsch-Benz, *Die jüdische Gemeinde*, p. 107
14. Ibid.
15. Josefine Koerner-Baumann, "Erinnerungen an jüdische Mitbürger," in *Schicksal und Geschichte der jüdischen Gemeinden Ettenheim, Altdorf, Kippenheim, Schmieheim, Rust, Orschweier*, ed. Bernhard Uttenweiler (Ettenheim: Historischer Verein für Mittelbaden, 1988), pp. 436–7, esp. p. 436.
16. Rosalie Hauser, "Erinnerungen," (MS), p. 27. The memoirs belong to the private archive of Frau E. Hotze, to whom I am grateful for granting me access. The memoirs have also been archived by the Leo Baeck Institute, New York.

17. On feasts see Kornelius Wieland-Gölz, "Jüdische Geschichte in der Gegenwart der christlichen Gemeinde. Die jüdisch–christliche Vergangenheit einer badischen Landgemeinde und ihre Bedeutung für die Gegenwart," Jahresarbeit I im Pfarrvikariat (MS), (n.p., 1996), p. 23; Dieter Weis, "Synagogen im früheren Amtsbezirk Ettenheim. Ettenheim, Altdorf, Kippenheim, Schmieheim und Rust," in *Schicksal und Geschichte*, pp. 68–156, esp. p. 147; Jürgen Stude, "Geschichte der jüdischen Gemeinden Kippenheim," in *Schicksal und Geschichte*, pp. 322–61, 345.

18. Marita Müller, "Mündliche Quellen zur jüdisch–christlichen Alltagsgeschichte in Gailingen vom Ende des 19.Jahrhunderts bis zum 2. Weltkrieg. Ortsgeschichtliche Grundlagen für die Erfassung der Kulturdenkmale in Gailingen," (Gailingen, n.y), 42.

19. Beate Bechtold-Comforty, "Jüdische Frauen auf dem Dorf – zwischen Eigenständigkeit und Integration," *Sozialwissenschaftliche Informationen* 18 (1989): 157–169.

20. Telephone interview with Hermann Schneeberg (name changed), Florida, who left the village in 1927 in order to become a butcher's apprentice in Frankfurt a.M. and then returned to Schmieheim in 1931.

21. Stadtarchiv Breisach/Bürgerliche Rechtspflege, Strafanzeigen vor dem Bürgermeisteramt.

22. Oded Heilbronner, "Der verlassene Stammtisch. Vom Verfall der bürgerlichen Infrastruktur und dem Aufstieg der NSDAP am Beispiel der Region Schwarzwald," *Geschichte und Gesellschaft* 19(1993): 178–201. It should, however, be noted that in the 1920s contemporary witnesses hardly mentioned these societies, most probably because they lost their integrative force after 1918. Yet voluntary associations in general (with the exception of Jewish associations) remained stable even after 1918 and outlived the worldwide economic crisis, unlike those in other regions in Baden. The historian Oded Heilbronner sees the crisis of bourgeois societies in the countryside as a starting-point for the organization of the NSDAP. Whether this can be maintained for villages in south Baden with significant Jewish minorities is less clear.

23. James F. Harris, "Public Opinion and the Proposed Emancipation of the Jews in Bavaria in 1849–50," *Yearbook of the Leo Baeck Institute* 34(1989): 67–79.

24. Generallandesarchiv Karlsruhe (Henceforth GLA) 231/1425.

25. This is based on Uwe Schellinger's views and insights.

26. Lothar Gall, "Die partei- und sozialgeschichtliche Problematik des badischen Kulturkampfes," *Zeitschrift für die Geschichte des Oberrheins*, 113(1965): 151–96, p. 154.
27. Reinhard Rürup, "Die Emanzipation der Juden in Baden," in R. Rürup, *Emanzipation und Antisemitismus* (Frankfurt: Fischer, 1984), pp. 46–92, and esp. p. 211, fn. 222.
28. A substantial Catholic majority means communities with 85 per cent or more Catholics.
29. Dagmar Herzog, *Intimacy and Exclusion. Religious Politics in Pre-Revolutionary Baden* (Princeton, NJ: Princeton University Press, 1996), p. 168.
30. Harris, "Public Opinion," p. 70.
31. GA Eichstetten, Rubrik IV, 3, 200; GA Kirchen, Rubrik XIII, GA Sulzburg, Rubrik XIII, 6.
32. The Oberamtmann of Ettenheim quotes the Gemeinderat of Altdorf when he says "the Israelites [had] the town council in their pocket."
33. Dagmar Schmieder-Friedrich and Eckhardt Friedrich (eds), *Die Gailinger Juden. Materialien zur Geschichte der jüdischen Gemeinde aus ihrer Blütezeit und den Jahren der gewaltsamen Auflösung* (Constance: Arbeitskreis für Regionalgeschichte, 1981), p. 30.
34. Staatsarchiv Freiburg, G18/1 LRA Müllheim, P.107 1337.
35. For the development of political anti-Semitism in Baden see Helmut Walser Smith, "Alltag und politischer Antisemitismus in Baden 1890–1900," *Zeitschrift für die Geschichte des Oberrheins* 141(1993): 280–303.
36. Schmid, *Verlorene Heimat*, p. 162.
37. See Gitta Reinhardt-Fehrenbach and Philipp Fehrenbach, "Die wirtschaftliche Entwicklung der Stadt Endingen," in *Endingen am Kaiserstuhl. Die Geschichte der Stadt* (Endingen: the authors, 1988), pp. 484–504; Philipp Fehrenbach, "Endingen, Weimar und Drittes Reich," ibid., pp. 169–85, esp. p. 175: Rinklin, Erinnerungen.
38. StAF L 50/1 15015.
39. Martin Liepach, "Zwischen Abwehrkampf und Wählermobilisierung. Juden und die Landtagswahl in Baden 1929," in Benz et al. (eds), *Jüdisches Leben*, p. 17.
40. The Center did not hold the majority of votes in all Catholic regions in Baden, as Oded Heilbronner has shown for the almost exclusively Catholic Black Forest (Hochschwarzwald): See Oded Heilbronner, "The Failure that Succeeded. The Nazi Party Activity in a Catholic Region in Germany 1929–1932," *Journal of Contemporary History*, 27,3(1992): 531–49.

Part VI
Afterword

–13–

Afterword: Living Apart and Together in Germany

Margaret Lavinia Anderson

"His [the Bürgermeister's] lady wife, a very cultivated woman, talked about the trinity: the pope in Rome and Luther and Moses."

Silberstein to Isenthal, in Theodor Fontane, *Mathilde Möhring* (1896)

Little Kempen am Niederrhein holds a celebrated place in the history of Western Christianity as the home of Thomas à Kempis (*d.* 1471), author of *The Imitation of Christ*. In the early years of the twentieth century, however, their famous son's message of brotherly love seemed honored more in the breech than in the observance. On Good Friday, when Protestants hurried into church to observe one of the most sacred days of their year, Catholic housewives gave the carpets their annual beating – making a loud and jarring counterpoint to the solemn harmonies of Bach. Their husbands took the opportunity to fertilize their fields, hauling dripping kegs of liquid manure (*Jauche*) through town and thereby releasing a smell noxious enough to penetrate even the thickest church walls. Thus were Kempen's calendars, seasonal and liturgical, Catholic and Protestant, divided. Was the annual offense to Kempener Protestants illegal? Certainly not. Was it intentional? Absolutely![1]

In Bad Oeynhausen, a small town in eastern Westphalia – but not only there – Protestant children were warned by their parents not to shop at the Catholic butcher or baker. Who could trust a man who might cheat you all week, confess and get absolution in time for Sunday mass, and then begin all over again on Monday morning?[2]

How long such customs had been "traditional" among Kempen's Catholics and Bad Oeynhausen's Protestants is anybody's guess. But as the chapters in this volume demonstrate, such markers of confessional difference would have surprised no one in the nineteenth century. Not always mutually hostile, sometimes even cooperative, the members of Germany's three officially recognized religions were nevertheless acutely aware of each other's presence – and difference. A well-developed internal radar registered confessional inflections not only in the calendar or shopping patterns, but in pronunciation, dress, and of course political choices.[3] Such inflections were embedded in every aspect of life, from the ways people imagined themselves as men or women, as Róisín Healy has suggested, to such scholarly monuments as Germany's dictionary of national biography (the *Neue Deutsche Biographie*), which as late as the 1970s carefully noted "*kath.*" "*evang.*" and "*hebr.*" after each entry. For a century and more, nothing could be said or done in Germany that was not said or done by a Protestant, a Catholic, or a Jew. The designations testify to contemporaries' belief that these distinctions were real ones, with real consequences, and not simply conventional or customary, the moldy relics of ancient quarrels.

Consciousness of difference, experienced in religious terms, had always been part of the internal radar of Jews, the archetypal European minority. Until the nineteenth century, however, most Christians in Germany had been insulated from such challenges by Reformation settlements that had bought peace at the price of confessional apartheid (*cuius regio, eius religio*). But the political foundations of these settlements were destroyed by Napoleon, and subsequent map-makers at Vienna boldly joined what those at Augsburg and Westphalia had so carefully kept asunder. Thus political and confessional geography no longer coincided, a demographic fact of the first importance as, over the course of the century, democratization brought populations into political decision-making.

If the new political settlements heightened confessional sensitivities, religious developments set off alarms. Among Protestants, the "Awakening," as it was called, provoked resistance among rationalist critics that contributed to a nervous sense of vulnerability within both wings of German Protestantism. Among Catholics, recovery from the traumas of Jacobinism and the collapse of the *Reichskirche* was accompanied by an unprecedented centralization of ecclesiastical authority and celebrated with a flamboyance that set others' teeth on edge. Feast days were marked by parading the sacrament through town, resplendent in its gold and silver monstrance and followed by a train of priests in eucharistic vestments and companies of equally gaudy brotherhoods, swinging their ensigns, waving their banners, and piping their horns.

The Church of Rome's conspicuous re-occupation of Germany's public spaces represented, in the eyes of outsiders, the objective correlative of an overweening political ambition that challenged the very sovereignty of the state. Although not everyone went so far as the liberal Swiss jurist,

Johann Caspar Bluntschli, who bluntly declared Catholics "criminals against mankind," Hegel was convinced "that with the Catholic religion, no rational constitution is possible." Even Queen Victoria responded to the news that a Catholic hierarchy was being re-established in England with shock: "Am I Queen of England or am I not?"[4]

Into this mix stepped Germany's third recognized denomination, the Jews, whose own self-conception had been transformed by the eighteenth-century *Haskala* and who began to demand a release from their remaining civil disabilities as well as integration, on the basis of equality, into civic life. Arguments for emancipation made Germany's Jews, although their numbers remained tiny, "present" to their fellow countrymen to a degree unknown in the past.

A third feature of the century that sharpened confessional awareness was the progressive extension of civic life itself, with the entry of the "public" into arenas that had previously been reserved to the Crown or attached to corporate bodies. A religious community's relationship to the state (whatever England's queen may have believed) diminished in significance as the importance of its relations to other groups grew. The ability of Germans to express themselves collectively through petitions, the press, and – increasingly – parliaments, provided a megaphone for opinions that would previously have been heard only at the *Stammtisch* or the *Marktplatz*. "Democratization" in its various forms stimulated self-consciousness all around, as each group reflected on its own and others' advantages in a world losing the securities of a segmentary old regime.[5] The confessional self-consciousness of the nineteenth and early twentieth century was thus a thoroughly modern phenomenon, possible because these groups now shared the same spaces – markets, rights, spheres – and, at least potentially, vied for the same power.

Political power in the German Empire was also inflected confessionally: because bureaucratic structures were increasingly important, and still dominated by Protestants (even, for much of the century, in Bavaria); because elections, nationally, rewarded the organized, which meant the Catholics; and because elections, municipally, advantaged those who paid more taxes, which in some places might well mean the Jews.[6]

These processes were much the same in the rest of Western Europe, but Germany's confessional makeup departed significantly from a perceived (Franco-British) norm. France (as the *mot* of a perhaps apocryphal bishop put it) was blessed with 100 different sauces and only one religion – while England, which could boast only one sauce, had 100 religions. The formation of new "denominations," the Anglo-American solution to the problem of conformity versus dissent, was not an attractive option in

Germany, where three, but only three, religions were recognized by the state. The result was that in Germany religious differences were often expressed, not as binomial conflicts between Self and Other, but in triangular struggles. And in a triangle, the Jews (as Fontane's Silberstein recognized when he reported approvingly on Mathilde Möhring's "trinity" to his friend Isenthal), need not always be on the bottom.

In fact, Germany's Jews became, willy-nilly, a third party to many of the conflicts within and between the two other confessions. As Protestant piety became increasingly "divided," in Lucian Hölscher's phrase, both traditionalists and rationalists might gain leverage by accusing the other of being, theologically, "like" the Jews.[7] Challenges to Catholicism, such as the Rongean anti-celibacy crusade, might become, once they became matters for political decision, a vehicle for Jewish equality – as Dagmar Herzog has shown for Baden. And the Protestant-led movement against "confessional" (i.e., Catholic) fraternities that burst onto the public stage in 1904 sometimes improved the social status of Jewish students, by integrating their organizations into student councils that excluded Catholics. In Breslau, the entrance of the Jewish "Thuringia" into the student council, a direct consequence of the anti-Catholic *Hochschulstreit*, led to the anti-semitic *Verein deutscher Studenten's* vacating its own seats – a most welcome by-product for Thuringia's members, who had long seen the V.D.St. as "the worst representative of anti-Semitism."[8]

In places where they were both minorities, Catholics and Jews might find their demands directly pitted against each other. "Conspicuous," writes Till van Rahden, describing the controversy over whether the new *Gymnasium* in Breslau was to be interconfessional, "was the active role of Jewish liberals" – conspicuous to the historian and, not surprisingly, to Breslau's Catholic minority as well, which suddenly saw its long-standing hopes for parity in secondary education being finessed by the Protestant-dominated city council's decision for Jewish inclusion. Here as elsewhere, Jews and Catholics pursued, under different rubrics, the (quite legitimate) interests of their own group. No one stood for that "poor bare, forked animal," "the thing itself; unaccommodated man."

Confessional controversies were complicated by the century's nationalism.[9] More precisely, the effort to define a German nation inevitably projected contemporary communal struggles on to the past. At the same time, it integrated past religious conflicts into narratives that became a central part of what it meant to belong to the new national community. Anthony Steinhoff has read one such narrative in the architecture and liturgy of Strasbourg's "new" Protestant Church. Scholarship was also the site of competing narratives – and a battleground of competing legitimacies. As Wolfgang Altgeld has shown us, professional historians were not ashamed to join the fray. But just as important as the narratives of architects and scholars were the stories that people told about themselves, as Kevin Cramer, with his analysis of the cult of Soldier-King Gustavus Adolphus, has demonstrated. The prospect of Protestant ownership of all the important national holidays concentrated Catholic minds wonderfully. Who can be surprised that they soon discovered their own candidate for founding martyr, one who pre-dated the Reformation: Saint Boniface, the Benedictine monk whose conversion of the "Germans" to Christianity in the eighth century was proposed as the birthday of the German nation?[10] More than 100,000 pilgrims streamed to his gravesite in Fulda in 1855 during the celebrations marking the 1,100th anniversary of his martyrdom. The discourse excoriating German division and "disunity," employed to great effect by Protestant nationalists, could be now be wielded by Catholics, as they contrasted the *"blos in Stämme sich zerfasernde Germanentum,"* which had confronted Boniface, with the "spiritual foundations of their civic unification" that was his legacy.[11] The irony of a German national narrative as a competition between a Swedish soldier and an English missionary was not lost on contemporaries.

Denis Donoghue, the Irish-born critic, has drawn our attention to the connection between the imaginative power of narrative and the vitality of religion itself.

> When we say that Ireland is a Catholic country, we mean that most of its people have received their sense of the world in narrative terms, the life, death, and resurrection of Christ, the lives of the saints, the commemoration of Christ's life in the sacraments, as elucidated by the teachings of the Church through its doctrines and rituals. In Ireland, Sunday Mass is the clearest form of customary knowledge. To the extent to which this knowledge has been eroded, the erosion has come about not mainly because of secularism at large, but because, for many people, narrative has lost its power. All that remains of the mystery is the tale, and now, for those people, not even that.[12]

In nineteenth-century Germany, we see no sign that narrative had lost its power.[13]

The master narratives of our own age, especially those that seek to explain the horrors that began after 1933, have tempted historians to include among their explanations a presumed confessional *Sonderweg* in the nineteenth century.[14] But we must be careful not to exaggerate Germany's peculiarity. English Protestantism was *also* riven by competing orthodox and rationalist strains (as the very Anglican W. E. Gladstone noted when he commented dryly that "Mr. [Matthew] Arnold combines a genuine love of Christianity with a capacity so to state its tenets as to be recognizable by neither friend nor foe"). And Gerard Connolly's study of the Midlands suggests that most of the themes familiar to us from German Catholicism found their counterparts in England: the role of the priest ("omnicompetent") and his political and social activism ("as comfortable on Anti-Corn Law League platform as he was in the pulpit"); the transformation of the irenic piety of the eighteenth century, which emphasized personal ethics and good interconfessional relations, into a militant ultramontanism intent on doctrinal truth and waging "a Jihad against all things non-Catholic" in the nineteenth. Even the "milieu," over which so much German scholarly ink has been spilled, had its Victorian counterpart: by erecting its own set of separate educational and social institutions, the Church in England held the faithful in "protective custody."[15]

And for all the notoriety of Friedrich Julius Stahl's theory of Prussia as "a Christian state," the same designation was invoked in England, and less self-consciously.[16] Although the integration of Britain's proportionally much smaller Jewish minority (less than 0.01 per cent of the population) in the first half of the century was not accompanied by the violence and mass protests that we see in Germany in those years, its peaceful course cannot be attributed to a more secular mentality. Even enthusiastic anglophiles in Germany winced at Victorian England's *"geschraubte Kirchlichkeit."*[17] And emancipation there was slow: only in 1846 were bequests to Jewish foundations enforced by the courts, did the synagogue become a legal establishment, was Judaism a religion recognized by law.[18]

Nor was Germany alone in coupling emancipation of its minorities with continued disabilities. Only in 1871 could a Jew or Catholic take a degree at Oxford, Cambridge, or Durham – three of the four English universities. The same 1829 Relief Bill that opened parliament to Catholics required of candidates for all other offices a declaration denying transubstantiation – a central article of Catholic belief. The use of streets and squares for their processions, claimed so boldly by German Catholics, was explicitly denied them in England in 1829, a denial that remained in force for nearly 100 years.[19]

It is the fate of religious minorities to see foreign questions through a different optic than the majority – and thus to face painful questions about their (dual) loyalty. English Jews found themselves stranded during the tidal wave of national indignation in 1876, when the Ottomans, who had a tradition of protecting Jews, were massacring Bulgarian Christians. German Catholics had experienced the same isolation five years earlier, over the Roman Question.[20] As for that perennial source of conflict, the schools: *The Jewish Chronicle* rejected the Forster Education Act of 1870, one of the great achievements of Gladstone's first ministry.[21] It espoused instead a position analogous to that of Breslau's Catholic press on the interconfessional *Johanneum* (and, *ceteris paribus*, a position opposite to that of Breslau's Jewish community). Educational tangles such as these reveal less about national differences or confessional prejudices than about the inherent difficulty of emancipating individuals without creating conditions that undermine the integrity and vitality of the groups to which they belong.

That religious loyalty might breed communal violence was no secret to the nineteenth century. While the outbursts of vandalism and rioting that occurred in Western Europe were incidental compared to the pogroms that were soon to become regular features of minority–majority relations further East – against Jews, against Armenians, and between neighbors on all sides of the recurrent Balkan wars – hindsight might suggest that they foreshadowed the intractable blood-letting in Northern Ireland, and the worse abominations to come from the very heart of Europe.[22]

Perhaps it was with these terrible futures in mind that the nineteenth century's broils have been seen by Olaf Blaschke as marking the beginning of a "*Second* Confessional Age." The phrase deliberately recalls the first "Confessional Age" of the sixteenth and seventeenth centuries, and reminds us of parallels with the past that (we have seen) were never far from contemporary minds. In 1824 a worried Christian Karl von Bunsen predicted to his mentor, the historian Barthold Georg Niebuhr, that "our children will see religious wars."[23]

But while a useful illustration of the over-heated anxiety that sometimes gripped contemporaries, Bunsen's prophesy should alert us against taking these parallels too literally.[24] Graveyards might be vandalized; they were not uprooted. Churches might be shut (more often, forcibly shared), and synagogues even on occasion set on fire: but they were not razed by an arm of the state.[25] Refractory priests were carted off to jail in "culture wagons," nuns and other religious orders were forced either to dissolve their congregations or to go abroad; but dragoons were not quartered on the population, nor were whole populations expelled from their cities and driven into exile. The one exception, admittedly a significant one, was Prussia's expulsion in 1885–6 from its eastern regions of *c*.30,000 undocumented aliens – Catholic Poles and Eastern Jews: a measure overwhelmingly condemned by the *Reichstag*. But for all the Center Party's attempts to paint the measure as an extension of the *Kulturkampf* (and thus to arouse a silent Vatican), the measure appears to have been a piece of nationality – rather than religious – policy.[26]

The most important fact about the culture wars of the nineteenth century, even in Germany where they were fiercest, is that they weren't *wars*.[27] For all the anger and suffering they brought to individuals and groups, the religious conflicts of the nineteenth century were not even a dim reflection of the Reformation and Counter-Reformation eras.[28]

The reason for the greater moderation lay not in intensity of belief, which was arguably just as strong, but in the more benign context. Not least important was the fact that the very social and institutional developments that publicized and thus increased confessional tensions – the popular press, the public assemblies, the parliamentary elections – also worked to channel and contain them. "In the nineteenth century," we are told, "religion was politicized as never before"[29] – which is certainly true. But we must remember that politics itself – if by "politics" we mean the exercise of power – was *also* politicized as never before: that is, subjected to processes that were competitive. A confessional age the nineteenth century certainly was; but confessional self-consciousness blossomed in a context that was felt to be "the Age of Improvement."[30]

In these evolving democratic contexts, even confessional conflict could have salutary features. As J. P. Parry has argued, for many people, democratic politics was itself perceived as "an activity of significance mainly because religious issues were so prominent."[31] Parry was referring to England, but his observation is no less true for Germany. An "unintended consequence" of the politicization of religion was to strengthen people's attachments not only to their own group, but also to the institutions – press, public, elections – that made their loyalties effective.[32]

"Aggressive social exclusion of those of different faiths" often poisoned the atmosphere in Germany, as in other lands. But contributors to this volume have also shown us signs of cooperation and mutual respect that had themselves become conventionalized, yes, even traditionalized: "social institutions," in Uli Baumann's phrase. The boundaries between confessions were not an "iron curtain."[33] No squadrons of armed *Volkspolizei* patrolled the confessional borders. They were hardly necessary, since confessional boundaries – unlike the involuntary boundaries of the Cold War – were very much self-enforced. Although in the twenty-first century it may seem remarkable that "as late as 1910 scarcely ten percent of those Germans who married dared [*sic*] choose a partner from a different faith," such rates were not unusual. In the American "melting pot," the percentage of endogamous marriages was even higher: in 1950, 97.1 per cent of US Jews married within their own group, as did 93.8 per cent of America's Catholics.[34] We should guard against assuming that low rates of inter-marriage are necessarily evidence of inter-group conflict, or even of disrespect. Conversely, while high rates of intermarriage are plausibly taken as evidence of a minority's successful integration, they may also be harbingers of its disappearance.

Integration may indeed be a bigger threat to a group than exclusion. For if any group, including a religious group, is not to disappear, it must have boundaries. It will have to assert its own vision against the surrounding culture. The existence of more than one community in a given social and political space will cause friction. Is this a bad thing? George Santayana once observed that

> any attempt to speak without speaking any particular language is not more hopeless than the attempt to have a religion that shall be no religion in particular. . . . Every living and healthy religion has a marked idiosyncrasy. Its power consists in its special and surprising message and in the bias which that revelation gives to life. The vistas it opens and the mysteries it propounds are another world to live in; and another world to live in – whether we expect ever to pass wholly over into it or no – is what we mean by having a religion.[35]

Our own generation congratulates itself on its commitment to diversity and its embrace of multicultural values. But if "multicultural" is to mean anything at all – that is, if we really do prize difference – then we can hardly desire to erase entirely the "bias" that comes with belonging to a particular religious community and participating in the "special and surprising message [its] revelation gives to life."[36]

Notes

1. Told to me by Frau Prof. Ruth Becker, a Catholic, who grew up in Kempen, learned it from her father, and confirmed it with her sister. The non-observance of Good Friday by Catholics was not universal, and, after the Second World War, Catholic practice increasingly conformed to that of Protestants.
2. Related to me in 1990 by Prof. Reinhard Rürup, a Protestant, with the agreement of his wife and others in the same company – Protestant academics from Franconia and Moravia.
3. Confessional accents: memoirs of the diplomat Rudolf Rahm, quoted in Manfred Vasold, "Konfessionales Afrika," *Frankfurter Allgemeine Zeitung*, 11 October 2000.
4. G. F. W. Hegel ("daß mit der katholischen Religion keine vernünftige Verfassung möglich ist") from *Vorlesungen über die Philosophie der Geschichte. Theorie-Werkausgabe*, XII. (Frankfurt a.M.: Suhrkamp, 1970), p. 531, quoted in Ralf Roth, "Katholisches Bürgertum in

Frankfurt am Main 1800–1914. Zwischen Emanzipation und Kultur-kampf," *Archiv für mittelrheinische Kirchengeschichte* 46 (1994): 207–46, quotation on p. 231. Bluntschli quoted in Stefan-Ludwig Hoffmann, "Brothers or Strangers? Jews and Freemasons in Nineteenth-century Germany," *German History* 18/2 (2000): 143–61; quotation on p. 157; Queen Victoria quoted in Harold J. Laski, *Studies in the Problem of Sovereignty* (New Haven, CT and London: Yale University Press, 1917), p. 163.

5. Arguing that the experience of Italy, where as late as 1912 only 7 per cent of the population was enfranchised, suggests that emancipation of minorities was smoothed by the absence of mass politics: Stephan Wendehorst, "Emancipation as Path to National Integration," in *The Emancipation of Catholics, Jews, and Protestants. Minorities and the Nation State in Nineteenth-century Europe*, ed. Rainer Liedtke and Stephan Wendehorst (Manchester and New York: Manchester University Press, 1999), pp. 188–206; at p. 200.

6. In Breslau, although Jews constituted in 1905 only 4% of the population, their wealth gave them 40% and 35% of the votes in the city's first and second voting classes, respectively: Till van Rahden, "Words and Actions: Rethinking the Social History of German Antisemitism, Breslau, 1870–1914," *German History* 18/4 (2000): 415. In Frankfurt city politics, their power was similar and in Berlin, even greater.

7. Men like Ernst Troeltsch and Adolf von Harnack, on Protestantism's theological "left," saw the purification of religion, says Uriel Tal, in "freeing Christianity from . . . Jewish excesses within Christianity . . ., that is, from such phenomena as dogma, doctrinal codifications, sacraments, moral laws": "Debatte um das 'Wesen' des Judentums," quoted in Gangolf Hübinger, *Kulturprotestantismus und Politik* (Tübingen: Mohr Siebeck, 1994), p. 274n. 39.

8. I owe this information to Lisa Fetheringill Swartout, who is completing a dissertation at the University of California, Berkeley, on relations between Jewish, Catholic, and Protestant students in German universities.

9. Helmut Walser Smith, *German Nationalism and Religious Conflict: Culture, Ideology, Politics, 1870–1914* (Princeton, NJ: Princeton University Press, 1995).

10. *Missionsvikar* Eduard Müller published his pugnacious *Bonifacius Kalender* in order to assert the presence of a "Church which in 1517 was everywhere bestowing its blessings where those who *currently* confess it are treated as interlopers": "'Dann laß ich 5 Fuß tiefer graben,'" *Bonifacius Kalender*, 1883, p. 2.

11. For the Boniface cult, pilgrimage figures, and the contemporary quotation, I am indebted to Siegfried Weichlein, who puts them in the context, however, not just of the Gustavus Adolphus, but also of the Hermann (Arminius) cult: Weichlein, "Die Bonifatiustradition und die Rekonfessionalisierung des deutschen Katholizismus zur Mitte des 19. Jahrhunderts," in O. Blaschke (ed*.*), *Religionskrieg in der Moderne? Renaissance und Rückgang des Konfessionalismus von 1800 bis heute* (Göttingen: Vandenhoeck & Ruprecht, 2001).

12. Denis Donaghue, *Warrenpoint* (New York: Alfred A. Knopf, 1990), p. 171.

13. Rainer Erb and Werner Bergmann's discussion of local memories and memorializing – especially those touching relations between Jews and Christians.

14. An explicit link to 1933 is suggested by Hölscher, in this volume, and by Olaf Blaschke, "Das 19. Jahrhundert: Ein Zweites Konfessionelles Zeitalter?" *Geschichte und Gesellschaft* 26 (Jan.,–Mar. 2000): 38–75; here at p. 67 (basing himself on the argument of M. Rainer Lepsius), and esp. p. 40, which refers to the "*verheerenden Konsequenzen*" of these lines of conflict "*etwa im Blick auf die Nazi-Diktatur.*"

15. G. Connolly, "The Transubstantiation of Myth: Towards a New Popular History of Nineteenth-Century Catholicism in England," *Journal of Ecclesiastical History* 35/1 (Jan. 1984): 78–104; quotations, pp. 94, 96, 97. Gladstone on Arnold was related to me by my first *Doktorvater,* Klaus Epstein, who received his Ph.D. in British history.

16. Valuable on the "Christian state": David Cesarani, "British Jews," in R. Liedtke and S. Wendehorst (eds), *Emancipation*, p. 39. Cesarani's implication, that British Jews had it as bad as continental (and therefore, by implication, German) Jews, cannot be sustained. Stereotypes in fiction and lingering legal inequalities simply do not compare to the insecurity of residence, property, and even life suffered by German Jews in many places before 1850. Cf. Erb and Bergmann, *Nachtseite*, esp. pp. 1–25, 97–108, 217–68. The multiple meanings of the word "emancipation" lead Cesarani to argue, p. 38, that the emancipation of British Jews was "comparatively slow" compared with the emancipation of the slaves(!). His real target is the notion that liberal England meant a secular England: a straw man that finds little support in either the perceptions of contemporaries or in scholarly literature.

17. Count Barby, in Theodor Fontane, *Der Stechlin* (1898), Goldmann Klassiker Taschenbuchausgabe, Munich, n.d., p. 108.

18. H. S. Q. Henriques, quoted in Cesarani, "British Jews," p. 41.
19. Until 1926. Ian Machen argues that Catholics remain in an inferior position even today. "British Catholics," in Liedtke and Wendehorst (eds), *Emancipation*, pp. 13–14, 31.
20. Liberal impatience with British Jews' preference for Turkey (Cesarani, "British Jews," pp. 50–53) is analogous to German Liberal incomprehension at the Catholic desire for aid on behalf of a dispossessed Holy See.
21. Cesarani, "British Jews," p. 47.
22. Certainly the "robust and rowdy" traditions of a mob-enforced "moral economy," celebrated by E. P. Thompson in *The Making of the English Working Class* (London, 1963), pp. 59, 63–7, look less appealing when the wealthy target of broken windows and threatening letters is not a (perhaps dissenting) Englishman but a German Jew. Cf. the *"hergebrachte[n] Vorstellungen einer 'gerechten politischen und wirtschaftlichen Ordnung,'"* in Erb and Bergmann, *Nachtseite*, p. 257. Anti-Catholic riots in Britain: Machin, "British Catholics," pp. 11–32; 26, 27, 28, 32.
23. Quoted by Vasold, "Konfessionelles Afrika."
24. Oddly, Blaschke argues that "Second Confessionalization" is preferable to the term "Re-confessionalization" (advanced by others) because the latter, he says, "remains metaphorical." "Das 19. Jahrhundert," p. 49.
25. As early as 1819 the states sent in soldiers and/or police to protect threatened Jews. Erb and Bergmann, *Nachtseite*, pp. 223–7, 233n. 51, 234 and 234n. 58, 235, 236, 239n. 72. Königshütte, Upper Silesia was put under military occupation for two months in the summer of 1871, after a mining strike ended in the torching of buildings and looting of (mostly Jewish-owned) shops. *Görlitzer Anzeiger*, from 29 June through to 15 August, 1871: nrs. 149–52, 154, 159, 162f., 168, 171–3, 189. Cf. Neustettin and neighboring areas in 1881: Christhard Hoffmann, "Politische Kultur und Gewalt gegen Minderheiten. Die antisemitischen Ausschreitungen in Pommern und Westpreußen 1881," *Jahrbuch für Antisemitismusforschung* 3 [1994]: 93–120.
26. Bismarck: "We want to get rid of foreign Poles because we have enough of our own;" and he replied to protests that the government was expelling "the Jews," that it would have looked confessionally suspicious if the government had said, "we're getting rid of all the Poles – except the Jews or Protestants." Nevertheless, anti-Semitic motives were unmistakable, even as Progressives mourned the loss of *c.*9,000 Jews, whose children, "experience teaches us, would have

strengthened the German element": Helmut Neubach, *Die Ausweisungen von Polen und Juden aus Preussen 1885/86: Ein Beitrag zu Bismarcks Polenpolitik und zur Geschichte des deutsch–polnischen Verhältnisses* (Wiesbaden: Harrassowitz, 1967), pp. 108, 109, 111.

27. The Swiss *Sonderbund* War in 1847 pitted Catholic against Protestant cantons, but the issues were not primarily religious, it lasted only 25 days, few lives were lost, and reconciliation was easy.

28. Nor did they match the inter-ethnic conflicts in the United States, where the mere prospect of sharing equality with African-Americans (i.e., genuine emancipation) produced about two lynchings a week from 1890 to 1920. A reminder of just how draconian the "first" confessional age was: Arno Herzig, "Die Rekatholisierung in deutschen Territorien im 16. und 17. Jahrhundert," *Geschichte und Gesellschaft* 26 (2000): 76–104.

29. Blaschke, "Das 19. Jahrhundert," p. 67. A telling analysis of the use of the new democratic measures for illiberal ends is in James F. Harris, *The People Speak! Anti-Semitism and Emancipation in Nineteenth-Century Bavaria* (Ann Arbor, MI: University of Michigan Press, 1994).

30. Admittedly, for many German Jews this age would begin only toward the end of the period in British history (1783–1867) examined under that name by Asa Brigg in his famous 1959 synthesis.

31. J. P. Parry, *Democracy and Religion: Gladstone and the Liberal Party, 1867–1875* (Cambridge: Cambridge University Press, 1986), p. 5, quoted in Eduardo Posada-Carbó, "Limits of Power: Elections under the Conservative Hegemony in Colombia, 1886–1930," *Hispanic American Historical Review* 77:2 (1997): 271n. 121-2.

32. Most recently: Hermann-Josef Große Kracht, "Religion in der Demokratisierungsfalle? Zum Verhältnis von traditioneller Religion und politischer Moderne am Beispiel des deutschen Katholizismus im Kaiserreich," *Geschichte in Wissenschaft und Unterricht* 51 (2000): 140–54.

33. "Iron curtain" (pp. 63, 74), "aggressive social exclusion" (p. 67), are the terms of Blaschke, "Das 19. Jahrhundert."

34. German figures and quotation: Blaschke, "Das 19. Jahrhundert," p. 65, which also gives the intermarriage figures for Germany in the 1950s as "around 20%." US figures from August B. Hollingshead, "Cultural Factors in the Selection of Marriage Mates," *American Sociological Review* XVI/1 (October, 1950), cited in Will Herberg, *Protestant, Catholic, Jew. An Essay in American Religious Sociology* (New York: Doubleday, 1956), p. 47.

35. *Reason in Religion*, Vol. II of *Life of Reason: The Phases of Human Progress* (New York, 1962), pp. 10–11, quoted in Clifford Geertz, "Religion as a Cultural System" in idem, *The Interpretation of Cultures* (New York: Basic Books, 1973), pp. 87–126; here at p. 87.
36. Anthony Appiah has argued that American academia can be the world's loudest champions of cultural diversity precisely because they are culturally so homogeneous: "The Multicultural Misunderstanding," *New York Review of Books*, 9 Oct. 1997.

Index

Adolphus, Gustavus, 18, 26, 98–113, 323

Allgemeine Zeitung des Judentums, 221–2, 227, 228

Allgemeines Landrecht, 81

Altermatt, Urs, 5

Altgeld, Wolfgang, 80, 122

Anti-Jesuit Law, 257

Anti-Semitism, 12, 15, 20, 58–60, 67, 85, 218, 219, 297, 306–312

Archiv für Reformationsgeschichte, 6

Arndt, Ernst Moritz, 52, 54

Arnold, Matthew, 324

Arnoldi, Wilhelm, 124

Ascher, Saul, 59

Autobiographies, 37

"Awakening," 46, 71–74, 80, 320

Bachem, Julius, 127

Baden, Lower Chamber, 186, 189, 192–193, 196–201, 203, 207

Barthold, Friedrich Wilhelm, 108–109

Baumeister, Martin, 127

Baumgarten, Otto, 34

"Berlin Awakening," 71–73

Berlin Society for the Promotion of Christianity Among the Jews, 72, 77–79, 82

Bireley, Robert, 134

Bildung, 40, 217, 224, 232

Bildungsroman, 37

Blackbourn, David, 15, 129, 156

Blaschke, Olaf, 8–9, 14, 325

Böhtlingk, Arthur, 173

Boniface, Saint, 323

Borromäusverein, 128–132, 134

Bötticher, Wilhelm, 109

Braun, Fr. Johannes, 129

Braun, Lily, 38

Breitenfeld, Battle of, 100–103, 110

Brentano, Clemens, 125

Breslauer Hausblätter, 218, 225

Bretschneider, Karl, 54–5, 56

Buchmann, Jakob, 229–230

Bunsen, Karl von, 325

Burg, Meno, 70

Busch, Wihelm, 165

Buß, Franz Josef, 190, 197–198, 201, 203, 207, 247

Busst, A.J.L., 160

Capuchins, 246–248

Catholic Center Party, 156, 254, 306

Catholic emancipation in England, 324–325

Catholic folk education movement, 126, 128–129, 133

Catholic Reading, 20

Cattle traders, Jewish, 300

Celibacy, 185, 189–192, 194

Centralverein für Deutsche Staatsbürger jüdischen Glaubens, 84

Christ, Anton, 204

Christian Schools, 15, 20, 69, 78–84

Communion, 35, 39, 271–273, 281, 283, 285

Confessional inculturation, 121, 134

Confirmation, 38

Contact zones, 14–16

Conversion, 57, 68–70, 85

Declaration of faith, 37–38

Democratization and religious coexistence, 321–322

Demography, religious, 41–44, 51–52, 272–273

Deutschkatholiken, 193, 195–204, 208

Devotional culture, 35–37, 40, 44

Dohm, Christian Wilhelm, 3, 68

Droysen, Gustav, 112–113

Index

Education and religion, 40–41, 217–234, 122, 125–129, 131
Elsner, Moritz, 220
Elvenich, Peter, 218
Engels, Friedrich, 39–40
Enlightenment, 3, 36, 39, 41, 44, 45, 54, 58, 67, 69, 73–74, 85, 99, 121–123, 125, 153, 157, 175, 176, 186, 190, 195, 219, 246, 247–52
Evangelischer Bund (Protestant League), 53, 156, 158–159, 163, 170, 172–173
Expulsion of 1885–1886, Prussian, 325

Falk, Adalbert, 171, 227–228
Feast of the Tabernacle, 301
Franco-Prussian War, 269, 286
Frederick William III, 70–74, 81–82, 85
Frederick William IV, 77–78
Ficker, Julius, 57
Flathe, Ludwig, 109
Förster, Friedrich, 104
Forckenbeck, Max von, 228–9
Foucault, Michel, 157
Fout, John, 162, 169
Franciscans, 246–249
François, Etienne, 3
Frevert, Ute, 157
Fries, Jacob, 55

Geertz, Clifford, 14–15
Geiger, Abraham, 6, 233
Geiger, Ludwig, 6
Gender, 154–164, 173–175
German Protestant Women's League, 170
Gfrörer, August Friedrich, 110–111
Goerres, Joseph, 52
Graetz, Heinrich, 6
Grimm, Jacob, 55
Grossman, Gottlob, 102, 105
Gurs, 297
Gustav-Adolf-Verein, 105, 107, 111

Haerter, Gustav, 284
Hahn-Hahn, Ida, 125
Hainauer, Julius, 231
Harnack, Adolph von, 33–34
Harris, James F., 305
Hartmann, C.H.F., 105
Haskala, 321

Hausen, Karin, 158
hecker, Fredrich, 187, 195, 203–5
Hep Hep Unrest of 1819, 59
Hesing, Albert, 111–112
Hertling, Georg von, 128
Hillebrand, Joseph, 250–251
Hinrichs, Carl, 7
Hintertreppenromane, 131
Hirsch, Samuel Raphael, 13
Hirscher, Johann Baptist, 196
Historisch-politische Blätter für das Katholische Deutschland (HpB), 111
Historisches Jahrbuch, 6
Hobrecht, Arthur, 224
Hochland, 127
Hochschulstreit, 322
Honigmann, David, 221, 224
Hübinger, Gangolf, 127

Ihringen, 309
Illien, Albert, 300
Index of Forbidden Books, 121, 130
Israelitische Wochenschrift, 226–228

Jacobi, Otto, 101–102
Janssen, Johannes, 112
Jatho, Carl, 33–34, 171
Jeggle, Utz, 299–300
Jesuits, 18, 20, 123, 153–176, 195, 230, 246–240, 246–257
Jesuit Missions, social composition, 253–254
"Jewish Center," 11
Jewish communities among Christian communities 11–12
Jewish emancipation, 6, 15, 17, 19, 54, 58, 60, 67–68, 77
Jewish teachers, 221, 224, 226–228, 233–234

Kant, Immanuel, 3, 57–58
Kaplan, Marion, 175
Kapp, Johann Georg Christian, 205–8
Klopp, Onno, 111
Kopp, Gustav, 284
Kraus, Franz Xaver, 128
Kulturkampf, 9, 52, 58, 60, 126, 131, 155–156, 159, 175, 218, 254, 257, 308, 325
Kuhlemann, Frank-Michael, 13

Index

Laqueur, Thomas, 157
Lazarists, 246–248
Leblois, Louis, 278, 284
Lending libraries, 124–126, 128–133
Lenz, Max, 54
Lepsius, M.Rainer, 10, 14
Lessing, Gotthold Ephraim, 3
Liberale Reichspartei, 254
Liedhegener, Antonius, 12, 13
Liepach, Martin, 309
Literacy, 122, 123–124, 126, 130
Liturgy, 268–274, 276–286, 319, 322
Los von Rom movement, 59
Luther, Martin, 52–53, 57, 97
Lützen, Battle of, 100–102, 105–107

McLeod, Hugh, 174
Manliness, 163–164
Marpingen, 8, 15, 159
Marx, Karl, 39–40, 75
Masonic Lodge, 44, 155, 162, 172
Menzel, Karl, 108–109
Menzel, Wolfgang, 113
Mergel, Thomas, 129
Milieu, 5, 9–14, 50, 127, 129, 308, 310, 324
Missions, Missionaries, 72–74, 80–82, 85, 245–258
Mixed marriages (interfaith marriages), 13, 45–46, 80–81, 185, 191–195, 198, 206, 208, 326–327
Modernization, 4, 8, 16, 41–43, 49
Moser, Friedrich, 97
Mühler, Heinrich von, 222, 227
Müllheim, 306–307, 311
Muth, Karl, 127

NSDAP, 56, 309–310
National literature (canon), 123, 132
Nationalism, 4, 17, 50, 52–56, 58, 97–102, 105, 112, 123, 132, 156, 199
Nebenius, Karl Friedrich, 191
Neue Deutsche Biographie, 320
New Church of Strasbourg, 269–285
Nicolai, Friedrich, 3, 53
Niebuhr, Barthold Georg, 108
Nietzsche, Friedrich, 267
Nipperdey, Thomas, 4, 5, 234
Nowak, Kurt, 7

Old Lutherans, 75, 82
Old Catholics, 19, 230–231, 234
Ortner, Sherry B., 14

Papal infallibility, 34, 155
Pascal, Blaise, 154
Paulsen, Friedrich, 165
Petitions against Jewish emancipation, 303–304
Petition Storm against German Catholics, 200
Pietism, 7–8
Protestant Piety, divisions in, 34
Pius IX, Pope, 153
Pius X, Pope, 167
Pluralist Societies, 19
Protestant Association (Protestantenverein), 155, 157–158, 171
Protestant League (see Evangelischer Bund)

Rango, Friedrich Ludwig von, 101
Raumer, Erlass, 256
Raumer, Friedrich von, 108
Reconfessionalization, 8–9
Rechtsstaat, 81–82
Redemptorists, 8, 246–249
Regional history, 298
Reichsdeputationshauptschluss, 121
Reinkens, Joseph Hubert, 218, 230
Religion and democracy, 326
Religion, völkisch, 46–47
Religious socialization, 39–40
Revival, Protestant 247, 255–258
Revolution of 1848, 46, 80, 83, 125, 132, 220, 243, 245–247, 257
Richarz, Monika, 299
Rindeschwender, Ignaz, 201
Roepell, Richard, 221, 224
Rouge, Johannes, 192
Rürup, Reinhard, 304

Sacred Heart Cult, 159
Sahlins, Peter, 16
Salzburg Transaction, 7
Salomon, Emile, 278
Sander, Adolf, 187
Santayana, George, 327
Scheibert, Carl Gottfried, 222

Index

Schell, Hermann, 128
Schellinger, Uwe, 304
Schieder, Wolfgang, 5
Schinkel, Karl Friedrich, 106–107
Schleiermacher, Friedrich, 58, 157
Schlesische Zeitung, 226
Schmieheim, 302
Schmidt, Michael Ignatz, 109–110
Schmitt, Carl, 234
Schönstedt, 84
Secularization, 5, 8, 12, 17, 20, 49–50, 55–56, 163, 175, 219, 221–223, 253–255, 257–258, 323
Sengenwald, Jules, 275
Sewell, William H., Jr., 14
Sonderweg, German, 323
Spener, Philip Jakob, 15
Sperber, Jonathan, 5, 246–248
Stahl, Friedrich Julius, 78–81, 83–86
Stern, Fritz, 161
Stetter, Karl Gustav, 223
Stoltz, Alban, 12, 125, 190, 197–198
Strauss, David Friedrich, 163
Sulamith, 76
Sybel, Heinrich von, 53, 57–58
Syllabus of Errors, 1864, 155

Tal, Uriel, 83–84
Traub, Gottfried, 34, 171
Treitschke, Heinrich von, 6, 233

Troeltsch, Ernst, 41
Ungerer, Gustav, 278–279, 282
Universalism, 217, 233–234

Versen, Franz, 121, 130
Vicari, Hermann von, Archbishop of Freiburg, 120–191, 199
Violence, religious, 325–326
Virchow, Rudolf, 233
Vogt, Niklas, 99–100
Voluntary societies, Jews in, 302–303

Walker, Mack, 7
Wallenstein, 110
Wars of Liberation, 71, 74
Wartburg, 56–57, 59
Wartburgfest, 55, 59
Weber, Max, 5, 41
Weizel, Gordon, 200
Westenrieder, Lorenz von, 109–110
Windthorst, Eduard, 254
Windthorst, Ludwig, 58, 60
Working Circle for Contemporary Church History, 133

Yiddish, 301

Zeldin, Theodore, 156
Zittel, Karl, 193–194, 198, 199